# Mexico
and the
# Hispanic
# Southwest
in
# American
# Literature

Cecil Robinson

*Text Drawings by* H. Beaumont Williams

*About the Author . . .*

CECIL ROBINSON, for much of his career as writer and teacher, has used the Southwest borderlands as listening-post — a strategic location from which to hear what the two Americas have been saying about each other. This interpenetration of the two major cultures of the Western hemisphere has preoccupied the author since he received his doctoral degree in North and Latin American literature from Columbia University and began to apply the insights of cultural dualism on both sides of the border. Robinson has been director of a Chilean intercultural institute, founder of a program in North American literature at the University of Guanabara in Río de Janeiro, and a student, teacher, and lecturer in many parts of Mexico. In the early 1970s he began commuting from the English Department at the University of Arizona weekly to Hermosillo to lecture in Spanish on North American literature at the University of Sonora. He has been a director of institutes for teachers of Spanish-speaking and Navajo bilinguals, and has served as coordinator of the University of Arizona's Committee for Bilingual and Bicultural Studies.

1977 Edition

THE UNIVERSITY OF ARIZONA PRESS

Copyright © 1977 and 1963
The Arizona Board of Regents
All Rights Reserved
Manufactured in the U.S.A.

I.S.B.N.–8165–0593–4
L.C. No. 76-24082 paper

For Madeleine

## CONTENTS

Introduction  ix
Prologue  3

PART I  *Criollo* Mexico and Frontier America
  A Chronological Listing of Early Events  16
  1  Two Cultures Meet in the Borderlands  17
  2  Mexican Traits — An Early Portrait  33
  3  A Discourse on Race, on Sex, on Death  69
  4  A Fragment of the Medieval World  103

PART II  Mexico and the Borderlands in Modern American Literature
  5  The Passing of Enríquez  137
  6  Mexican Traits — A Later Look  164
  7  Children of the Earth  210
  8  Love, Fate, and Death  251
  9  Idols and Altars  280
  10  Chicano Literature  308
  11  The Southwest as a Literary Region: Local Color or Belles Lettres?  332
  Epilogue  353
  Notes  359
  Bibliography  375
  Index  383

# INTRODUCTION

Pressing upward from an extended border across the American Southwest, Mexico has produced a cultural storm front. Because it not only borders upon the United States but makes a deep cultural penetration northward from the boundary, Mexico's influence upon American literature has been unlike any other foreign influence. Mexico, its culture and its people, has been from the early nineteenth century an unavoidable presence in westward-moving America. From the days of the earliest cultural contacts, for all the turbulence of these encounters, American writers, far from wishing to ignore the presence of Mexico, have discovered a special fascination in the heightened color and intensity of Mexican life. Increasingly, the very degree of contrast has provided these writers with a useful setting for comment upon their own society.

Pioneer America could find little to approve of in the Mexican society it collided with, being affronted in all its major convictions by Mexican attitudes, real or alleged. Americans, in their Protestant individualism, in their ideas of thrift and hard work, in their faith in progress through technology, in their insistence upon personal hygiene, in puritanism and racial pride, found Mexico much to their distaste because of its hierarchical Catholicism and the extent of priestly power, its social stratification with pronounced sense of caste, its apparent devotion to pleasure and its seeming avoidance of work, its technological backwardness and its alleged ineptness with machinery, its reported indifference to cleanliness, and its reputation for pervasive sensuality. These early North Americans were also repelled by what seemed to them to be an element of ferocity in Mexico's people, by apparent addiction to crimes of violence and theft, by the alleged cowardice of Mexicans and their morbid doting upon death. Added to all this was the Anglo-Saxon's contempt for a people who had lowered themselves to a state of general cohabitation with the Indians and had thus forfeited the right to be considered "white."

The earliest literary references to Mexico, mainly in journals of adventure, exploration, and trade, show American writers to have been in general accord with the ideology of their own society. The Texas rebellion against Mexico in 1835 and the Mexican War from 1846 to

1848 generated propaganda with more than a note of high-flown patriotism and braggadocio. "Greaser" became a household word. It was only toward the end of the nineteenth century when the pace of American life had become increasingly harassing that Americans felt the impulse to portray and to read about Mexican culture in quite a different light. Exemplifying the tendency of new societies to seek roots in the traditional past, Californians began to conceive of their own old mission culture as a historic past. In fact, a nostalgia for quieter times and pastoral serenities made the mission culture greatly attractive to American readers in general. The aristocratic dons of an earlier California and a more characteristically Hispanic Southwest recalled amenities seemingly lost in America's gilded age.

Following closely upon the dealers in nostalgia came American writers prepared to write seriously about Mexico in ways which reflected an increasingly critical attitude toward their own society. In their growing sense of isolation, their uneasiness at the fragmentation of modern American life, their disgust with materialism and profiteering individualism, their sympathy with the primitive, the passionate, and the oppressed, and in their changed attitudes toward sex and death, modern American writers have tended to find intriguing and salutary the very aspects of Mexican society which had most disgusted the early writers of journals, and the nationalistic novelists, poets, and essayists of the second half of the nineteenth century. In each period there have been interesting counter-currents of thought, and there has been a growing realization that the Hispanic Southwest provides an alternative to New England and the South as a source of tradition and folklore from which a literature can arise.

The vitality of Mexico as it extends itself culturally into the American Southwest first impressed me when as a very young man I entered the area and, during a stint at manual labor, associated intimately with Mexican-American workers. It was through these quite humble but articulate and vivid representatives of a complicated and subtle culture that I first received a vision of the extended "America" to which we are now awakening. As is often the case, a condition which society in general is just coming to recognize was sensed considerably in advance by creative writers. A remarkable number of North American writers have felt compelled to deal with Mexican culture as found within the borders of the United States or in Mexico proper, and they have expressed increasingly a sense that the continental experience will remain incomplete until the attainments of Ibero-America are incorporated into our literature. In recent years a long step has been taken toward this completion. The Mexican-Americans, the Chicanos, have found their voice.

It is the fruitful new genre of Chicano literature that is providing a sinewy cultural link between the Americas. Whitman heralded a continental culture enriched by Mexican sensibility. Many of the writers whose works are examined in this book have advanced the fulfillment of Whitman's prophecy. It is my hope that this book also may serve to bring closer the day when the term "American literature" will be taken to mean the interacting literatures of North and Hispanic America.

CECIL ROBINSON

# PROLOGUE

# Prologue

The peoples of Post-Columbian America, North and South, have a common experience in their history: the conquest of a new world, of indigenous peoples, and of vast and often inhospitable terrain. Varying greatly according to the kinds of Europeans involved, the various Indian cultures encountered, and the many faces of nature in the Western Hemisphere, nevertheless in an important psychological respect, the experience has been one. As such, it has needed some quintessential expression in the literature of the Americas. Among the many tales of conquest, one seems to stand alone, lofty and detached from the details of historical context or from the general fabric of story and lore surrounding the period of discovery and colonization. The destruction of Tenochtitlan, ancient capital of the Aztecs, by the army of Cortez, is, in its charged atmosphere of triumph and pathos, the very prototype of the conquest of the New World.

In literature, the story of the Conquest of Mexico has been an important link between North and Hispanic America. North American writers, hardly less than Latin Americans, have felt its power and sensed its importance as a type of the New World experience. The Spaniard destroying in his rage for gold a savage, brilliant, and innocent people, has served North American writers as an analogue for the later continental epic of the destruction of the wilderness. Although the early Spanish writers in reporting home about the strange and marvelous city of Tenochtitlan emphasized that its high state of development was such as to make the most sophisticated European gape with wonderment, the North American writers who later took up the theme often saw fit to emphasize for their own purposes the savagery and innocence which underlay this dazzling display of civilization.

However, in order to portray the Aztecs as a part of a virginal America soon to be despoiled, North American writers obsessed with this idea had to mute certain of the darker phases of Aztec life, the grisly side of its religion with its torture and human sacrifice.

Though Prescott more than any other writer influenced American authors writing about the Conquest, he gave little encouragement in

*The Conquest of Mexico* to contemporary and later writers who were to present the Aztecs as a case of innocence betrayed. While not minimizing Spanish barbarities, Prescott insisted that the Conquest was in the main a deliverance from the terrors of the god Huitzilopotchli to the mildness and love of the Virgin of Guadalupe. A modern writer, Frances Gillmor, who has combined creative gifts with dogged and ingenious scholarship in recreating the lives and times of two Aztec leaders, insists that she too is not to be identified with the concept of the Aztec as noble savage betrayed. Her two books dealing with Aztec themes are written in the manner of biographical narrative. They are *Flute of the Smoking Mirror*[1], a study of the poet-statesman of Texacoco, Nazahualcoyotl (1402-1472), and *The King Danced in the Market Place*[2], a biography of Huehue Moctezuma Ilhuicamina, grandfather of the famous Moctezuma II and the leader who first made the Aztecs into a formidable power extending their domain over neighboring peoples. These books admirably convey to the reader the author's sense of the color and tone of Aztec society and the psychology of the people. A society and its leaders are dealt with as worthy in themselves of recording and interpretation, leaving untouched the question of innocence or betrayal. However, Frances Gillmor has verbally stated that Indianists inside of Mexico and without are guilty of distortion in underestimating the role that Spanish culture and Christian idealism have played in the development of Mexican society. George Vaillant, on the other hand, in his small and classic volume, *The Aztecs of Mexico*,[3] while reporting fully on the horrors, placed them in their proper context in a complex and affecting religious symbolism ranging from the gayety of flower festivals to the sacrificial stone and the obsidian knife. He insists that with the destruction of Tenochtitlan a uniquely aesthetic vision of life perished.

A cherished myth, of course, is not to be overthrown by facts or by rationalistic analysis. Furthermore, the idea of the Conquest as the destruction of innocence, which has flourished in American letters for over a century, certainly expresses a truth if not the whole truth. The very imminence of total disaster has made every knowable detail of Moctezuma's city seem especially precious to novelists and poets. Brooding in the approved manner of early nineteenth-century romanticism over the lost glories of the Aztecs, Robert Montgomery Bird, somewhat in the spirit of Whitman's "Muse in the New World," heralds the Aztecs as a source of new-world mythology for literature and theorizes that

> nature, and the memory of strange deeds of renown, have flung over the valley of Mexico a charm more romantic than is attached to many of the vales of the older world; for though historic association and the spell of poetry have consecrated the borders of

Leman and the laurel groves of Tempe . . . [yet does our fancy, in either, dwell upon objects which are not so much the adjuvants of romance as of sentiment; in both, we gather food rather for feeling than imagination; we live over thoughts which are generated by memory, and our conceptions are the reproductions of experience.] But poetry has added no plenary charm, history has cast no over-sufficient light on the haunts of Montezuma;[4] on the Valley of Lakes, though filled with the hum of life, the mysteries of backward years are yet brooding; and the marvels of human destiny are whispered to our ears, in the sigh of every breeze. . . . One chapter only of its history (and that how full of marvels!) has been written or preserved; the rest is a blank. . . . This is the proper field for romantic musings.[5]

Two modern American poets have recited, one in prose, the other in verse, long lists of objects of commerce and art that were to be found in the ancient capital of Mexico at the time of Moctezuma. The objects are rendered almost tactile to the reader, and the naming is the poetry. In his book of essays, *In The American Grain,* William Carlos Williams assesses "The Destruction of Tenochtitlan" as a significant event in the American experience. Of that city he writes:

Here "everything which the world affords" was offered for purchase, from the personal services of laborers and porters to the last refinements of bijouterie; gold, silver, lead, brass, copper, tin; wrought and unwrought stone, bricks burnt and unburnt, timber hewn and unhewn, of different sorts; game of every variety, fowls, quails, partridges, wild ducks, parrots, pigeons, reed-birds, sparrows, eagles, hawks, owls, likewise the skins of some birds of prey with their feathers, head, beak and claws; rabbits, hares, deer and little dogs, which they raised for eating; wood and coals in abundance and brasiers of earthenware for burning coals; mats of various kinds; all kinds of green vegetables, especially onions, leeks, watercresses, nasturtium, sorrel, artichokes and golden thistle; fruits, fish, honey, grain — either whole, in the form of flour or baked into loaves; different kinds of cotton thread of all colors; jars, jugs, pots and an endless variety of vessels, all made of fine clay, most of them glazed and painted; eggs, cakes, patés of birds and fish; wine from the maguey, finally everything that could be found throughout the whole country was sold there, each kind of merchandise in a separate street or quarter of the market assigned to it exclusively, and thus the best order was preserved.

To Williams the epic of Cortez and Moctezuma was the very stuff of "the American grain." He goes on to enumerate the gifts which Moctezuma sent to Cortez in an effort to placate him and forestall his march on the capital:

. . . a gold necklace of seven pieces, set with many gems like small rubies, a hundred and eighty-three emeralds and ten fine pearls, and hung with twenty-seven little bells of gold. Two wheels, one of gold like the sun and the other of silver with the image of the moon upon it, made of plates of those metals, twenty-eight hands in circumference, with figures of animals and other things in bas-relief, finished with great skill and ingenuity. — A headpiece of wood and gold, adorned with gems, from which hung twenty-five little bells of gold, and, on it, instead of plume, a green bird with eyes, beak and feet of gold. — Several shoes of the skin of deer, sewed with gold thread, the soles of which were made of blue and white stones of a brilliant appearance. — A shield of wood and leather, with little bells hanging to it and covered with plates of gold, in the middle of which was cut the image of the god of war between four heads of a lion, a tiger, an eagle and an owl, represented alive with their hair and feathers. — Twenty-four curious and beautiful shields of gold, of feathers and very small pearls, and four of feathers and silver only. — Four fishes, two ducks and some other birds of molten gold. — A large mirror adorned with gold, and many small. — Miters and crowns of feathers and gold ornamented with pearls and gems. — Several large plumes of beautiful feathers, fretted with gold and small pearls. — Several fans of gold and silver mixed together; others of feathers only, of different forms and sizes. — A variety of cotton mantles, some all white, others chequered with white and black, or red, green, yellow and blue; on the outside rough like shaggy cloth and within destitute of color and nap.— A number of underwaistcoats, handkerchiefs, counter panes, tapestries and carpets of cotton, the workmanship superior to the materials of which they were composed. — And books made of tablets with a smooth surface for writing, which being joined might be folded together or stretched out to be a considerable length. . . .

Needless to say, all these gifts rather than deterring Cortez aroused his cupidity the more and strengthened his resolve to conquer the heart of the Aztec empire.

The other poet, Archibald MacLeish, in his narrative poem *Conquistador* speaks with the voice of Bernal Diaz del Castillo, veteran campaigner who had fought under Cortez in all the battles of the Conquest. Bernal Diaz's account of the Conquest, *La Verdadera Historia de la Conquista de Nueva España,* was the source upon which Prescott relied the most. Directly or indirectly through Prescott it has influenced most American writers dealing with the Conquest. It was written in the form of a memoir in the soldier's old age, and MacLeish catches much of the spirit of the original chronicle in its nostalgia and testiness as well as in its clarity, matter-of-factness, and eye for detail. Bernal Diaz retained a remarkable memory for the minutia of life in Tenochtitlan as it was first seen by Cortez and his men. In *Conquistador* MacLeish has him speak of the varied commerce of the city:

> Merchants of sweet nuts and of chives and of honey:
> Of leaves of dock for the eyes: of a calf's bone for
>
> Gloss of the hair as the hand draws it: of dung
> For salt for the tanning of leather: sellers of yarn:
> Old men with the sun-bleached hair and the bunches of
>
> Herbs: of lettuces washed cool: of garlic
> Dried brown on a withy of plaited grass:
> Sellers of cooked dough by the coal-fires larding the
>
> Stained skirt with the spittle of burning fat:
> Those the makers of robes: Those that shredded the
> Silken down of a seed and their fingers fastened the
>
> Stone to the twist of it turning the scarlet thread:
> Sellers of good dreams: of blue clay for the
> Baking of gods: of quills of the gold: of hennequin:
>
> Sellers of beetles for red dyes: makers of
> Stone masks of the dead and of stone mirrors:
> Makers of fortunate knots: magistrates in the
>
> Swept porch — and they kept the names of the year:
> They took the tax on the red stones and the herons:
> They judged of the levies of salt: venders of syrups:
>
> Of harsh drugs for the old from the coupling of hares:
> Of dry seeds: of sweet straws. . . .

The contrast of elegance and barbarity arouses wonder. Pursuing his reflections on "The Destruction of Tenochtitlan," William Carlos Williams writes of Moctezuma: "Surely no other prince has lived, or will ever live, in such state as did this American cacique. The whole waking aspirations of his people, opposed to and completing their religious sense, seemed to come off in him and in him alone: the drive upward, toward the sun and the stars. He was the very person of their ornate dreams, so delicate, so prismatically colorful, so full of tinkling sounds and rhythms, so tireless of invention. Never was such a surface lifted above the isolate blackness of such profound savagery."

Another modern American writer, John Houghton Allen, in the novel *Southwest,* an original work savoring authentically of the borderlands, treats a similar theme in a strange way. He writes of the capital city of the Toltecs, predecessors of the Aztecs, and, perhaps because of his Catholic background, has a character in the novel present these people not as splendid and innocent barbarians but as victims of a fall from grace. The book, written in the first person, is mainly about the borderland between Texas and Mexico. The principal characters are Mexican rancheros and ranch hands among whom the author was raised. Loosely constructed and drawling its way from tale to tale in the manner of campfire reminiscences, the book is loaded with the lore, proverbs, and turn of speech of the borderlands and meanders back and forth through the first decades of the twentieth century as various characters remember tales of great bandits or heroes of the revolution such as Pancho Villa and his *dorados*. But there is an unexpected interpolation toward the end of the book, nightmarish, Poe-like in its weirdness and convincing other worldliness. One remembers that Allen is quite consciously Southern, by way of Texas. "We had a weird story told to us by a dope addict," writes Allen, casually getting his tale under way, "around the campfire at Agua Dulce one Christmas Day. Perhaps we were the sort of men who attracted weird and violent tales, but the fact remains, if you told us a story it had to be good." The Mexicans present had celebrated their Christmas the night before in traditional style "at the posada and by going to their annual Mass." Now they were back at work on the ranch and "*crudos*," i.e., suffering from hangover. "It was a pitch-dark night, and the day had been gray as a fog, with the brush twisted and tortured and bare under overcast skies. . . ." The men sitting around the fire were "passing the bottle, because of the nip in the air, and because after all, it was Christmas," when suddenly a man from out in the darkness lurched past the rim of firelight startling all hands. It turned out that he was a harmless and pitiable creature, known to be a smoker of marihuana, "one of those grotesques that are awry and jangled from smoking this humble weed." After eating like a glutton and praising the cook "— and that alone took a *boca-de-ora* [sic] —" he launched into his story. Once as a young man he was forced to flee into the mountains west of Torreón because of a knifing. He mounted high into practically inaccessible regions of mountain wilderness, passed over a summit, and descended into an unknown valley where he discovered the "city of the Toltecs." He sneaked, full of dread, past the huge, "hawk-nosed" sentinels, who, clothed in gorgeous raiment, stood erect and looked straight ahead as though paralyzed by some enchantment. The people in the streets were frozen still, having been suddenly caught by some spell while in the attitudes of daily living. In terror the narrator fled into the principal temple where he found a throng of people kneeling and bowed frozen in an attitude of "mysterious penance" before a high priest on a throne. Horrified all the more, he escaped into a side room and found himself in a seraglio of temple maidens, all of them remarkable in that they were blondes with golden hair that fell below their waists, and fine blue eyes like clear water, and the brave laughter that would not be heard again in the Western World. They were like Valkyries, the music of Wagner. Perhaps they had been sent as tribute to the monarchs of the Western World from the greenland colonies a thousand years ago — for they were Vikings, and they were beautiful, the tropic sun had never touched their loveliness. There was peace about their eyes, and they were the golden thighs of Paradise. The sight of them affected me with a bitter nostalgia, and again I remembered, as we all remember, what the Spanish have lost in the Western World. They were like the blue-eyed, golden-haired Spanish descended from the Visigoths, that we all in our subconscious remember. It is not that we are people dark by nature, attracted by the light, the tall and the fair; it has been with us since we first came to the Indies, that we suffered a fall from grace — for the Captains of Cortés were massive men with red beards and light hair and blue eyes and voices like Thor— and we would remember the Visigoths. We have a bitter nostalgia for blondness, we brown little men, we yearn back to our ethnos, we would dream of the fair people with blue eyes, that even the Indians believed in — and we have remembered the Visigoths.[6]

These temple maids were imprisoned by some spell and seemed to long for the release that a Christian benediction might have given them,

> but the very idea gave me a cold sweat, and I came away from the temple maidens and I found myself in the streets again, rushing through the streets of that awful city, the people crying havoc, for they seemed to cry after me to stop and heal them with a Christian benediction — this was what they had been waiting for, a thousand years! ... I imagined the dismay on their faces, I dared not look at them from fear and shame, but they cried aloud, at last. There was a babble of voices for a moment, and then silence. They had waited for a Christian a thousand years, and I ran.[7]

The theme of the failure of the European in his relations with the original people of America is still here, but the point of view is different. The European did not dare bestow real Christianity upon those who desperately needed it.

Though early American novelists dealing with the Conquest relied almost entirely on Prescott and Bernal Díaz for their source material, they did not match either of these writers in enthusiasm for the great conquistador. In the main, the Spaniard was the despoiler, and American writers have tended to find a community of spirit with that aspect of the Mexican soul which has not permitted to this day a statue of Cortez to be erected throughout the length and breadth of Mexico. The modern Mexican historian, Wigberto Jimenez Moreno, has said that the Mexican psyche still bears the scars of the trauma caused by the rape of the

Indian mother by the Spanish father. A recent and rather startling revelation of how close to the surface is the intense feeling which survives in Mexico about the fate of the Aztec was the furor caused by the discovery in the south of Mexico of the alleged bones of the last of the Aztec emperors, Cuauhtemoc (this Nahuatl name also has various spellings in English). Of a very different metal from his uncle, Moctezuma II, Cuauhtemoc defied the Spaniards while his city was reduced to rubble, block by block, and his people subsisted on rats. He never surrendered but was captured and promised honorable treatment. Cortez brought him along on one of his expeditions to the south, not daring to leave him in the capital. In the course of the expedition, Cortez had Cuauhtemoc hanged, claiming that the Aztec leader was plotting treason. In an early American novel, Robert Montgomery Bird mourns the fate of Cuauhtemoc or Cuatimozin as that writer names him: "Four years after the fall of his empire, and at a distance of several hundred leagues from his native valley, he expiated upon a gibbet, a crime that existed only in the gloomy and remorseful imagination of the Conqueror. And thus, with two royal kinsmen, kings and feudatories of Anahuac, he was left to swing in the winds, and feed the vultures of a distant and desert land. He merited a higher distinction, a loftier respect, and a profounder compassion, than men will willingly accord to a barbarian and infidel."[8] In a long and idyllic novel written a decade after Bird's, Joseph Holt Ingraham celebrates the rise and love of the first Moctezuma whose descendant was to lose "his power, his empire, and his life, by the hands of an invader, whose coming was from the rising sun, and whose pathway was deluged with blood."[9] Published the same year as Ingraham's book was Edward Maturin's *Montezuma, the Last of the Aztecs,* which conjured up the vision of a pastoral, innocent, and serene Tenochtitlan on the eve of the Conquest:

> Nor had nature, in the caprice which sometimes characterizes her loveliest creations, lavished these beauties for her own solitary enjoyment, or the isolated honours of her own worship. Towns, studding the bosoms of the lakes, or bordering their margins, lent the busy and populous aspect, to this sylvan elysium, of worshippers assembled at the great altar of nature, to pour forth their hymns of gratitude, or solemnize their simple rites in honour of her who had made their happy valley one rich panorama of her beauties, and endowed the temporary sojourn of earth with the fadeless joys, the unwithering hues, and beatific visions of heaven! Clustered with flowers, or embowered in shade, lay these cottages; their quiet inhabitants occupied in the various employments afforded by their pastoral retreat: some of them engaged on their *chinampas* in rearing fruit, flowers or vegetables for the market of

Tenochtitlan. Alas! little did they deem their days of happy seclusion in that valley-retreat were so rapidly drawing to a close: its smiling orchards and gardens so soon to be trampled by the iron-heel of the conquerer, or laid waste by his desolating ambition; the crystal waters of its lakes darkened and defaced by the smoke of the lombard and the quiet depths of their paradise re-echoing the blast of the war-trumpet or the remorseless battle-cry, "God and St. Iago!"[10]

Again in *Conquistador,* MacLeish depicts the Spanish soldiers recognizing that in Mexico they would forever be strangers:

We praised the trampling of sun as a gilt cock;
Our hearts were singing as hammered bronze and our mouths with

Sound as the corn is where the wind goes: and we mocked the
Shape of love with our thumbs: We cried aloud of the
Great sky: of the salt rock: of the land. . . .

And nevertheless it was not so: for the ground was

Silent against us: on our foreign hands
The dust was a solemn and red stain: our tongues were
Unskilled to the pulp of their fruits as a language of
Sullen stones in our mouths: we heard the sun in the
Crackle of live trees with the ears of strangers. . . .

William Carlos Williams absolves Cortez of personal blame, calling him the agent of "the spirit of malice which underlies men's lives and against which nothing offers resistance. And bitter as the thought may be that Tenochtitlan, the barbaric city, its people, its genius wherever found should have been crushed out because of the awkward names men give their emptiness, yet it was no man's fault. It was the force of the pack whom the dead drive. Cortez was neither malicious, stupid, nor blind, but a conqueror like other conquerors."

And yet, of course, all was not destruction. From practically the first day that Cortez and his men landed in Vera Cruz a racial fusion began which was to produce a remarkable new culture. In fact the very prefiguration of the new Mexican race was the relationship between Cortez and his Indian mistress, Malinche, known to the Spaniards as Doña Marina. She gave him access to the Indian world, not only in its stratagems and intrigues but in its traditions and its psychology. Indianists in Mexico have long hated Malinche as a traitor to her people. The modern painter Siqueiros presents her in a large mural being lasciviously fondled by Cortez, as she snickers at the destruction of her people, her earth-brown body making sharp contrast with the startling whiteness of the skin of the Spaniard. And yet Malinche had real grievances. The daughter of a small chieftain on the rim of Tenochtitlan, she was dispossessed of her inheritance at the connivance of her mother. Her father died while she was a child and her mother remarried and had a son for whom she was very ambitious. If he was to inherit the chieftainship, Malinche had to be removed; so the mother sold her into slavery and staged a mock funeral to prove that she was dead. It was as a slave girl in the region of Vera Cruz that Cortez came upon her. While undoubtedly she paved the way for his successes, she also gave him an understanding and respect for the indigenous cultures of Mexico. For Cortez, unlike Pizarro, although he felt impelled on occasion to use harsh methods, had no love of cruelty per se. The histories of Mexico and Peru might be expected to have run a parallel course. In each area the Spaniards came upon highly developed and flourishing Indian civilizations, but Mexico produced a genuine fusion of races and cultures, while in Peru a Spanish oligarchy still uneasily rules from Lima a dispossessed mass of Indians whose resentment is rising to a dangerous pitch. The nature of the conquest in each area and more particularly the characters of the leading conquistadores provide a key to this situation, and Malinche deserves no little credit for the road that colonial Mexico embarked upon. In the opening lines, MacLeish in *Conquistador* presents Bernal Díaz faced with the fact of *mestizaje,* a racial mixture, in the persons of his own children:

> . . . my children
> Half-grown: sons with beards: the big one
> Breaking the small of his back in the brothel thills
> And a girl to be married and all of them snarling at home
> With the Indian look in their eyes like a cat killing.

In a modern novel, *Step Down Elder Brother,* the author, Josephina Niggli, considers the social situation of the state of Neuvo León and especially its capital, Monterey, the industrial center of Mexico. Nuevo León had long prided itself on being *criollo,* that is of pure Spanish blood though born in the New World. With the industrialization of the area, *mestizos* (mixed-bloods) poured into the region from the south. They came as laborers, but within two or three generations and especially after the great revolution which began in 1910 and lasted a decade, many of the *mestizos* became petty bourgeois and began vigorously challenging the older families. The protagonist of the novel, Domingo Vasquez de Anda, though a scion of one of the great families, has come to recognize and accept the inevitable triumph of the *mestizos*. He is saturated in the history of Mexico, and as he stands over a sleeping servant girl, Serafina, who has been made pregnant by his brother, and notices for the first time the Indian caste of her features, he muses upon her lineage somewhat extravagantly: "Perhaps on Serafina's bone there was stamped the memory of Cortés' entrance to Mexico City; of Montezuma's litter with the coverlet woven from hummingbird's feathers. In her might still remain echoes of the poet-emperor, greatest of the Aztecans [Nezahualcoyotl], who, like David, came from the fields to sit on the throne and there compose psalms to God."[11] Serafina's child, though rejected by its own father, is to become, through Domingo's insistence, a recognized member of the family.

But apart from the partial survival of the Aztecs in the blood line of living Mexicans, what if anything survives of Tenochtitlan? A number of American writers have dealt with the subterranean continuance of Indian attitudes and ritual in the religious life of modern Mexico, a subject which will be treated later; but quite aside from this consideration, several American writers, some of whom are in no way regionalists, have felt impelled to re-emphasize and reinterpret the epic of Tenochtitlan as important for the self-understanding of even English-speaking America. Hart Crane ended his long poem, *The Bridge,* which had aimed at capturing all of America for the imagination, with a somewhat enigmatic reference to the eagle and the serpent, the ancient insignia of the Aztecs which is reproduced on the flag of modern Mexico. Evidently Crane felt that in the summing up of his epic this cultural symbol was not to be omitted. In another poem addressed to the stone statue of the Aztec flower god, Xochipilli, Crane challenges the reader to avail himself of that which was enduring in the life of a "dismounted people":

>           . . . If you
> Could drink the sun as did and does
> Xochipilli — as they who've
> Gone have done, as they
> Who've done . . . A god of flowers in statued
> Stone . . . of love —
> If you could die, then starve, who live
> Thereafter, stronger than death smiles in flowering stone —
> You could stop time, give florescent
> Time a longer answer back (shave lightning,
> Possess in hale full the winds) of time
> A longer answer force, more enduring answer
> As they did — and have done . . .[12]

Not only in "The Destruction of Tenochtitlan," but in other essays William Carlos Williams has returned to the theme of the Aztecs and their relationship to the American consciousness. In discussing the type of the "New World Man," he rejects the notion of T. S. Eliot's enervated J. Alfred Prufrock as being representative. "Prufrock is a masterly portrait of the man just below the summit, but the type is universal; the model in his case might be Mr. J. No. The New World is Montezuma or, since he was stoned to death in a parley, Guatemozin, who had the city of Mexico leveled over him before he was taken."[13] As to the legacy of Tenochtitlan, Williams says: "One is at liberty to guess what the pure American addition to world culture might have been if it had gone forward singly. But that is merely an academicism. Perhaps Tenochtitlan which Cortez destroyed held the key. That also is beside the point, except that Tenochtitlan with its curious brilliance may still legitimately be kept alive in thought not as something which *could* have been preserved but as something which was actual and was destroyed."[14] The theme has been with us almost from the beginning of our literature; it exists in countless popular forms and has been reappraised by serious modern American writers. We have not seen the end of it, as it is enduringly a part of the matter of America.

PART ONE

# Criollo Mexico and Frontier America

*Chronological Listing of Events in the Histories of the United States and Mexico which have been reflected in the early record of Mexico in American Literature*

| | |
|---|---|
| 1519–1521 | The Conquest of Mexico by Spain. |
| 1800 | Philip Nolan leads a filibustering expedition into Texas, still under the Spanish crown, and is defeated. |
| 1807 | Zebulon Pike and party wander by mistake into Spanish territory, are arrested but soon released. |
| 1813 | Augustus Magee leads the Republican Army of the North into Texas and is defeated by Spanish troops under General Arredondo. |
| 1810–1821 | Mexican wars of independence against Spain. |
| 1821 | Trade along the Santa Fe Trail from Independence, Missouri, to Santa Fe, New Mexico, becomes legal. |
| 1835 | The Texas Revolution. |
| 1841 | The Texan-Santa Fe Expedition. |
| 1846–1848 | War between the United States and Mexico. |
| 1849 | The California gold rush. |
| 1857 | Benito Juárez becomes president of Mexico. |
| 1861–1865 | The American Civil War. Both the United States and Mexico are absorbed in rending civil conflicts. Contacts between the nations are largely suspended. Taking advantage of the Civil War in the United States, which renders that nation incapable of enforcing the Monroe Doctrine, the French intervene in Mexico and set up Maximilian as emperor. |
| 1867 | Unable to crush the national armies of Juárez and facing pressure from the United States under President Johnson, the French abandon Mexico and Maximilian, who is executed that year at Querétaro. Juárez and his liberals are victorious. The *criollo* era in Mexico is over. The United States emerges from the Civil War as a powerful, industrialized country. Two transformed nations resume relations with each other. |

CHAPTER ONE

## Two Cultures Meet in the Borderlands

Despite the impact of the story of the Conquest of Mexico upon North American writers, the long, subsequent history of colonial Mexico remains virtually unrecorded in the works of contemporary English-speaking writers in North America. It is almost awesome to contemplate the fact that Spain's colonial rule of Mexico lasted for three hundred years, a span considerably longer than the entire history of the United States. And these three hundred years, in which a vivid people were working out their destiny in an extended terrain to the south, were three centuries of silence in terms of the consciousness of English-speaking North America. To be sure, reports of colonial Mexico figured, tangentially, in the news and historical accounts of the colonial rivalries of England, France, and Spain. But in any sense which could be called literary, the space that might have been occupied by colonial Mexico was a vacuum in North American letters. This lack of a literary record is due to the fact that New Spain was an abstraction in the minds of people in the United States until the early part of the nineteenth century. Then, at the eve of Mexico's break from Spanish rule, Mexicans and Americans in the flesh encountered each other in the borderlands of the Southwest. From this encounter developed a cultural involvement between the United States and Mexico, continuing to the present.

In 1803, the Louisiana Purchase removed the barrier of the French-owned Louisiana Territory, comprising most of the present midwestern states, from the path of U. S. expansion, and the push to the West and Southwest began in earnest. The result was inevitable collision with Mexico in the desert region of what is now the American Southwest. The early American writers who reported on this collision, the chroniclers and novelists of the frontier, reveal, in the simplicity of their characters, far more of themselves than of the Mexico of their day. Yet there is, in their accounts, much interesting and valuable reporting, the chroniclers and writers of memoirs having produced, by and large, better literature than the novelists. But Mexico had other uses beyond providing a new field for the reporting of strange scenes. It was the perfect foil by which young America could re-enforce its image of itself. It brought out all the swagger, the braggadocio, the grand disdain, or the self-righteousness of mountain man, explorer, Santa Fe trader, military man, journalist, or plain forty-niner. Other early American writers using Mexican themes but drawing their material secondhand reproduced for the most part the attitudes found in the original sources.

Early happenings in the border region, foolhardy, cocksure adventures, naïve in spirit, and prompted by a fancy as limitless as the plains of Texas, reflected unmistakably the character of the frontiersman. These first incidents of contact between Mexicans and Americans were unofficial and violent. American freebooters with outlandish schemes of empire staged filibustering raids into Texas when the area was still under the Spanish crown. In 1800 Philip Nolan and a small party attempted to arrange a compact with the Comanches to join forces in driving out the Spanish royalist troops. The enterprise ended disastrously for the Americans, but one member of the expedition, Ellis Bean, from Natchez, Tennessee, has left a picaresque memoir of his experiences in Mexico. In 1813 a more serious attempt was made by a large force of Americans under the command of Augustus Magee, a graduate of West Point. After initial successes, the "Republican Army of the North" was finally defeated by Spanish troops under General Arredondo, but its exploits haunted the memory of the border region and became part of its folklore. The colonization of Texas by Americans while the area was under Mexican rule at first proceeded in an orderly manner under the guidance of that most un-Texan of Texans, Stephen F. Austin. But with all his skill as a diplomat and his understanding in dealing with an alien culture, he could not forestall the inevitable. The words *Alamo* and *Goliad* became and still are battle cries to make the blood rise. This contest with Mexico produced the archetype of the hero as frontiersman exemplified in its pure form by Bowie, Crockett, and Houston. In this concoction, a liberal admixture of Mexican villainy was an essential ingredient. Nor was much fabrication needed here. Fannin's unarmed men were massacred at Goliad. Greatly outnumbered, they finally capitulated to the Mexicans after having received assurances that they would be treated honorably as prisoners of war.

The ill-fated Texan Santa Fe Expedition of 1841 was about as naïve an enterprise as was ever launched in the borderlands. Texas, during its short life as a republic, maintained a shadowy claim to the Territory of New Mexico. Faced with an empty treasury, President Mirabeau Lamar of Texas decided to make a move which he hoped would capture for Texas the lucrative trade of the Santa Fe Trail. Accordingly, he outfitted and armed an expedition of some three hundred men, who were to cross from Austin to Santa Fe through a wilderness never before penetrated

*Cultures Meet in the Borderlands* 19

by Americans and known only in part by scattered plains Indians and a few Mexican hunters and traders. The ostensible purpose of the expedition was to be trade. But the leaders carried with them documents signed by Lamar exhorting the people of New Mexico to throw off the tyrannous rule of Mexico and join the free Republic of Texas. Lamar fully explained in these documents to any New Mexican readers who might construe the expedition to be a military invasion that the leaders of the expedition were instructed to employ force only if the people sided with them against the officials of Mexican rule. If the people did not favor the cause of Texas, then the whole venture was to be converted into a peaceable mission of trade. When the Texans, more dead than alive from hunger, thirst, and exhaustion, finally reached the first New Mexican settlements, they were met by emissaries of Governor Manuel Armijo of New Mexico. Here was a man who embodied in his person all that was showy, guileful, and disarming in the Mexican personality. He appears again and again in American writing, and his character is still being examined with fascination by contemporary novelists. The Texans on their part met Mexican guile with a specious frankness. It was outrageous that they should be treated as anything but peaceable traders. Armijo had been forewarned of this expedition and its aims by his agents in Texas, some who had acted as outfitters and guides for the Texans. His captain, Salazar, disarmed the Texans by ruse. He met them with a great show of courtesy, commiserated over their condition, and said that unfortunately, purely as a matter of form, he must ask them to surrender their arms temporarily. This was an action he explained, that the Governor insisted on with American traders as an act of good faith on their part, and the arms were always returned shortly and in good condition. Having thus naïvely allowed themselves to be disarmed, the Texans were completely at the mercy of Armijo and Salazar, two men notably lacking in this quality. Once deprived of their weapons, the Texans were declared prisoners of war and herded to Santa Fe where some of them were summarily executed. The rest were to be sent all the way to Mexico City on foot, as living testaments to the Mexican capital that Manuel Armijo was intrepidly upholding the sovereignty of Mexico on the northern frontier. The first lap of the journey, a real *jornada de muerte,* was made under the command of Salazar himself. He drove the prisoners mercilessly, starved them systematically, while pocketing the funds which were to be spent on supplies, shot all stragglers but kept their ears to help him with his final accounting. Upon arriving in El Paso, the prisoners came under a new jurisdiction. Salazar handed them over to the military commandant of the region and stood dumbfounded while that Mexican officer, white with rage, condemned him as a barbarian and disgrace to the country. The American frontiersmen were experiencing another Mexico as they drew closer to its center of culture. After several days of rest during which they were treated with much kindness, especially by the priests and women of El Paso, the prisoners resumed their journey toward Mexico City, this time mounted. From here on, their progress took on the air of a triumphant procession. Communities along the way turned out to welcome the young men from the north, and prominent citizens vied for the privilege of entertaining them. The Texans acquired a lot of Spanish and many ideas about the country and the people. After a period of imprisonment in Mexico City, they were released.

Accompanying the expedition from the beginning was a young newspaperman, George Wilkins Kendall. A New Englander by birth, he had wandered throughout the country from the time he was seventeen years old, working first as a printer and later as a reporter. When only twenty-eight years old, he established, in 1837, the New Orleans *Picayune*. This newspaper, which was to do so much in later years to foster regional writing in America, was "the first representative in the South of the vigorous, rollicking 'Penny Press.' "[1] As such, it became immensely popular and much imitated. Having gotten wind of Mirabeau Lamar's scheme to take over New Mexico, Kendall joined the expedition in Austin, much in the manner of a foreign correspondent. Upon his return from the imprisonment in Mexico City, he wrote an account of the experience of the expedition. The *Narrative of the Texan Santa Fe Expedition* was immediately taken up by the American public, and it has since served as basic source material not only for historians but for writers of fiction. Popular historical novelists such as Hervey Allen in *Anthony Adverse* and Elliot Arnold in *The Time of the Gringo* have found it ready to hand. More importantly, both Harvey Fergusson and Paul Horgan, contemporary American writers who have done significant studies of the Southwest in fiction and in social histories, have made wide use of Kendall's account in their novels and cultural histories. Fortunately for the purposes of this study, Kendall was unhampered by any notions of scholarly objectivity. With all his prejudices intact, he was pristine America caught in the maze of a complex and totally alien culture.

Ventures like the filibustering invasions of Nolan and Magee and the Texan Santa Fe Expedition were expressions of one aspect of the American character of the time and region. Another side, characteristic of Americans at any time, was also very much in evidence in the borderlands, the concern with commerce. The Santa Fe Trail, extending from Independence, Missouri, to Santa Fe, was functioning as a trade route between western America and northern Mexico even before the establishment of the Mexican Republic. Though it was Spain's policy with her colonies to prohibit their trading anywhere but with the mother country, it was not easy in the farthest reaches of her empire in North America to enforce this policy. Though officially discouraged and at times even stopped, a clandestine trade had been carried on along the Santa Fe Trail ever since Major Zebulon Pike published his report on the Santa Fe-Taos region in 1810. In 1821 Captain William Backnell returned from an expedition to Santa Fe to report a complete change in the attitude of the authorities in New Mexico toward American traders. Spain was out of Mexico and Iturbide had been proclaimed emperor. Mexico was eager to trade with the United States, and the Santa Fe Trail was now wide open. From 1821 onward the volume of trade along the Trail increased to such an extent that in time New Mexico became dependent for its revenue upon the American traders. Considerably before the formal annexation of New Mexico, the Territory was in fact an economic colony of the United States. This situation was one which Governor Armijo, for all his show of authority, recognized completely and which contributed to his detestation of all Americans.

The literature of the Santa Fe Trail is extensive and includes that early volume of American fiction *Prose Poems and Sketches* by Albert Pike, published in 1834, containing among other things short stories with a New Mexican locale. A number of journals and memoirs about life on the Trail survive. Among the better are James Josiah Webb's *Adventures in the Santa Fe Trade,* covering the period between 1844 and 1847, and Lewis H. Garrard's *Wah-To-Yah and the Taos Trail,* originally published in 1850. But the undoubted classic of the literature of the Santa Fe Trail is Josiah Gregg's *Commerce of the Prairies,* 1851. Gregg plied the Trail for many years and was successful in his commercial enterprises, but essentially he was an intellectual, detached and lonely in a pioneer society. He filled notebooks with his botanical and zoological observations gathered along the Trail for proposed scientific treatises that never got into print. But his keen eye for detail is in evidence throughout the *Commerce of the Prairies,* and he has given to American literature a literate and comprehensive account of life among the Mexicans and Americans along the Santa Fe Trail and in its terminal cities. Paul Horgan in *The Centuries of Santa Fe*[2] gives a thinly fictionalized sketch of Josiah Gregg as "the Missouri trader." While admiring much in the quality of the man, Horgan, a Catholic writer, satirizes Gregg's commitment to a rather barren rationalism, his scientism and puritanism, and his total inability to respond to the aesthetic aspect of New Mexican life in its music, dances, and religious ceremonies.

At about the same time that the Santa Fe Trail was first being traveled, another sort of frontier with Mexico was being opened, a commerce by sea in which American vessels went all the way around the tip of South America to trade along the west coast of South America, Central America, and Mexico as far north as California. While Spain still held her colonies, the merchant seamen met the same opposition as did the Santa Fe traders from the Spanish authorities. Sea-going Sam Slicks, sailing out of Boston, have left ludicrous accounts of their various ruses in pulling the wool over the eyes of Spanish port officials in South America and Mexico. The earliest of these accounts and typical of its kind is William Shaler's *Journal of a Voyage Between China and the Northwestern Coast of America Made in 1804.* Another Yankee seaman, Richard Cleveland, a great friend of Shaler's, wrote in 1855 a similar journal, *Voyages and Commercial Enterprises of the Sons of New England,* dealing with the same time and region. The most consciously literary and the best known narrative of New England trading in California waters is Richard Henry Dana's *Two Years Before the Mast,* 1840. Shaler, Cleveland, and Dana encountered a California which, being remote from the centers of Mexican civilization, had developed a regional variation in culture. Here tendencies generally present in the culture of Spain and her extensions in the New World were exaggerated. The aristocratic pretense, conspicuous leisure, and absolute abhorrence of work among the Californians astounded the sons of New England. Another sea-going account of Mexico, *Los Gringos,* 1849, was written during the Mexican war by an American naval officer, Lieutenant H. A. Wise. Unfailingly jaunty, Wise was determined to be amused rather than annoyed by what he claimed to be the ubiquitous rascality of Mexican men, which was, he felt, more than compensated for by the vivacity and allure of Mexico's women.

Aside from the relatively conventional trade carried on by the Santa Fe trader and the New England sea captain in the Southwest, there were the feverish prospecting of the forty-niner and the eccentric, freebooting career of the mountain man, who went alone into the wilderness to trap beaver. These men too had their brushes with Mexican civilization and have left their records. There are a number of accounts still in existence written by forty-niners. Most of them are devoted primarily to the rigors of the journey to California with harrowing tales of those who died, went mad, or resorted to cannibalism in the attempts to cross Death Valley, or to accounts of the avarice and debauchery witnessed in the diggings. One of these narratives, however, is less preoccupied with the immediate business at hand and has a good deal to say about Mexicans encountered in Chihuahua, Sonora, and California. This account, *Mexican Gold Trail, the Journal of a 49-er,* by George W. B.

Evans had long been unavailable but was published in 1945 by the Huntington Library in a volume edited by Glenn S. Dumke. Evans was intelligent and sensitive and very much a product of his middlewestern, Protestant environment, one which in its emphasis on literal adherence to high standards of personal conduct made him completely unappreciative of the flamboyance with which some northern Mexicans whom he encountered disregarded conventional morality. Another literary record of California diggings and one from a rather unexpected source was *The Shirley Letters from the California Mines* by Louise Amelia Smith. The author, who assumed the *nom de plume* of Dame Shirley, was a New England schoolmistress, friend of Margaret Fuller and Emily Dickinson. She had followed her husband to California during the gold rush and wrote a series of letters to her sister, letters obviously intended from the outset for publication. In the introduction to the 1949 edition of the letters published by Knopf, the editor, Carl I. Wheat, quotes statements from Charles Warren Stoddard and Josiah Royce to the effect that the *Shirley Letters* give a much truer picture of life in the California mines than does anything written by Bret Harte. Though at times somewhat stilted and pretentious in diction, these letters are full of unabashed references to the ructions in the local saloons and other aspects of life in a rough and generally womanless society. They also reveal a generosity of spirit toward the often ill-treated Mexicans rare for on-the-scene reports in that period. One of the mountain men, James Ohio Pattie, who left Kentucky to wander throughout the Southwest, published in 1831 *The Personal Narrative of James O. Pattie of Kentucky*. This book was edited and probably to a considerable degree prompted by Timothy Flint, a Congregational minister who knew Pattie personally. But the flavor of the author is very much there, and there is no prudery or evasiveness. Franklin Walker, in the *Literary History of Southern California,* says of Pattie's narrative: "Although its accuracy has been questioned and its spirit criticized, it remains the epic of the mountain men, perhaps more truly representing their attitudes, their experiences, and their adventures than any other book which has appeared on the subject."[3] Pattie devotes a good deal of space to accounts of Mexican life, but despite its fascination for him, he can find little to admire in Mexico except its skill in horsemanship and the beauty of its women.

Official travelers, bearing commissions to explore or fix boundaries, have also left testaments to their first encounters with the northern fringes of Mexican society. Major Zebulon Pike in 1807 was given command of an expedition which was to explore the western reaches of the territory acquired by the United States through the Louisiana Purchase. By accident he and his men passed over into Spanish territory where they were taken into custody and marched through the wilderness into Santa Fe. The Spanish authorities, satisfied that the Americans had not intended to transgress, treated Pike and his men with great courtesy and entertained them royally. Soon released from custody, the expedition headed back for the American border. Pike's account of this sojourn into Spanish territory, published in 1810, was one of the first reports on the Hispanic Southwest to reach the American public. Pike was thoroughly appreciative of the courtesies he had received and graciously acknowledged them in his report, but his thorough-going puritanism made him gag on what he observed of life in Taos and Santa Fe, such as the fandangos which made no effort to conceal what dancing is all about and the almost Moorish attitude he observed among the men, who tended to regard their women as purely sexual objects to be kept at home and kept quiet, while they themselves discussed those things which were exclusively their domain, politics and horses. Some hedonistic and unconventional priests of the region were to Pike simply incredible. His account stirred interest for the first time among American readers in the Hispanic lands beyond the border. Another army officer and explorer, John Charles Frémont, the famed pathfinder, was of quite a different character. There was much of the mountain man in his makeup, and his memoirs of early explorations in California reveal a delight in the color, dash, and good horsemanship of the early Californians. John Russell Bartlett, appointed in 1850 by President Zachary Taylor as commissioner to survey the boundary between the United States and Mexico, wrote a two-volume narrative of his experiences in the Southwest. He had a wealth of information about conditions that were ripe for change. In his treatment of Mexican society he was arrogant and completely ethnocentric. An equally choleric account of Mexican life can be found in *Audubon's Western Journal: 1849–1850,* written by John Wodehouse Audubon, younger of John J. Audubon's two sons. Some of the most interesting reports to come out of the Southwest in the 1860's were written by a transplanted Irishman, J. Ross Browne, who wandered freely throughout the area, sometimes on his own and sometimes on government commission. An excellent writer, Browne was a humorist, satirist, and skillful descriptive narrator. He was as scornful of Mexicans as was Bartlett but much more colorful in his descriptions of them. Browne's two volumes dealing in whole or in part with the Southwest, both published in the 1860's, are *Crusoe's Island . . . With Sketches of Adventures in California and Washoe,* and *A Tour Through Arizona, 1864, or Adventures in the Apache Country.*

Some early American writers who had never been to Mexico dealt with Mexican themes. Novelists who used the epic of the Conquest to provide material for fiction such as Bird, Maturin, and Ingraham have already been mentioned. Prescott himself, because of serious eye trouble, was unable to travel and had never visited the Spanish-speaking lands of which he wrote. Despite his admiration of both the Aztecs and the conquistadores, he shared in the general American disparagement of the Mexicans of his own time. "Those familiar with modern Mexicans," he wrote in his history of the Conquest, "will find it difficult to conceive that the nation should ever have been capable of devising the enlightened polity which we have been considering. But they should remember that in the Mexicans of our day they see only a conquered race; as different from their ancestors as are the modern Egyptians from those who built — I will not say, the tasteless pyramids — but the temples and palaces, whose magnificent wrecks strew the borders of the Nile, at Luxor and Karnac."[4] Continuing the analogy, he saw the contemporary Mexican to be as remote in quality from his Aztec forbears as the "degenerate descendant" of the ancient Greek was from the Athenian of the age of Pericles. The earliest American novel with a Mexican background, *Francis Berrian; or the Mexican Patriot,* published in Boston in 1826, was produced by Timothy Flint, a writer who also had never been to Mexico. Flint was the Congregational minister who later edited James Ohio Pattie's narrative. Harvard-trained, he moved to Cincinnati where he edited a periodical concerned with the westward movement and also published four novels dealing mainly with Western life. He never saw the country about which he wrote, relying on second-hand and untrustworthy information. The careful reader can discover geographical inaccuracies in *Francis Berrian*. The novel is bad melodrama, but it does give a lively picture of Mexico during its war of independence, with the intricacies of its factional disputes. Operating also at second hand in treating of Mexico, were Washington Irving and James Fenimore Cooper. Irving's *The Adventures of Captain Bonneville, U.S.A.* includes an account of the captain's exploratory trip into California. Benjamin Louis Eulalie de Bonneville was born in France in 1796, immigrated to the United States and was graduated from West Point in 1815. Most of his life was spent on the frontier. In romanticizing his picturesque career, Irving reworked Bonneville's journals with additions from such sources as Lewis and Clark to produce what Stanley T. Williams has called "another potboiler,"[5] designed to feed the unappeasable public appetite for accounts of the opening West. The rough-hewn Mexican *rancheros* of northern Mexico turn out, in Irving's account, to have a remarkable resemblance to the gallant and picturesque *caballeros* of Irving's earlier Spanish sketches. Cooper, in the novel *Jack Tier,* has created in Señor

Montefalderón a Mexican gentleman who has all the stiff dignity and elaborate punctilio of the stock figure of the Spanish don.

The high-spirited and jaunty voice of nationalism in early nineteenth-century America split into different registers when the westward-pushing frontier collided with Mexico. There was on the one hand the rabid racialism and mounting ferocity against the "greaser" and on the other the pontifical tones of the doctrine of Manifest Destiny. Walt Whitman, who some thirty-five years later was to write so glowingly of the Latin contribution to the composite American man, was in 1846 in tune with the spirit of the age. "What has miserable, inefficient Mexico," he wrote in the *Brooklyn Daily Eagle,* "with her superstition, her burlesque upon freedom, her actual tyranny by the few over the many — what has she to do with the great mission of peopling the New World with a noble race? Be it ours, to achieve that mission! Be it ours to roll down all of the upstart leaven of old despotism, that comes our way!"[6] In Congress a Representative Trimble made an announcement expressing sentiments which were rapidly becoming platitudinous. "The great engineer of the Universe has fixed the natural limits of our country, and man cannot change them. That at least is above the treaty-making power. To that boundary we shall go; peaceably if we can, forcibly if we must."[7] During the same period Ralph Waldo Emerson felt obliged to visit a friend who had spent the night in the Concord jail for refusing to pay the annual polltax in protest against America's war with Mexico. "Henry, why are you here?" Emerson is said to have asked in astonishment. "Why are you *not* here?" was the emphatic reply credited to Henry David Thoreau, whose writings along with James Russell Lowell's *Bigelow Papers* represent a small body of opinion which opposed itself to the tide of Manifest Destiny. Recognizing the psychological unity in prevailing attitudes toward the Negro and the Mexican, Thoreau, in his essay "Civil Disobedience," writes of the merchants and farmers of Massachusetts that they are "more interested in commerce and agriculture than they are in humanity, and are not prepared to do justice to the slave and to Mexico, *cost what it may,*" that they "even postpone the question of freedom to the question of free-trade, and quietly read the prices-current along with the latest advices from Mexico, after dinner, and, it may be, fall asleep over them both."[8] It is ironic that the Anglo-Americans in Austin's colony, before the revolt of Texas from Mexico, while ever ready to curse the tyranny of Mexico's rule, were outraged at the mounting hostility of the Mexican government toward the institution of Negro slavery that had been transplanted onto its territory. One of the aims of the Texas revolt was to secure Texas for slavery.

The feverish nationalism created by the conflicts with Mexico together with the general public interest in the westward movement created a market for a special kind of popular literature which soon deluged the country. A great amount of this literature was supplied by the publishing house of Beadle and Adams, which first gave America the *Dime Novel*. The guiding spirit behind this publishing venture was Erasmus Beadle, a man of old Yankee stock but born and reared in Otsego, New York, where he operated his first printing press. Beadle combined business acumen with a professed sense of duty to advance the cause of patriotism and, beginning in 1859 and continuing through the eighties, flooded the country with a pulp literature which in catering to the spirit of nationalism achieved tremendous popularity. The *Dime Novels* were adventure stories of all kinds with a marked emphasis on tales of pioneering days and border conflicts. According to the bulletin of the New York Public Library, which contains the only full collection of this material, Beadle and Adams achieved "a pioneer literature which has now wholly vanished but which, for a generation, exercised a profound influence on the country's thought, character, and habits of mind."[9] The editor of the series was Orville J. Victor, a man with a certain reputation for scholarship who had assisted President Lincoln in the preparation of some of his speeches. Victor's professed standards as editor were accuracy in the portrayal of the pioneer spirit and consistency in the use of incidents and known conditions of the period and region in which they occurred. The publishing house hired as writers or collaborators men with considerable experience in the West, well known in their time. Among them were Dr. Frank Powell, Captain "Bruin" Adams, "Buffalo Bill" Cody, Major Sam Hall (known as "Buckskin Sam"), Major St. Vrain, Joseph Badger, Prentiss Ingraham, Captain Alfred Taylor, T. C. Harbaugh, Major Henry B. Stoddard, Lieutenant H. Randolph, Captain Frederick Whittaker, Lieutenant Alfred Thorne, Captain Jack Crawford (the "poet scout"), Lieutenant James Magoon, William R. Eyster, Oll Coomes, Ned Buntline, J. B. Omodhundroo ("Texas Jack"). Many of these were military men who had done service in the border region; others were aging frontiersmen and mountain men, glad to have found a source of livelihood as the wilderness of their youth vanished. Their intimate knowledge of the realities of Western life did not save them from producing remarkably bad literature, stock melodrama with conventionalized plots governed by a Victorian code of sex morality, all of which bore little relationship to what had been happening on the frontier. These men, of course, were not writers to begin with. They were hampered by prevalent notions of what a story should be, and they were made to conform to the editorial policy of Beadle and Adams.

Nevertheless, the modern reader can find things of interest in these tales. Much of the dialogue and humor is probably true to what was current on the frontier. In the attitudes expressed, this pulp literature reveals more openly than most records of the time the naïve and cocky sense of superiority with which young America regarded itself. The "greaser" provides a most apt foil for the projection of such an inflated self-image, and the dime novels are full of incidents in which Saxon intelligence, strength, and purity of motive triumph over the guile and treachery of the degenerate "yellow belly." But the response to the Mexican in this literature is not as simple as it might at first appear. There is an interesting ambivalence. While the ordinary Mexican encountered every day in the border country was treated with unremitting scorn, the aristocratic owners of the large haciendas in the interior of Mexico were objects of interest and curiosity to the writers of the dime novels, who treated them with a combination of hostility and respect. Affronted in their American egalitarianism, these writers were at the same time dazzled by the spectacle of a feudalistic society whose privileged members had style, wealth, leisure, and limitless opportunity for self-indulgence. The Mexican women of these stories, beautiful señoritas all, seem to have been in accidental proximity to the rest of their race. Their proper place was beside the blond and noble giants from the north who have rescued them from the connivings of deceitful, cowardly, and dowry-seeking Mexican suitors.

A more pretentious literary genre but actually little better than the dime novels was the body of Texas romances, published in hard-cover volumes during the same period. The writing is somewhat better and provides some excellent samples of frontier humor as well as some realistic accounts of life among the cattle raisers of Texas in early times, but it displays, in its treatment of the Mexican, as much arrogant racialism as do the dime novels. Some of the more prolific writers of these Texas romances were George Lippard, Anthony Ganilh, Charles Wilkins Webber, Samuel Hammett, and Jeremiah Clemens.

The periods of the Texas revolt and the Mexican War produced some letters and memoirs of sufficient quality to remain a permanent part of the literary record of early America. The letters of Stephen F. Austin[10] give the reader access to accounts of the day-by-day working out of one of the strangest ventures Americans ever entered upon. For ten years, while the Anglo-Americans in Texas were under Mexican rule, Austin almost single-handedly kept the lines of communication open between Mexican officialdom and his unruly frontiersmen. His biographer, Eugene C. Barker, says of Austin that "he possessed the faculty, rare in Americans of any time and in his day almost unknown, of sympathy with an alien race, and willingness and ability to adapt himself to its national mannerisms and sensibilities."[11] Many of the letters are written in excellent Spanish and show everywhere a studied observance of the sort of punctilio Mexicans expect. One may read a letter addressed to the political chief of the area, Saucedo, discussing in great detail a recent decision that Saucedo had made in an altercation between one of Austin's colonists and a Mexican concerning the sale of a burro. Austin had taken up the matter because he believed that Saucedo, in giving judgement to the Mexican, had violated one of the the provisions of Mexican law, thus setting what Austin believed to be the dangerous precedent of rendering decisions subjectively, outside of the law, and of confusing the executive and judiciary powers. While in effect taking Saucedo to task, Austin addresses himself to the Mexican official with constant and elaborate protestations of respect and submission. In another letter he warns a Methodist preacher in the colony not to go in for noisy evangelism, reminding him that the Anglo-Americans of the colony were all supposed to be Roman Catholics, the adoption of Catholicism being one of the terms of admission to the colony. Austin goes on to explain that the Mexican government was probably not too particular about the facts of the matter as long as the forms were not too flagrantly violated. Throughout the letters one finds a subtle mind at work. A cousin of Stephen Austin, Mary Austin Holley, records in a series of well-written letters the rising tension between Anglo-American and Mexican that she observed during a visit to Austin's colony in 1831.[12]

In 1955, in a Connecticut antique shop a handwritten and aged manuscript was discovered. The handwriting was precise, elaborate, and whorled as in a monk's scroll. Throughout the pages of the manuscript were scattered sketches, some of them colored, of remarkable freshness, skill, and vividness, depicting scenes of the Mexican War and of the countryside, buildings, and people of northern Mexico, Texas, and Arizona in the 1840's. The Battle of Buena Vista is portrayed in color, with the ornateness of Santa Anna's cavalry contrasting with the tight-fitting, business-like garb of the American soldiery. American cavalry is shown trotting across the worn cobblestones of a Mexican plaza to line up for review in front of a churrigueresque cathedral. There are hogarthian scenes in cantinas and bordellos, featuring the swarthy and menacing faces of Mexican brigands, and a boudoir escapade showing a surprised and furious Mexican man in night-shirt advancing with knife in hand upon an American intruder, the author himself, while two señoritas cower under the bedclothes. Such were the illustrations which accompanied the original manuscript of *My Confession, the Recollections of a Rogue,* by Samuel E. Chamberlain. Sam Chamberlain, a Yankee from New Hampshire, had taken part in most of the major engagements of the Mexican War before he had reached the age of twenty. Everywhere he went he sketched, and years later, after the Civil War in which the erstwhile Private Sam Chamberlain had risen to the rank of general, he wrote his memoirs into which he incorporated the sketches. Interestingly, these memoirs have nothing to say about the Civil War. They deal only with those years which had obviously stirred Chamberlain most deeply, the years during and immediately after the Mexican War. Roger Butterfield, the editor of *My Confession,* which was published with sketches included by Harper in 1956, believes that it had been Chamberlain's original intention to publish his book but that he decided against publication in view of the position of respectability he had attained in his native New Hampshire as civic leader and family man. In many ways Chamberlain was a typical product of his time, as sure of the Manifest Destiny of his country and of himself as any character in a dime novel or Texas romance. The book is full of references to the connivings and cruelties of the "greasers," but there are also accounts of the many atrocities committed by the American forces, especially the Texas volunteers and the "Rackansackers," volunteers from Arkansas. Furthermore, Chamberlain gives full credit to the bravery and effectiveness of the Mexican troops at the Battle of Buena Vista, a battle which the Mexicans came within a hair's breadth of winning. The American line broke at several vital points as groups of volunteers fled in panic, leaving the thinning line of regulars to stretch themselves out further to close the gaps. These volunteers, so unreliable in battle, were the ones who perpetrated most of the atrocities later. The Texas volunteers were in a class by themselves. Vociferously remembering the Alamo, they killed Mexicans with demonic fury, on or off the battlefield. After the war Chamberlain joined, as a means of deserting a peacetime army which had begun to bore him, a renegade band composed of Americans, Mexicans, French, Canadians, and Indians which had adopted the trade of scalp hunting. It was employed by General Urrea, military commandant of the state of Sonora, the same general who had supervised the massacre of Fannin's surrendered troops at Goliad. The scalp hunters, under the incredibly depraved John Glanton and "Judge" Holden, were paid fifty dollars for every Indian scalp they delivered to Urrea. Glanton was justified in his confidence that he could include a few Mexican scalps in any bale without detection. Chamberlain, at least by his own account, took little part in the band's professional operations and quit in disgust as soon as he was able to. In time he became so attracted to Mexico that he considered marrying a Mexican woman and becoming a citizen of the country. Despite the bravado which gives an air of puerility to a book which was written in mature years, *My Confession* is the work of a man who was as good a writer as he was an artist. Roger Butterfield says of Chamberlain that he was "a fascinating, complex character — part ruthless Yankee and part incorrigible dreamer and boaster — who left us a book that is more revealing than most formal histories of his time."[13]

Early American writers and chroniclers in dealing with Mexico generally mistook a part for the whole. The Mexico they knew was the northern frontier of that country during an epoch of great internal disorganization in which the capital was so bedeviled by uprisings that the North lay almost totally neglected, cut off from any effective communication with the center of government and culture. In 1828, the Mexican government sent one of its few commissions to the Anglo-American colonies in Texas. The ostensible purpose of the commission was to adjust boundaries, but its director, General Manuel Mier y Teran, was charged with investigating and reporting on the attitudes of the American colonists. Rumors of seditious activities in Texas had already reached the capital. In his report to the president of Mexico, Mier y Teran wrote:

> It would cause you the same chagrin that it has caused me to see the opinion that is held of our nation by these foreign colonists, since, with the exception of some few who have journeyed to the capital, they know no other Mexicans than the inhabitants about here, and excepting the authorities necessary to any form of society, the said inhabitants are the most ignorant of Negroes and Indians .... Thus I tell myself that it could not be otherwise than that from such a state of affairs should arise an antagonism between the Mexicans and foreigners, which is not the least of the smoldering fires which I have discovered.[14]

This appraisal of the state of social relations between the peoples of the border region is completely borne out by the attitudes expressed by the American chroniclers of the early Southwest. The more or less ragged fringes of Mexican society were not such as would favorably impress American frontiersmen, who by and large held the plains Indians in higher regard than they did the Mexicans. Such nomadic warriors as the Apaches and Navajos had certain stoic virtues which could be readily understood and appreciated by the rather simple frontiersman, yet even the most forlorn Mexican represented to a degree a complex culture that these Americans either could not or would not understand. Nor were all the Mexicans encountered by Americans in the Southwest low-caste primitives. There were also the ingrown and somewhat decadent aristocracies of California and New Mexico, families which had the lineage but no longer the real culture of the old colonial elite. They had been completely out of touch with the cultural centers of Mexico for generations, and some of the most pretentious of them could barely read or write. Their way of life, however, was thoroughly aristocratic, a leisure society based on feudalistic land tenure and peonage. These landed families represented the last vestige of a colonial society which was soon to disappear. They were the *criollos,* people born in Mexico of good family, and boasting pure Spanish descent. This claim of *pureza de sangre* has been largely discounted by modern investigators, but the *criollos* if they did not inherit a pure blood line from Spain certainly did inherit and greatly cherish the institutions of the mother country. These *ricos,* the wealthy landowners, were as distasteful to the American frontiersman as were the impoverished, knife-wielding tatterdemalions, the *leperos,* for the *ricos* displayed to a superlative degree the "legerdemain" noted by the modern novelist Wright Morris of "Mother Mexico." They were impractical yet cunning, mystical but erotic, fierce yet evasive, obsessed with a concept of honor but, to the Americans, seemingly incapable of the truth in the homespun, American sense of the word. They were quite too much for the "pasteurized stranger from the north."

CHAPTER TWO

## Mexican Traits — An Early Portrait

However naive and ethnocentric, the early accounts of Mexico written by Americans mark the opening phase of a lasting cultural involvement. They are worth examining, for they provide more than a mere catalogue of ideas and attitudes. In the savor and character of the language used, they vivify the emotional environment surrounding events which have had important consequences. An attitude toward Mexico frequently expressed by these writers and one with which we are still familiar in America's response to alien cultures was one of contempt for Mexico's ineptness with machinery and indifference to technological progress. The mud adobe houses, those characteristic Mexican dwellings which have been so greatly praised in recent years as marvels of adaptation to environment, singularly failed to impress George Wilkins Kendall. "They have neither windows or floors," he wrote in the *Narrative of the Texan Santa Fe Expedition,* "and in point of comfort and convenience are only one degree removed from the rudest wigwam of the Indian."[1] While in Mexico City, Kendall observed a group of Mexicans working to secure fast the folding door at the hospital of San Lazaro. "A Yankee, with a strip of board, a hammer, and half a dozen nails, would have securely fastened this large door in half an hour — it took a dozen Mexicans, with tools and timber enough to build a small dwelling, an entire day to perform the same operation. . . . This little circumstance will serve to show the state of many of the mechanic arts throughout Mexico."[2] Paul Horgan in *The Centuries of Santa Fe* presents a scene in which the "Missouri trader" is watching contemptuously as the Santa Fe militia gathers before the palace of Governor Armijo. In recording the Missouri trader's reactions, since this characterization of an unnamed trader is actually a portrait of Josiah Gregg, Horgan draws directly from the *Commerce of the Prairies.* "He was amazed," writes Horgan, "at their weapons in that year of 1822. 'Most of them were armed with bows and arrows. A few had guns which looked as though they had been imported by Cortez, while others had iron hoops fastened to the ends of poles, which passed for lances.' "[3] The traditionally pastoral nature of much of Mexican society, a kind of primitiveness which was later to attract American writers seeking escape from the evils of industrialism, comes in for a good deal of contempt in this early period because of backward methods used in agriculture. George Evans, the puritanical forty-niner, compares American and Mexican methods in the Southwest. "Although wagons are used by the American residents here, the Mexicans adheres to the heavy, wooden-wheeled cart, the wheels of which are a load for any one pair of oxen. Their plows are still the same in form and materials as were those used by the agriculturalists of ancient times, without the addition of a single point of improvement."[4] John Russell Bartlett, boundary commissioner in the Southwest from 1850 to 1853, writes of the community of Casas Grandes in Chihuahua: "Its whole dependence is upon the rich and luxurious valley, which is here about two miles wide, and which among Mexicans would be said to be in a high state of cultivation. This is speaking comparatively; for what in Mexico is considered superior cultivation, would be thought very slovenly tillage in the United States."[5] Commenting on the Mexican system of transport which supplied San Antonio, Bartlett writes:

> At present the supplies of merchandise are brought from the coast by the slow medium of ox carts. These are driven by Mexicans, and in a favorable condition of the roads make the trip in six days. The business of freighting almost entirely supports the Mexican population of the city and its vicinity. The American people are too much imbued with the spirit of progress to engage in any business that partakes of the past. The idea of carrying on commerce with ox carts, and making 130 miles in six days, over an excellent road, might do for the past century, not for this steam and lightning age.[6]

In comparing the stages of development of Mexico and the United States, Bartlett goes back to the colonial policies of Spain and England and renders a thoroughly pragmatic judgement:

> What a marked difference there is in Spanish and English colonization! Here the zealous missionary preceded all others, planting the cross along with the banner of his country. Then commenced the work of baptizing; and as soon as a sufficient number of converts had been made, a fertile valley was chosen and a church erected with buildings to accommodate some hundreds. Next came the colonists, whose main efforts were to support the Mission and its priests. The Anglo-Saxon pioneer entered the wilderness with his axe, his plough, and his rifle; and after he had erected his own dwelling, the mill and blacksmith's shop rose up. Lands were brought into cultivation, the mechanic arts flourished; and when the colony became large enough and rich enough to support a pastor, a church was built. For the results of the two modes of colonization, compare Texas, New Mexico, California, Sonora, and Chihuahua, before the first three became annexed to the United States, and the states of

Ohio, Indiana, Illinois, and Michigan. The latter had attained more wealth, more population and importance, and had done quite as much toward promoting Christianity in the first ten years after their settlement, as the former had in two centuries.[7]

Ideas expressed somewhat pompously in the journals often appear again in the raffish prose of the dime novels or Texas romances. In one of the dime novels, a Vermont Yankee, "of that great Anglo-Saxon stock," finds himself lonely for worthy companionship as he walks through Mexico and says to himself: "Course, there's plenty of greasers and yellow jackets, but who wants to be jabberin' with such heathen? They laff right in a filler's face if he talks o' railroads, and, as for 'lectric telegraphs or locomotives, I guess they'd as soon believe in harnessing chain lightning to their old go-carts."[8]

The technological backwardness of Mexico was due, these early writers were convinced, to the total indolence of the people. Modern writers in condemning compulsive aspects of American ambition have frequently used the Mexican as an example of a type of unhurried human being, great in his capacity for life enjoyment, content with few material possessions, and unharried by the constant urge to acquire. However, to the early writers the Mexican was just plain lazy and deserved to lose out, as he surely would, to the energetic, productive northerner. In 1804, Captain William Shaler noted of the Californians that "they are of an indolent, harmless disposition, and fond of spirituous liquors. That they should not be industrious, is not surprising; their government does not encourage industry."[9] The government in this case was still the Spanish monarchy. With the publication in 1840 of Richard Henry Dana Jr.'s *Two Years Before the Mast,* the American public became aware of the existence in California of a feudalistic society in which "the Indians being slaves and doing all the work," the landowning class lived in conspicuous leisure. Whatever was being done in the way of trade was already at this early date in the hands of Yankees who were marrying into the old California families, adopting Catholicism in order to be acceptable. Dana was amazed at the Californians' refusal to develop the resources of a bountiful region. He noted that though the country abounded in grapes, the native Californians bought "bad wine" made in Boston and sold to them at an "immense price." California hides were exchanged for small manufactured goods worth only a fraction of the value of the skins. Since these hides were never processed in California, the people bought shoes from American traders, which were "as like as not made of their own hides, which have been carried twice around Cape Horn," at exhorbitant prices.[10] After having considered the rich soil, good climate, and excellent harbor of the area, Dana concluded that "nothing but the character of the people prevents Monterey from becoming a great town."[11] Reporting on Mazatlán, a seaport on the west coast of Mexico, during the Mexican War, Lieutenant H. A. Wise wrote of the people that they were "beyond comparison the laziest and most ignorant set of vagabonds the world produces. They were a quiet people also, never so far forgetting their natal sloth, as to go through the exertion of making a noise. Even their knife fights were conducted with a certain show of dignity and decorum."[12] James Ohio Pattie, the mountain man, wrote concerning an area in northern Mexico that "this province would be among the richest of the Mexican country, if it were inhabited by an enlightened, enterprising, and industrious people. Nothing can exceed the indolence of the actual inhabitants. The only point in which I ever saw them display any activity, is in throwing a lasso, and in horsemanship. In this I judge, they surpass all other people. Their great business and common pursuit, is in noosing and taming wild horses and cattle."[13] George Wilkins Kendall, buoyantly confident of world salvation through technology, could only pity the Mexicans for their ineffectiveness:

> Strange that with a country as fair as any upon the face of the earth, abounding in every species of soil and climate, fruit and mineral, the Mexicans will not profit by the lessons and adopt the systems of their Saxon neighbors. They pertinaciously cling to the customs of their forefathers, and are becoming every year more and more impoverished — in short they are morally, physically and intellectually distanced in the great race of improvement which is run in almost every other quarter of the earth. Give them but tortillas, frijoles, and chile colorado to supply their animal wants for the day, and seven-tenths of the Mexicans are satisfied; and so they will continue to be until the race becomes extinct or amalgamated with Anglo-Saxon stock; for no political change, no revolution, can uproot that inherent indolence and antipathy to change, which in this age of improvement and advancement must sooner or later work their ruin and downfall. In these wonder-working days of steam, to stand still is to retrograde.[14]

J. Ross Browne, Irishman turned Western adventurer, reacted to the Mexicans in Sonora in a manner quite unlike the later Steinbeck enchantment with Mexican vagabondry. "All day long they sit by the doors of their filthy little adobe huts, smoking cigarritos and playing cards. I fancy they like it better than working. At least they live by idleness. Industry would kill them. When these mixed races are compelled to work, they sicken and die."[15] Bartlett, in describing the city of San Antonio, reported that it had at the time of his visit a population of about six thousand of which two-thirds were Mexican, German, and

French. However, the character of the town, he insisted, was essentially American. "Mexican indolence cannot stand by the side of the energy and industry of the Americans and Europeans, and the newcomers are rapidly elbowing the old settlers to one side. Some few of the Mexicans have the good sense to fall in with the spirit of progress; but the great majority draws back before it, and live upon the outskirts of the town in the primitive style of their forefathers."[16] This conspicuous lack among Mexicans of the urge for self-improvement along lines of the example set by the progressive United States could occasion only contempt on the part of Americans or at best an attitude of enlightened superiority. Horgan's Missouri trader, making the first of many trips along the Santa Fe Trail, decided on what attitude he would adopt toward an alien people:

> The young trader was conscious of his country's strong romance for the west, and he felt representative of it. He felt, also, a conviction of superiority to those other human beings whom he encountered on his travels, the various parties of Plains Indians, and — now as they came into hailing distance — the men from New Mexico. He believed that an enlightened superiority was the best point of view from which to examine new or unfamiliar exercises of the Divine Will, and he derived his own from two sources. One was his citizenship of the United States. The other was the tone of his mind, for which he could be persuaded to take the credit, as it was the product of his unceasing diligence in self-improvement.[17]

One Mexican, however, who could not be accused of lacking an urge for self-improvement, in his own sense of the term, was Governor Manuel Armijo of New Mexico. Born of a poor family, he started his career as a shepherd on the vast range owned by the rich and socially prominent Chavez family. It is reported that he regularly stole Chavez's sheep and sold them. Eventually he was able to afford a sheep ranch of his own, but he still continued to steal Chavez's sheep and even, as he later boasted openly, sold many of them back to Chavez himself. Reports of Armijo are to be found in many American accounts, few of them having anything good to say of him. But James Josiah Webb in *Adventures in the Santa Fe Trade, 1844–1847* sees Armijo as a sort of Mexican Horatio Alger. "From a long acquaintance with him, and from the representations of other traders who had a more intimate acquaintance with him, I am satisfied the American opinion of him, derived from the manner of his obtaining the position of governor and [from] the account of him given by Kendall in his *Expedition,* is unjust . . . He was emphatically a self-made man, and rose from the position of pastor, or sheep herder, to that of governor by his own energies, without aid, counsel, or even sympathy from those in higher position."[18] Thus energy, no matter how applied, was sufficient to bring forth admiring comment from a Yankee trader.

While most of the chroniclers saw in Mexico the horrible example of what a society could sink to which ignored the American ideals of hard work and attention to business, the earliest American novel treating Mexican themes, *Francis Berrian,* 1826, prefigures modern American attitudes toward Mexico. The author, Timothy Flint, begins his story describing a trip down the Mississippi in a steamboat. During this trip the narrator meets an interesting and somewhat exotic-looking young man, Francis Berrian, who tells of his years spent in Mexico, including a period with the patriot forces of Morelos fighting against the Spanish royalist troops. His motive for going to Mexico in the first place, Berrian claims, was to find relief from a too materialistic and pragmatic society and to look for adventure. " 'You matter-of-fact people here in the States,' " he says to the narrator, " 'are, I am sensible, inclined either to ridicule romantic feeling and adventure, or, still worse, to view it as having immoral tendencies, and tending to unnerve the mind, and unfit it for the severer and more important duties of life.' " The narrator strongly disclaims any such feelings: " 'Have no fear upon that score, ' " . . . " 'for I, at least, am not one of them. It is so long since I have heard of nothing but dollars and cents, the mere mercenary details of existence, that I languish to be introduced to another world. ' "[19]

One of the most frequent subjects for comment among these early writers was the seeming unconcern with personal hygiene among Mexicans of all classes. In one of the early short stories of American literature, "The Inroad of the Nabajo," by Albert Pike, published in 1834, the women of Santa Fe are described as "scudding hither and thither, with their black hair flying, and their naked feet shaming the ground by their superior filth."[20] Lieutenant Wise observed that "with the denizens of Monterey, even the wealthiest, cleanliness was an acquirement very little appreciated or practiced, and I should presume the commodity of soap to be an article 'more honored in the breach than the observance.' "[21] One of the writers of Texas romances, Samuel A. Hammett, describes a testy old army officer from San Antonio, Colonel Fontleroy, as being "naterally good-humored as a she-bar when her cubs is meddled with." His disposition was in no way improved as a result of his having been "sent out among the fleas and Mexicans, and gettin' the ager so powerful that it fairly shuk him outer the country."[22] Jeremiah Clemens, another writer of Texas romances, gives his version of the origin and appropriateness of the term "greaser":

> An American whose ill fortune has made him for any number of days, a sojourner in the city of Metamoras [sic] can have no difficulty in tracing the origin of the term "greaser," originally applied by the old Texans to the Mexican Rancheros, and subsequently extended to the whole nation. Narrow, muddy, filthy streets, swarming with men, women and children as filthy — enlivened by an eternal chorus of little dogs without hair, except about the muzzles, and the tips of their tails — houses without floors, built of mud and straw, and inhabited by fleas and other vermin, in the proportion of fifty to the square inch — disgusting sewers — rotting offal, and a hot, sickly atmosphere, make up an assembly of discomforts compared with which the purgatory of an orthodox Catholic is rather an agreeable kind of place. The people look greasy, their clothes are greasy, their dogs are greasy, their houses are greasy — everywhere grease and filth hold divided dominion, and the singular appropriateness of the name bestowed by the western settlers, soon caused it to be universally adopted by the American army.[23]

Further in the same book Clemens considers the situation of a Mexican enclosure in which the house, flower garden, and a fountain are crowded up against the stables, pigsty, and chicken coop. He is struck by the ambivalence of "these evidences of a refined and cultivated taste" and the spectacle of so much dirt, and concludes that the condition is not chronic but due to political and religious exploitation:

> In nearly every house in Mexico, may be witnessed the same admixture of filth and cleanliness; of order, and disorder; of the beautiful and the disgusting. It is the struggle of intellect and refinement against governmental misrule and priestly superstition. In such a land the same house, of necessity, contains the biped, and the quadruped; for there alone is there any assurance of safety for either; but the fountain playing by the pig-stye, and the flowers blooming around the dung hill have each a voice to proclaim how high in the scale of civilization the people might attain under happier auspices.[24]

Early Americans, priding themselves on their straight forwardness and down-to-earthness, disliked particularly in the Mexican character that which was formalistic, ritualistic, showy, given to high-flown professions, especially when these professions seemed not to be borne out by the reality of action or underlying motive. Timothy Flint in *Francis Berrian,* describes one of the camps in which the forces of the rebel general, Morelos, were presumably preparing for action against the Spanish royalists. Francis Berrian, American adventurer in Mexico, had been attracted to the cause of the rebels because of the ardor with which their leaders had professed their devotion to the idea of freedom. Once having joined them and having become acquainted with their way of life,

Berrian became disillusioned by the difference between their professions and their actions:

> Every new view of the men gave me more disheartening apprehensions of the issue of a cause, depending upon such leaders. Had they listened to Morelos, they would have had subordination, discipline, system, economy, and sufficient supplies of provisions for a siege. But there was no compulsion, and no subordination. The resources of a month were wasted in the riot of a week. The camp rang with patriotic songs, and the reckless gaiety of young men, who felt themselves far from all restraint; and presented an aspect of frolic and mirth, that was peculiarly fascinating to such a people. Even under the massive dome of our quarters, new stories of intrigues were constantly getting air, and their intrigues, and their pride, and their parties, and their heart-burnings, furnished ample materials for the thousand and one narratives of scandal. Almost every night brought its balls and fandango. . . . The country for twenty leagues round was put in requisition to furnish the requisite good cheer. The poor plundered peasants had no other redress, than to imprecate curses, equally, on the heads of Royalists and Patriots.[25]

The elaborateness of Mexican manners was suspect and thought to be insincere. Kendall remarked that on entering a well-bred Mexican's home everything is put at the visitor's disposal, and should he admire anything it is immediately given him. "Such is Mexican etiquette — polite but unmeaning."[26] Of the Missouri trader, Horgan wrote that "in the manners of the New Mexican, who meant to be amiable, courteous, and cheerful, he found only 'a false glare of talent, eminently calculated to mislead and impose.' "[27] As part of their general showiness, a proclivity to idle boasting was cited against the Mexicans. William V. Wells, one of the early contributors to the *Overland Monthly,* describes the last days of the French army in Mexico:

> The French soldiers, who had been originally so enthusiastic for the Mexican expedition, soon grew discontented with a field utterly barren of military renown. Wearied with continual hide-and-seek combats, among mountain ravines and impenetrable jungles, they longed to return to *La Belle France,* or face death in some less ignoble form. They were sometimes worsted in these insignificant encounters; and it was refreshing to observe the bombast of the Mexicans after any such advantage. Nothing will ever change the national character in that respect. There is a Mexican history of the war with the United States, in which nearly every engagement is set down as a Mexican victory; but prudence counseled a retreat for strategic considerations. Santa Anna always insisted and conclusively proved that he won all his battles against Scott and Taylor; and the bells of Saltillo and Monterrey are rung to this day on the anniversary of the great Mexican victory of Buena Vista. The Mexicans achieved a good many brilliant victories of that kind

over the Chasseurs d'Afrique and Zouaves, by which, as they assert, the invaders were driven away. The facts are, that when Napoleon decided to abandon the ill-starred expedition, the order was given to concentrate the troops in Central Mexico, preparatory to their embarkation at Vera Cruz. As the French or Austrians marched out of a town, the Mexicans, at a respectful distance, marched in at the other side, with the usual paroxysm of aguardiente, shooting and robbing. The idea of any credit being due to the United States for its moral weight in bringing about the exodus of the French, is hooted at as absurd. With their departure, Mexican gasconade may be said to have reached its climax.[28]

Not all the early American writers, however, looked upon Mexican style as mere sham. James Fenimore Cooper in the novel *Jack Tier*, which was written during the Mexican War, describes a Mexican charactor, Senior Montefalderón, as "a man of polished manners, as we maintain is very apt to be the case with Mexican gentlemen, whatever may be the opinion of this good Republic on the subject just at this moment. . . ."[29] Don Juan Montefalderón was "a soldier and a gallant cavalier" who was imbued with that kind of patriotism which "would defend his home and fireside, his altars and the graves of his fathers, from the ruthless steps of the invader." He was a "grave and thoughtful man," who had something about him of the "exaltation of the Spanish character; the overflowings of a generous chivalry."[30] Dana was also impressed by Mexican style, which remained grand even when exhibited by a person who was destitute. "Every rich man looks like a grandee, and every poor scamp like a broken-down gentleman . . . . I have often seen a man with a fine figure, and courteous manners dressed in broadcloth and velvet, with a noble horse completely covered with trapping; without a 'real' in his pockets, and absolutely suffering for something to eat."[31] This grand manner extended to all levels of society. "A common bullock-driver, on horseback, delivering a message, seemed to speak like an ambassador at an audience. In fact, they sometimes appeared to me to be a people on whom a curse had fallen, and stripped them of everything but their pride, their manner, and their voices."[32] Perhaps it was natural that a woman should view the courtesies and flourishes of Mexican society somewhat differently than would the frontiersmen and traders. Susan Magoffin, wife of a Santa Fe trader from Missouri, in one of the few surviving accounts of the Santa Fe Trail written by a woman, was continually charmed by Mexican civilities and graces:

> What a polite people these Mexicans are, altho' they are looked upon as a half-barbarous set by the generality of people. This morning I have rather taken a little protegé, a little market girl — Sitting at the window and on the look out for vegetables, this little thing

came along with green peas the month of *Sept.*; she came in and we had a long conversation on matters and things in general, and I found that not more than six years old she is quite conversant in all things. On receiving her pay she bowed most politely, shook hands with a kind *'adiós' and 'me alegro de verte bien'* [I am glad to see you in good health], and also a promise to return tomorrow. Just to see the true politeness and ease displayed by that child is truly [amazing], 'twould put many a mother in the U. S. to the blush. And she is so graceful too, her rebozo was thrown to one side and a nice white napkin of peas set down from off her head with quite as much grace as some ladies display in a minuet.[33]

As most of the early American commentaries on Mexico were written by men, it was the Mexican women who showed to advantage in their accounts. These men were clearly delighted to have escaped, if only temporarily, from the prevailing atmosphere of womanhood in their own society which in its puritanical strictures was not only anti-erotic but also anti-aesthetic. James Ohio Pattie emerging from the wilderness into the glitter of Mexican society was pleased to find that his mountain man's garb was not held against him. "It may be imagined that we did not cut a particular dandy-like figure, among people, many of whom were rich, and would be considered well-dressed anywhere. Notwithstanding this, it is a strong proof of their politeness, that we were civilly treated by the ladies, and had the pleasure of dancing with the handsomest and richest of them."[34] That Mexican women were often handsome and most desirable has been attested to by even those American chroniclers who could find nothing else to say in favor of Mexico. Lieutenant Wise in *Los Gringos* regularly digressed from his principal theme, the scoundrelly nature of Mexican men, to enlarge upon the beauty and allure of Mexican women. Describing the women of Guadalajara, he became so caught up in the rapture of his vision that he lapsed into a naval imagery that came natural to him as an officer of the line:

They were so tastefully attired in full flowing and becoming skirts, with no awkward stays or corsets to cramp the grace of motion — the coquettish *ribosa,* never quiet an instant, but changing its silken folds, and half revealing the glancing neck and arm! — The hair, too; such hair! *ay de mi!* no odious bonnets to conceal God's fair handiwork! — Then their arched tiny feet, kissing the marble pavement, with so firm, so light, yet dignified a tread — and then the elders, sailing majestically astern of their lovely convoys — like ships of the line — regarding with wary eyes privateers in disguise of gay young cavaliers, crossing their track. Hola! What blockade could intercept those softly audible murmurs! or the light downy touch of dimpled fingers, quick as a swallow's kiss to his mate! or, more than all, withstand the languid, lightening glances flashed from their upper deck of eyes! *Ave purissima!.* The waking hours by day, and sleepless ones by night, that Spanish maidens have caused me![35]

Seventeen-year old Lewis H. Garrard, recently having arrived in Santa Fe from his native Cincinnati, warmly admired in the women of Santa Fe a habit which would have marked for a prostitute any woman in his home city.

> Though smoking is repugnant to many ladies, it certainly does enhance the charms of the Mexican señoritas, who, with neatly rolled-up shucks between coral lips, perpetrate winning smiles, their magically brilliant eyes the meanwhile searching one's very soul. How dulcet-toned are their voices, which, siren-like, irresistibly draw the willing victim within the giddy vortex of dissipation! And these cigarillos they present with such a grace, and so expressive an eye, so musical a tongue, and so handsome a face, that it was impossible to refuse.[36]

J. Ross Browne, whose usual tone when dealing with Mexican men was one of grand disdain for "these mixed races," softened considerably when describing the women of the nation.

> Many of the señoritas were pretty, and those who had no great pretensions to beauty in other respects were at least fitted with fine eyes and teeth, rich brunette complexions, and forms of wonderful pliancy and grace. All, or nearly all, were luminous with jewelry, and wore dresses of the most flashy colors, in which flowers, lace, and glittering tinsel combine to set off their dusky charms. I saw some among them who would not have compared unfavorably with the ladies of Cadiz, perhaps in more respects than one. They danced easily and naturally; and, considering the limited opportunity of culture they had enjoyed in this remote region, it was wonderful how free, simple, and graceful they were in their manners.[37]

Even the complacent and unbending John Russell Bartlett acknowledged the quality of Mexico's women: "The Mexican like the Spanish ladies have a natural gracefulness of manner, which has been observed by all travelers, and has captivated most foreigners who have taken up their residence in the country."[38]

Though commenting freely and in the main derogatively on Mexican style and manners, early American writers seldom took up that other aspect of society in the borderlands, the manners of Americans towards Mexicans. One early writer, however, who did record observations in this area was Louise Amelia Smith, "Dame Shirley" of the California mines. In her letters she used the word *Spaniards* when referring to Spanish-speaking miners because not all of them were Mexican. Some were Chileans who had come to California on ships that had rounded the Cape. However, by far the majority of "Spaniards" in the California diggings were Mexicans, mainly from Sonora. "Dame Shirley" in one of her letters took up the question of communication between "Spaniards" and Americans in the mines:

> By the way, speaking of language, nothing is more amusing than to observe the different styles, in which the generality of the Americans talk *at* the unfortunate Spaniard. In the first place, many of them really believe, that when they have learned *sabe* and *vamos,* (two words which they seldom use in the right place,) *poco tiempo, si* and *bueno,* (the last they will persist in pronouncing *whayno,*) they have the whole of the glorious Castilian at their tongue's end. Some, however, eschew the above words entirely, and innocently fance, that by splitting the tympanum of an unhappy foreigner, in screaming forth their sentences in good solid English, they can be surely understood; others, at the imminent risk of dislocating their own limbs and the jaws of their listeners, by the laughs which their efforts elicit, make the most excruciatingly grotesque gestures, and think that *that* is speaking Spanish. The majority, however, place a most beautiful and touching faith in broken *English,* and when they murder it, with the few words of Castilian quoted above, are firmly convinced, that it is nothing but their "ugly dispositions" which make the Spaniards pretend not to understand them.[39]

Of the words used by early American writers to describe Mexicans, one of the most frequent to appear is the word *cowardly.* In the case of the writers of journals or diaries, the charge of cowardice is usually presented not as an abstraction or generalization but as the inevitable conclusion to be drawn from given instances of Mexican behavior. Here is a strange report upon a people who from both the Spanish and Indian lines of their inheritance might have been expected to retain something of the stoic cult of physical courage. Furthermore, quite apart from the psychological consideration that there are undoubtedly no ethnic or national groups of people who are inherently either brave or cowardly, there remains the evidence in Mexican history of many acts of rash and headlong courage. The explanation of any seeming inconsistency lies in the fact that here as elsewhere the early American writers in dealing with aspects of Mexican character mistook a part for the whole. To understand the behavior of Mexicans in the borderlands at the time of the earliest contacts with American frontiersmen, one must be able to view this behavior as a manifestation of the special plight of Mexico's northern region during the era of *criollo* rule, one of the most demoralized periods in the long history of Mexico. It is unfortunate, at least from the point of view of a possible mutual esteem, that these two societies first encountered each other at a time when the United States was bumptiously self-confident, and Mexico was undergoing a period in which its national morale was at a very low ebb.

The upswell of popular revolt which took the form of the first phase of the independence movement in Mexico soon dissipated itself as the movement passed into the hands of the *criollo* class exclusively. The

Indians and mestizos who had ardently followed the early revolutionary leaders Hidalgo, Morelos, Guerrero, and Guadalupe Victoria found that their needs and desires were of no concern to the aristocratic *criollos* who had appropriated the revolution. The time had not yet come when the descendants of the Aztecs could reclaim their heritage. Meanwhile, they could serve as cannon fodder as rival betasseled generals rended the new republic in pursuit of their political ambitions. With a new general in the president's office every few months and with what little money was available being spent to bribe officers to secure their political loyalty, there was small inclination on the part of the various governmnets to attend to the affairs of the remote northern frontier of Mexico. In this region, isolated adobe presidios manned by neglected, unpaid garrisons and surrounded by immense wastes were charged with holding for the republic the northern tier of Mexican states against two formidable enemies. The first of these were the Apaches, who had adopted none of the culture of the Spaniards but had acquired from them the arts of shooting and riding a horse, accomplishments which converted them from relatively defenseless tribesmen into marauders who became the terrifying scourge of the desert. The second of the enemies were the Americans pushing toward the Pacific, who could not take these isolated presidios seriously as obstacles to the fulfillment of their Manifest Destiny.

Continual reference is made in the American chronicles of the borderlands to the wretched appearance and scoundrelly nature of Mexicans encountered in the region. The ragged soldiers of the presidios are the special objects of contempt, with many accounts of their cowardice in the face of the Apaches. One reason for the poor performance of the Mexican military can be seen in the provisions of a decree of the congress of Coahuila and Texas, September 29, 1826: "The *ayuntamientos* with the assistance of armed force will proceed to make levies; vagabonds and disorderly persons shall be taken in preference for military service, recruits may be obtained by entrapment and decoy."[40] Troops of this caliber could do little to protect those few settlers who clung to the presidios. A diary which was written by a Mexican army officer in 1828 and 1829 gives a clear account of the situation of the garrison at San Antonio, Texas, during its last years under Mexican rule:

> Although the land is most fertile, the inhabitants do not cultivate it because of the danger of Indians which they face as soon as they separate themselves any distance from their houses, to which these barbarians come often in the silence of the night to do damage without fear of the garrison, for when it becomes aware of this damage, which is irreparable, it is unable to apply any other remedy than the mounting of a continual watch, because of the sad

fact of a total lack of equipment, especially military, that leaves no other recourse. These unfortunate troops have often gone for months, even years, without pay, without clothes, and continually engaged in desert campaigning against the savages, maintaining themselves with the meat of buffalo, deer, etc., exhausting themselves in the hunt, with no alleviation from these hardships forthcoming from the government, in spite of continuous appeals.[41]

The rambunctious nature of the first Americans to encounter Mexicans in the borderlands is illustrated by James Ohio Pattie's account of meeting a Mexican army officer in northern Mexico. If the mountain man's recording of the conversation is accurate, it is evident that each party in his own style was out to nettle the other.

[The officer] said, still in a very civil manner, that he had had the command of some troops in Guanaxuato, but was now on his way to the city of Mexico, to take charge of the 6th regiment, which was ordered to the province of Texas, to find out among the Americans there, those who had refused obedience to the Mexican laws. He added, that when he succeeded in finding them, he would soon learn them to behave well. The last remark was made in rather a contemptuous tone of voice, and with something like an implied insult to me. This warmed my blood, and I replied in a tone not so gentle as prudence might have counselled a stranger in a foreign land to have adopted, that if himself and his men did not conduct themselves properly when they were among the Americans, the latter would soon despatch them to another country, which they had not yet seen; as the Americans were not Mexicans, to stand at the corner of a house, and hide their guns behind the side of it, while they looked another way, and pulled the trigger. At this he flew into a passion. I did not try to irritate him any further, and he rode on and left us.[42]

Pattie summed up elsewhere in his narrative his opinion of Mexican courage: "I have no faith in the courage of these people, except where they have greatly the advantage, or can kill in the dark, without danger to themselves. This in my view is the amount of a Spaniard's bravery."[43] In a scene in the largely apocryphal *Colonel Crockett's Exploits and Adventures in Texas,* Crockett is approaching San Antonio for the first time, accompanied by frontier eccentrics like himself, among them a man named Thimblerig and an ex-seaman called the old pirate. A group of horsemen is sighted at some distance. " 'Look out for squalls,' said the old pirate who had not spoken for an hour; 'they are a scouting party of Mexicans,' 'and are three or four times our number'; said Thimblerig. 'No matter,' replied the old man; 'they are convicts, jail birds, and cowardly ruffians, no doubt, who would tremble at a loud word as much as a mustang at the sight of a lasso.' "[44] Evans, the forty-niner, tells of an incident which occurred in the city of Santa Rosa in northern Mexico. A Dr. Long, an American who had a Mexican wife, discovered that his father-in-law, a political "out," had been charged with treason by local officials and sentenced to death. Long gathered ten men and, equipped with rifles and two wagons, moved on the city demanding that the authorities release his father-in-law. "Mexican cowardice came under, and at the end of the stipulated time [Long] had the proud satisfaction of seeing his aged relative, at the head of the city authorities, coming forward to negotiate a peace . . . This timely movement of the doctor's party saved the life of his wife's father and gave the doctor an ascendancy over the cowardly population of the city such as few men possess. He lives a nabob among them, and his word is generally of more force than Mexican laws."[45] Lewis Garrard in *Wah-To-Yah and the Taos Trail* delivers himself of a sweeping condemnation of the inhabitants of New Mexico. "The New Mexicans, when weakest, are the most contemptibly servile objects to be seen; and with their whining voices, shrugs of the shoulder, and dastardly expression of their villainous countenances, they commend themselves unreservedly to one's contempt. But, when *they* have the mastery, the worst qualities of a craven's character are displayed in revenge, hatred, and unbridled rage. Depraved in morals, they stop at nothing to accomplish their purpose. The extreme degradation into which they are fallen seems a fearful retribution upon the destroyers of the Aztec Empire."[46]

During the period of westward expansion, American policy toward the Indian, whatever it might have been in theory, was in practice simply one of extermination. Frontiersmen and troops of the Western garrisons in their continual battle with the plains Indians developed traits in common with them. These Americans in the Western outposts became tough, wily, fearless, and merciless. As they came to resemble each other, these opponents grew in a way to respect each other. Both, in the no-quarter-given attitude of their Spartan code, came to have the most withering contempt for the Mexicans. The Apaches used to boast that the Mexicans were their shepherds and that the only reason the Mexicans were permitted to survive at all was that it suited the convenience of the Apaches to have the Mexicans raise sheep, cattle, and horses for the Apaches to expropriate at will. So feeble had Mexican control of its northern provinces become that the Mexican governments finally resorted to the practice of paying tribute to the Apache chieftains to buy for their northern garrisons a brief and uncertain immunity from raids. Lt. José María Sánchez in his diary *Viaje a Texas* records his feeling of humiliation as he witnessed the Mexican garrison at Laredo, Texas, paying tribute money to leaders of the Lipan Indians, an offshoot of the Apache tribe. In time, depending upon the reactions of the Apaches, Mexican policy varied from paying tribute for peace to hiring armed bands to take Apache scalps for bounty. Many of these bands were composed of renegade Americans and other Indians. It will be recalled that Sam Chamberlain had joined the notorious scalp-hunting band led by John Glanton, which was paid fifty dollars a scalp by General Urrea, military commandant of Sonora.

Pattie relates that his party entered Santa Fe to find the city in an uproar because Indians had raided and carried off four girls, including the daughter of a former governor. According to Pattie's account, his group developed a plan by which it was to join forces with the Mexican troops of the city to ambush the Indians. The joint force succeeded in surprising the Indians, who immediately charged to break through the ambush. At this point, so the account goes, the New Mexican troops broke and ran, leaving the Americans to deal with the situation alone. Despite the defection of the New Mexicans, the girls were rescued and returned to their parents. In the short story, "The Inroad of the Nabajo," Albert Pike creates a similar scene. A report had reached Santa Fe, while still under Mexican rule, that a band of Navajos was approaching. Mexican soldiers gathered in formation with much swagger, and a group of Americans who happened to be in Santa Fe — mountain men and traders — joined them to help with the defense of the city. When the shrieking Navajos came into sight and bore down upon them, "the heroes who had been chattering and boasting in front of the Americans, shrunk in behind them, and left them to bear the brunt of the battle."[47]

George W. B. Evans in *Mexican Gold Trail* contrasts Mexican cowardice to American bravery in the matter of coping with the Indians. Commenting on another Indian massacre in northern Mexico which occurred within eighteen miles of his temporary quarters, he writes:

> Turn to the west, and you find the same news repeated, and money, mules, and packs driven off; and notwithstanding these repeated injuries the government makes no effort to rid her people of the *Appache* [sic] *wrongs,* although they have many soldiers quartered in the city without employment or activity for the body or mind. These reports of countrymen having been waylaid, murdered, and scalped afford food for an hour's conversation, and then the subject, with all its horrors to an American mind, is dropped and rests with the things of the past. Would this be the case in our government? Could Indians come within eighteen miles of the city of Columbus, and there commit wrongs of this character, and the whole transaction be passed by our people without more than a murmur? Would Americans, on the receipt of such news, ride to the seat of disaster, and there look upon the gory, gaping wounds of the body before them, and hear the sounds

speaking from every gaping gash, "Revenge me, my countrymen, revenge," without a swelling heart, a fixed determination, and a vow registered on high that this night's bloody deeds should return in a fourfold manner upon the heads of the perpetrators? I answer confidently for my countrymen, "No, never." Cowardice is not inherent with us, but here it is—hence the difference.[48]

Several pages further in the journal, Evans takes up the subject again:

> The whole country seems to be governed by the Appache nation, and those pretending to rule dare not say that they are masters. Gomaz, the Appache chief, is said to be a Mexican, and they have offered the Americans a reward of $1,000 for his scalp. But he is too smart for his brethren, and, unless he should be taken by Americans, he will live to a good old age, honored and respected by his followers because of the many Mexican scalps dangling at his belt. This daring chief has laid the town of Ceyammi under an annual contribution, and draws from that and other similar sources a large amount of revenue. 'Tis said that this city makes him an annual payment as a peace purchase. Would Americans suffer this? No! not if every tree in the forest served to shield an Indian, and they stood upon the ground as thick and numerous as the blades of grass. It may be thought that too much is claimed for Americans, but a moment's reflection, a retrospective view of the fields of Lexington, Bunkerhill, Monmouth, Yorktown, and later still, of [Resaca] de la Palma, Sacramento, Buena Vista, etc., will convince any doubter that Americans will not submit to injustice from any source but under all circumstances defend their rights manfully.[49]

Though less numerous and not as well organized as the Apaches, the Comanche Indians also preyed upon the northern settlements of Mexico with devastating results. Evans tells of witnessing the return to a Mexican village of the lone survivor of a Comanche attack. "One was left to return and tell of the butchery of his companions. This is but a sample of the treatment these poor, cowardly Mexicans receive from the Comanche Indians. This tribe has sworn eternal enmity against Mexicans, and they are executing their threats; and the poor, miserable, driveling Mexicans must meet their fate, for they have no American government to protect them."[50] Bartlett, commenting on an incident in which Mexicans had fled abandoning comrades to the Apaches, writes: "This narrative exhibits the poltroonery of the Mexicans in no stronger light than do incidents continually taking place. I have been told by many Mexican gentlemen and military officers, that ten Apaches will put a hundred of the lower class of their countrymen to flight. They become panic-stricken; and if forced to discharge their guns, they do so at random, turning their faces and generally closing their eyes."[51]

The Texas romances and dime novels echo the journals and diaries on the theme of Mexican cowardice. A Texas colonel in one of the romances, *The Prairie Scout* by Charles W. Webber, declares the Mexican eagle to be a fitting symbol for the flag of Mexico. "The Mexican eagle is a dirty, cowardly creature that feeds upon carcasses, and will hardly attack a live rabbit — a perfect buzzard! And there is such close affinity between their habits and the Mexican character, that I don't wonder at their hoisting a carrion-bird upon their national standard."[52] The hero of Jeremiah Clemens' *Bernard Lile* launches into a diatribe on the cowardliness of the Mexican people and the clear duty of the United States to take possession of a nation which does not have the courage to defend itself. This outburst is occasioned by an incident during the Mexican War in which Bernard Lile discovers that he has been resting on a tombstone which bears the inscription "el sepulcro de mi madre."

> With a feeling of bitter contempt, the soldier ran his eye over the letters. "My mother's grave," he muttered. "Shame upon the coward wretch who had feeling enough to rear this monument, but lacked the nerve to defend it. The hand which traced these words was in all probability trembling behind the town's defenses, while the slab its owner ought to have died to protect from insult, was the couch of a foreign foe. Great God will such a people long be permitted to hold dominion over the fairest portion of the globe? Will the eagles now perched upon its hill tops, or screaming over its valleys, again wing their flight to the northward of the Rio Grande? Will party strife at home, or a weak fear of senseless censures from abroad, recal [sic] the immortal army which has planted the standard of the republic upon the regal hill of Chapultepec, and flung its glorious folds to the breeze from the halls of the murdered Montezumas? A high mission will be unfulfilled if one foot of the Aztec empire is restored to the despot and his slaves. A great work will have to be commenced anew; but it *will be* commenced, and it *will* be completed! This land was not meant to be the home of those who will not defend the spot where reposes a mother's remains.[53]

In Samuel A. Hammett's *Piney Woods Tavern,* a Texan named Milward discusses the Mexican War. "Put your Mexican on horseback and he will cavort with the best, become quite troublesome with his ugly lance, even blaze away considerably with his escopette — at least until some one drops — and then he's off! Plant him behind a safe wall, and he will shoot you a cannon as well as the next man; but never trust him at close quarters, where bayonets and bowie knives are in fashion. He can't stand it and will not. Perhaps, like the Frenchman, he may be ticklish, and does not like to have sharp things pointed at him."[54]

The villain of a dime novel entitled *The Serpent of El Paso,* by Major

Sam Hall, is a Mexican named Martínez, who, resplendently dressed and exquisite in his courtesies, escorts the beautiful American girl, Lize, to a dance on the Mexican side of the border. When the dance is shot up by some loutish Americans, Martínez, terrified, drops to the floor for safety, leaving Lize exposed. She is rescued from this precarious position by Frontier Frank, a noble Saxon, who is later severely wounded in a sneak attack by the humiliated Martínez.[55] Elsewhere in the same book "Buckskin Sam" Hall, the author, comments on Mexican fear of the Apaches: "The war cry of a party of Apaches invariably paralyzes the male portion of a Mexican village, and either causes them to run like cowards and desert their women and children, or renders them incapable of resisting the merciless red men."[56] Another dime novel hero, seeing dust being raised across the mesa, shouts to his partner: "So — a dust cloud coming this way, lance points, that means red-skins, then, for devil a greaser ever had pluck enough to carry lance so far from their holes."[57]

Being generally honest reporters, however limited in their point of view, the early chroniclers of the borderlands, so often disparaging in their treatment of Mexicans, did record instances of Mexican courage. Young and inexperienced as he was, seventeen-year-old Lewis H. Garrard was nevertheless able to perceive the full irony of a situation which developed in Taos during his stay in the region, an irony which can be better understood upon examination of the events which led up to this situation. When Colonel Kearny marched his forces into New Mexico he faced the prospect of having to pass through canyons which had been reported bristling with Mexican defenses. Yet when the Americans reached these passes, they found the defenses dismantled and the defenders gone. New Mexico was occupied without a shot being fired. The causes for this sudden evaporation of the will to resist in New Mexico have not been established beyond all doubt, but records of the period strongly indicate that the blustering Governor Manuel Armijo accepted a large bribe from the American government to hand over the area without a fight. The agent through whom this bribe was purportedly arranged was a Missouri trader named James Magoffin, brother-in-law of the Susan Magoffin whose diary has been quoted above. Magoffin, one of the subtlest personalities in the early history of the American Southwest, married a New Mexican woman, settled in Santa Fe, and learned to speak a Spanish which was so fluent, idiomatic, and well-pronounced that he seemed to have been born to the tongue. His many Mexican acquaintances tended to forget that "Don Jaime" was an American. All the big houses along the Rio Grande valley were open to this witty and thoroughly engaging Irish-American, and he was on intimate terms with New Mexican politicians. He particularly cultivated a friendship with

Governor Armijo. Concealed behind Magoffin's front of gregarious affability was a spirit which was not only intensely nationalistic but undoubtedly opportunistic as well. He was eager to see the Americans take over New Mexico and kept American authorities informed on events and attitudes in that territory. From the point of view of his business, he clearly stood to gain by an American occupation, as Armijo's government exacted high duties on American goods. Before Kearny marched his troops into New Mexico, he sent as his emissary to Santa Fe a Captain Philip Cooke. Cooke was instructed to first contact Magoffin, who was to arrange for an interview with Armijo. After introducing Cooke to Armijo, Magoffin discreetly retired to the governor's outer office, leaving the two men to confer privately. Cooke read a statement from Kearny imploring Armijo to avoid the spilling of blood in a futile resistance. Armijo answered in grandiose terms, referring to his personal honor and the honor of Mexico. He sternly rejected Kearny's proposal and dismissed Cooke from his presence. As Cooke was leaving he saw Magoffin, who had been waiting outside, enter the governor's office. What transpired between Armijo and Magoffin on this occasion is not definitely known, but most historians of the period believe that Magoffin offered, on the part of the United States government, a sizeable bribe for the peaceful delivery of New Mexico to Kearny's forces. In *The Time of the Gringo,* a historical novel better than most of its kind, Elliott Arnold develops a scene in which Magoffin explains to Cooke, in reference to the separate interviews each had had with Armijo, the workings of Mexican psychology:

> "With the Mexicans what is done is not so important as the manner in which it is done. The style is everything. Anything may be done if it is done in the proper style. And the style is part of the honor, and the honor must be served before all else . . . Now, you know all about honor. You are an officer. But this is a different kind of honor. I see it in my own sons. There is certain face that has to be maintained, like that of the orientals. Of all the things I said tonight to Don Manuel, only one thing carried any weight, and that was the amount of money he was being offered to get out. But it was necessary to prefix it with the argument that resistance was useless, which is debatable . . . I had to save Don Manuel's face for him, to himself, even as I offered a bribe. On his part Don Manuél upheld his honor when he officially rejected Kearny's demand . . . All of this was necessary, and if you fail to see it also was sincere, you miss the point entirely. Colonel Kearny understood this even better than I did. That is why we were sent jointly, with identical demands but with separate weapons, and that is why I planned it so you would see Armijo first, and alone. Don Manuél was able to make the required chivalrous reply to you. And he was also able to listen to me."[58]

Kearny's occupation of New Mexico had seemed so simple and appeared to be so generally accepted by the New Mexican public that a small holding force was left in Santa Fe while Kearny and the main body of his troops pushed on to California. Now was the time for those who were unreconciled and ashamed of the passive acceptance of the conqueror to show their hands. Chief among the unreconcilables was Father Antonio José Martínez, pastor and dominating political figure of the Taos area. This is the Father Martínez of Taos so masterfully portrayed in *Death Comes for the Archbishop*. Martínez was deeply humiliated by the presence of the American forces. He saw in it not only a thwarting of his own strong political ambitions but also the end of the great privileges and power of the clergy in New Mexico. He gathered Mexican followers and plotted a revolt against the Americans which was to be managed by inciting the fierce Taos Indians into a general uprising. For days the conspirators circulated among the Indians, passing out liquor and exciting their natural animosity toward foreigners. Finally, after a night of orgiastic drinking and inflammatory speeches, the whole pueblo arose in arms. Indians and Mexicans besieged the house of the American governor, Charles Bent, murdered his wife and children and finally scalped him. The mob then took over the whole area, and all Americans who could be found were butchered. An American force was rushed from Santa Fe to Taos, and the revolt was easily put down. Because of Father Martínez's great prestige and power in the region, the American authorities chose not to prefer charges against him, though they were well aware of his complicity in the revolt. Instead they arrested his principal followers. Garrard witnessed the trials of these Mexicans and was struck by the irony of seeing men declared guilty of treason for having resisted a foreign invader.

> It certainly did appear to be a great assumption on the part of the Americans to conquer a country, and then arraign the revolting inhabitants for treason. American judges sat on the bench, New Mexicans and Americans filled the jurybox, and an American soldiery guarded the halls. Verily, a strange mixture of violence and justice — a strange middle ground between the martial and common law. After an absence of a few minutes, the jury returned with a verdict of 'guilty in the first degree' — five for murder, one for treason. Treason, indeed! What did the poor devil know about his new allegiance? But so it was; and, as the jail was overstocked with others awaiting trial, it was deemed expedient to hasten the execution, and the culprits were sentenced to be hanged the following Friday — hangman's day. When the concluding words *"muerto, muerto, muerto"* — "dead, dead, dead" — were pronounced by Judge Beaubien, in his solemn and impressive manner, the painful stillness that reigned in the courtroom, and the subdued grief mani-

fested by a few bystanders, were noticed not without an inward sympathy. The poor wretches sat with unmovable features; but I fancied that under the assumed looks of apathetic indifference, could be read the deepest anguish. When remanded to jail till the day of execution, they drew their sarapes more closely around them, and accompanied the armed guard. I left the room, sick at heart. Justice! out upon the word, when its distorted meaning is the warrant for murdering those who defend to the last their country and their homes.[59]

Garrard was present at the execution and has left a record of the courageous and defiant manner in which one of the condemned men met his death. "The one accused of *treason*," he wrote, "showed a spirit of martyrdom worthy of the cause for which he died — the liberty of his country; and, instead of the cringing, contemptible recantation of the others, his speech was firm asseverations of his own innocence, the unjustness of his trial, and the arbitrary conduct of his murderers. With a scowl, as the cap was pulled over his face, the last words he uttered between his gritting teeth were, 'Caraho, los Americanos!' "[60]

Among other early American writers who commented on instances of Mexican courage was John Russell Bartlett, who had so often and with such relish declared the cowardice of Mexicans when attacked by Indians. He described in his *Narrative* an occasion in which his wagon train was crossing the desert in Chihuahua guarded by five Mexican soldiers. When the train was attacked by Apaches, "the five Mexican soldiers, who were on foot, stood up to the fight manfully, and were in the thickest of it. They did much, too, toward saving the last wagon, which had got separated."[61]

Washington Irving, in *The Adventures of Captain Bonneville*, described in sentimental terms the gallant heroism of a young Mexican named Loretto, who had rescued a "beautiful Blackfoot girl" from a band of Crow Indians and then made her his wife "after the Indian style." Loretto and his wife were traveling with a band of trappers when they came across a group of Blackfeet which included the girl's brother. Brother and sister rushed into each other's arms, but meanwhile the trappers and the Blackfeet Indians had begun shooting arrows at each other. Loretto ran through a hale of arrows to be by his wife's side. However, the girl's brother took charge of her and denied that Loretto had any claim to her at all. At this point, the chief of the Indian band, admiring Loretto's courage, allowed him to return unmolested but alone to the positions of the trappers. Later the lovers were reunited.[62] Though these events had purportedly been witnessed by Captain Bonneville in his travels, Loretto's "in-laws" are too much in the literary convention of the noble savage and Loretto himself too much the romanticized gallant of the southern races to make the tale believable, at least in Irving's version.

The society of *criollo* Mexico which the American frontiersmen encountered tended to promote irresponsibility in the members of its two main social divisions. The aristocratic *ricos* tended to be irresponsible because they were never held to account; the demoralized peons had nothing to lose, and therefore no cause for self-restraint. As to the question of bravery or cowardice, these peons saw nothing in the social organization under which they were forced to live worth defending except their own skins. There were, however, some Mexican types who were in neither one class nor the other. The muleteers, or *arrieros,* were a class to themselves. They sold their services and were beholden to no one. Their profession was a dangerous one, as they were often called upon to pilot mule pack trains across isolated wastes where they were subject to Indian attack. As a group, they were brave, responsible and entertaining. Americans who came in contact with them liked and respected them. "The 'arrieros' of Mexico," wrote Kendall, "are the most hardy, brave, generous and trustworthy of her inhabitants — a class of men in whom the utmost reliance can be placed, and whose calling, requiring them to be constantly roaming from point to point and mixing with the world, provides them with a fund of anecdote and the legendary lore of the country, and renders them well informed and exceedingly entertaining companions. From what I saw and heard of them they are universally to be trusted with any charge, and their word may be invariably depended on — which is a good deal more than can be said of any other class, as a body, in Mexico, whether civil, military, or ecclesiastical."[63] Josiah Gregg in *Commerce of the Prairies* tells of an incident in which he and his party suffered a surprise attack by Commanches. A Mexican muleteer, seeing the danger to Gregg's two favorite riding horses which were tethered within a few paces of the Indians, "rushed out and brought safely in the most valuable of the two, though fusil-balls were showering around him all the while."[64]

Another group which was neither rico nor peon was the class of rancheros. The rancheros, as mentioned above, were a type distinctive of northern Mexico. They were cattlemen who owned their small ranches and worked their own stock rather than depend upon overseers as did most of the ricos. The rancheros, mainly a mestizo group, were tough and skilled cowhands, self-reliant and resistant to oppression. They furnished many revolutionary leaders, especially in the last great uprising, and have provided leadership out of proportion to their numbers in the governments that followed. Gregg, taking note of the frequent charge of cowardice made by Americans in reference to Mexicans, wrote: "While this may well be true of wealthier classes and city-bred caballeros who become the officers whose conduct decides battles, nevertheless the rancheros, the yeomanry of New Mexico, often display hardiness and bravery."[65] Gregg ascribed the fact that Mexican troops often did not hold fast in battle to their lack of confidence in their leaders and to their poor armament.

A gift for telling falsehoods, often with some flair, was commonly credited to the Mexicans. Kendall writes that members of the Texan Santa Fe expedition could not decide whether to trust a Mexican who was acting as a guide and who claimed to know the country through which they were passing. Those who argued in favor of placing confidence in him claimed that he had been employed as a mail carrier between Austin and San Antonio for several years and had been found to be trustworthy. Kendall comments that "this circumstance was related when his claims as a person entitled to credit were canvassed in camp, and went far to establish for him a character for probity which few of his countrymen of the same class receive or deserve."[66] Further in the account, Kendall describes a Mexican servant as a man whose "leading characteristics were great good-nature, extreme idleness, and a proneness to telling the most outrageous falsehoods — the two latter very common failings with his countrymen."[67] Lt. Wise writes of the Mexican army officers he encountered that "a few of them were pleasant, conversible, intelligent gentlemen; but generally speaking they were dirty, ill-bred persons, without moral principle, and the greatest liars in existence, and they invariably taxed one another with being cowards." [68]

Mexicans, according to the early American accounts, were the sort of people who would steal anything that was not nailed down. "The adroitness of the Mexicans in thieving equals that of the rascals at Naples." wrote John W. Audubon,[69] who owned up to a "hatred of all things Mexican."[70] His *Western Journals* are full of accounts of Mexican depravity. On one occasion a member of his party, a Lieutenant Browning, "had his pistol stolen from his holster, while standing within three feet of his mule. This made the fifth lost in this way. He drew his revolver and ordered the [Mexican] crowd off, and in an instant the ground was clear, and the fear that characterizes these miserable creatures was shown as they hurried off, holding their hats to shield the back of their heads." [71] Bartlett ruefully described the loss of some luggage which he had carelessly left unguarded for a moment. "The articles lost were not of much value; but it was provoking, notwithstanding all my care, to be robbed by this rascally people wherever I went."[72] In the matter of having things stolen from him, Lt. Wise characteristically maintained a whimsical tone. "Thieving and pilfering were practiced among the lower orders, in an almost equal degree to knife combats. Leperos are thieves and liars by profession, and their coarse serapes serve to conceal all their peccadillos ... and as the leperos, as a body, are not fond of work, they exercised their ingenuity in appropriating property of others. I had escaped their depredations so long, that I fancied there was nothing worth filching in my possession, or innocently supposed there was some kind of freemasonry established between us. However, I was soon undeceived ... but eventually I became more of a philosopher — was robbed at all times unmercifully and looked upon it as a destiny."[73] One of the few early American writers to acknowledge the relationship between stealing and poverty in discussing Mexican conduct was James Josiah Webb who had the following entry in his *Adventures in the Santa Fe Trade:*

> In a conversation with Dr. Connolly some years after the establishment of the Territorial government, and after his marriage to the widow Chavez, he was boasting of the improved condition of his servants under his liberal management. He had raised the wages of his shepherds from two and three, to four and six, dollars a month, and the peons on the hacienda to six and eight, and teamsters with his wagon train to ten; and some of the best and most industrious laborers he had allowed to work a portion of the land on shares. And he flattered himself that he was treating them with great generosity and kindness, and was doing more to improve the condition of his servants than any of his neighbors.
> "Well, doctor," [I said], "how many servants have you on your hacienda?"
> "Big and little, 108."
> "Well, I suppose you furnish them all [with] work through the winter?"
> "Oh no. The crops are all gathered and stored, and I have no further work for them until time to plant the [?] . . ."
> "Of course they have a good store of corn and other provisions laid up for the winter?"
> "Not an ear — not a thing."
> "But how are they to live with nothing in store, and nothing to do to earn a living?"
> He saw the point, and laughingly replied, *"Steal from Otero."*
> "And how are Otero's servants to live, who you said were not as well cared for as yours?"
> "Oh, they will steal from me — if they have the chance. It is considered dishonorable to steal from the master, but neighborly stealing is no disgrace."
> This was the condition of the laboring classes of old New Mexico, and in view of the example set by the religious fathers, and their entire dependance upon their masters, is it strange [that] they were, as John Randolph very truly but uncharitably called

them, "a blanketed nation of prostitutes and thieves?" Let us withhold our denunciations until we in imagination have put ourselves in their places, and ask ourselves what we would do.[74]

The early writers of the American Southwest did not incline to take a tolerantly amused view of picaresque rascality. In a short story entitled "A Mexican Tale," Albert Pike writes of a character, Santiago Sandoval, who had won a position for himself in Santa Fe by practicing various kinds of chicanery, that "men did not cry out against him, or point to him as an example to be shunned, and by which their children might take heed to their steps. No, he had no such reputation. He had been a man of much *diligencia,* as the Spaniards call a faculty which they possess and exercise — in our language, *swindling.*"[75] Evans describes a trip he took to the town of Presidio del Norte, now Júarez, with a young American named Hall, who knew Spanish well. The mayor of this Mexican town was attempting to make Evans pay an extra two dollars to have his passport countersigned when Hall interposed and indignantly denied the justice of such a procedure. "By this interference," writes Evans, "my $2.00 was saved and Mexican rascality exposed to the scorn of strangers. Conscience has nothing to do in a Mexican's estimate of the value of his property or his services, and when an attempt is made by any of these harpies to extort money for real or imaginary services, the only thing necessary to be done is to take a firm stand at your own price and give them that or nothing."[76] Such was the usual American reaction to an alien people who, perhaps from the Arabic legacy in southern Europe, delighted in oblique maneuvering. These were a people to whom transactions were not simply a means of accomplishing business efficiently but occasions for a by-play of wits within a code which would allow no lapse from good manners. This seeking for the strategic advantage while maintaining an almost deprecating grace of manner exasperated Anglo-Saxon Americans, who cried foul and charged all Mexicans with hypocrisy and deceit. "They have no stability," wrote Josiah Gregg, "except in artifice, no profundity except for intrigue: qualities for which they have acquired an unenviable celebrity."[77]

Part of the optimism of nineteenth-century America was based on the belief that it had established a social order founded upon reason and restraint. Comparatively speaking, America in the early nineteenth century with its homogeneity in Anglo-Saxon tradition and its commitment to the principles of the Age of Reason was in fact an ordered society. People were not accustomed to scenes of violence in their daily lives and took little cognizance of the subsurface savagery which in more restrained societies takes the form of an often disguised vindictiveness. The open display of ferocity in Mexico both appalled early American observers and gave them cause to feel complacently superior. In the novel *Calavar* by Robert Montgomery Bird, published in 1834, a Mexican priest says to an American visitor: "The barbaric romance which loiters about the brains even of European nations, is the pith and medulla of a Mexican head. The poetry of bloodshed, the sentiment of renown — the first and last passion, and the true test, of the savage state — are not yet removed from us. We are not yet civilized up to the point of seeing that reason reprobates, human happiness denounces, and God abhors, the splendour of contention. Your own people — the happiest and most favoured of modern days — are, perhaps not so backward."[78]

Nineteenth-century American travelers in Mexico reported that murder was not only a common occurence but that it was generally practiced with impunity. James O. Pattie writes that during a three-day stop over in a Mexican village the bodies of ten people who had been murdered during the night were brought into town. "Part of the number were supposed to have been killed on account of having been known to carry a great deal of money with them, and part to have had a quarrel about some abandoned women. This last is a most common occasion of night murders, the people being still more addicted to jealousy, and under still less restraints of law, than in old Spain, in the cities of which, assassination from this cause are notoriously frequent."[79] In one of the Texas romances, *Mexico Versus Texas,* written in 1838, the author, Anthony Ganilh, combines the theme of Mexican savagery and guile with that of clerical cupidity and callousness toward murder. An American, Mr. Faring, is traveling by coach through northern Mexico in the company of two Mexican friars. In a little village they meet a crowd which is accompanying a man to a grave-site. This person, from another village, has claimed that he had experienced a vision in which it was revealed to him that a man lay buried at the site together with a considerable sum of money. The villagers help him dig, and together they disinter the body of a man with two bullet holes in the head. Beside the body is found a bag containing a large sum in coins. The man of visions proceeds to distribute some of the money to the villagers, makes a donation to the friars, and goes off with the greater part. Faring, disinclined to believe in revelations, approaches the friars and declares his belief that the enterprising visionary must have had a hand in the murder. He suggests to one of the friars that the man be arrested and handed over to the authorities at Saltillo and volunteers to assist in the arrest himself. To this proposal the agitated friar answers:

> I advise you not to meddle with this man, nor to do a thing which would be accounted exceedingly foolish, and might perhaps subject you to considerable delay and great expense. Why it would be acting the part of Don Quixote, who went about avenging wrongs and redressing injuries! What should we come to in this country, if it were thought necessary to apprehend all who act similar to this man? I have known in my time, that is to say since I was a novice, no less than sixty or seventy corpses thus disinterred, between Durango and Zacatecas, and never before heard that anybody interfered, though, to be sure, people would sometimes smile and significantly shake the head, when a fellow returned enriched from one of these expeditions. Moreover, I think you wrong this poor man, by your suspicions; he is innocent I dare say. He appears very mild, and is certainly exceedingly charitable, for he has bestowed forty dollars, out of six hundred, for masses to be said on behalf of the deceased. A murderer or robber would not think of the like, I am sure.[80]

In *Bernard Lile,* another of the Texas romances, Jeremiah Clemens describes a man "with the ear marks of a greaser" as being "born a thief, and I reckon counts the stealage as the best part of his wages.... He would murder his brother for a peso, and betray anything but his priest for half the money."[81]

The dime novels generally portray the average Mexican as a man of brutal insensibility. In a typical example of the outpourings from the press of Beadle and Adams, *The Serpent of El Paso,* by Buckskin Sam Hall, a Mexican, Lorenzo Castro, plans to kill his rival in love, the American Lieutenant Moore. To camouflage his action he plans a general shooting fray at the dance hall and gathers a group of Mexicans to assist him. Having gained a temporary victory against the Americans at the dance hall, the Mexicans break into a store, roll out some kegs of whiskey and begin a mighty debauch while their own friends and confederates in the recent action lie wounded and dying.

Private Sam Chamberlain, between battles in the Mexican War, rather relished the Hogarthian aspects of Mexican life as he encountered it in the north Mexican states. He was a great frequenter of saloons and bordellos and has left some lively accounts and sketches of these places. On one occasion he dropped in on one of his favorite haunts, a combination of bordello and dance hall, run by two sisters. One of them Ramonda, tried to warn him to get out. But Sam, "being overwise and obstinate from the effects of muscal [sic]," refused to leave, "thinking that there was a lover in the matter." Elbowing past Ramonda, he forced his way into the dance hall. "One look was enough! I was completely sobered, cold chills shot all over me, succeeded by a deathly faintness. How I wished I had taken Ramonda's advice and was now flying for

## Mexican Traits: An Early Portrait    61

camp. Around the room smoking and drinking was seated at least twenty as villainous looking cutthroats as ever drank pulque . . . ." These men crowded around Chamberlain and were all for doing away with him immediately when one of the group, who was both a priest and a brigand, intervened. Fr. Martínez (whose name Sam persisted in spelling *Martiznes*) was a thoroughly picaresque fellow. He had frequently been a drinking companion of Chamberlain's, and during the course of many sessions of drinking pulque and mescal the two had become fast friends. Martínez, in order to improve Sam's chances of survival suggested that it would be more sport to have a man-to-man knife contest with bets taken on the outcome. The men agreed to this arrangement, and an elderly but savage-looking man with one eye, El Tuerto, volunteered to oppose Chamberlain.

> The brigands prepared the room for the conflict, the heavy tables were pushed back against the wall, and to my great surprise half a dozen [sic] smiling Señoritas in scant night dresses appeared and grouped themselves on the tables. We were to peel to our buff and soon stood with nothing on but our pants. The "greasers" were highly elated, and bet freely on the result and to my surprise I seemed to be the favorite. I felt cool, and now my foe was stripped I was satisfied that I should come out all right, for he appeared weak and emaciated. . . . The holy relic, the gift of Franceita [a former mistress] that I wore around my neck attracted attention, and was examined with much interest, and when for effect I kissed it there were cries of, *"El soldado no herético, mucho bueno Cristiano!"* while the ladies all took sides with me and chattered away like magpies.[82]

Sam won the contest by ignoring his knife and poking El Tuerto in his one eye with a left fist. Though he was given safe conduct from Ramonda's place, there was an aftermath to Sam's adventure among the bandits. El Tuerto had a young and beautiful wife whom he treated, at least according to Chamberlain, with great brutality. Chamberlain abducted the girl, "Carmeleita" [sic], and took her to live with him at his camp. (United States Army establishments, evidently, were considerably less formal in those days.) After some weeks of blissful cohabitation, Sam and Carmeleita discovered that El Tuerto had complained to the Provost Marshal. Though Sam described to the authorities the fate which undoubtedly awaited the girl if she were returned to El Tuerto, the Army could hardly deny the legitimacy of the old man's complaint and returned his wife to him. The two disappeared, and for weeks Chamberlain tried to find out what had happened to them. Finally his friend Fr. Martínez told him a "tale of horror." El Tuerto had joined the notorious Canales gang of outlaws and "had carried Carmeleita to a lone ranch where she was outraged by Canales' whole gang of demons and then cut to pieces!"[83]

The Mexican habit of violence manifesting itself in overt cruelty is commented upon by Washington Irving in *The Adventures of Captain Bonneville*. The captain had come upon a group of Mexicans in California who talked freely of the outrages they had committed against a tribe of primitive Indians called "Root-Diggers." "The Mexicans, very probably, charged them with the sin of horse-stealing; we have no other mode of accounting for the infamous barbarities of which, according to their own story, they were guilty; hunting the poor Indians like wild beasts, and killing them without mercy. The Mexicans excelled at this savage sport; chasing their unfortunate victims at full speed; noosing them round the neck with their lassos, and then dragging them to death."[84] The theme of Mexican cruelty also finds its way into Whitman's "Song of Myself," in which the poet recounts in spare, reportorial style the capitulation of a group of Texans to Mexican forces during the Texas revolt. The Texans sign terms of honorable surrender but, having once laid down their arms, are massacred. The events are described without comment, but the account in its very leanness heightens the reader's sense of outrage. Whitman emphasizes that this scene did not take place at the familiar Alamo. What he in fact describes is the massacre at Goliad.[85]

Special attention has been given by some American writers to a particular kind of cruelty ascribed to Mexicans, that of cruelty to animals. Irving Babbitt in recent years has even theorized on this subject as it pertains to the general culture of latinity: "Insensibility to the suffering of animals, though general in Spain, is not any greater, so far as my own observation goes, than in other Latin countries. Possibly, medieval religion, in so exalting man above other creatures, in refusing to recognize his relations to the rest of nature, tended to increase this lack of sympathy with brute creation."[86] Among the several frontier writers who took up the theme of Mexican cruelty to animals was James Ohio Pattie, who has left a clear and detailed report of bull and bear baiting in northern Mexico. The spectacle obviously interested him, but beyond giving the facts, which are shocking enough, he declined to pass judgment.

> Five large grey bears had been caught, and fastened in a pen built for the purpose of confining the bulls, during a bullbaiting. One of the latter animals, held by ropes, was brought to the spot by man on horseback, and thrown down. A bear was then drawn up to him, and they were fastened together by a rope about fifteen feet in length, in such a manner, that they could not separate from each other. One end of it is tied around one of the forefeet of the

bull, and the other around one of the hind feet of the bear. The two were then left to spring upon their feet. As soon as this movement is made, the bull makes at the bear, very often deciding the fate of the ferocious animal in the first act. If the bull fails in goring the bear, the fierce animal seizes him and tears him to death. Fourteen of the latter lost their lives, before the five bears were destroyed.[87]

The art of the bullfight, which was later to excite so much interest among American writers, was regarded at this early stage as just another example of Mexican savagery. Bartlett, upon entering Chihuahua City for the first time, was informed that one of the show places of the city was the bullfight arena and that there would be an exhibition of the art during his stay. "But having once witnessed one of these cruel sights in El Paso," he wrote in his *Narrative,* "I had no desire to be present at another."[88] During a visit to Mexico City, William Cullen Bryant discovered that the bullfight had been suppressed by the reform laws of Júarez. In applauding this action, Bryant wrote in the essay, "A Visit to Mexico," that "there is scarce any public entertainment so well adapted to encourage and cherish a spirit of cruelty in a people as the bull fights of Spain."[89]

Whatever their degree of hostility, the early chroniclers of the borderlands in their persistent references to the alien people to the south gave evidence of their lasting interest in things Mexican. Nor was the fascination of Mexico's women the only occasion for a favorable report. Major Zebulon Pike in 1807 was greatly moved by the hospitality that the people of New Mexico bestowed upon him and his men as they were being marched through small settlements on the way to Santa Fe under the custody of Spanish troops. "We were frequently stopped by women, who invited us into their houses to eat; and in every place where we halted a moment, there was a contest who should be our hosts. My poor lads who had been frozen, were conducted home by old men, who would cause their daughters to dress their feet; provide their victuals and drink, and at night, gave them the best bed in the house. In short, all their conduct brought to my recollection the hospitality of the ancient patriarchs, and caused me to sigh with regret at the corruption of that noble principle, by the polish of modern ages."[90] The short story writer, Albert Pike, also gives testimony to the sense of hospitality that the New Mexicans entertained toward Americans before the latter by their rowdyism outwore their welcome. "It was supposed that an American could be guilty of no crime—no meanness. Did he want a store?—rooms in abundance were offered him gratis. Did he eat and sleep at a Spanish house while traveling? — no pay was received; and everywhere the people possessed that character of hospitality which they still preserve, at a distance from the large towns. In fact, I have never, at a single door, requested food and lodging, by the untranslatable expression, *tengo posada?* (literally, have I a tavern?) without being promptly answered in the affirmative; that is, in the little country settlements."[91]

John Charles Frémont, the Pathfinder, responded with quick sympathy to the Mexicans of California. He insisted, and was in many respects right, that these people were a breed apart. They had long been so separated from the main currents of Mexican life that they had grown used to living a genial life in an abundant countryside, unmolested by the governmental authorities except for their own elected officials who were as relaxed as the people they governed. "They were a happy people." wrote Frémont, "living without restraint or vexatious authority, one large family, with kinships ramified throughout the whole. Mostly, in the towns, the evenings were spent in social gatherings, with only the light refreshments of the wines of the country. Healthy and good-tempered, they had their pleasures in the friendly meeting and the dancing, for other amusements there were none. And each one had the old Spanish pride in his personality, for every ranchero was a grandee of the country. Such a people, free to range at pleasure by night as by day, would hardly endure any restraints upon that personal liberty, where any oppression is most quickly felt."[92] On the basis of this very aversion to authority, Frémont had expected that the Mexican Californians would freely throw in their lot with the democratic United States. In this expectation he was wrong, however, as the feeling of these people toward Mother Mexico turned out to be strong at the very last moment of decision. After an initial show of passivity toward the American invasion, the Mexican Californians rallied and made a desperate last stand against the forces of Manifest Destiny.

A counter theme to that of Mexican cruelty and brutality and one which appears even in those reports which have devoted much space to the darker sides of Mexican life is that of the kindness and charity to be found among Mexico's people. Seven years before Zebulon Pike and his men were being marched into Santa Fe under guard, the remnants of Philip Nolan's unsuccessful filibustering attack on Texas were being herded through the Mexican countryside as prisoners of war. Ellis Bean of Natchez, Tennessee, one of that ragged crew, wrote of the Mexican people: "We noticed that everywhere they were mixed with Indian, but of a kind and friendly disposition. They were all exceedingly kind to us, presenting us with fruits, clothes, and money."[93] In 1841 the people of northern Mexico were again afforded the spectacle of tattered-looking Americans being pushed along by their Mexican captors. Kendall reported that the captured members of the Texan-Santa Fe expedition were the objects of much pity on the part of the Mexican populace. Perhaps in that era of *criollo* rule, the impoverished people of Mexico could identify themselves more readily with the captured foreigners than with the officials of their own government. "The mild and subdued eyes of the poor Indians," wrote Kendall, "were turned upon us invariably in pity, while the crowd through which we passed, in all the large cities, appeared rather to be actuated by commiseration than triumph or hatred, Jews and heretics though they thought and termed us . . . . This speaks much for the lower orders, when it is understood that they might at any time have practiced many acts of insolence towards us with impunity."[94]

Kendall, though constantly inveighing against Mexican officialdom, was in fact considerably impressed by some qualities he discovered in the masses of the poor in Mexico. In one of the observations he made in his *Narrative* he anticipated an attitude which was to appear frequently among modern American writers treating of Mexican themes. He described as "an excellent trait in the character of the Mexican people" that "poverty is certainly no crime, is never insulted . . . . No concealment of poverty is attempted — the poor Mexican family, unlike that of the Americans or English in similar circumstances, never impoverishes itself still further by forced endeavors to conceal its real necessities. Yet they are hospitable to the extent of their means, explaining simply: 'somos pobres.' "[95] Some of the most effective scenes in Kendall's narrative were those describing the patients at the hospital of San Lazaro in Mexico City. This hospital was mainly for lepers, but a group of the Texan prisoners were sent to a separate ward in San Lazaro when smallpox had broken out among them. Kendall was able to observe the daily life of the lepers, and he praised their courage, good cheer, and ingenuity in providing entertainment for themselves. On the feast of San Lazaro, crowds poured into the hospital, and gifts were bestowed upon all the patients. These charitable people were in many cases not friends or relatives of the patients but complete strangers. The Texans were amazed to find that even they, prisoners accused of conspiracy and invasion, were not excluded when the presents were being passed around. In a somewhat begrudging tone, Kendall concluded that "as an offset to their many vices, the Mexicans certainly possess charity and hospitality in an eminent degree — virtues which cover a multitude of sins, and which are not only professed but practised in that country."[96] He described these traits among the Mexican people as being the result of the emphasis which Roman Catholicism always places upon works of charity and urged the Protestant denominations in his own country to follow the example. George W. B. Evans was impressed by the charity that Mexicans showed toward beggars: "There is one thing creditable amongst this people. I noticed the approach to the market of a host of beggars who never applied to anyone without receiving alms. Many of these are blind and live upon the gifts of others from day to day."[97] Josiah Gregg, too, remarked upon the general almsgiving among Mexicans and wrote that there was "scarcely a race of people on the face of the earth more alive to dictates of charity."[98] He then proceeded to vitiate this praise by declaring that this prevalence of almsgiving was more due to religious instruction than to any real sympathy.

From the earliest days of border contact Americans writing about Mexico have been attracted, even fascinated, by the picturesque qualities of the Mexican style of life — the capacity for investing even the ordinary affairs of daily living with an air of dramatic intensity. Occasion for countless clichés and rococo passages of badly-written prose, this persistent theme has often been used to contrast Mexican life to the routinized and unaesthetic aspects of life in the United States.

Much as it has been overworked, however, the theme has been effective in the hands of some writers with an eye for detail and with a feeling for the psychology which underlies the Mexican sense of the dramatic. Among the early American writers, Mexican bravado and swagger, often treated with contempt or amusement, seemed at its most attractive in Mexican horsemanship, which was universally admired. "The Mexicans and half-breeds of California," wrote Washington Irving in *The Adventures of Captain Bonneville,* "spend the greater part of their time in the saddle. They are fearless riders; and their daring feats upon unbroken colts and wild horses, astonished our trappers; though accustomed to the bold riders of the prairies." Irving, while purporting to be only reworking the journal of Captain Bonneville, apparently let slip some evidence of the general license he had been taking with the original text when he compared the Mexican horseman in California to the "vainglorious caballero of Andalusia," as Irving himself had never been to California and presumably Bonneville had never been to Spain. This horseman of the Far West as Irving portrays him is as cocky in his deportment as he is colorful in his regalia. He decks himself out in a huge *sombrero,* braided around the brim in gold or silver, wears a tight-fitting velvet jacket, also heavily enlaced with braid, and sports a pair of elaborately carved leather boots with enormous silver spurs attached. "Thus equipped and suitably mounted, he considers himself the glory of California and the terror of the universe."[99] Frémont also greatly admired the horsemanship to be found among Californians. In his memoirs he recalls an occasion upon which, together with a Californian friend, Francisco de la Guerra, he was watching a noted figure among hacienda owners of the region, Don Pedro, manage a practically unbroken horse: "Of course, like all Californians, Don Pedro was a splendid horseman. He sprang lightly into the saddle, which was that of the country, with the usual *mochila* or large, stiff leather covering to the saddle. But his right foot had not reached the stirrup when the gray commenced. He bucked from the start, going a round in a circle about thirty yards across, bucking right along and with so much force that he jerked Don Pedro's sword from his scabbard, the pistols from the holsters and the *mochilas* from between him and the saddle. Everybody applauded his horsemanship. Francisco de la Guerra cried out 'Todavía es Californio!' ('He is a Californian still.')"[100]

One of the most memorable accounts of Mexican style and sense of pageantry to be found in early American writing is Sam Chamberlain's description of Santa Anna's army as it moved into position for the Battle of Buena Vista, so nearly lost by the American forces.

> The sun rose bright and clear behind the Sierra Madre on the morning of the 23rd of February, 1847. It shone on a scene well calculated to stir one's blood to a fever heat with warlike enthusiasm and make a coward brave. I doubt if the 'Sun of Austerlitz' shone on a more brilliant spectacle than the Mexican army displayed before us — twenty thousand men clad in new uniforms, belts as white as snow, brasses and arms burnished until they glittered like gold and silver.
>
> Their Cavalry was magnificent — some six thousand cavaliers richly caparisoned in uniforms of blue faced with red, with waving plumes and glittering weapons, advanced towards us as if they would ride down our little band and finish the battle at one blow.
>
> They formed in one long line with their massed bands in front, and then a procession of ecclesiastical dignitaries with all the gorgeous paraphernalia of the Catholic Church advanced along the lines, preceded by the bands playing a solemn anthem. The air was so clear we could see every movement: The Infantry knelt down, the Cavalry lowered their lances and uncovered, and their colors drooped as the benedictions were bestowed. This ceremony offered a striking contrast to conditions in our lines; there was not a Chaplain in our army![101]

Not only was the tone of Mexican society thought to be different from that of the United States in its heightened sense of drama but it was also credited with a greater degree of aesthetic sensibility. In this notion, some early American writers anticipated ideas later to be expressed by such moderns as Waldo Frank. George Wilkins Kendall, immediately after having ridiculed the Mexican carpenters for their clumsy efforts at fastening a large door at San Lazaro, took up the subject of the lepers who were decorating a hall in the hospital in preparation for the feast of San Lazaro.

> And here the Mexicans excel. Festoons, flags, and devices, cut in paper of all colours, were hung about the walls, and the lamps were decorated in the same way. The word "caridad" — charity — was also neatly cut in paper and pasted about on the different utensils, and in places where it would readily strike the eye of visitors. The floor was stained with a yellow tint, and on the ceiling long strips of red, white, and blue muslin were tastefully arranged in bows and different fanciful forms, giving relief and beauty to the general appearance. Flowers also were entwined about the cots, and, considering the material with which the lepers were provided, I doubt whether any other people under the sun could have given the room an appearance as beautiful.[102]

In piecing together a composite portrait of the Mexican as he appeared to early American writers, this chapter has examined in considerable detail the reactions of these writers to an alien civilization with which frontier America was unavoidably involved. These early chroniclers and novelists have been freely quoted in order to reproduce the tone, the atmosphere in which these first cultural contacts took place. Yet there have been important omissions. Little has been said of the biological universals of human life, sex, and death, and the differing ways in which the two principal cultures of the borderlands coped with them. The question of race, an obsessive theme in early America as it is today, has only been touched upon. Finally there remains to be examined the juxtaposition of widely divergent institutional patterns, religious and political, that took place in the borderlands. These matters, to the extent that they have been used as themes in early American writing and in the works of moderns relating to this early period, will be the subject of the next two chapters.

CHAPTER THREE

## A Discourse on Race, on Sex, on Death

With all the talk of a melting pot, the United States, if not in its genes at least in its attitudes, remains a predominantly Anglo-Saxon country. The conditioning of the past, in which the American consciousness has been affected by both the insularity of Britain and the polarity of master and slave in America, has produced in the mind of the dominant American type a characteristic distortion. The dark-skinned man is rarely seen, even by those who wish him well, in the reality of his individual being. To a considerable extent he continues to be the "invisible man," in Ralph Ellison's sense of the term. The conditioned response of the white American toward the Negro was to a great measure simply continued in a different setting and toward a different people when Americans first settled beside Mexicans in the Southwest. In certain ways the Mexican, though much has been made of the picturesqueness which his presence has given to the Hispanic Southwest, remains an invisible man to a large majority of the "Anglo" population hurrying about its business in the now burgeoning cities of the area.

Significantly, in a census taken in 1834, it was revealed that 81 per cent of the Anglo-Americans who had settled in Texas came from the slave states.[1] Since, as General Mier y Teran noted in his report to the president of Mexico, many of the Mexicans encountered by the Anglo-Americans in Texas bore evidence of an Indian strain, it was all the easier for these predominantly southern Americans to transfer ready-made attitudes toward an anomalous race. The role that racial feeling played in the Texas revolt against Mexico has been cited by Eugene C. Barker, Texan historian: "The Texans saw themselves in danger of becoming the alien subjects of a people to whom they deliberately believed themselves morally, intellectually, and politically superior. The racial feeling, indeed, underlay and colored Texan-Mexican relations from the establishment of the first Anglo-American colony in 1821."[2] Southern traditions remain strong in Texas today and have carried over to some extent into New Mexico and Arizona. California, in its attitude toward its heritage from Mexico, suffers from a split personality. On the one hand it reveres and thoroughly commercializes the "Spanish" past, and on the other it tends to scorn or simply ignore the living representatives of this past in its midst. On festive occasions for purpose of pageantry it can still trot out representatives of the old, aristocratic "Spanish" families to ride along with the rest of the parade in ten-gallon hat and braided jacket. Two modern writers on social themes, Carey McWilliams in *North From Mexico*[3] and Ruth Tuck in *Not With the Fist*,[4] appear to have enjoyed themselves thoroughly as they somewhat playfully but emphatically exposed California's schizophrenic state of mind toward Mexico and the "Spanish" past. Both writers traced the genealogies of the old "Spanish" families to discover these "aristocrats" to have been of ordinary origin, *mestizo,* and as Mexican as tortillas and beans.

If the Mexican in the American Southwest has been overlooked in the flesh, he has certainly not been ignored in American writing. But even here the reality of the man has often been sacrificed to the type, and in many cases the various types of Mexicans to appear in American writing in different periods have been significant principally in revealing the psychic needs of the writers who have produced them. The American writer, especially in recent years, has often turned to the Mexican out of a sense of his own deficiency or of the deficiencies of the society in which he grew up. In either case, the Mexican and his culture have been used as compensation. Furthermore, under the compulsion of a sense of guilt in the name of his own race-proud society, the modern American writer has tended to oversimplify his Mexican characters in the direction of some stoic or primitive ideal. The resultant literary images of the Mexican as one of various types of noble savage, or as the emotionally unhampered, picaresque product of an unsterilized society, or yet as a graceful representative in the New World of the mellower culture of traditional Europe are often as unreal in their overemphasis as the earlier stereotypes of the brutal, dirty, cowardly Mexican of the border chronicles and first novels of the Southwest.

In recent years the portrait of the Mexican in American writing has become more and more accurate, but the principle of selection, the kinds of Mexican characters which American writers have chosen to portray, remains revealing in terms of the inner needs of the writer. Lesley Byrd Simpson, the author of several good studies of Mexican civilization, quite properly chose as the title for one of his books, *Many Mexicos.*[5] The underlying theme of the book is that Mexico is an extremely complex civilization with its rather subtle social stratification in the vertical sense, and horizontally with its numerous, diverse, and semi-autonomous regional cultures scattered throughout the wide extent of the Mexican earth. Hart Crane, despite his limited acquaintance with

Mexico, was another American writer who clearly perceived the cultural complexity of that nation. In a letter to Samuel Loveman, written in the town of Mixcoac in 1931, he exclaimed: "It seems incredible, but Mexico is more vast than you can ever realize by looking at a map and more various in its population than any country on earth. Layer on layer of various races and cultures scattered in the million gorges and valleys which make the scenery so plastic and superb."[6] Because of this very complexity and also because of his own inner dictates, the modern American writer, like the early chronicler of the borderlands, often mistook a part for the whole in terms of Mexican character and culture, even though his representation of what he knew of Mexico might have been quite accurate. Yet there are no real grounds for complaint in the fact that modern American writers have so frequently used Mexico as a foil to emphasize deficiencies in their own society. These writers knew well enough that they were fortunate in having a neighboring culture which could serve so admirably for this purpose; and whatever may have been their motivations, they have produced a steadily more clear and more accurate image of this important civilization to the south. In doing so they have attested, in the very persistence of their choice of Mexican subject matter, to the permanence of the cultural involvement of Mexico and the United States.

The feelings of guilt and inadequacy which have characterized modern American writers in their approach to Mexico are notably absent in the work of the first Americans to leave literary records of the Mexican scene. These early writers often allowed themselves to express quite unabashedly their distaste for Mexicans on purely racial grounds. The backwardness, uncontrollable passion, and chronic instability attributed to Mexico, were, according to such writers, predictable manifestations of the biological inferiority of Mexico's mixed race. In *The Oregon Trail,* Francis Parkman records his reactions to the Mexicans he encountered along the banks of the Missouri River, men in the employ of various Santa Fe trading companies. "On the muddy shore stood some thirty or forty dark, slavish looking Spaniards, gazing stupidly out from beneath their broad hats."[7] Crossing the river, he met a boat in which "the rowers, swarthy, ignoble Mexicans, turned their brutish faces upwards to look, as I reached the bank."[8] Further in the narrative, Parkman describes coming across "two or three squalid Mexicans, with their broad hats, and their vile faces overgrown with hair."[9] Much the same tone is taken by J. Ross Browne in his Western travel books. His aversion toward Mexicans, an outright physical repulsion, was such that there was no room left for any feeling of compassion for the inhabitants of Sonora who, when he was wandering through the area in 1864, were being continually victimized by the Apaches who were quick to take advantage of the weakened military position of both the United States and Mexico in the Arizona-Sonora region during that period. The American garrison in Arizona had been greatly depleted as troops were drawn off to bolster both of the contending armies during the Civil War. In Mexico, all military forces were engaged in regions farther south than Sonora, as the French and Mexican supporters of Maximilian attempted to cope with the increasing guerrilla activities of the Republican army loyal to Júarez. Sonora lay totally at the mercy of the ferocious Apaches, and many of its inhabitants attempted to flee to Arizona for protection. Of this situation Ross Browne said that "Arizona possessed at least the pretense of military protection. It soon became infested with the refuse population of Sonora — the most faithless and abandoned race, perhaps, on the face of the earth."[10] These people, Browne discovered, were not only deplorably fecund but given by long custom to forming sexual alliances with the Indians. "Occasionally some beneficent Padre goes through the country doing up a long arrearage of marriages, putting together in the holy bonds of wedlock all who desire to secure by the rites of the Church the partners with whom they chance at the time to be on terms of domestic intimacy. For this reason I think Sonora can beat the world in the production of villainous races. Miscegenation has prevailed in this country for three centuries. Every generation the population grows worse; and the Sonoranians may now be ranked with their natural compadres — Indians, burros, and coyotes."[11] Many of the Sonora settlements at this time had been totally abandoned, while in other places, usually around a decayed presidio or mission church, a few settlers clung together, if not for protection at least for company. Of one such grouping Browne wrote: "A more desolate-looking place than Cocospera does not perhaps exist in Sonora. A few Mexican and Indian huts, huddled around a ruinous old church, with a ghostly population of Greasers, Yaqui Indians, skeleton dogs, and seedy sheep, is all that attracts the eye of a stranger . . . ."[12]

The modern reader accustomed to current standards of taste might well be amazed by finding constant references to a neighboring people, in respectable mid-nineteenth-century American publications, as being totally loathsome. And yet the very insensitivity of an earlier American public in matters of race did confer upon writers of the time the freedom to write vividly and perhaps more honestly about racial antipathies, including their own. The editors of the fashionable *Overland Monthly* undoubtedly had no qualms about publishing a story in which a character was described as being "a ragged, dirty Mexican, whose matted hair was a model of a cactus-fence, whose tattered blanket served to make more evident his nakedness, an unmistakable, unredeemed 'greaser.' "[13] It would be a veritable curmudgeon among modern public officials who would write of Mexicans in the state of Sonora as did J. R. Bartlett, early boundary commissioner in the Southwest. He described these northern Mexicans as being "of a dingy, opaque, olive green, which shows there is no friendly mixture in the blood of the Spaniard and the Indian. They appear to be the same squalid, flabby, mixed race which is observed in almost every part of the Mexican coasts."[14] Such language, of course, was only to be expected in the dime novels or Texas romances. Even the aristocratic General Santa Anna did not escape the association in the Texan mind of Mexican with Negro. A pugnacious Texas woman, Mrs. Jim Sprott, in Samuel Hammett's *Piney Woods Tavern* refers to Santa Anna as "that yaller nigger."[15]

The complacence with which writers of the frontier compared Mexicans with Americans to the total advantage of the latter is typified in a passage in the early American novel *Francis Berrian*. Timothy Flint puts the comparison into the mouth of one of his Mexican characters, Doña Martha, having her bear witness against her own people in favor of the noble Saxon. Referring to her engagement to the American Francis Berrian she says: "Since I have been acquainted with this man I have learned to read English; I have been deeply engaged in the American history. What a great country! What a noble people! Compare their faces and persons with those of the people here, and what a difference!"[16]

A dissenter among early American writers in this matter of racial aversion toward Mexicans was Albert Pike, who prefigured in his sensibility those modern writers who have seen an interesting and aesthetically satisfying combination in the interplay of Spanish and Indian strains that make up the Mexican physique and temperament. Describing a young man from New Mexico, Pike wrote in the short story "A Mexican Tale" that "his eyes, like those of all his people, were keen and black; and his face, though by no means angular or striking, might be accounted handsome. Mixing in his veins the blood of the Spaniard and the Indian, he possessed the energy and the indomitable fierceness of both races, united to the simplicity of character, which, as yet, had met little to corrupt it."[17]

Several mid-nineteenth-century American writers commented upon race and status in Mexican society. Latin America, in pointing the finger at racial discrimination in the United States, often declares itself to be free of racial prejudice. Certainly there has been a rather general admixture of European, Indian, and Negro stocks throughout Hispanic America, with considerable variation in this matter from country to country. However, since the days of the Conquest, people of prevailingly Spanish or Portuguese descent have dominated and still dominate Latin America. This situation exists to some extent even in Mexico where those of pure Spanish blood are a small minority and the *mestizo* is clearly the prevalent type. Now that revolutionary ardors have cooled in Mexico and the grandeurs of the Indian past are evoked less often, a lighter complexion can be counted on to be an advantage in society and in business. Francis Parkman, surveying the human types he encountered in Colorado, would not accord to any of the Mexicans he met the distinction of being "white." "The human race in this part of the world," he wrote in *The Oregon Trail,* "is separated into three main divisions, arranged in the order of their merit: white men, Indians and Mexicans; to the latter of whom the honorable title of 'whites' is by no means conceded."[18] Other early writers, however, observing Mexicans in less primitive settings than did Parkman, perceived the variation in racial types and the consequent gradations of social status. George W. B. Evans in *Mexican Gold Trail, The Journal of a Forty-Niner,* wrote of the Mexicans he had encountered just below the Texas border that "there are, as near as I can learn, three classes. The first are the regular descendants of Castilian or Spanish blood and are characterized by a desire to gain knowledge, and are ambitious and industrious and generally intelligent. The next class comes from a mixture of Spanish and Indian blood — and if an American makes anything off these in trade, he may be pronounced an early riser. The last class is of Negro and Indian origin, indolent and very cowardly."[19] Richard Henry Dana in *Two Years Before the Mast* described the stratification of society in California. An aristocracy existed composed of a few upper-class families which intermarried, "keeping up an exclusive system in every respect." They were proud of a purely Spanish descent, thus maintaining a sense of caste which, according to such modern writers as Carey McWilliams, Ruth Tuck, and Harvey Fergusson, was founded upon illusion. "From this upper class," wrote Dana, "they go down by regular shades, growing more and more dark and muddy, until you come to the pure Indian."[20]

A certain ambiguity creeps into the work of these early writers when they consider the social position of the man of mixed blood in Mexico. On the one hand there is the general tendency to react with hostility to the spectacle of a feudalistic caste system with its hereditary rank and privilege. Such a system was an affront to American egalitarian ideals. On the other hand, it seemed most natural to these writers that the *mestizos* and Indians should be fixed in the lower order of society. This ambiguity, of course, arises directly from the central contradiction in American democracy by which a professedly egalitarian society maintains a caste system on the basis of race. The abhorence of miscegenation has been called the one enduring American taboo and while the feeling against it is most strong in terms of alliances between Whites and Negroes, it carries over to include the mating of Whites with dark peoples other than Negro. The squaw man, the White who had settled down with an Indian woman, was a stock object of derision in the literature of the American West. Even Cooper in *The Last of the Mohicans* could not allow his noble Uncas an uncomplicated love relationship with Cora, daughter of an American army officer. Their affair had to remain unconsummated. Even to permit them to display a sexual attraction to each other, Cooper had to invent a secret shame for Cora, a rather remote Negro strain. In another novel, *The Prairie,* Cooper comments on the nature of half-breeds, men born of Indian women by white fathers. "This race has much of the depravity of civilization without the virtues of the savage."[21] A similar idea was expressed by Bartlett in reference to Mexican *mestizos* compared to the "Spanish" families who had entertained him in El Paso. "These are a few respectable old Spanish families at El Paso, who possess much intelligence, as well as that elegance and dignity of manner which characterized their ancestors. . . . A vast gulf intervenes between these Castilians and the masses, who are a mixed breed, possessing none of the virtue of their European ancestors, but all their vices, with those of the aborigines superadded."[22]

The *Overland Monthly,* which was to be Western America's answer to the *Atlantic Monthly* and which had pretensions to being a formulator of opinion in the West, carried a number of stories and articles on Mexico, most of them uncomplimentary. In one of these articles, "In the Backwoods of Mexico," the author, W. T. Pritchard, expressed the commonly held opinion that there was a cause and effect relationship between racial admixture and moral deficiency: "I did not like the looks of the fellow Ignacio, and very soon suspected he was up to mischief — there was too even an admixture of Spanish and Indian blood in him to be of much good."[23] The cowardice so often charged to Mexicans was explained by some writers as the result of Mexico's having weakened her stock through racial mixture. In an article entitled "The French in Mexico," which appeared in the *Overland Monthly* for September, 1868, William V. Wells accounted for the superiority of the French army over its Mexican opponent on the grounds of the racial inferiority of Mexico's army. "In the open field, a charge of disciplined troops usually sufficed to put to flight the collection of frowzy-headed mestizos, leperos, mulattoes, Indians, Samboes, and other mongrels now, as in the time of our own war with them, composing a Mexican army."[24] The same theme is to be found elsewhere in early American writing. William Gilmore Simms in the verse play *Michael Bonham or the Fall of Bexar,* published in 1852, displayed the Southerner's pride of race when he had one of his characters, a Texan defender of the Alamo, shout: "They fly before us. They can hold no ground with the old Saxon stock."[25]

As might be expected, William Cullen Bryant, as a cultivated man of letters from the abolitionist Northeast, expressed himself on the subject of race in Mexico in a manner quite different from the vulgar racialism of early Southern and Western writers. While attending a meeting of the Geographical and Statistical Society in Mexico City, a society devoted to cultivation of the arts and sciences, Bryant took note of the vice-president of Mexico, Ramírez, and the distinguished Mexican historian, Altamirano, both Indians. These examples of men of indigenous stock who had risen to positions of eminence in Mexico occasioned him to write in the essay "A Visit to Mexico" that "many of these descendants of the people subdued by Cortés are men of cultivated minds and engaging manners. The greater part of the works of art in the galleries of which I have spoken [Mexican Academy of Arts] are from their hands."[26]

The fact that Mexicans in the border region refused to treat Negroes in the manner prescribed by white Americans was a source of irritation to American frontiersmen, and some of the grumbling on this score is to be found in early Southwestern writing. Josiah Gregg, dedicated as he was to the rationalistic ideals of the enlightenment, was nevertheless outraged at the deference that he observed being paid to some Negroes in northern Mexico. He felt positively humiliated by the social success of an American Negro named George who, having married the sister of a Mexican officer, emerged as Don Jorge and became a gallant figure in local society and great favorite with the ladies.[27] One of the Texas romances, *Mexico Versus Texas* by Anthony Ganilh, published in 1838, includes a polemical justification of Negro slavery delivered by a Texan to a Mexican army officer. The Texan has been arguing the moral superiority of Americans to Mexicans. To this claim, the Mexican officer answers:

> "And tell me, if you please, how does it happen that so moral and chaste a people have so many mulattoes amongst them? — You may travel the whole extent of Mexico, without meeting so many individuals of mongrel heritage, though, amongst us, marriages between the various castes are neither prohibited by law, nor stigmatized by public opinion. And your slavery! — What have you to say to that?" "Ah, ah," replied the other, "there you think you have embarrassed me; but I can produce good arguments to prove that negroes are an inferior race, made purposely to be hewers of

wood and drawers of water to the whites. Do you wish scripture authority? — I can quote the curse of Noah against one of his sons and his posterity, and nothing prevents us from supposing that our negroes are descended from Ham. In that case, we do nothing more than fulfilling the scripture, you know. Do you wish for philosophical proofs? — Dissect a black man, and you will find the internal structure of his body somewhat different from that of the whites. It is somewhere about the lumbary regions, anatomists say! Does this not make my assertion good, and prove them to be intended by nature to serve us as playthings? — If you want metaphysical arguments, we can show that negroes are inferior to us in judgement, and though some of their fanatical friends represent them as naturally superior in warmth of fancy and quickness of imagination, we are not bound to acknowledge the truth of the fact. But let us drop this subject. It is dangerous to treat of it, even in the coolest manner. My neighbours might mistake you for an abolitionist, and in that case you would become hateful. The suspicion of abolitionism operates like the plague here."[28]

Several modern American writers have used the records of this early period in the borderlands to provide material for the writing of short stories and novels. Of these writers, Harvey Fergusson has shown himself to be particularly interested in the history of racial conflict in the Southwest from the earliest days of American penetration into the area. This conflict provides the principal theme for a twentieth-century trilogy later assembled in one volume under the title of *Followers of the Sun*.[29] The novels in the trilogy are arranged chronologically by period rather than by date of publication. The first part of *Followers of the Sun* is the novel *Wolf Song,* which deals with the mountain men in New Mexico, the first Anglo-Americans to become acquainted with the region. *In Those Days,* the second part, is a novel which in covering the adult life of its central figure, Robert Jayson, pioneer trader and businessman, recounts the swift conquest of New Mexico by the Americans and the consequent destruction of the wealth and traditional way of life of the old Mexican landholding families of the Rio Grande valley. *The Blood of the Conquerors,* the last part, although actually the first written of the three novels, shows the old Mexican families of the Albuquerque region in full decay and in the final stage of what was to become an almost total dispossession. The protagonist of the novel, Ramón Delcasar, a young Mexican-American and last in the line of a once proud and powerful family, attempts to reverse the tide and compete with the "gringos" on their own grounds. He is successful for a while. His motive, however, in struggling against the fate which has overtaken his people is not the usual competitive profit urge of the "gringos" but rather a desire to make himself acceptable to an Anglo-American girl.

When the girl's family moves east in order to prevent her marriage with a Mexican, Ramón Delcasar loses the will to fight and quickly lapses into the stagnant condition of the rest of his people.

When the mountain men, disheveled, disorganized, and totally individualistic, first showed up in the cities of Santa Fe and Taos, they probably did not strike the local inhabitants as being the advance guard of an invasion, and yet they were thoroughly disliked for their arrogance. These fur-trappers lived isolated lives in the wilderness punctuated by occasional wild sprees in frontier settlements. Money earned by pelts was spent orgiastically by men who consumed enormous quantities of liquor and who considered all women to be theirs for the taking. Their contempt for the "greasers" was boundless. Fergusson in *Wolf Song* describes the disruption caused by a group of mountain men riding into Taos.

> Around the plaza brown men slouched sulky and resentful in doorways, with serapes pulled up and sombreros pulled down, with corn husk cigarettes hanging from secretive mouths. More came out from bars and stores and stood and looked. Some got up from squatting comfort against shady walls and some left games of cooncan, but none gave a greeting.
> 
> A Cockfight at the corner, that was right in the way, blew up into running cursing men and fluttering squawking birds.
> 
> The mountain men rode straight through it and saved some rooster's life.
> 
> "Out of the way, you greasers! You can't shine now!"[30]

A young man named Gullion serves in the novel to typify the character of the mountain man. In one scene he starts a fracas in a Taos dance hall which erupts into a general fight between mountain men and Mexicans. These dance hall ructions almost invariably occurred when the mountain men swept in on Santa Fe or Taos.

> Gullion was arguing noisily with a slick little Mexican over the red-skirted girl Gullion had been dancing with most of the evening. The crowds whirled and parted around them. The girl stood on one foot looking modestly down while the white man blustered and the dark one stood his ground, insisting with a politeness that covered a hatred old and overripe. Gullion ended the argument by flattening a great hand against the Mexican's expostulating mouth, knocking him down and away with a long shove.
> 
> "Off the floor, you goddam greaser," he roared. "You can't shine here...."[31]

Occasionally a mountain man settled down with a Mexican woman, but in doing so he generally lost caste with his fellows. In *Wolf Song*, an old mountain man, Rube Thatcher, warns a young friend of the danger in taking a Mexican girl too seriously.

> I ain't lived in these mountains since the Rio Grande was a spring branch fer nothin'. I seen many a good man marry Mexican and I ain't seen one yit that wasn't sorry. Them women breeds like prairie dogs an' jest as careless. They look good when they're young but after they've calved a time or two they swell up like a cow in a truck patch an' you need a wagon to move 'em. They do nothin' but eat and holler like a guinea keet .... And all their kids is jest as Mexican as they are.... I mind Joe Thomas that was as good a mountain man as ever set a float stick and he went loco over a brown gal in El Paso. Her family hated gringos, so he snatched her up in his saddle and ran to Socorro with her. I seen him there about six years later settin' in a barroom lookin' sad and peaked as a moulted rooster. He looked out the window kind of sorrowful. "Yander comes five goddam greasers," he says. "Who are they?" somebody asks. "M' wife and the four kids," says Joe.[32]

In the second novel of the trilogy, *In Those Days,* a character named Tom Foote argues with the protagonist, Robert Jayson, that he should leave the little New Mexican town where he has been working in a store to join Foote in a partnership to start a business in Albuquerque. "If a man stays around these little towns," Foote says, "he jest goes greaser himself. He gets him a Mexican girl and she don't egg him on like a white woman would. He lickers up when he likes and nobody minds. It's a lazy country and it makes a man lazy."[33]

Of course, not all Americans viewed "going Mexican" as a form of degeneracy. The famous Judge Roy Bean, "the law west of the Pecos," submerged himself, during periods of his youth, into the Mexican population of Texas. In fact, he eventually married a Mexican woman. C. L. Sonnichsen, in his savory biography of Roy Bean, gives this account of Bean's early life in San Antonio:

> SAN ANTONIO is today the closest thing to an old Spanish town in the United States. Seventy-five years ago it was as Mexican as chili peppers. Patriarchal clans with melodious names ran the commercial and social life of the place in the old-fashioned way. Politics was a family matter. There were a great many Germans and Frenchmen and Americans who moved in their own tight little circles, but everybody picked up the Spanish language and slid into Spanish ways.
> 
> Roy Bean liked that. He liked the way people loafed half a day at a time on the shady side of an adobe house telling stories. He liked the smoke and clatter of the *cantinas* in the evening. He liked the green mesquite-studded Texas landscape on which the town sat so comfortably — the clear streams of water puttering cheerfully along the busiest streets — the *lavanderas* washing clothes on the banks —

the small boys scandalizing the washwomen by swimming naked under their noses.

He liked the people — the proud men and the beautiful girls with their brilliant eyes and the soft, dark bloom on their cheeks.

He liked the Mexican view that every man had a right to his own vices.

And so he left the Frenchmen and the Germans and the Americans to enjoy their own society while he went Mexican.[34]

An interesting comparison can be made, when viewed in terms of shifts in American public attitudes, between the freedom felt by nineteenth-century American writers to be coarsely opprobrious in racial matters, and their acceptance of prevailing taboos in matters of sex. The early American writers who lingered over the repugnant aspects of the Mexican physique often expressed with a hurried avoidance of detail their shock at the openly erotic tone of Mexican society, an atmosphere which in its pervasive voluptuity confirmed them in the belief that the Mexicans were a racially defective people. The unself-conscious acceptance of the body which is part of a Mexican's attitude toward life caused offense. Susan Magoffin in her diary recorded her shock at what she regarded to be the lax tendency toward exposure among Mexicans.

> The women slap about with their arms and necks bare, perhaps their bosoms exposed (and they are none of the prettiest or whitest). If they are about to cross the little creek that is near all the villages, regardless of those about them, they pull their dresses, which in the first place but little more than cover their calves — up above their knees and paddle through the water like ducks, sloshing and splattering everything about . . . it is repulsive to see the children running about perfectly naked, or if they have on a chemise it is in such ribbands it had better be off at once. I am constrained to keep my veil drawn closely over my face all the time to protect my blushes.[35]

Bernard DeVoto in *1846 The Year of Decision* drew upon Susan Magoffin's diary and satirized in a rather good-humored manner her puritanical reaction to Mexican life, giving a picture of her as she winced her way through a Santa Fe fiesta.

> Susan could not approve the abandon of those dances in which the women were so fervently embraced. She was not reconciled to the native costumes which, though prettily colored, were not reticent about a woman's limbs and exposed so much of the bosom that Susan turned her eyes away from what she considered open incitation of the baser instincts. All the women smoked corn-shuck cigarettes, too, and fat priests drank wines and *aguardiente* and displayed an unclerical mirth that distinguished them sharply from the parsons she knew. But worst of all La Tules was there, Doña

Gertrudes Barcelo, a handsome, urbane female. Everyone seemed to like her although she owned and personally managed the town's biggest gambling hall. She had, the distressed Susan wrote down, "that shrewd and fascinating manner necessary to allure the wayward, inexperienced youth to the hall of final ruin."[36]

Susan Magoffin was not the only one to leave a record of the doings of La Tules. Josiah Gregg could not avoid running across her on a number of occasions, and he viewed her with great distaste. The entries in his journal on the subject of this defiantly unconventional woman form part of the material which Paul Horgan used in developing his portrait of the Missouri trader in *The Centuries of Santa Fe*.

> The most famous gambling house he [the Missouri trader] saw was that located at Number 37, Calle de la Muralla, or Rampart Street. It was run by a woman of strong temperament and tolerant shrewdness called La Tules. He saw her many times, never without condemning her in his thoughts or afterwards in his notes. She seemed like an animal predator to him. At first she "lived (or rather roamed) in Taos." She was a female "of very loose habits," who "finally extended her wandering to the capital. She there became a constant attendant upon one of those pandemoniums where the favorite game of *monte* was dealt *pro bono publico*. For some years she spent her days in lowliness and misery." But her luck changed, she opened a bank of her own, and "she gradually rose higher and higher in . . . affluence, until she found herself in possession of a very handsome fortune." In the end, she was "considered the most expert *monte* dealer in Santa Fe," and — he was shocked — she was "openly received in the first circles of society" calling herself "Señora Doña Gertrudes Barcelo." He could imagine what would be thought of her "among the gentility and the chivalry" of American cities. He had an exasperating notion that she would not care what was thought of her, there, or anywhere, so long as the money continued to flow across her *monte* boards into her black alpaca bags with their stout drawstrings.[37]

Part of this general disapproval of La Tules stemmed no doubt from the peculiarly Protestant aversion to gambling, which relates to the notion that a person should only possess what has been gained by hard work and also to the sense that life should be viewed as a predictable, orderly experience. The Mexican fascination for gambling, on the other hand, might well express the feeling that life is at bottom chaotic and that human successes are largely a matter of chance. But quite apart from the fact that La Tules became a successful professional gambler she was in bad odor with the community of American traders and their wives in Santa Fe because she was a notoriously "loose woman." Among the ways in which this looseness expressed itself was her love of dancing. She was a great frequenter of the dance halls, and these were an abomination. Albert Pike in the short story "The Inroad of the Nabajo" gives a picture of a fandango held in a dance hall in Santa Fe as it impressed the central figure of the story, the American visitor.

> On the evening after my arrival in the village, I went to a fandango. I saw the men and women dancing waltzes, and drinking whiskey together; and in another room, I saw the monte bank open. It is a strange sight — a Spanish fandango. Well-dressed women — (they call them ladies) — harlots, priests, thieves, half-breed Indians — all spinning round together in the waltz. Here, a filthy, ragged fellow with half a shirt, a pair of leather breeches, and long, dirty, woolen stockings, and Apache moccasins, was hanging and whirling round with the pretty wife of Pedro Vigil; and there, the priest was dancing with La Altegracia, who paid her husband a regular sum to keep out of the way, and so lived with an American. I was soon disgusted.[38]

The fact that the Mexicans loved dancing and made no effort to conceal the basically sexual nature of it brought forth other prim comments from American chroniclers of the early Southwest. George W. B. Evans noted that at Presidio del Norte, now Juárez, "our boys enjoyed themselves at a Mexican fandango, or Spanish dance, where rude things were indulged in, although the fandango was held at the residence of the city alcalde, or mayor."[39] Harvey Fergusson, writing of the dances held at the haciendas of the Rio Grande valley in the mid-nineteenth century, described the Cuna or cradle waltz. "The whirling dancers embraced each other loosely about the shoulders, making a cradle, 'which was never bottomless' as one shocked observer from Missouri remarked."[40] Another such observer, Horgan's Missouri trader, reacted characteristically to dancing in Santa Fe, expressing the mixture of puritanism and sophistication in his make up. "In his driftings about the city he could not but observe how warmly and frankly the inhabitants dealt with what in other connotations he called 'the Gentle Passion.' He made a note on the dancing of the Santa Feans, and sent it to *Niles's National Register,* where it was published in 1841. 'The fandango is a lascivious dance, partaking in part of the waltz, cotillion, and many amorous movements, and' — he used a worldly tone — 'is certainly handsome and amusing. It is the national dance. In this the governor and most humble citizen move together, and in this consists all their republican boast.' "[41]

Harvey Fergusson in the novel *The Conquest of Don Pedro* returns to the subject of the dances held at the great Mexican houses along the Rio Grande valley. More than any other American writer, Fergusson has examined the feudalistic Mexican aristocracy which once flourished in the Southwest. He has described it in the last moments of its fullest flowering, shown it in decline, and recorded its final ruin at the hands of encroaching American entrepreneurs. In the seventies and eighties, the period dealt with in *The Conquest of Don Pedro,* the big house in the Rio Grande valley still had considerable vigor, but its authority to rule the region over which it presided had been challenged. Leo Mendés, Jewish peddler turned shopowner, is shown experiencing the inner workings of this Southwestern aristocracy as he gradually gains social acceptance among its leading families. He becomes familiar with the round of social events that takes place in the big houses in the region of the Texas-New Mexico border.

> There were square dances of the utmost complication, led and called by a young man from El Paso who had an astonishing repertoire and generalship, handling his dancers like a well-trained army, throwing them into spasms of laughter by his sudden changes of pace and movement, then deploying them into a whirl of waltzing couples. Later, a gifted young woman mounted the platform and made impromptu verses about each couple as they danced past her. It was easy to make verse in Spanish, but her wit and resource were astonishing and she repeatedly broke up the dancing in a burst of applause. Everyone laughed and clapped more and more as the evening lengthened and the crowd madness of music and rhythm seized them all. Leo was again impressed by the great capacity these people had to enjoy themselves, to seize and devour the moment....[42]

While Fergusson saw the destruction of the old Mexican order in the Southwest in terms of social, economic and political pressures, the early American writers of the Southwest were inclined to moralize and to see the downfall of Mexico in this area as the inevitable price to be paid for degeneracy, especially for sexual immorality. In the Texas romance, *Mexico Versus Texas,* Anthony Ganilh presents one of his Texans explaining to a Captain of the Mexican army why it has become the special mission of the United States to regenerate Mexico by means of military conquest.

> In point of chastity, also, the most important and influential qualification of Northern nations, we are infinitely superior to you — Lust is, with us, hateful and shameful; with you, it is a matter of indifference. *This* is the chief curse of the South: the leprosy which unnerves both body and mind. It is what caused the Roman empire to sink under the assaults of the Northern barbarians. Notwithstanding all the science, policy, and refinement of the *Queen of the Earth,* she was struck, as with a moral consumption, by this vice; and all her strength was swept away by a deluge from the North. A mighty wave is again starting from the same point, and it will sweep even to the Equator. The Southern races must be renewed,

and the United States are the *officina gentium* for the new Continent.[43]

Bernard Lile, hero of another of the Texas romances, clearly fitted the role of agent for this regeneration of the southern race. Lile was a stern Texas warrior, totally dedicated to the killing of Mexicans. Not for him were the occasions of dalliance with Mexican women which some of his less consecrated compatriots indulged in between battles. "In these light scenes," wrote Jeremiah Clemens, "it is needless to say that Bernard Lile did not mingle. To him the fountain of pleasure was as bitter as the waters of Marah, and he turned from it in sad and severe reproof. Other employment better suited to his taste was at hand."[44]

Occasionally a more worldly approach to the subject of sexuality was taken by an early American commentator on Mexican life. Lt. Wise, in *Los Gringos,* observed that "the native society of Mazatlán cannot certainly boast of a very elevated tone of morality. Indeed I have good authority for asserting that there were not fifty legitimately married couples in the town — rather a small proportion for ten thousand inhabitants; perhaps the marriage formula is considered a bore . . . Still this system of *relatione* [sic], as so generally practiced in Mazatlán, appeared to work well, and we never heard of lawsuits for children."[45]

Hispanic society has always insisted on clearly differentiated roles for the sexes. Members of such a society in order to be acceptable and successful feel impelled to emphasize the expected attributes of sex. The ideal of *machismo,* a word which signifies masculine aggressiveness and sexual virility, is a compelling one for men in Mexican society. Women must be as emphatically feminine, wise in the ways of sexual allure and submissive to masculine authority. In contrast, the United States in pursuing egalitarian ideals perhaps to a *reductio ad absurdum* has gone a long way toward abolishing social distinctions on the basis of sex, thus producing individuals whose aura is considerably more neutral. The loss to a great extent of assigned roles for man and woman in domestic life has resulted in the rather unique character of the American marriage, often unstable and crisis-ridden because of blurred lines of authority and yet potentially fruitful in opportunities for individualized expression. In the first account of Mexican life in the Southwest to reach the American public, Major Zebulon Pike in the familiar tones of American puritanism and egalitarianism described the treatment of Mexican women by their men:

> The general subjects of conversation among the men are women, money, and horses, which appear to be the only objects, in their

estimation, worthy of consideration, uniting the female sex with their money and their beasts, and from having treated them too much after the manner of the latter, they have eradicated from their breasts every sentiment of virtue and ambition, either to pursue the acquirements which would make them amiable companions, instructive mothers, or respectable members of society, their whole souls, with a few exceptions, like the Turkish ladies, being taken up in music, dress, and the little blandishments of voluptuous dissipation. Finding that the men only regard them as objects of gratification to the sensual passions, they have lost every idea of the feast of reason and flow of soul, which arise from the intercourse of two refined and virtuous minds.[46]

Harvey Fergusson in his novels and in the cultural history *Rio Grande* has devoted a good deal of space to examining patterns of sexuality among the Mexican aristocrats of the Rio Grande valley during the period of the dominion of the big house. The novel *Wolf Song* deals with an epoch which began shortly after Zebulon Pike's visit to Santa Fe and Taos in 1807. One of the characters of the novel, Lola, daughter of a wealthy Mexican landowner, is described as becoming restive under the almost Arabic cloistering enforced by ancient custom. "Lola was guarded," writes Fergusson, "from men and from the world by a tradition centuries old that had come unchanged across the ocean. She was part of an ancient stream of woman-feeling that sensuous men had long guarded behind thick walls and barred windows, keeping it pure and dangerous for their delight."[47] Lola's fiance was Ambrosio Guitiérrez, a young man also of good family. Ambrosio was in no hurry for the wedding; no date had been set, and the engagement had dragged on for some time. The reason that Ambrosio was in no haste for marriage was that he was enjoying himself thoroughly leading the life of freedom and pleasure available to a young *rico* of one of the privileged families of New Mexico in that period.

> Gayety his spirit craved and he knew it in *bailes* and fandangos. Dressed in purple velvet trimmed with silver braid, his flaring trousers slit to show his white linen drawers, he waltzed nimbly half the night. Full of music wine and desire, he wandered about the town with his fellows, twanging under windows until he found a pillow to share ... For he craved love and it was never denied him. The bodies of slave women were his for the taking and among the bored wives of his friends he carried on complicated and dangerous intrigues with a knife in his belt, always ready to fight and to die if need be. He sinned much and for the most part pleasantly and every week he muttered in confessional the words that brought him absolution and smoothed his path to paradise.[48]

By established custom among the *ricos* of New Mexico at this time, a young man engaged to be married was expected to present his fiancée with an Indian slave girl to be her personal servant. This act was not only considered to be a proof of the chivalrous desire to provide service for the beloved; it was also in early times a proof of the young man's courage and skill in combat. These slave girls were originally obtained by raiding the Navajos, Comanches, and Apaches. Since these tribes were the most fierce warrior peoples of the Southwest and since the young man was required to make the capture himself, though of course he would be a member of a raiding party, the gift of an Indian girl was indeed proof of courage and skill at arms. However, as time went on the requirements for the manner of obtaining a servant girl were relaxed, and it became accepted practice for a young man to simply buy an Indian girl to present to his fiancée. Such was the case with Ambrosio, who went to Sonora and bought a girl named Abrana and presented her to Lola. Abrana served Lola hand and foot, but in her secret thoughts the Indian girl had a considerable degree of contempt for her mistress.

> Lola was a magnificent vessel but an empty one in Abrana's eyes. She envied Lola her beauty and despised her for being a virgin at eighteen. Abrana was also eighteen and she had known three men and borne one baby. She despised Lola for being a virgin and hoped that she would long continue to be one, for she was herself one of the *queridas* of Ambrosio Gutiérrez. He had bought her in Sonora for five hundred dollars as a present for Lola and had taken her to his bosom on the way home. Ambrosio made *versos* for Lola and twanged a guitar beneath her window. He sang to Lola of his heart and his soul but he lay with Abrana on warm nights in the orchard and gave her many useful presents.[49]

Lola became increasingly impatient with the situation she found herself in, though it was the usual one for a girl of her class. She was tired of waiting and was becoming bored with seeing Ambrosio "squatting on his purple hams" outside of her window and singing the old *versos* of courtship which had in them an element of taunt:

> Though you see me with other women
> Do not blush as you pass me by.
> Many go to the fair to look
> Who do not stay to buy.

He seemed to her like a "tomcat watching a tabby with the endless subtle patience that tomcats have, uttering now and then a yearning meow, roaming widely between times." She chafed bitterly when she compared his freedom to wander with the perpetual confinement which she must endure, reflecting that "it would be the same when she was married except that she might take lovers after her husband began to be tired of her, provided he was complacent. If he was not he might punish her in many ways. He might even cut off her ears as old Pedro Sánchez had done with his young wife. Sánchez was a brute, to be sure, but he went unpunished. No man ever lost his ears . . . ." In her mother she saw "the image of her destiny." Lola too would "grow fat on idleness, chocolate and wine and sad on neglect." Thinking of these things, she suddenly remembered another old *verso*:

> Your love is like a little dog
> That runs whoever calls.
> My love is like a heavy stone
> That stays just where it falls.⁵⁰

Lola rebelled and went off with an American. But later, at the insistence of her powerful family, the American joined the church and married Lola properly in a church ceremony, thus becoming absorbed into the system of the big house. However, Lola's victory was considerable. She could look forward to more personal freedom than she would have had married to one of her own people, and she would be living with a man less likely to take the polygamous life as a matter of course. Whether or not Fergusson in creating the rebellious Lola was guilty of inserting an American mind into a Mexican woman, he did verify in the contrasting descriptions of the lives of Lola and Ambrosio an ancient social pattern transplanted intact from Europe and rooted in the North American soil centuries before the disrupting arrival of Anglo-Americans into the Southwest.

The women of Mexico, however, were far from being the passive victims of the predatory sexuality of their men. They could always generate a considerable amount of heat themselves, and the glow of their sexual vitality immediately struck the first Anglo-American men to enter the Southwest. Many of them took to living with Mexican girls, and not a few of them married into Mexican families. However, the "immodesty" of Mexican women called forth some dour comments, which remain in the written records of this early period. Louis H. Garrard in *Wah-To-Yah and the Taos Trail* acknowledged that the allure of the women of New Mexico was victimizing many a good American man, a fact which brought forth the following priggish remarks:

> I must say that there is much romance to a superficial observer in having a Mexican wife; but, were we to come down to sober reality, the affair would show forth in a different light. From the depraved moral education of the New Mexicans, there can be no intellectual enjoyment. The only attractions are of the baser sort. From youth accustomed to a life of servitude and vitiated habits, we look in vain for true woman's attraction — modesty — that at-

tribute which encircles as a halo the intelligent, virtuous, and educated woman. Surely 'twas pardonable pride in me to notice, by contrast, the superiority of those of my own country.[51]

George Wilkins Kendall also takes up the question of modesty and the Mexican woman and gives a charming account of his gradual conversion to her greater naturalness of dress.

> On first entering the country, the Anglo-Saxon traveler, who has been used to the gentler sex of his native land in more full, and perhaps I should say more becoming costume, feels not a little astonished at the Eve-like and scanty garments of the females he meets; he thinks that they are but half-dressed, and wonders how they have the indelicacy, or, as he would deem it at home, brazen impudence, to appear before him in deshabille so immodest. But he soon learns that it is the custom and fashion of the country — that, to use a common Yankee expression, the women "don't know any better." He soon looks with an eye of some leniency, at such little deficiencies of dress as the absence of a gown, and is not long in coming to the honest conclusion, as the eye becomes more weaned from the fastidiousness of early habit and association, that a pretty girl is quite as pretty without as with that garment. By-and-by, he is even led to think that the dress of the women, among whom fate, business, or a desire to see the world may have thrown him, is really graceful, easy — ay, becoming: he next wonders how the females of his native land can press and confine, can twist and contort themselves out of all proportion, causing the most gracefully curving lines of beauty to become straight and rigid, the exquisite undulations of the natural form to become flat or angular, or conical or jutting. . . . He looks around him, he compares, he deliberates — the result is altogether in favor of his new-found friends.[52]

Though the lines of the dresses worn by Mexican women of that period were simple when compared to the frills, bustles, and hoops of the women in the United States at the time, they were fashioned with considerable craftsmanship and often made use of bright, rich, or "gaudy," as Kendall put it, colors, and jewelry was much valued. Richard Henry Dana archly observed that the excessive fondness for dress among the women of California was often their "ruin." "A present of a fine mantle, or of a necklace or pair of earrings, gains the favor of the greater part of them."[53] This high coloration in the externals of dress favored by Mexican women was matched by the combustion from within. J. Ross Browne has left the following striking portrait of a Mexican woman he saw at a dance in California.

> The belle of the occasion was a dark-eyed, fierce-looking woman of about six-and-twenty, a half-breed from Santa Barbara. Her features were far from comely, being sharp and uneven; her skin

was scarred with fire or small-pox; and her form, though not destitute of a certain grace of style, was too lithe, wiry, and acrobatic to convey an idea of voluptuous attraction. Every motion, every nerve seemed the incarnation of a suppressed vigor; every glance of her fierce, flashing eyes was instinct with untamable passion. She was a mustang in human shape — one that I thought would kick or bite upon very slight provocation. In the matter of dress she was almost oriental. The richest and most striking colors decorated her, and made a rare accord with her wild and singular physique; a gorgeous silk dress of bright orange, flounced up to the waist; a white bodice, with blood-red ribbons upon each shoulder; a green sash around the waist; an immense gold-cased breast-pin, with diamonds glittering in the centre, the greatest profusion of rings on her fingers, and her ears loaded down with sparkling earrings; while her heavy black hair was gathered up in a knot behind, and pinned with a gold dagger — all being in strict keeping with her wild, dashing character, and bearing some remote affinity to a dangerous but royal game-bird.[54]

When, during the Mexican War, American men in large numbers, many of them from puritanical rural areas, first encountered the women of Mexico, they were both fascinated and much taken aback. "The Missourians," wrote Bernard De Voto, "were shocked by the paint on their faces, their familiarity and easy laughter, and, the truth is, by the charm they gave to what had to be considered vice. They showed their breasts and, it was believed, in fact it was soon proved, they could be easily possessed — for pay, for kindness, or for mere amenity. An instructed prudery showed itself: sex ought not be decorative."[55]

Yet the situation described by De Voto was the irregular one of war time. For all her intensity, the Mexican woman who is not a professional prostitute does not usually give herself casually. There is the combination of passion and formalism, the marked respect for convention, the sense of propriety, and yet the interest in intrigue. Sex manners vary in Mexico, as elsewhere, according to class and are most complex among the most cultivated people. Fergusson's novel *The Conquest of Don Pedro,* one of his most recent and best works, contains a study of several Mexican women of the Rio Grande area in the 1870's and 80's. The reader becomes acquainted with these women as their lives touch upon the career of the central figure of the book, Leo Mendes, a remarkably conceived character who represents an interesting and significant type in the history of the Southwest, the Jewish peddler and trader of frontier days. As a type he was as persistent and intrepid as any of the figures associated with the westward expansion of America, and his descendants today form the merchant prince families of many

Southwestern cities. But the figure of Leo Mendes is more than a projection of a frontier type. He appears in the novel as a highly individualized personality while remaining always a representative of the Jew in a Christian society. In his detachment and intelligence, he is a fit commentator upon the scene around him and provides the consciousness through which the reader is made to appraise the Mexican culture of the Southwest as it was in that period. Fergusson introduces his protagonist briskly and in a way calculated to arouse the immediate interest of the reader.

> Leo Mendes was a strong, stocky man of medium height with handsome heavy features, thick black eyebrows and thick curly hair. His complexion was naturally swarthy and darkened by long exposure to the sun. His blue cotton shirt and denim trousers and his wide black hat did not distinguish him from most of the natives and neither did the Apache boot-moccasins with hard cowhide soles and turned-up toes which he found the most comfortable of walking shoes. He might easily have passed for a Mexican and often did so, for he spoke Spanish not only fluently but with an instinctive mastery of native idiom, gesture and inflection. He had a gift for taking on the color of his environment without effort and without conscious intention. So he was often taken for a native, but he never pretended to be one if he was asked. By remote origin he was a Portuguese Jew and by birth a New Yorker. He looked like a Mexican and sounded like a Mexican, and sometimes briefly he even felt like a Mexican — but only briefly. At heart he was always and everywhere a stranger, with the reticence, the detachment and skepticism of the man who can mingle in any society but feels he belongs to none.[56]

Leo came to understand early in his career in New Mexico that there existed here a psychological adaptation, difficult for northerners to comprehend, by which the Mexican gave full rein to the body without abandonment of the religious sense. Leo had adopted the Mexican custom of coming to the plaza in Santa Fe on summer evenings. Saturday night was an especially colorful time at the plaza. A Negro band belonging to the American army gave a concert, and "this event was perhaps more appreciated by the populace than anything else the conquerors had done." The whole city turned out. Groups of young men circled the plaza in one direction and young women the other. If a man broke away from his group and began walking beside a young woman and she permitted him to, the couple from that moment would be considered affianced. "But challenging glances and even quick words could be exchanged without hazard of matrimony. Saturday night in the plaza was a mass flirtation. All the town's most gorgeous prostitutes were there, as well as all its finest ladies. The air was filled with the squeal and giggle of feminine excitement, with the perfume of feminine presence." Leo never joined the parade but always sat quietly on a bench enjoying the sight. One day he noticed a solitary woman walking around the plaza. "She was a large handsome woman of indeterminate age, with a fine brown skin, heavy black hair and a deep bosom. She had the gliding walk of an Indian and also the perfect bearing. She might have carried a cup of water on her head without spilling a drop." Having once noticed her, Leo saw her quite regularly at the plaza, always walking by herself, looking straight ahead, never exchanging glances with anyone. His curiosity was aroused, and he made inquiries. The woman was Dolores Pino, famed and feared as a witch. She was the daughter of a Navajo slave girl captured by one of the aristocratic Pino family. "This girl fought her captor like a wildcat, and he had great sport subduing her to his desire. So the girl Dolores was born of rape and nursed on hate. That was her legend." She eventually left the Pino household and set herself up as a witch, telling fortunes, giving advice and charms, embarrassing her father's family by maintaining the name of Pino, and making a good living in her profession. There were many tales circulated in Santa Fe about the occult powers possessed by Dolores Pino. Many people came to her secretly. Publically she was shunned. It was said that once she looked a man in the eyes he would involuntarily follow her and would never be heard from again. One evening when Leo was sitting on a bench in the plaza, Dolores Pino turned her head as she walked by and looking at him directly in the eyes gave him a long and steady look. Leo returned the look without flinching, and Dolores Pino passed on, but Leo knew that some form of communication had been established. On another evening in the plaza shortly after this occasion, Dolores Pino again turned to look at Leo. As she turned away, there was a faint smile on her lips. Leo got up from his bench and followed. She led him to a small house concealed in the apple trees. He knocked on the door and was invited into a neat room with good Navajo blankets covering the bed and the floor and a large, wooden image of the Virgin of Guadalupe standing in a niche in the wall. She greeted him cheerfully and announced that she was in the process of making hot chocolate for him. They talked at length. She told Leo that in spite of rumors about her evil powers she was a good and pious woman who went to church and confessed her sins, who paid her tithes and gave to the poor, and who never harmed anyone. She told him much about his past and his destiny, ending by saying that it was part of his destiny to come again the following evening. Leo accepted this announcement of an assignation without comment. The next evening he approached the house.

There was no light! He stopped, feeling at first as simply disappointed as a child denied his candy, and then a righteous anger against this woman who had fooled him. Obviously, she was not even there. He was about to turn away, but on second thought he decided to go and knock on her door, just to make sure. The door, to his surprise, stood slightly ajar. He knocked on it and stood listening, but heard no sound except a faint breeze in the apple trees. Something strongly impelled him to push the door open and enter. He stepped into solid darkness and a silence in which he could hear his own quick breathing. Then, after she had enjoyed his suspense for a full minute, he heard her laugh softly. He did not say anything but went groping toward the sound with slightly tremulous hands. She had made down her pallet and lay there naked, and when he put his hands upon her she did not laugh any more or say a word, but when he had stripped and mounted her she made a continuous guttural sound deep in her throat. It seemed to have in it nothing of her usual voice or of any human voice but to be a subhuman music of desire, of the pure and innocent lust that is common to man and beast. Between their embraces she lay silent, and when finally she spoke it was in her usual crisp and positive way, as though she had come out of a trance or up from some abysmal depth of abandon to resume her personality.

"Put on your clothes," she told him firmly. "I may commit carnal sin, for the flesh is weak and God will forgive me, but no man has ever seen me naked and none ever will."[57]

"I admire your principles," Leo said.

In this way began an affair between two people who had in common an intrinsic solitude.

Leo at this stage of his career went on long trips throughout the New Mexican countryside, eking out a living by peddling and trading, exposing himself to the dangers of Indians and bandits while traveling through isolated wastes. He came to understand the people with whom he was dealing. His survival depended upon a comprehension of their ways, and among other things he grew to recognize the ambiguity of their sexual code.

> Leo saw women every day, yet knew they were not for him. The better he came to understand these people the more clearly he saw that he must address himself to the men and leave the women alone. For these were a highly erotic people with a strict morality, which was always violated, a pious people who sinned with passion and confessed and repented with passionate sincerity. Unmarried girls were guarded with firearms and sometimes locked up for safe keeping with ferocious dogs, but the boys and girls of a village nevertheless contrived to explore the wonders of love at an early age, as Leo had opportunity to observe. Men were always ready

to fight for the purity and fidelity of their wives, yet adultery had almost the status of an institution. Husbands had to be much away from home and wives were sly and cunning.

Desire was not to be denied, and without sin how could there be repentance and divine forgiveness? To these people sin and repentance were the drama that kept faith alive and life exciting.[58]

Leo ceased being an itinerant peddler when he established a small store in the New Mexican village of Don Pedro. Until his arrival, Don Pedro and the area surrounding it had been completely dependent upon the hacienda owned by the Vierra family which gave employment and supplied provisions. In order to remain in Don Pedro, Leo had to stand his ground against Don Augustin Vierra, the *patrón,* who, striding haughtily into the store, had given Leo a time limit to get out. Leo faced Don Augustin coolly on this occasion. Refusing to be terrorized, he judged that the *patrón* was not as formidable as he tried to make himself out to be. As often before, Leo had accurately appraised the character of the person with whom he was dealing. He remained and flourished. His expanded store became indispensable to the economy of the region. Don Augustin's own account at the store became so large that Leo had to take over to a considerable degree the managing of the *patrón's* financial affairs, becoming something of a personal banker and loan agent to the Vierra family. His conquest of Don Pedro was complete when Doña Lupe, wife of the proud Don Augustin, chose to begin a sexual intrigue with him. Through Lupe, Leo came to understand another type of Mexican woman.

> Lupe came of a class and race of women for whom sex had been their whole profession and relation to life for centuries, and they had made an art of it and of every phase of it, from the first faint smile of flirtation to the final spasm. She was the heir of a great and ancient erotic tradition but her silky skin and her gift of touch were her own. She was truly an artist of love. It seemed to him that along with her clothes she had shed her whole social personality, with its prides and poses, had become another creature, all desire, pure and shameless, and one that captivated him completely . . . . She was supremely discreet, cunning as a coyote and happily free of guilt. Sin she accepted as a necessary part of human life on earth. For her, every act of passion was both a fall and a redemption, leaving her pure and pacified.[59]

Leo Mendes met the next woman who was to be important in his life when she was still a child of ten. She was Magdalena Vierra, niece of Doña Lupe, who took to spending hours in Leo's store watching him deal with his many customers of such diverse origins. These included not only Mexican people of different classes but cowboys, foremen, and owners of large Anglo-American cattle spreads, and enlisted men and officers of the American army. Leo's store provided Magdalena with a view of another world quite different from that of the big house with its ancient and prescribed ways, and a latent capacity for rebellion in her nature was stirred by the spectacle. Being generally perceptive as well as proudly conscious of her status in local society, she dominated a group of girls of her age. She and her friends loitered around the store to such an extent that Leo finally cleared away a corner for their use. They brought in specimens of desert reptiles and young birds, and Leo would allow them to keep the animals in the store for a while before he would insist that they be let loose again. Feeling an old interest in natural history awakened, he would explain the nature and habits of these animals to the girls, even bringing down a book on natural history from Santa Fe to show to them. Magdalena was by far the most apt of his pupils, and she, knowing her prerogatives as a Vierra, would refuse to allow herself to be shooed out of the store with bribes of candy as did the other girls when Leo felt they had gotten too much under foot. Since she insisted upon staying behind, Leo felt impelled to continue the lessons for her benefit alone.

> Leo knew that he was abetting Magdalena in a variety of adventures that neither the Vierras nor the Padre would have approved. He felt some faint twinges of conscience about this, but was sustained by a strong sympathy for her freedom and her delight in it. He knew that if her destiny was typical this was the only freedom she would ever have, except such as she might achieve by stealth and cunning. A Mexican girl was often allowed to run at large as a child, but the stroke of puberty suddenly and permanently transformed her life. She then became a lady, and a Mexican lady was more an institution than a person. She first took communion and then made a social debut, more or less formal according to the wealth and social importance of her family. After that she was forbidden to see any male person alone, except members of her family, or to go abroad unaccompanied or to engage in any physical activity except dancing. By the time she was sixteen, if lucky, she might be married, often to a husband chosen by her parents and always to one approved by them. Mexican women in general accepted this destiny with grace and resignation, as the will of God, but Leo felt that it was probably going to be difficult for Magdalena, with her rebellious temper, her love of action and her versatile curiosity. For curiosity in particular there seemed to be no place in a life of faith and status. It was essentially an unquestioning life.[60]

Leo realized that with the rapidly changing character of New Mexico, a knowledge of English would be of great value to Magdalena and would aid her in the process of self-liberation.

> On his trips to Santa Fe and Albuquerque he hunted for books that might catch her interest. This proved difficult. Magdalena was a gifted talker but no student. She was bored with Mother Goose rhymes and also by the classical fairy tales. The few juvenile stories he found were all designed to elevate the character and morals of the young, and these she repudiated decisively. She had no taste for self-improvement. Leo at last offered her some of the dime novels of Ned Buntline which were then just beginning to flood the market, most of them based on the exploits of Kit Carson, who was still living in Taos as an old man and read the Buntline version of his own exploits with amused astonishment. These epics of slaughter and gallantry delighted Magdalena. She had been raised on tales of Indian battles, had always known the Apaches and Comanches were the natural enemies of her people.[61]

On such literary fare her English vocabulary increased rapidly and she was soon able to converse with Leo completely in English. However, in due time Magdalena was sent to convent school in Santa Fe, partly to get her away from Leo and his influence. It was expected that when she returned some three years later she would be the finished product of a Mexican lady. Leo felt desolate at her departure and thought that she had gone out of his life completely. When finally she came back to Don Pedro at the age of sixteen, a grand ball was arranged for her by the Vierras. She was to be formally introduced to local Mexican society, and the big house was never more splendid than on that occasion. Leo was the only non-Mexican invited. Local society, almost all of whose members were on his books, could not afford to snub him. Astounded and suddenly made timid by the transformed and now beautiful Magdalena, Leo remained on the outskirts of the party while the young men crowded around her. When she saw him, she came over to him, greeted him warmly and with the old habit of command informed him that she would be at the store on the following day and wanted to see him alone. When she arrived at Leo's office, she poured out to him her discontent with convent life and her boredom with Mexican society. She was far from being the resigned Mexican lady, and Leo was captivated. Before he knew it, he had been maneuvered into proposing marriage. She had hardly left the room, however, when he was seized with a sense of the impossibility of such a union. Family and church would withhold their sanction. Leo, as his friend Padre Orlando had put it, did not have the believing mind. A church wedding was out of the question. Yet Magdalena was not one to let institutions stand between her and what she desired. She took to going to Padre Orlando's at night on the pretext that she wanted more religious instruction. Church was the one place to which a Mexican woman could go alone. One day she informed Leo that on her way back from church she would drop in at the store to say hello. Leo understood immediately that the seemingly casual remark was in fact an assignation. Magdalena, however she might have been influenced by American ways, had not lost the Mexican talent for sexual intrigue. That night it seemed to Leo "that both of them were free of the past and of the world and that this was their wedding."

Later they were married in a civil ceremony. Their menage, a large household, took on many of the external trappings and a considerable amount of the ceremony and routine of the Mexican big house. Leo himself felt that in many ways he had become a Mexican gentleman. Yet Magdalena had her way in most things and was completely free in a manner that would have been inconceivable had she married a Mexican. Though Mexican families at first shunned her because she had not been married in the Church, they in time forgave her and began flocking to her house. Local Americans — army officers, cattlemen, and government agents — also came to the parties at the house of Leo Mendes, which was becoming famous for the splendour of its entertainments. Magdalena dazzled the Americans with her beauty and made them feel at home with her perfect command of American idiom. This house was the one place in the region where Mexican and Anglo-American society mingled.

Yet in a matter of a few years Magdalena became totally absorbed in a young and impressive looking Texan named Robert Coppinger. He was from people who were, as Padre Orlando put it, "much like her own in everything but race — cattle people who own the earth and have the habit of command." She carried on a secretive affair but not without qualms, as her affection for Leo was very real. In this situation Magdalena was again following her strong urge toward self-fulfillment. As Padre Orlando observed in summing up the affair, Magdalena had always remained a child in her relation to Leo, and Leo himself, maintaining his capacity for detachment even in this crisis, recognized the justice of the observation. He surrendered her to Coppinger, who became a Catholic in order to marry her with the full approval of her people. Before this church wedding took place, Leo sold his store in Don Pedro. The region had lost its savor for him. Farther north, in the cities of Santa Fe, Albuquerque, and Las Vegas things were changing rapidly with the arrival of the railroad, and there would be much opportunity for a man of Leo's resourcefulness. Furthermore, as Leo put it in his final visit to Padre Orlando, he had always remained a peddler at heart, and he now felt as though Don Pedro had been only a longer stop in his travels. Riding northward, he had to cross again the vast wasteland known as the Jornada de Muerte, the journey of death. It had formerly terrified him when he had first crossed it going south, appalled by the dreadful isolation, conscious of the money belt strapped around his waist, and aware of the possibility of attack by bandits or Indians. "Now as then he felt cut off from everything, suspended between a life he had left and one unkown. But otherwise he was not the same man at all. He was one who had outlived his fears, and for the first time in his life he was glad of wilderness, of space and solitude."

In *The Conquest of Don Pedro,* Harvey Fergusson has used the figure of Leo Mendes to make his most thorough analysis of Mexico's erotic tradition, one which in its combination of passion and stylization is so different from the rather amorphous situation of sexual mores in American culture. Even Dolores Pino, the outcast, had her strong sense of the proprieties while at the same time recognizing that conventions, however appropriate, express only the surface of human life. In Doña Lupe, Fergusson gives his portrait of the Mexican woman of the big house par excellence, completely attuned to the nuances of the manners of her society and conventional even in her subterfuges. Magdalena represents the result of the impact of two cultures. Leo Mendes, the wandering Jew, was for her a kind of catalytic agent between these two societies. Without consciously meaning to exploit him, she sought him instinctively as the way to freedom, and under his guidance she achieved in her personality a synthesis which might well represent the author's vision of an eventual cultural fusion in the American Southwest.

Along with the complex erotic tradition that Mexico has maintained there has been a corresponding preoccupation with the concept of death. With the counterpull of love and death as a central theme, Mexican culture has exerted a powerful fascination upon the modern mind. Contemporary American writers have proclaimed a cult of death in Mexico and have seized upon it to fling at their countrymen in order to shame them for their euphemistic evasions of the fact of death. This expression of polarity in Mexican culture has inevitably been associated with Freudian theory. Also, the apparent obsession with death in Mexico has been ascribed to the heavy sense of fate attributed to Indian cultures, and indeed Mexican fatalism has come into a good deal of attention from American writers as a fit antidote to the American "optative" mood. With amazement and intense interest American writers have watched the festive and often burlesquing treatment of the theme of death common to Mexican folkways and have accounted for it variously as the triumphant and mocking assertion of the life force in the face of and in the full acknowledgment of death or, in terms of Christian other-worldliness, as a dramatization of the faith in a possible triumph of the human spirit over evil and damnation.

As might have been expected, early American writers have paid much less attention to the death infatuation of Mexico than have modern writers. The tendency among early American observers of Mexico has been to treat as isolated phenomena aspects of Mexican culture which modern writers have seen as parts of a constellation of attitudes formed around the central themes of death and fate. Thus the festive air of Mexican funerals has been seen by some early American writers as just another example of Mexican morbidity and brutal insensibility. Others have taken it as a further indication of the general and giddy fondness among Mexicans for the gaudy trappings of religious ceremonial unaccompanied by any proper sense of the reverence due on the occasion of a Christian burial. The Mexican passion for gambling was noted at length by these writers and always with marked disapproval, but the implication in terms of ideas of fate or destiny inherent in the great attraction of gambling for the Mexican was never pursued nor probably even thought of. Modern American writers treating of this early period of Mexican-American relations have tended to feature scenes dealing with death which were lightly passed over by the first American recorders.

Several modern American writers in their attempts to interpret Mexican attitudes toward death have traced them back to elements in the psychology of the Aztecs as revealed in religious rite and symbol, subjecting these cultural manifestations to careful and respectful analysis. But William H. Prescott as a man of his times, for all his thoroughness in marshalling known facts about the Aztecs, simply deplored without further exploration the death obsession of these people and the influence it had retained upon the later culture of Mexico. "Familiarity with the bloody rites of sacrifice steeled the heart against human sympathy, and begat a thirst for carnage, like that excited in the Romans by the exhibitions of the circus. The perpetual recurrence of ceremonies, in which the people took part, associated religions with their most intimate concerns, and spread the gloom of superstition over the domestic hearth, until the character of the nation wore a grave and even melancholy aspect, which belongs to their descendants at the present day."[62]

And yet the celebration of death in Mexico is often anything but melancholy. Dana in *Two Years Before the Mast* expressed his amazement at the gayety displayed at the funeral of a young Mexican girl in

California. The father had given a wake the night before in which guests had had a gala time eating and drinking great quantities. All during the festivities the body of the child, increasingly ignored, had been on display. The pall bearers at the funeral were a group of young girls dressed in white who made no effort to restrain their giggles. To the young observer from Boston, the whole thing was in deplorable taste.

George Wilkins Kendall, who for all his Yankee cockiness had a considerable degree of sensitivity, watched with astonishment and a measure of awe as the lepers at the hospital of San Lázaro in Mexico City cavorted during a festival given in their quarters. Most of these men, as Kendall described them in the *Narrative of the Texan Santa Fe Expedition,* were in the advanced stages of leprosy and at the very threshold of death, a fact of which they were quite aware. And yet during this fiesta a number of them were gaily playing cards, showing incredible dexterity as they shuffled them with defingered hands. Others were nimbly dancing with crutches, some of them singing lustily at the same time, though their voices were horribly distorted.

But the rituals celebrating death in Mexico could be grim as well. Most of the early American chroniclers of the Southwest who reported on the Santa-Fe and Taos areas had something to say about the Penitentes, members of a religious sect famed for its observance of the passion of Christ by actually crucifying one of its own. Usually the surrogate Christ survived the ordeal but sometimes not. Suspension from the cross was managed by tying the arms of the sacrificial victim to the crosspiece, though it has been reported that on occasion nails have been used. Before the crucifixion, the member of the sect impersonating Christ was fiercely whipped during long processions so that by the time he reached his calvary he was a mass of blood. As would be expected, the reaction of early American chroniclers to this spectacle was uniformly one of horror and disgust. The Penitentes still function clandestinely in remote areas of New Mexico, and their rituals have been the subject of a considerable amount of analysis by modern American writers. At one time the *hermanos penitentes* constituted a powerful force in the New Mexico area and practiced their rites openly in spite of the disapproval of the Church. The membership of the sect consisted of the primitive and independent small farmers of the mountain area. These impoverished but hardy people resisted the encroachments and attempts to dominate on the part of the *rico* landowners of the Rio Grande valley. The Penitentes continued as a political power even after the American occupation was established, and as late as the first decade of the twentieth century ambitious politicians would subject themselves to the whip lashings which are part of the initiation ceremonies of the Penitentes in order to be able to say to the mountain people that they too were *hermanos*. In *Rio Grande,* Harvey Fergusson writes of the order of Penitentes that "as a religion, although its rules and its songs came straight from the mediaeval church and were never changed, it became more and more a primitive penance and a primitive worship of death. The church formally pronounced against it in the eighties and it must have suffered the opposition of many of the padres long before that for its tendency was to free the common man from their exactions. It was the flower of a spiritual integrity which had its roots, lower and deeper than those of any church, in an ancient sacrifice of blood, in the ecstatic acceptance of pain and death." [63]

It has seemed to some American observers that there is an element almost of voluptuousness in the manner in which the Mexican beholds the spectacle of death. This essentially modern notion has been injected as it were retroactively into reenactments by contemporary American authors of early scenes of contact between Mexicans and Americans. Paul Horgan in his fine, panoramic and yet subtle interpretation of the history and culture of the Southwest, *Great River,* presents a scene in which he conveys this sense of the almost libidinal search on the part of Mexicans for the opportunity to witness death. During the period in which the memories of the Texas revolt and the Mexican war were still fresh, there continued to be a considerable amount of unofficial warfare throughout the border region. The contestants were often Texans and Mexicans, and occasionally armed Texas units would unite with one Mexican faction against another, the aim being, aside from the pure love of battle, to weaken the central government of Mexico which had not totally abandoned hope of regaining some of the territory lost to the United States. Horgan writes of a battle which took place on the plains before the city of Saltillo, capital of the state of Coahuila and a city not far from the Texas border, in which Texans under Colonel Jordan had joined forces with the troops fighting for the cause of a Mexican separatist movement of the north under Colonels Lopez and Molano. The inhabitants of Saltillo knew that a battle was to take place between the Centralists and the forces of the proclaimed Rio Grande Republic on the plains before their city where it could be easily viewed. The city, as Horgan described it, busily prepared itself for the spectacle in "the golden October weather." "Its flat roofs were prepared for the spectators of the coming battle, and hillsides too were occupied by civilians. Everyone was an amateur of the arts of battle. Opposing forces moving in tight formations made grand patterns that were easy to follow. The spectacle would have amplitude, with land for a theater, bullets for dialogue, and death for many climaxes, much to the Mexican taste."[64]

In the historical novel *The Time of the Gringo*, Elliott Arnold described an Indian insurrection which took place in the early nineteenth century. The Taos Indians had revolted from Mexican rule and for a while took over the government in Santa Fe. Mexican officials were hunted down and tortured to death. Arnold presented a scene which fitted the historical fact, the death by torture of two New Mexican officials in the plaza in Santa Fe. However, somewhat extravagant in his version of the reaction of New Mexican bystanders to the spectacle, he gave an example of the tendency of modern American writers to overplay the theme of Mexico's love of death: "Soon after the Indians began their torture a small crowd of New Mexicans collected around them, at first in a wide perimeter. After a while the victims ceased to be men of their race. The affinity for death that was contained in every drop of their Spanish blood made the New Mexican spectators part of the ceremony. . . . When the two men were dead and hung limply from their bonds in what in the night seemed to be a weird distortion of the crucifixion, the New Mexicans who had looked on felt hollow and purged as though they had undergone a religious experience."[65] In another part of the book, Arnold dealt with the historical personage, James Magoffin, whose activities in New Mexico have been mentioned before. In one scene Magoffin was witnessing a crude version of the bullfight which was practiced in New Mexico. It was a dangerous game in which the contestant tried to overturn the bull by twisting its tail. As he watched, "Magoffin was aware again of the preoccupation with death which was the birthright of the people. Death was not the inevitable. Death was not something to be awaited, but must be courted during life. . . ." A New Mexican woman named Soledad, noting Magoffin's absorption in the spectacle, said to him, "I know Americans believe it is uncivilized with us — this and the bullfighting. . . . We have no fear of death, Don Santiago. He is an old friend!" Magoffin answered in the tones of American pragmatism that there might be other ways " 'to which an unconcern for death might be more usefully put.' 'But there must be no use to it!' she said stamping her foot. 'That is the whole thing, the uselessness of it.' "[66]

There is a duality, almost a dichotomy of function, in the institutions man makes use of in coping with the biological universals, love and death. In some ways these institutions uphold the attitudes of a culture toward the inescapable: in other ways such institutions may conflict with the expressions people give to biological necessity. The cultural situation becomes more complicated when, as in the American Southwest, sets of institutions expressing quite different attitudes toward human affairs collide. The Anglo-Americans first entered the Hispanic Southwest traveling, as the Mexican General Mier y Teran put it, with their Constitution in their pockets. Though they were interested in and sometimes amazed by the deeply rooted institutions which Mexico had planted in the Southwest, they had little inclination to make any real concessions to a strange way of life. The institutional conflict in the American Southwest, as it was experienced in the early period of Anglo-American penetration into the area, will be dealt with in the following chapter to the extent that this conflict has provided themes for a lasting body of American writing.

CHAPTER FOUR

## A Fragment of the Medieval World

When the first Anglo-Americans, the advance guard of a boisterous frontier democracy, burst into the Hispanic Southwest, they shattered the surface calm of a totally isolated society which was, as Harvey Fergusson has described it, "wholly feudal in form and spirit — in all essentials a fragment of the mediaeval world, surviving long after the rest of that world was dead."[1] The cultural anthropologist Edward H. Spicer has made an important and interesting observation about the nature of the civilization brought by the Spaniards to the New World. In *Cycles of Conquest* he wrote: "The Spanish culture brought by Spaniards to Mexico consisted of a number of elements believed by high state and church officials to be essential for the civilizing process. . . . What had been implanted was not Spanish culture but a European distillation made largely by Spaniards."[2] Colonial Mexico was, therefore, intended to be an idealization of late mediaeval Europe. Spicer however, makes the following qualification: "Besides selected elements regarded by Spaniards as essentials in the Spanish way of life and constituting a sort of 'refined' form of the culture, there were miscellaneous elements that came in through individuals of widely varied backgrounds [different tools, religious festivals, and other objects or customs from the various regions of Spain]. . . . In such ways ranging from handicrafts to religious practices, additional elements of Spanish culture, not in the blueprints, were transferred and combined."[3] Thus what Spain set up in Mexico was not really "New Spain" but an interesting amalgam of the essence of mediaeval Europe with regionalized Spanish flavoring at the folk level.

It was a society based on the old patriarchal analogue. The king of Spain was still emperor of the Americas and the surrogate of God. The light of divine authority shone through the Spanish monarchy to be refracted throughout the fixed descending order of civil rule. In microcosm this same order prevailed in the family, in which the father exercised unquestionable authority by divine right. "This was a lazy and voluptuous people," wrote Fergusson, "but everyone knew whom he

[ 103 ]

had to obey, from the humblest peon up to the Governor and Captain-General who was the representative of the king who derived his power from God. . . . If one obeyed his masters it mattered little what else he did."[4] This outpost of Hispanic civilization in the southwestern part of the North American continent was "the last expansive thrust of religious empire in America. Faith in God and King had been its spiritual nourishment and both were on the wane."[5] Zebulon Pike, whose report was to result in the opening of the Santa Fe trail, was conducted into Santa Fe by Spanish troops on the very eve of Mexico's revolt against Spain. Yet the Spanish system established in this area survived the formal break with Spain and was unaffected for a while by the nominal republicanism of the Mexican government. But even before the deluge of North Americans brought about radical changes in the area, the feudalistic caste system of the Hispanic Southwest had entered a stage of crisis from within. The first American chroniclers and novelists to report on the Hispanic Southwest were hardly aware of the crisis, so impressed were they by the unaccustomed sight of an aristocratic society. Yet one does discover in some of the dime novels scenes in which lower-class Mexicans take action against their Mexican overlords. The producers of this popular fiction, for all their inadequacy as writers, frequently did have a thorough familiarity with the area about which they were writing. Modern American writers with the record before them and with the typically modern sensitivity to social change have paid a good deal of attention to the internal crisis within the Mexican society of the borderlands in that period. After the American annexation of the Southwest, the formal structure of the old order, pressed from within and from without, crumbled rapidly; but some of the cultural attitudes it fostered survive among the descendants of these early Mexican settlers as well as among later arrivals to the area from Mexico. Many of these people experience within themselves a conflict which is the result of the overlaying of the culture of the United States upon the earlier Hispanic foundation. Among these people there is a groping for a cultural synthesis, and this conflict and the attempts at resolving it have produced an important theme in the literature of the American Southwest.

The conflict finds its most immediate and severe expression in relationships between members of the family, with the father frequently attempting to assert the patriarchal claim against children in revolt. The times are certainly against the old-style Mexican father in the American Southwest, and, especially in urban areas, his equivocal position in the household presents a strong contrast to the role of the earlier family head, who took his position of absolute authority for granted and invested it with a regal grandeur which could be alternately casual and fierce. As Fergusson describes this early patriarch in the province of New Mexico, he was a man whose children, no matter what their age, "uncovered when he approached and they dared not smoke in his presence. He could chastise a grown son or give his daughter in marriage as easily as he could sell a horse or kill a slave. His power sprang from his loins and multiplied with his family. One man had thirty-six legitimate children by three wives and almost all had large families of a darker shade by Indian concubines."[6] Life was arranged for the pleasure of these men, and commerce, "except in slaves, horses and the products of their own lands, was beneath them, as were the professions. In 1831 the province contained only one doctor and no lawyers. There were almost no books except bibles."[7]

For all its rigidity of form, this society was not lacking in grace. The poor were as perfect in their manners as were the rich, and no one was so poor as to be unable to find joy in taking part in the richly ceremonial life around him. In commenting on the love of ritual among these people, Fergusson observes that in this they were typical of Latin-Americans at any time among whom "the established forms of human conduct seem never to go dead as they do among us where formality is almost a synonym for dullness."[8] Manners were not only elaborate and invested with a genuine charm, they were expansive and gave room for some originality of expression. Salutation had become an art. " 'May you live to be a thousand sir! ' 'And may you, sir, live to see the last of my years!' " "Where men go armed," comments Fergusson wryly, "they speak with exaggerated deference."[9] These people "were not afraid to touch each other. When old friends and relatives met, all embraced and kissed. . . . Girls publicly embraced and kissed male friends whom they would never see alone unless in marriage or by stealth. Men embraced each other, kissed on the cheek, and expressed the degree of their affection by the heartiness with which they hammered each other on the back."[10]

Among the *ricos* of the Rio Grande valley in this early period, the family, for all its warmth and spontaneity, was very much of an institution, as the occasional American who tried to breach its wall of ceremony and etiquette soon found out. In the novel *Grant of Kingdom,* Harvey Fergusson presents the situation of Jean Ballard, an American mountain man of the eighteen thirties, who was attempting to initiate a courtship with Consuelo, the daughter of the wealthy and established Coronels.

> For the first time in his life he felt the massive, inert resistance of old established things, of a people fortified by wealth and custom and tradition, by a way of life stronger than they were, a social pattern which was a power in itself. They did not hate him as a person but they hated anything alien. Family was everything to them. Their whole society was a great family and it was organized to repel intrusion. They did not have to insult him or reject him or even close a door to him. They could freeze him out and wait him out. He might come and sip chocolate for months and even for years and never pass any of the barriers of custom and manner that were set up against him.[11]

In *The Conquest of Don Pedro,* Fergusson examines the families of the *ricos* of New Mexico as they were in a later period, in the seventies and eighties. Leo Mendes, the merchant from New York, was able to achieve a degree of acceptance from the established Mexican families of the Rio Grande valley. He accomplished this, however, by first holding his ground against the *patrón,* Don Augustin Vierra, who would have liked to have driven him from the area, and secondly by eventually having most of the leading families of the area in his debt, a situation which augured the fate of the Mexican aristocracy of the Southwest. When Mendes married Magdalena Vierra and established an estate of his own in Don Pedro, he assumed many of the outer trappings of a *rico* of the Rio Grande valley, but no one knew better than Leo Mendes himself that he had not been made over into a Mexican *patrón,* nor did he wish to be. He knew that he

> lacked the gift of autocratic authority which is the first essential of a patriarchal lord. . . . He had acquired power in spite of himself — the power of money and debt, and the power of an employer over his underlings — but he had never learned to like it. His orders always had the accent of request and his instinct was rather for compromise than ultimatum . . . . Worst of all he lacked the air of command — the peremptory voice, the menacing brow and flashing eye, the sweeping gesture. With admiration and awe he had watched Don Augustin manage his vaqueros on a roundup. No military commander could have been more absolute . . . . This gift of command was the product of an ancient tradition, rooted in faith, nourished in isolation, handed down from father to son — and it was one custom of the country Leo could neither acquire nor imitate.[12]

However, the ancient tradition was being undermined in the province of New Mexico even before the territory was annexed by the United States. Not only was the rule of the old families being challenged by a vigorous, upstart *mestizo* element, it was facing something of a mutiny from within. Maxwell Anderson's verse play *Night Over Taos* deals with the crisis within an old Mexican family just before the war between Mexico and the United States. The family head, Pablo Montoya, is a traditional Mexican patriarch who is a leader of the forces preparing to resist the United States. He recognizes that his enemies are not only the government and military forces of the republic to the north but also those native New Mexicans influenced by ideas which were entering New Mexico by way of the Santa Fe Trail. Even his nominal ally, the familiar Padre José Martínez of Taos, had done much in his sermons and in his newspaper to propagate ideas hostile to the old order. Martínez, who so oddly combined absolutist and liberal ideas in his thinking, was eventually to secede from Rome and set up his own church. Yet he was the very core of the resistance to the American encroachment. Much of the dialogue in *Night Over Taos* consists of ideological debate between Martínez and Montoya. However, Montoya's concern with upholding Spanish tradition is not only a matter of abstract principle. A widower, he has recently become engaged to a woman much younger than he, in fact approximately the same age as his younger son Felipe. Felipe and his father's fianceé fall in love. Her engagement to Montoya had been arranged by her family without deference to her own feelings. Felipe respectfully but firmly stands up to his father and announces the radical idea that people have a right to choose whom they are to marry and that love takes precedence over parental decree. In his rage, Montoya accuses his son not only of betraying a father but of committing an act of treason to the whole cause of Spanish-Mexican culture and of showing readiness to side with the enemy to the north. Felipe answers:

> How could I be for the north
> When all my people, all my friends, and my life
> Are rooted in Taos? I've fought on your side and mine,
> And I'd do it again . . . but still I'm not so blind
> But what I can see that if the laws of the north
> Were to judge between us, my father would be in the wrong,
> And I'd be in the right! And it would be just! but here
> A girl goes where she's sent by her father, and when
> She's chosen by an old man who can pay for her
> Or who has her at his mercy, she's his, and a slave,
> And all the women are slaves here!
>     (That's why you can't trust them!)
> And the men are slaves! Yes, I am myself no better
> Than a peon . . . [13]

In presenting the case to Padre Martínez, Montoya declares that Felipe's defiance is more than a personal matter, it is a threat to the entire established order:

> The north wins in Felipe
> If he has his way! When sons turn against their fathers

> And get their will by it, all our rule goes down
> And order with it. Our state's built on that ... but no more
> Not if Felipe can defy me, and keep
> What he got by defiance! You fool, the north itself
> Attacks us from within, and if it conquers
> In Taos, what will it matter if Taos is taken
> And conquered from the outside?[14]

Aside from ideological conflicts within the big house itself, the ancient and threatened order of the Southwest had long been weakening because of a corrosion of the sense of responsibility and of the sense of function among the masters of the big houses. In accounting for the state of decay that had come upon the society of the Rio Grande valley in the first half of the nineteenth century, Harvey Fergusson noted that the proud *ricos* "had increasingly neglected their obligations as leaders. They were hated and feared by their retainers whom they left at the mercy of savages."[15] One is reminded here of the distinction that Lionel Trilling has made between pride of function and pride of status. In his discussion of social attitudes, in the essay "Manners, Morals, and the Novel,"[16] he points out that the hauteur of the early feudal lords of Europe, however distasteful it may have been to underlings, was at least grounded in a legitimate pride of function. These lords upheld their end of the unwritten feudal bargain by providing needed protection in return for servitude. In the later ages of Europe when the centralized governments of the national states took over the role of protecting the people, the feudal lords relinquished this function. As they came less and less to have a raison d'être in society, they insisted more and more upon special privileges. A legitimate pride of function had degenerated into a pride based solely upon social status. Such a claim for recognition on the basis of assumed status rather than upon the competent exercise of function, talent, or skill constitutes Trilling's definition of the word "snobbery." Thus in failing to provide for the protection and well being of their social inferiors while maintaining an excessively pretentious way of life, the privileged people of the Rio Grande valley had increasingly become snobs, and the forms of their society had become obsolete. As Fergusson describes the inequities of the system, the "law held the peon but not the patron. It provided that officers in the army and priests of the church could be tried only by their own peers. The army in New Mexico was at best a few hundred ragged peons but it provided berths and immunities for young men of the right people as did also the church, and the powerful landowner was just as immune as these by reason of his property. Always less than a thousand soldiers, priests and gentlemen ruled the country."[17]

Modern writers dealing with the Mexican-American war have pictured the dandified Mexican officer as failing in his duty toward his men. In *The Great River,* Paul Horgan writes: "What a difference, noted the military critics, there was between the Mexican officers and men! The officers were elegant, elaborately uniformed, full of style and address—and almost to a man incompetent. They did not really lead their troops, or see to their welfare, or use their endurance wisely. The common foot soldiers were marched thirty miles a day, sometimes fifty, while the American infantryman averaged perhaps fifteen. The dark little Mexican Indian was courageous, and 'with an able general would make a good fight,' as Lieutenant Grant said."[18] Bernard DeVoto contemptuously describes the panoply of General Arista's officers as they confronted Taylor at Palo Alto. "Throughout the war the Mexicans had difficulty in getting soldiers who could shoot and greater difficulty in supplying them with food and powder, but their armies were always beautifully costumed. These are the shakos, pompons, plumes, buckles, aguillettes, pennons, epaulettes, and saber sashes you saw pictured in your grandfather's books when you were a child. They glittered in the noon sun like a battle piece by Benjamin West and, after tranquilly watering his troops, Taylor formed a line and moved out to attack the haberdashery. He intended to use his favorite weapon, the bayonet."[19]

Thus the society of the *ricos,* epitomized by the showy and irresponsible Santa Anna, failed Mexico in its hour of need. The shock caused by military defeat and loss of great territory convulsed Mexico and began a process of social revolution which culminated in the great upheaval of modern times, the much venerated "Revolución." With Santa Anna fled to exile in Cuba, the new face of Mexico was that of the grave, indigenous Benito Juárez. The whole turn of events had caught the *ricos* very much by surprise. As Ralph Roeder observed in *Juárez and His Mexico,* "foresight was not among the faculties of Santa Anna." Neither the "benemerito de la patria," as Santa Anna had himself called, nor the others of his class could have recognized Juárez as the coming man in Mexico. Santa Anna first encountered the Indian Juárez during the early period of the *criollo* general's rise to power, when the taste of political and military glory was still fresh. In 1829, Santa Anna was feted at a supper given in his honor by a professor of an educational institute for young men in Oaxaca. Students of the institute were waiting on table, one of these being Benito Juárez, an impoverished boy in white smock and bare feet. Lacking the gift of prophecy, Santa Anna had no inkling that in the person of Juárez he had looked upon the face of that redoubtable Mexico which was to reassert itself upon the passing of his own ephemeral and betasseled era. But having the "flair of the expert politician for names and faces," he remembered the meeting. Years later when Scott's army had entered Mexico City, Santa Anna, fleeing southward, sought asylum in the state of Oaxaca. The governor of that state, who had always thought that Santa Anna was bad news for Mexico, closed the state to "that wandering germ of civil war." The governor was Benito Juárez. In assessing the situation later in his Cuban exile, Santa Anna characteristically missed the point. According to Ralph Roeder, he was not only bitter but baffled by the affair. "Years later he recalled that rebuff as the most bitter of all those which he had suffered because he could not explain it. With the taste still bitter on his tongue, he wrote, rinsing his mouth of the name of Juárez: 'He could not forgive me because he had waited on me at table in Oaxaca, in December 1829, with his bare feet on the floor and in his linen smock and trousers. . . . It is amazing,' he added, 'that an Indian of such low degree should have figured in Mexico . . . .' "[20]

Coincident with the passing of the era of Santa Anna was the decline of the big house in what had now become the American Southwest. A society was falling into ruins which for all its inequities had developed a pervasive charm. As Fergusson defines this elusive quality, "charm in human society is a cumulative thing and it does not survive rapid change. It depends upon the faithful observance of customs and traditions, slowly perfected. It requires that men shall live for generations in the same houses, tilling the same lands, having the same relations of class to class and man to man. Perhaps this aristocratic ideal was never more completely realized, on a small scale and in a rude way, than it was along the Rio Grande when the wars with the pueblos were over and the great valley was settled."[21]

The great houses of the *ricos* in New Mexico were situated mainly in the lower valley of the Rio Grande in the southern part of the state, the territory known as the Rio Abajo, the lower river. The domain of these feudal lords extended southward along the fertile Rio Grande valley into Texas. In northern New Mexico, the Rio Grande trickles its way through a mountainous region, known as the Rio Arriba, the upper river, which has historically been the stronghold of the Pueblo Indians and of a hardy, though poor, Mexican yeomanry which stubbornly resisted the encroachments of the *ricos*. The political centers of the small farmers and sheep raisers of the Rio Arriba were the lodges of the Penitent Brothers. Though the Penitentes have received considerable publicity because of their bizarre and savage rites, they have not been generally recognized in terms of their social significance. The members of this dissident religious sect can be compared to the Methodists and Anabaptists of the lower classes of England, who defied the established church that had allied itself to such an extent with the wealthy and the privileged. Though the great houses of the Rio Abajo have disappeared without a trace, "the Penitent Brothers still lash their bare backs every holy week.... The life of the humble still goes on much as it did a hundred years ago.... Here once more the mighty have fallen and if the meek have not inherited the earth they have at least clung to some of it with astonishing tenacity."[22]

Leo Mendés, when he first arrived in Santa Fe as an itinerant peddler, found that he could get along well with the poor of the city because "these people, like his own, had a history of oppression. They had the same quick compassion and feeling of responsibility for each other, the same mordant humor and fatalistic outlook. He was not one of them, but they treated him as though he were, and he could understand and appreciate them."[23]

The mountain people of the Rio Arriba, as they were in the 1830's, have a role in Fergusson's novel *Grant of Kingdom*. A former evangelist named Laird from the mountains of Tennessee, though many years resident in New Mexico, had gotten into trouble for having aided Mexican tenants in a movement against their landlord. He escaped into the mountains of the Rio Arriba confident that he would find asylum among a people whose hostility to the *ricos* was so similar to the bitterness felt by his own mountain people in Tennessee toward the great plantation owners of the lowlands. He did not fear the mountain Mexicans although he knew that many of them were bandits. "They were not criminals in their own eyes. They had lived here for generations partly by preying on the flocks and herds of the *ricos* in the valley. To them the rich were legitimate objects of plunder."[24] As he had expected, Laird was warmly received by the people of the Sangre de Cristo mountains, who were unstinting in their hospitality toward him.

The *ricos* in attempting to maintain their position of dominance not only had to contend with the resistance of the men from the Rio Arriba, they had also to cope with usurping upstarts in their midst. Though the best of the *ricos* still preserved something of Spanish chivalry, a sense of honor and motivations beyond gain, the class as a whole had become by the eighteen thirties effete and irresolute. In their increasing ineffectuality, the *ricos* were less and less able to stave off the encroachments of a vital, coarse, and utterly opportunistic *mestizo* group which was reaching for power. This new group was epitomized by Governor Manuel Armijo and his right hand man, Salazar. In the novel *The Time of the Gringo*, Elliot Arnold treats Armijo somewhat sympathetically as a sort of social protest figure. Certainly he was a prototype of a kind of Latin American tyrant whose era is coming to an end. These *caudillos* have been interim figures filling the vacuum of power left by the weakening aristocracy. Most of them came from obscure origins and gained initial popular support as champions of the people against the privileged. Such mid-century figures as Trujillo, Perón, and Batista were representative of this breed. In *Rio Grande,* Harvey Fergusson gives this description of the man who was governor of New Mexico at the time of the Mexican-American war.

> Governor Manuel Armijo of Albuquerque, who had the honor of presenting New Mexico to the United States, was one of the earliest and one of the most perfect specimens of this Spanish-American demagoguery. His significance is not reduced by the fact that he performed in a small theater and his career had the advantage that it can be examined in detail and in a long retrospect. Although he shed much blood he was essentially and even consciously comic for he was a professing rogue who elevated cowardice to the dignity of a philosophy and practiced treachery as an art. It is almost as though he had set himself to enact a bloody satire on Democracy, war, diplomacy and all the other creaking machineries of government.[25]

The *ricos* hated Armijo and suspected that he was about to betray them to the Americans, but they were further weakened by doubt and ideological conflict in their own circle. It is ironic that the man who led the abortive uprising against American rule, Padre Martínez, should himself have been one of the sowers of doubt. In *Night Over Taos,* Maxwell Anderson presents the following dialogue between Martínez and his aristocratic friend Pablo Montoya:

MARTÍNEZ

The times are changing. Mexico's a republic.
The English to the north broke from their kings. We're here
Like a little island of empire, and on all sides
The people have a share in what happens.

MONTOYA

And that's what you've meant
By your printing press . . . and your teaching the peons to read!
Do you want a republic here?

MARTÍNEZ

I want to save
What we have, Pablo. They're not all peons. They look
To the north and south, my friend, and take stock of themselves,
A little, and wonder why one class of men,
Or one man out of that class, has it all his own way
In the province of Taos.

**MONTOYA**

If so, it's because you've taught them
To think they can think.

**MARTINEZ**

Not so. It came without asking,
Like an infection. There's only one cure for it,
And that's to seem to offer them from within
What's offered them outside. Give them books and schools,
And the franchise if they want it.

**MONTOYA**

You're my friend, José
And have been, but this difference between us
Is deep as hell, and as wide. You fight the north
Because you want to keep your place. In your heart
You want what the north wants! But I fight the north
Because I despise what it stands for! Why should they think
About government, these peons? They're happier
With someone thinking for them! Why should the young
Take rank above their elders?

**MARTINEZ**

We must give them the shadow
Or they'll want the substance.

**MONTOYA**

Begin to make concessions
And they turn to a mob and tear you to pieces! Show them
You're afraid of them, and they're wolves! But let them see
That you're the better man and they're sheep, and your dogs
Can herd them without fences! . . . And shall women choose men?
Are they so much wiser? All your reforms fall in
With this plague from the north that enfeebles us. God's name
I think you mean well! You've been my friend, but what
You teach is poison to me!

**MARTINEZ**

An enlightened people
Could be ruled more simply . . .

**MONTOYA**

All rule is based on fear . . .
On fear and love . . . but when they know too much
They neither fear you nor love you! Teach them too much
And you tear your empire down, and what you have left
Is what there was before there were empires! This

> Is all your progress ... and they won't thank you for it.
> Nor will the women. They don't want freedom! But they'll take it,
> And laugh at you for giving it.[26]

Martínez was indeed a manipulator, one who in the interest of retaining his own position of power in changing times would willingly give the people the shadow lest they later demand the substance. He was, however, an extremely complex man of powerful will and intellect and genuinely interested in radical ideas. Montoya's charge that the reforms advocated by Martínez "fall in with this plague from the north that enfeebles us" parallels the anguished cry of the aristocratic Mexican statesman, José María Tornel, upon the loss of Texas to the Americans:

> Too late have we come to know the restless and enterprising neighbor who sets himself up as our mentor, holding up his institutions for us to copy them, institutions which transplanted to our soil could not but produce constant anarchy, and which, by draining our resources, perverting our character, and weakening our vigor, have left us powerless against the attacks and the invasions of this modern Rome.[27]

Something of the discontent of lower class Mexicans with the feudal order of *criollo* society is reflected in the dime novels. In one of them, a humble Mexican buffalo hunter or *cibolero* triumphed in the riding contests at the fair of San Marcos. He laid his trophy at the feet of a beautiful young woman of the landed gentry. When he received a smile of encouragement from her, he forgot, in his infatuation, that "he was nothing but a cibolero, whose sole fortune was a horse, a bow, and his empty hand. He forgot that she was of the 'sangre azul,' that her father, the proudest in the land, could trace their descent far beyond Cortez and his Conquistadores — forgot that they could buy ten thousand such as he and still be rich."[28] The woman amused herself with him for a while but later conspired with her real lover, a man of her own class, to have him hanged. Cut down by a passer-by from the tree from which he was hanging, the *cibolero* recovered and as the "Mad Chief" of an Apache tribe devoted his life to terrible vengeance against the *ricos*. The same theme appears in another dime novel which fictionalizes the life of the California bandit, Joaquín Murrieta. As an ordinary soldier in the Mexican army he quarrels with a superior officer who dismisses him contemptuously: "You dare to challenge me — a Spanish gentleman! ... you a nameless low-born boy."[29] Murrieta, deeply humiliated, deserts the army and becomes a bandit in the style of Robin Hood, plundering the rich and aiding the poor. The authors of these works, in their frontier republicanism, invariably side with the humiliated lower-class Mexicans against their haughty Mexican overlords. An artist of humble origins named Lorenzo tries to break up a fight between two young aristocrats by deflecting a sword thrust with his guitar. He is angrily thrust aside by one of the duelists: "How dare you, base peasant, arrest my sword?"[30] The quarrel was over a woman, but it is Lorenzo who finally goes off with her. In another example, an aristocratic Mexican woman, Marietta, asks her *criollo* suitor, Pedro Mercedo, to get her a glass of water. Pedro, in his pride of caste, is offended that he should be asked to perform a menial task and therefore summons a half-naked peon to fetch the water. Marietta is enraged on two counts: first, that Pedro should be too proud to perform a small service and, second, that this tattered peon should be allowed to enter her patio. The peon is sent away in the most contemptuous manner. But this seeming Mexican laborer is in reality a disguised member of a marauding band of Apaches. Hiding in the brush, he ambushes Pedro Mercedo and stabs him to death.[31]

Episodes of this sort are undoubtedly an expression of the authors' determination to emphasize Mexico's degeneracy by comparing arrogant and effete Mexican aristocrats with ruggedly egalitarian American frontiersmen. But quite possibly these naïve tales indicate as well an awareness on the part of the Western writers employed by Beadle and Adams that there existed in the society of the Mexican borderlands a good deal of popular discontent with *criollo* feudalism.

Though the weakened society of the big house succumbed rapidly after the American annexation of the Southwest, something of the spirit of the old feudal contract remains. Fergusson sees this lingering heritage in the readiness of Mexican-Americans to lapse into a state of dependency.

> If you hire a Mexican to work for you he is likely to regard you as a potential source of all things needed and to become a somewhat importunate solicitor of favors. Give him half a chance and he will get himself into your debt and stay there. In a word, he will relapse into peonage. Doubtless the tradition of his experience accounts for both of these attitudes . . . . Both political and economic life in New Mexico still suffer from his instinctive love of a feudal relationship to some leader. Shrewd politicians have built up some of the most perfectly working and perfectly corrupt political machines that ever existed by taking proper care of their henchmen.[32]

The inevitable attitude of American frontiersmen toward the hierarchical society that they encountered in Mexico can be found expressed in the earliest records of border contact. A survivor of the Philip Nolan filibustering expedition into Texas when it was still under the Spanish crown, the picaresque "Colonel" Ellis P. Bean, sets the tone in a letter written in 1813. Bean had escaped imprisonment in Mexico and had joined the patriot forces of Morelos in the early phase of the Mexican struggle for independence. He claimed to have received an offer from a royalist officer to desert the cause of Mexican independence and join the royalist army. Bean includes the following letter in his memoirs, his purported response to this offer:

> Sir: I have had the pleasure of receiving your letter, dated December the 20th 1812: and in answer to the same, I have to state that I am very poor, but for all that, your king has not money enough to buy me, or make me a friend to a tyrant, when I have been rocked in the cradle of liberty from infancy.
>
> Your ob't servant, Bean[33]

Some forty years later the same kind of sentiments are being recorded. George W. B. Evans, the forty-niner, describes his reaction to the social situation of northern Mexico:

> These northern towns are, in fact, nothing but colonies; the wealthy owners residing in the large and rich cities of the south whilst the people here are peons — poor, miserable slaves of their rich and noble masters, toiling and risking life and limb that they and their families might roll in wealth and luxury. But such is the case. Shut out from the mind of man the truths of the Bible, the knowledge derived at school, the intelligence gained from, and widely disseminated by the free, untrammeled press, and you at once blot that people, as it were, out of the world. You shut them from everything like an intelligent existence, and open the door to abject slavery and fully prepare them for the fetters ready for them. Thank God that my fate has cast me among the free and intelligent of the earth, that I am an American by birth and in feeling, and can fully appreciate the blessings conferred by our Republic.[34]

James Fenimore Cooper saw the Mexican-American War as a movement of liberation by which an enlightened United States would free Mexico of feudalistic oppressions.

> Providence, however, directs all to the completion of its own wise ends. If the crust which has so long encircled that nation, inclosing it in bigotry and ignorance, shall now be irretrievably broken, letting in light, even Mexico herself may have cause hereafter to rejoice in her present disasters. It was in this way that Italy has been, in a manner, regenerated; the conquests of the French carrying in their train the means and agencies which have, at length, aroused that glorious portion of the earth to some of its ancient spirit. Mexico, in certain senses, is the Italy of this continent; and war, however ruthless and much to be deplored, may yet confer on her the inestimable blessings of real liberty, and a religion released from *"feux d'artifice,"* as well as all other artifices.[35]

Whatever the complacency of this statement, it had its prophetic element. Mexico did in fact enter a regenerative stage after the defeat. And though the United States was not in any direct sense an ideological mentor, the great Juárez was influenced in his concepts of jurisprudence by American political thought.

The fact that the American frontiersmen encountered in the Southwest a society which was not only authoritarian but also radically different in its social arrangements has had its lasting effects. In *North From Mexico,* Carey McWilliams ascribes the uneasy relationship between Mexican and "Anglo" in the modern Southwest to the fact that "a large part of the Anglo-American influx to the borderlands after 1846 was made up of middle-class elements in the sense that they were neither very rich nor extremely poor. In the borderlands, these elements did not find their Hispanic 'opposite numbers.' " Instead they found a few aristocrats with whom, because of great difference of tradition and outlook, they could establish no rapport, and a mass of semi-savage peons. "The absence of local self-government and the presence of a population that was seven-eighths illiterate in 1850, predisposed the Anglo-Americans to form an extremely negative opinion of the Mexican lower classes who constituted nine-tenths of the population."[36] Thus was established the image of the "greaser" to be perpetuated as a tradition of the Southwest.

Early American arrivals to the borderlands not only disapproved of the social order they encountered but also looked with contempt upon Mexican public officials whom they saw as universally corrupt. Kendall was impressed by the fact that everything he saw in Mexico seemed old and deteriorated and that there were no buildings to be seen in process of construction. He blamed this situation on the nature of the people and on their rulers who were "jealous, selfish, and ambitious."[37] Naval Lieutenant Wise, stationed in Mazatlán during the Mexican war, describes the population of the city as being disheartened at the news that the American occupation forces were going to be withdrawn, leaving the people again at the mercy of their own corrupt officials.

> In the month of March the first positive information relating to rumors of peace reached Mazatlán. It was agreeable news to a few former *empleados* of the customs and courts, all idle and disaffected vagabonds, but the majority of peaceably-disposed citizens and foreign residents were averse to our departure. They had so long been oppressed by Mexican misrule, intrigue, and extortion, that the law, order, and tolerant state of things existing under our sway, presented a too pleasing contrast not to sigh for a continuance of it.[38]

Jeremiah Clemens, in the Texas romance *Bernard Lile,* wrote of the Rio Grande country that "it was the home of a people whose substance had been wrung from them by the tyrant and the priest, and whose energies had been withered by the baleful conviction that any provision for the morrow would only serve to pamper their oppressors."[39]

Modern writers treating of the early period of border contacts give the same picture. In *The Time of the Gringo,* Elliot Arnold has Armijo say: "Of course I appropriated funds. I took all that I could get. Who in government does not appropriate funds? . . . . At least I produced results."[40] Fergusson, examining the psychology underlying Mexican procedures, digresses in the novel *Grant of Kingdom* to describe the role of the ubiquitous "coyote" as that of "a negotiator, one who arranges difficult matters and always for a price. All Mexican society abounds in coyotes and of many different kinds and degrees. For the Mexicans are not a direct people, they are deviously and elaborately indirect. They love both ceremony and intrigue for their own sakes, and they hate the blunt and the obvious. So the professional go-between has a large part in their lives."[41]

Judicial procedures in Mexico occasioned a good deal of bitter comment by early American writers. Part of the acrimony was due to a misunderstanding of the basis of Mexican law. Kendall refers to an incident in which two "foreigners" in New Mexico "accidentally" shot a New Mexican boy. They brought his body into Santa Fe and reported the incident. Armijo had them jailed and set a trial in which they should be "held responsible for murder unless they could prove themselves innocent."[42] This procedure seemed to Kendall not only abominable but typically Mexican. However, the concept of justice by which a man is considered guilty unless he can prove himself innocent derives from the Roman law of continental Europe and is still the underlying concept of the legal systems of southern Europe and Hispanic America. Josiah Gregg describes having been brought to court because of an argument with a wealthy New Mexican landlord, Don Angel, who claimed that Gregg's servant had robbed him. No definite charges were made against him. "All I knew was that I had offended a 'rico'. . . . It is not unusual, however, in that 'land of liberty,' for a person to be arrested and even confined for weeks, without knowing the cause. The writ of Habeas Corpus appears unknown in the judicial tribunals of Northern Mexico."[43] Elsewhere in the narrative, Gregg complains that justice is "an article of traffic" in New Mexico. Litigants who cannot apply the "silver unction" are very unlikely to win their cases.[44] Thus the poor have very little chance against the rich in court. The *fueros,* special courts for the clergy and for the military, were particularly offensive to Gregg. Though no priest or soldier could be tried in a civil court, ordinary citizens could be tried in the *fueros,* and the decisions rendered there would supersede any former judgements, which may have been passed by civil courts. "It is no wonder then," concluded Gregg, "that the cause of freedom has made so little progress."[45] In a similar vein, Dana in *Two Years Before the Mast,* after describing arbitrary judicial practices among early Californians, summed up with the statement that "as for justice, they know no law but will and fear."[46]

This rule of fear was enforced by a ubiquitous military establishment whose prestige and power was clearly above that of the civil, a situation which jarred the republican sensibilities of early American reporters even when this power was used beneficently in order to oblige them. The Spanish officer, Lieutenant Mulgares, who conducted Pike and his men through small New Mexican settlements toward Santa Fe in one of the most genteel of arrests, had the most hospitable of intentions when he sent off the following order, as reproduced in Pike's account, to the mayors of surrounding villages. "Send this evening six or eight of your handsomest girls, to the village of St. [sic] Fernández, where I propose giving a fandango, for the entertainment of the American officers arrived this day." That such an order should have been sent out to civil authorities affronted Zebulon Pike in two important aspects of his cultural make up, his deeply ingrained republicanism and his puritanism. "This order," he wrote in his account, "was punctually obeyed, and pourtrays [sic] more clearly than a chapter of observations, the degraded state of the common people."[47]

Kendall reports a similar experience. One of the more humane of the Mexican officers conducting the prisoners of the Texan Santa Fe expedition was a Major Roblado. Taking pity on the foot-weary Texans, he ordered the mayor of a small town to provide a hundred mules. When the mayor protested the poverty of his town, he was told by the Mexican officer that if the mules were not provided by morning the major would make a jackass out of the mayor by making him carry the heaviest prisoner himself. The mules were provided, and there was no compensation. Kendall, while much relieved to be finally mounted and feeling genuinely grateful to Roblado, nevertheless reflected on the significance of the incident in terms of the nature of Mexican society. "Roblado," he wrote, "manifested as little compunction on the occasion as a bear would while robbing a beehive."[48] Later Kendall witnessed a young Mexican being seized, tied up, and carried off by a recruiting officer despite the despairing cries of the young man's mother. "This," wrote Kendall, "in a republic which boasts of its freedom, and cannot issue the most trifling despatch without tacking 'God and Liberty' to some part of it."[49]

The *Overland Monthly* published an article in October, 1870, designed to acquaint an American public unaccustomed to such extensions of the military function with the Mexican institution of the "pronunciamiento." The author, W. R. Turnbull, defines this phenomenon of Latin American politics by giving a very lively account of his personal experience in the Mexican city of Puebla when General Negrete pronounced against the government of Juárez. Turnbull considers this a classic instance and gives a detailed account of the intrigue involved in luring, with promises of plunder and promotion, city commanders to join the rebels. Once in command of the city, Negrete systematically extorts large sums of money from all citizens reputed to have any means. Though most of the garrison commanders cynically and greedily betray their trust in joining Negrete, there are heroes in the account. Colonel Campillo refuses to join the rebels and gallops out of the city through a hail of bullets. Colonel Yepez, in charge of a large "conducta" of gold heading toward Puebla, is contacted by an agent of Negrete. Yepez pretends to go along with the revolt but later maneuvers his men into a good position, rallies them to the cause of Juárez, and defeats the rebels, who had been counting heavily on the gold. This defeat marks the turning point in the fortunes of the rebels. Turnbull admires the dispatch with which Juárez handled such a serious uprising. He concludes that Mexico, having learned the value of unity through its experience with the French, was moving away from the former blend of opera-bouffe and savagery in politics toward a new stability. The essay, written in an excellent prose, vivid in its use of incident and characterization, is by a man obviously attuned to the nuances of the Mexico of his day.

While the critical attitude taken by Americans toward the Mexican society of the early nineteenth century was inevitable and in some respects justified, it was also ethnocentric to a considerable degree. There was much swagger, bombast, and ignorance in the "patriotism" of the American frontiersmen as it expressed itself in a derision of all things Mexican. Mary Austin Holley, a New England cousin of Stephen Austin, visited the American colonies in Texas in 1830 and described in her letters a "goodly portion" of the American colonists as being "full of pretensions and overflowing with 'patriotism' often the veriest 'demagoguery'; accustomed at home to vent their spleen on rulers and obnoxious measures, they were not slow to infuse into the before contented community the spirit of resistance on the slightest provocation, until the subject of their declamation, by exciting distrust and jealousy, became real. They forgot the genius and the habits of the Mexican people; their newness to self-government, their jealousy of the Anglo-Americans . . . ."[50]

Stephen Austin himself, though sophisticated and to a considerable extent tactful in his relations with Mexican officials, occasionally expressed himself in his letters to Mexican dignitaries with considerable complacence. In criticising things Mexican he used as the implied standard of perfection the institutions, attitudes, and customs of his own Anglo-American tradition. In a letter to the Mexican general Ugartechea he wrote: "Listen, if all the people of this nation [Mexico] had the same industry in farming, and the love of liberty and for the constitution and the laws that the people of my colony have, there would be more national prosperity and fewer revolutions."[51] Though Austin might well have been right in this assertion, the tone of the letter, written by one who had solicited permission to settle in Mexico, could hardly have been pleasing to Ugartechea. On another occasion, Austin included a lecture to the Mexicans in the preface of a bill that he submitted to the legislature of Texas and Coahuila proposing the establishment of a school of modern languages in Texas. The Mexicans were told that they must come out from under "those dark clouds of the centuries past which to this day obscure the political atmosphere of Mexico." They must rid themselves of "ideas that are crude, fanatical, servile and obsolete."[52] So much for the Hispanic tradition!

The first Americans to make contact with the Mexican civilization of the Southwest were homogeneous in their Anglo-Saxon Protestant tradition in a way that Americans have not been since. They approached Mexican Catholicism with a pre-existing hostility. Furthermore, in the Catholic Church of the Mexican borderlands they encountered a clergy so remote from the centers of ecclesiastical authority that it had fallen into corrupt practices which could be carried on with impunity. A number of the priests of this area were heavy drinkers, gamblers, extortionists, and men who maintained mistresses. But the censure of Mexican Catholicism to be found in the early American chronicles of the borderlands goes beyond disgusted references to corrupt practices. There is a cultural confrontation here in which a multiple, and thus anti-authoritarian, Protestantism, puritanical and anti-aesthetic in its outlook, surveys with disapproval a Catholicism which is hierarchical, mystical, ornate, and dramatic.

There is a good deal of comment in early American writing upon the position of power held by the Mexican clergy and upon the unquestioning obedience rendered to the clergy by people of all classes. Austin saw in Mexican devotion to the Church "a fanaticism" that "reigns with a power that equally astonishes and grieves a man of common sense."[53] Zebulon Pike, after discoursing on the great power of the military in Mexico, adds that "to a stranger it is impossible to define the limits of the military and ecclesiastical, in every affair which relates to the citizens, and in fact with the soldiery, the force of superstition is such that I am doubtful whether they would generally obey one of their officers in a direct violation of the injunction of their religious professions."[54] George Evans writes that "to the behests of the priest all Mexicans pay attention, in no case violating his commands or transgressing the requirements of their religion. In this respect they are always true, and by their blind devotion are easily kept poor and ignorant...."[55] Warming up to the subject, Evans goes on to say that "there never existed a people on the face of the globe so completely, so emphatically, the worshipers of idols, and so entirely controlled in all their acts by priestly dictation as these Mexicans. They uncover their heads or bend the knee to every cross, wherever met with, and all persons who neglect or refuse to bow to these absurd notions are looked upon as heretics and regarded with disdain."[56]

In a passage remarkably like the prose emanating from present-day California, James Ohio Pattie rhapsodizes upon the scenery and climate of that region, saying that "this country is more calculated to charm the eye, than any one I have ever seen." He goes on, however, to add that "its inhabitants are equally calculated to excite dislike, and even the stronger feelings of disgust and hatred. The priests are omnipotent, and all things are subject to their power."[57] Pattie in his journey through California played quite self-consciously the role of the resourceful Yankee among a backward people. On one occasion he contracted with the Franciscan head of an Indian mission to vaccinate all the inhabitants of the region controlled by the mission. After having completed the job, he was handed a note by the priest acknowledging a debt to the agreed upon amount and adding that this debt would be paid upon Pattie's becoming a Catholic and a Mexican subject. These attached conditions set the mountain man to sputtering:

> Prudential considerations were sufficient to withhold me no longer, and I answered in a short manner, that I felt at that moment as though I should rejoice to find myself once more in a country where I should be justly dealt by. He asked me what I meant when I spoke of being justly dealt by? I told him what my meaning was, and wished to be in my own country, where there are laws to compel a man to pay another what he justly owes him, without his having the power to attach to the debt, as a condition upon which the payment is to depend, the submission to, and gratification of, any of his whimsical desires. Upon this the priest's tone became loud and angry as he said, "then you regard my proposing that you become a Catholic, as the expression of an unjust and whimsical desire!' I told him 'yes, that I did; and that I would not change my present opinions for all the money his mission was worth....' When I had thus given honest and plain utterance to the feelings, which swelled within me, the priest ordered me to

leave his house. I walked out quickly, and possessed myself of my rifle, as I did not know, but some of his attendants at hand might be set upon me; for if the comparison be allowable the priests of this country have the people as much and entirely under their control, as the people of our own country have a good biddable dog.[58]

Pattie, embodying so much of the presumptuous swagger of the mountain man, was hardly the kind to make any concessions to the culture of the people through whose country he was being permitted to travel. He enjoyed baiting Mexicans of all classes, insisting on the inferiority of Mexican character and institutions. In his narrative he reports with relish the following encounter:

> I amused myself at times with an old man, who daily fell in my way, who was at once rich and to the last degree a miser; and yet devotedly attached to the priests, who were alone able to get a little money out of him. He often spoke to me about the unsafeness of my religion. Instead of meeting his remarks with an argument, I generally affronted him at once, and then diverted myself with his ways of showing his anger. I told him that his priest treated him as the Spanish hostlers do their horses. He asked me to explain the comparison. I observed, "you know how the hostler in the first place throws his lasso over the mule's neck. That secures the body of the beast. Next the animal is blindfolded. That hinders his seeing where he is led. Next step he binds the saddle safe and fast. Then the holy father rigs his heels with spurs. Next come spur and lash, and the animal is now restive to no purpose. There is no shaking off the rider. On he goes, till the animal under him dies, and both go to hell together!" At this he flew into such a violent rage, as to run at me with his knife.[59]

Bartlett's narrative also contains much of this same aggressive disdain for Mexican Catholicism. In referring to the remains of the mission of San José outside of San Antonio, Bartlett writes that "the work of ruin has been assisted by the numerous military companies near here, who, finding in the hands and features of the statues convenient marks for rifle and pistol shots, did not fail to improve the opportunity for showing at the same time their skill in arms and their contempt for the Mexican belief."[60]

One is reminded in reading some of the bitterly anti-Catholic passages in the early novel *Francis Berrian* that its author, Timothy Flint, was a Congregational minister in a period when religious hatreds were strong. The hero, Berrian, in a discussion with a Mexican, justifies his association with the cause of the patriot army of Morelos on the grounds of helping to liberate Mexico from the tyranny of the Church. Of the

Mexicans themselves he says, "they are ignorant and barbarous, I grant you. But what has made them so? Enlighten their ignorance; — break their chains — remove the threefold veil of darkness with which your priesthood have hoodwinked them."[61] Berrian in the course of his wanderings through Mexico falls in love with a young Mexican woman, but as a Protestant he has, in pursuing his courtship, a formidable antagonist in the chaplain attached to the young woman's wealthy, aristocratic family. Timothy Flint gives this portrait of the family priest.

> The father confessor, whom they called by the name Josephus, was a priest of high standing in the country, had been educated at Rome, and had all the external suavity and observance of a courtier, the training and adroitness of a Jesuit, and a sufficiency of intrigue to have been minister of the Grand Seignior. His form was noble, his voice deep and impressive, and every function of his ministry performed with an indescribable grace. Seen at a distance, his countenance and manner inspired respect. Contemplated more nearly and intensely, there was something in it sinister and repressing to confidence and affection. He regarded the spirit of the age, the fermenting germ of republicanism, and the slightest beginnings of innovation in the Catholic hierarchy, with a deep aversion, that savoured rather of a malignant nature, than of the prejudices of education. In the same proportion as his own enlightened mind had penetrated the absurdities of those points, which constitute the incredible and contradictory of the Catholic dogmas, was he bitter and strenuous, even to persecution, for retaining every jot and tittle of them in all their ancient strictness.[62]

Jesuit training is given similar recognition in one of the Texas romances, *Mustang Grey,* by Jeremiah Clemens. A Mexican named Bartolo Piedras, who is described as having "united in his own person the quadruple character of horse-trader, smuggler, slaver, and robber," had been educated in a Jesuit institution. "It is fair to presume," writes Clemens, "that the principles on which he acted were imbibed from the same source."[63]

The great power which the clergy exercised over all phases of Mexican life and which provoked such unfavorable comment among the early American chroniclers of the borderlands eventually brought on the first great wave of anti-clericalism in Mexico, a movement which led to the reform laws of Juárez. William Cullen Bryant was visiting Mexico City during the period of "la Reforma" and found in his conversations with Mexicans and others insistence upon the fact of the general corruption and idleness of the clergy. He was surprised to find a rather flourishing Protestantism in the capital. He also noted with benign approval the effects of Juárez's measures against the Church, the closing down of convents and monasteries, prohibition of clerical dress in the streets, the secularization of schools. He concluded of the members of the Catholic clergy that "they will become better men by the effect of adversity and the formidable rivalry to which they are now subjected."[64]

Not only did the early American chroniclers insist upon the extent of clerical power in the Mexican society of the borderlands, but they also took pains to record in detail incidents which could serve to exemplify the abuse of this power. A number of accounts mention exhorbitant fees charged by priests to perform marriages and to preside at burials. George Evans writes of having a conversation with the overseer of an hacienda, who informed him that almost all the peons were unmarried but were nevertheless living together in concubinage. When Evans asked "the reason for this violation of the doctrine taught by the Bible, and regarded with so much reverence by other denominations of Christians," he was told that the peons simply couldn't afford the marriage fees demanded by the priests. Evans then asked if the priests ever preached against the practice of cohabitation without benefit of clergy, to which the answer was no. Scandalized by such informal arrangements which "would be characterized as sins by our clergy," Evans concludes that in Catholicism, "where sins are so easily disposed of, such conduct is winked at by those in charge of the spiritual interests of the people, so long as their blind devotion keeps the church purse well filled and a cunning priesthood in absolute power and dominion."[65] Josiah Gregg reprints a letter which appeared in a Chihuahua paper in which a father complains about the fee demanded by the Church to perform a marriage service for his son. " 'Did I not pride myself,' " writes the father, " 'on being a true apostolic Roman Catholic, and were it not that the charming graces of my intended daughter-in-law have so captivated my son that nothing but marriage will satisfy him, I would assuredly advise him to contrive some other arrangement with his beloved, which might not be so ruinous to our poor purse.' "[66]

On the subject of burial fees, Gregg tells of a poor widow in Santa Fe who begged a little medicine for a sick child. " 'Not that the life of the babe imports me much,' " she wailed, " 'for I know the "angelito" will go directly to heaven; but what shall I do to pay the priest for burying it? He will take my house and all from me — and I shall be turned desolate into the street.' "[67] Because of exhorbitant burial fees, according to Gregg, indigent parents often resorted to hiding a child's body in a church. When the priest found it, he was forced to bury it gratis. On the other hand, if he discovered who were the parents, they not only had to pay the fee but also received "severe castigation."[68] Pattie reports that he witnessed an occasion in which the bodies of several Mexicans who had been murdered were paraded through the streets in order to beg money to pay the priests for a burial. However, there was no inquest of any sort held over the bodies. "This excited in me," writes Pattie, "still more disgust than the murders. I expressed myself in consequence, with so much freedom, in regard to this sort of miserable imposition, as to give great offence to my host, who, like most of the people, was rigidly devoted to the religion of the church."[69] In *Adventures in the Santa Fe Trade*, J. J. Webb gives his estimation of the effects of clerical cupidity upon the morality of the people. "An inflexible rule with the priests was: no money, no marrying; no money, [no] baptizing; no money, no burying.... As a consequence the poor were extremely so, and without hope of bettering their condition. The priesthood [was] corrupt, vicious, and improvident. Is it strange, then, that with such a heartless, demoralized, and utterly impious, yet very religious, priesthood, the people in such abject poverty could see no merit in virtue or honesty?"[70]

These borderland priests were culpable, according to American writers, not only in their greed but also in the flagrant violation of their vows. Zebulon Pike gives this shocked report of a swaggering Mexican priest: "The conduct and behaviour of a young priest who came in, was such as in our country would have been amply sufficient forever to have banished him from the clerical association, strutting about with a dirk in his boot, a cane in his hand, whispering to one girl, chucking another under the chin, and going out with a third."[71] Francis Parkman in *The Oregon Trail* gives an account of a conversation he had with a plainsman named Reynal. When asked whether he had married the Mexican woman with whom he was living, Reynal answered, "no, the priests don't marry their women, and why should I marry mine."[72] Gregg characterizes a "large portion of the 'pastores' " as "first at the fandango — first at the gaming table — first at the cock-pit — first at bacchanalian orgies — and by no means last in the contraction of those 'liaisons' which are so emphatically prohibited by their vows."[73]

This picture of a dissolute Mexican clergy is to be found also in early American fiction. The American protagonist in the short story "The Inroad of the Nabajo" by Albert Pike gives this report of a fandango in Santa Fe. " 'The people were afraid to get drunk on my first fandango night. I was astonished to find them so sober. The priest was there; and they feared to get drunk until he had done so. That event took place about eleven at night, and then aguardiente was in demand.' "[74] Jeremiah Clemens, ardent in his support of Texas and of Anglo-American Protestantism, describes with some verve the actions of a lecherous Mexican priest, Padre José, in the Texas romance *Mustang Grey*. The hero of this novel was in historical fact a Texan gun fighter, famous for his ruthless slaughter of Mexicans in border conflicts and in the Mexican War. In Clemens' version, a Mexican woman, Inez, in love with Mustang Grey, seeks the aid of Padre José in order to procure the escape of her Texan lover from his Mexican captives. She later describes to Grey what happened during her interview with the priest. "Gradually his manner grew more tender, and at length he clasped me in his arms, and pressed a hot kiss upon my lips.... His eyes absolutely glistened with lascivious fire, as they ran over my face and person."[75]

Not all of the early reports on the Mexican clergy were unfavorable, however. Richard Cleveland, that early New England venturer into California waters, gives this account of a California mission padre in his journal *Voyages and Commercial Enterprises of the Sons of New England,* which was first published in 1842.

> The more intimately we became acquainted with Padre Mariano, the more we were convinced that his was a character to love and respect. He appeared to be one of that rare class, who, for piety and the love of their fellow-men, might justly rank with a Fenelon or a Cheverus. His countenance beaming with the love and benevolence which were his prevailing motives of action, inspired immediate and perfect confidence, even with those who had seen as much of the Spanish character as it had been our lot to do. His mild and humane treatment of his domestics made their intercourse more like that of father and children, than of masters and servants. His regular observance, morning, noon, and evening, of his devotional duties, with his uncouth looking domestics assembled around him, and on bended knee, and with the utmost decorum, participating in his prayers to the throne of grace, was affecting, and might be received as a tacit reproach for indifference to such duties, by that part of his audience, whom his brethren would denominate heretics. But this good man was gifted with a mind too liberal and noble, and a benevolence too extensive and pure to pronounce condemnation for difference of opinions, or to believe in the monopoly of truth and goodness in any one sect of Christians.[76]

Cleveland clearly thought of Padre Mariano as an exception, but he generally credited the clergy in California with being amiable, though ignorant and bigoted. His assertion that the padre in his liberality would not claim unique and exclusive authority for his church simply indicates a misunderstanding of Catholicism.

Kendall was by no means uniformly hostile to the clergy. During the terrible march of the Texas prisoners, it was often the priests who were able to bring blankets and food to comfort them. The authority of these priests and their right of access to the prisoners could not be questioned by the Mexican captors. The frequency with which the padres aided these now humbled Texan invaders would indicate that in essential matters the Christian conscience was still active among many of the

Mexican clergy. Kendall, as a seasoned newspaperman and former resident of cosmopolitan New Orleans, took a sophisticated view of clerical lapses from prescribed conduct.

> That the good padres of that country have their "compañeras," or female companions, is well known ... and equally well known is it that they invariably make their selections with a discrimination which shows that they are most excellent judges of female beauty. ... I trust that the kind-hearted curas, from whom myself and companions received so many favors and attentions, will give me full pardon for thus exposing some of their weaknesses and frailties .... They will also excuse me, when I say to any of them, that they are a class of enlightened, generous, good-natured, discerning, hospitable, hail-fellow-well-met, penance-hating, women-loving men, prone toward the enjoyments of the table, holding fast in great scorn, addicted to occasional gambling and winebibbing, and pretending no ignorance in matters of cock-fighting and sports of a like nature; more particularly when I repeat that I entertain the best feelings towards one and all of them.[77]

James Josiah Webb, usually so severe in his treatment of the Mexican clergy, reports with good-humored amusement an occasion in which a Father Lliba took supper with Webb and some friends. There was "a good supply of liquors" for the entertainment of the "reverend guest" on hand, "of which he partook quite freely and became rather hilarious. On leaving camp, he mounted his pony and rode around the camp at the fastest run of his horse (two or three times), and coming to the road leading to town, struck off on it, raising his hat with a grand flourish, [and] gave us the parting [*Adiós.*] *Goodbye!* 'Go to hell!' and went off satisfied and happy."[78]

In his portrait of a New Mexican priest in the short story "A Mexican Tale," Albert Pike balances character defects and professional achievements.

> The Frai Luis, Muro was about thirty years of age, of features coarse and sensual, but regular; stoutly but firmly built, and of the medium height. Had he not been a priest, his character for virtue would have been little respected. He was grievously addicted to various sins; and among them was numbered the love of good liquor, and, at times, a forgetfulness of his vow of celibacy. Had he not been a priest, however, he would have been only a bon vivant, and a very good fellow as the world of New Mexico goes, and no crime or sin would have been laid at his door. To say the truth, the Padre Muro was infinitely superior to many or most of his brethren, who, in general, are in that country hardly as well educated as a boy of eight years in ours. Now the Frai Luis had been educated at the College of Guadalajara, and was a tolerable scholar in Latin and Greek. He was also well

versed in the now exploded systems of natural philosophy and chemistry; and was in fact a man of no mean talent — and of no great sanctity.[79]

Probably the most picaresque of the many unusual clergymen described in the literature of the borderlands was the swashbuckling guerilla chief, Father Martínez, in Sam Chamberlain's *My Confession*.

> One regular frequenter at Victorines [a bordello and dance hall outside of Monterey] was Martie Martiznes [sic], a priest and guerillar [sic]. He sought no concealment but seemed to court observation; dressed in the picturesque costume of the *ranchero rico* (rich rancher) he would come into the room, treat the [American] soldiers to *vino, pulque,* and *muscal* [sic] dance and flirt with the *poblanas*, "buck" at monte, in fact make himself the most popular man in the house. Between this typical Mexican *padre* and myself a strong feeling of friendship sprang up which proved of great service to me, more than once.[80]

The high coloration of Mexican Catholicism with its ritualized drama, its primitiveness, and its admixture with Indian modes of worship, characteristics which modern writers have admired, produced reactions of contempt or amusement from the early American writers of the borderlands. Kendall describes a religious procession that took place in the town of San Miguel near the eastern border of New Mexico. The second contingent of armed Texans was approaching the town, and the object of the religious service was to seek the protection of the patron saint from these invading strangers. Members of the first contingent had already been taken captive, Kendall among them, and observed the procession from the prison which fronted on the plaza. As the group of worshippers passed by the prison, the Texan inmates were highly amused to see an old and shabbily clad priest with what seemed to the Texans to be ludicrously oversized leather-rimmed glasses, preceded by a panoply under which doll-like images of the Virgin and San Miguel were carried. The image of San Miguel, loosened by many outings, wavered and bent with each step. Before went a queazy band and behind the ragged worshippers. "At each of the four corners, and at each of the four sides of the plaza did the procession stop, kneel down, and publicly thank San Miguel for thus keeping his charge out of the hands of heretics, and all this while the comical image, now arrayed with an extra load of furbelows, feathery, and finery, bowed his acknowledgement to the crowd of ragged worshippers in a style which would have done credit to any Merry-Andrew."[81] Kendall's reaction to the famous story of the appearance of the Virgin at Guadalupe was that it was "interesting as showing by what nonsensical superstitions and barefaced impostures the poor Indians were originally gulled by a crafty priesthood."[82] As for the existence of Indian elements in Mexican Catholicism, Kendall wrote that it accounted for the fact that "the religion of a large portion of the mixed classes is to this day but a blending of whimsical and grotesque ceremonies with the solemn and imposing observances which appertain to the religion of the Romish Church."[83]

Josiah Gregg, after having mentioned the welter of miracles reported in Mexico, including that of Guadalupe, concluded that "the popular creed seems to be the embodiment of as much that is fantastic and improbable in idolatrous worship, as it is possible to clothe in the garb of a Christian faith."[84] Gregg went to great lengths to avoid being passed by processions bearing the host, so he would not feel obliged to kneel. The veneration, kneeling, and ring-kissing accorded to a bishop visiting Santa Fe disgusted him. "The slavish obsequiousness of the lower classes towards these pampered priests is almost incredible."[85] He considered that "true devotion" was lacking and that Mexican religion was all form and ritual. Yet he presented, despite this thesis, a striking picture of all life coming to an abrupt standstill with the ringing of the vesper bell in Santa Fe. "An almost breathless silence reigns throughout the town, disturbed only by the occasional sibilations of the devout multitude."[86]

Commenting on the devotion of the people before an image of St. Francis, Bartlett wrote that "the faith of the people in this thing of wood and paint is astonishing. An old man told us with the utmost seriousness, that last May, when the Cholera visited the place, and was cutting off twenty a day, they had only to bring the image into the street, and the disease at once disappeared."[87]

The theme of Mexican idolatry also appears in one of the Texas romances. In *Mexico Versus Texas* by Anthony Ganilh there is a scene in which a Mexican woman is showing an American visitor through her house.

> On a mahogany table, in a corner, were placed three small statues of saints, exquisitely carved, decorated with gems, and in full dress of gold and silver tissue. These were "los santos de la casa," the household saints. Something like the penates amongst the ancient Romans.
> Our traveller, attracted by the delicacy of the sculpture, paid some attention to this, and the lady of the house, mistaking his curiosity for a religious feeling, explained at great length, all the miracles they had performed in behalf of the family; and, in order to manifest how grateful she had been for the benefits she had received, displayed before him a complete wardrobe, which she kept in one of the table drawers, for the use of the little figures. There were white satin gowns with silver fringe, to be used during Christmas and Easter weeks, red, for Whitsuntide! — purple for Lent and advent; nay, black velvet ones for holy week! — She had

necklaces and ear-rings for them, and treated them just as little girls treat their dolls. From her careless prattle, he even gathered that she attributed to them human passions, and thought them accessible to vanity and resentment; for, it was not without some self-complacency that she detailed how many times she had punished them, when deaf to her petitions, by taking away their finery, or stimulated them, by promises of costly ornaments.[88]

The gap between the actual behavior of Mexicans and their religious professions seemed, to early American writers, to be a very wide one indeed. With a Protestant suspicion of the aesthetic, the American chroniclers of the borderlands concluded that the Mexicans had become morally paralyzed by the sensuous enchantments of their religious rituals. Kendall, more in amazement than in admiration, gives a striking account of how the lepers in the hospital of San Lázaro in Mexico City were transported by their participation in the liturgical and sacramental life of the Church. On one occasion he observed them gathered around a highly decorated altar, chanting a litany. "Had the wretches been arrayed in habiliments befitting their unfortunate lot, and their deportment been of a character more consonant with their condition, the effect of the whole scene would have been different; but to see the wretches flaunting in gaudy apparel, and many of them joyous under the most horrible affliction which has ever been entailed upon humanity — all this formed a picture which may be imagined but cannot be described."[89]

In *The Conquest of Mexico,* Prescott credits the aesthetic and emotional aspects of Catholicism with being principal factors in the success of the missionary enterprise. "The Protestant missionary seeks to enlighten the understanding of his convert by the pale light of reason. But the bolder Catholic, kindling the spirit by the splendor of the spectacle and by the glowing portrait of an agonized Redeemer, sweeps along his hearers in a tempest of passion, that drowns everything like reflection.' "[90] Prescott gives the opinion that conversion was made easy by the fact that the religion of the Aztecs, with its pronounced emphasis on form and ritual, was similar in tone to Roman Catholicism. In accounting for the gap between profession and action in Mexican life, he brings to his analysis the point of view of a Boston Unitarian.

> To the more rational spirit of the present day, enlightened by a purer Christianity, it may seem difficult to reconcile gross deviations from morals with such devotion to the cause of religion. But the religion taught in that day was one of form and elaborate ceremony. In the punctilious attention to discipline, the spirit of Christianity was permitted to evaporate. The mind, occupied with forms, thinks little of substance. In a worship that is addressed too

exclusively to the senses, it is often the case, that morality becomes divorced from religion, and the measure of righteousness is determined by the creed rather than by the conduct.[91]

The self-immolating rites of the Penitentes, representing a provincial extreme in Mexican religious expression, quite naturally appalled American observers. There is a scene in Anthony Ganilh's *Mexico Versus Texas,* undoubtedly drawn from the author's own experience, which describes a religious procession held on Maundy Thursday in northern Mexico. The ceremony is rendered "shocking and repulsive" by a group of Penitentes leading the procession "naked from the waist upwards, and barelegged, tottering under the weight of a huge piece of timber, to which their arms are fastened, in the form of a cross. . . ." The Texas writer, adding the sentiment of racial antagonism, continues with the observation that "as they are generally Indians who perform this part, the deep, dark hue of their skins increases the disgust which such an instance of barbarianism is calculated to inspire; yet this is the share of the ceremony most admired. . . .'"[92] Josiah Gregg reports on a procession of Penitentes in Santa Fe during Holy Week. Three of them were carrying crosses weighted by stones, dragging chains embedded in the skin. One man was bleeding profusely as the result of being continually lashed as the procession proceeded. "Although the actors in this tragical farce were completely muffled, yet they were well known to many of the bystanders, one of whom assured me that they were three of the most notorious rascals in the country. By submitting to this species of penance, they annually received complete absolution of their past year's sins, and, thus 'purified,' entered afresh on the old career of wickedness and crime."[93]

One aspect of Mexican religion which has appealed to modern Americans suffering from a sense of rootlessness has been the comfortable familiarity of the Mexican approach to sacred things. Especially in rural Mexico, the Virgin and the saints are felt to be always close by. They are treated as confidants rather than as objects of fear or awe and can be upbraided if they do not perform to order. Ancient religious tradition permeates all the occasions of daily life, tending to obliterate the boundary between secular pursuits and specifically religious functions. The symbolism and the vocabulary of the Church flow throughout the home, the market place, and even the places of entertainment; and conversely something of the color and vibrancy of the streets and of the fiestas find their way back into the Church. This very intercourse between the mundane and the religious appeared to early American writers to be evidence of the blasphemous irreverence of Mexico. Gregg exclaimed: "But what most oddly greets, and really outrages most

Protestant ears, is the accompaniment of divine service with the very same instruments, and often the same tunes" as are heard at the fandangos.[94] Susan Magoffin described her first visit to a Mexican Catholic church in a similar way.

> The priest neither preached nor prayed, leaving each one to pray for himself; he repeated some Latin neither understood by himself or his hearers. The latter repeated their aves and pater nosters — ever and anon whispering to a next neighbour and giving a sly glance to the American spectators. Their music consisted of a violin, which all the time they continued to tune, and a thumbing, jingling guitar; the same tunes they had the other night at the fandango, were played. It is a strange mode of worship to a Protestant who has been raised to regard the Sabbath with strictest piety, not even to think of a dancing tune on a violin, let the hearing of it alone.[95]

Kendall was shocked by the use of religious names for public houses. "It was quite common for us to stop at the tavern of the Holy Ghost, or Hotel of the True Cross, and others, a translation of which would appear irreverent and almost blasphemous to my countrymen."[96] Bartlett was scandalized by the number of Mexicans who bore the name Jesús. "'This name is so common among the Mexicans, particularly the lower classes, that one can seldom get half a dozen of them together without finding a Jesús in the company. We had two of the name in the [boundary] Commission for a year; both of whom, I am sorry to say, proved entirely unworthy of it."[97]

The brusque contempt with which American frontiersmen treated the culture and institutions of that "fragment of the mediaeval world" which they had discovered in the Southwest reflected not only their confidence but also their innocence. In surveying the entire range of reactions of frontier America to the Mexican society it first encountered in the borderland, one can recognize the America announced by Whitman, messianic in its expansiveness, confident that it had rendered obsolete the customs and institutions of Europe. While the Southwest seemed to those frontier Americans who first came upon it to have been a sort of isolated museum of antiquities, these pristine wilderness types, in their turn, seemed to be a peculiarly isolated breed to that Europe from which these antiquities had been transplanted in the Southwest. Marching through the new Eden of the wilderness, the American frontiersmen had gotten beyond earshot of the European tale of the old Eden and the fall of man. When they encountered the story again in the Southwest, where it expressed itself in the concept of the need for fixed hierarchical authority to curb chronically sinful and limited mankind, they repudiated it immediately as the invention of an effete people bent on preserving privilege and obstructing progress. The later pillaging of the new Eden was to bring about a revision of thought on the subjects of the natural goodness of man and the automatic nature of progress. And yet this salutary revision was not, for the most part, to express itself among American thinkers in the form of a demand for the return to a patriarchal order but rather for a more realistic appraisal of the nature of man without abandonment of hope for a more just society. Taking part in this process of revision were American writers, more cosmopolitan, less sure of their own identity or of their proper relationship to society, who were to look upon neighboring Mexico and its cultural extension into the American Southwest in quite a different way than had the early American chroniclers and novelists of the borderlands.

PART TWO

# Mexico and the Borderlands
# In Modern American Literature

CHAPTER FIVE

## The Passing of Enríquez

Mexico and the American Southwest, so much in the public eye during the periods of the Texas rebellion and the ensuing Mexican War, were practically forgotten by Americans during the decades that followed. The Civil War with campaigns on both sides directed by officers who had gained their first battle experience in the Mexican War, absorbed American energies and attention. When this conflict was over, public interest was divided between the acrimonies of reconstruction and the exhilarations of the era of industrial expansion. Almost overnight a huge industrial plant was erected in a period remarkable for its energy and resourcefulness as it was for its spirit of plunder. The physical human force needed to stoke this industrial plant was provided by rural America and by Europe. Serious class conflicts developed as the United States produced for the first time a real proletariat. Many of the immigrants who comprised this new proletariat were Catholics and Jews, thus shattering the old racial and cultural homogeneity of America. The uprooted American farmers and the European immigrants flocking to the urban, industrial centers of America combined to produce that characteristic feeling of modern Americans, a sense of rootlessness. From now on Americans would bring a special self-consciousness to the word *tradition*.

Toward the end of the nineteenth century the Southwest was rediscovered. Many Americans, harassed and made anxious by the fiercely competitive and exploitative spirit of the times and disgusted by the materialism and fake, parlor-car splendor of the Gilded Age, were pleased to be told by prominent authors that the United States in annexing the territory of the great Southwest had fallen heir to an ancient, dignified, and serene tradition.

More influential than any other work in bringing about this rediscovery was Helen Hunt Jackson's *Ramona,* first published in 1884. This novel, which achieved an immense popularity, operates on two levels. It is, on the one hand, a nostalgic evocation of the old "Spanish" California, with its gentle Franciscan mission fathers, its chivalric dons and haughty, aristocratic doñas. On the other hand, it is an impassioned denunciation of Manifest Destiny America. In this aspect it is in direct line of descent from Uncle Tom's Cabin, charged with the same moral passion that fired the abolitionists. Helen Hunt Jackson, New Englander and close friend of Emily Dickinson, was a woman with a cause. She had observed in California the brutal dispossession of the communal, agriculturalized Indians by American cattlemen and farmers who had moved in to take over the land by right of conquest. These Indians were products of the paternal mission system established by the Franciscans in California. Christianized and Hispanicized, the California Indians were culturally Mexicans. Generations of quiet, communal, agricultural life under the supervision of the padres had left them ill prepared for the rough times to come when the Americans took over. Because most of these Indians could show no formal deeds to their ancestral lands, they were simply driven off by incoming American ranchers who had procured titles to these lands from a United States territorial government indifferent to the fate of the Indians. Unwarlike because of their long Franciscan conditioning, these Indians docilely allowed themselves to be dispossessed. Like modern refugees of war, Indian families lined the roads taking what possessions they could carry. Many of them simply starved to death. *Ramona* combined the story of an aristocratic "Spanish" household whose adjacent lands had been much depleted by plundering Americans and the account of Alejandro, a noble savage in the grand tradition, and his fellow California Indians driven to desperation because they had been forced off their lands. Though as literature *Ramona* with its "genteel" language and melodramatic contrivances has obvious deficiencies, it can, because of the genuineness of the author's compassion, still move the modern reader. Like *Uncle Tom's Cabin* it fired public indignation. The protests that poured into Washington could not be ignored, and some efforts were made to stabilize the land situation and resettle those Indians already dispossessed. Unlike the dime novels and the Texas Romances, *Ramona* gave the American public a view of the Mexican War not as a glorious revenge for the Alamo but as a war of conquest with the usual consequences of such a war.

Though undoubtedly many of Helen Hunt Jackson's contemporaries read *Ramona* in order to weep over the fate of Alejandro and his wife, Ramona, who had left her comfortable home in order to share the misfortunes of her Indian husband, others probably succumbed to another lure, the opportunity to escape the clanging new industrialism of nineteenth-century America by entering into the pastoral idyl of old California. Early in the novel Mrs. Jackson set the tone of this life of enchantment. "It was a picturesque life, with more of sentiment and gayety in it, more also that was truly dramatic, more romance, than will ever be seen again on those sunny shores. The aroma of it all lingers there still; industries and inventions have not yet slain it; it will last out its century. . . .[1] Here was a literary vein which was to be worked with considerable profit by a number of American writers.

In 1902 Gertrude Atherton published *The Splendid Idle Forties,*[2] a group of stories celebrating the "Spanish" California first encountered by American occupying troops. These stories are designed only to charm and are full of gallant caballeros, proud señoras, lovely chaperoned señoritas, and dashing American officers whose courtesy and delicacy mark their attempts to soften, in their social relations with the "Spanish Californians," the embarrassing fact of military conquest. Bret Harte in his shrewd sense of what would appeal to a contemporary reading public made wide use of Hispanic material in his California stories and sketches, often simply to give his readers a solid dose of quaint, Old World charm, though sometimes to use the confrontation of two cultures in order to make some incisive observations about American life. In "Bohemian Days in San Francisco," he reminisces in the style of Washington Irving.

> I recall . . . my wanderings through the Spanish Quarter, where three centuries of quaint customs, speech, and dress were still preserved; where the proverbs of Sancho Panza were still spoken in the language of Cervantes, and the high-flown illusions of the La Manchian knight still a part of the Spanish Californian hidalgo's dream. I recall the modern "Greaser," or Mexican — his index finger steeped in cigarette stains; his velvet jacket and his crimson sash; the many flounced skirt and lace manta of his women, and their caressing intonations — the one musical utterance of the whole hard-voiced city.[3]

Harte uses here the standard convention observed by promoters of the California idyl of making a distinction between the "Spanish Californian Hidalgo" and the Mexican "greaser," a distinction which is to be the occasion of some tart commentary on the part of later critics of this whole genre of California literature.

Charles F. Lummis, Yankee newspaperman turned ardent chronicler of the Southwest, in the very titles he chose for his books, such as *The Land of Poco Tiempo* and *Flowers of Our Lost Romance,* proved his devotion to the cause of romanticizing the Hispanic Southwest. " 'Picturesque' is a tame word for it," he exulted. "It is a picture, a romance, a dream, all in one. It is our one corner that is the sun's very own."[4] In *Flowers of Our Lost Romance* he compares the respective traditions arising from the settlement of the New World by the English and by the Spanish.

> The dour spirit of the Puritans made their taming of New England as unromantic as such a brave adventure could be. They despised Romance, and John Alden and Priscilla are about the one pathetic little flower of their century. The Spaniard, on the other hand, kept his childhood — his ideals and imagination and love of mystery and adventure, his chivalry and his warm humanity. He wasn't ashamed to show that he had feelings. It is no wonder that the discovery and the taming of the New World by such spirits has given us four centuries of uninterrupted and infinitely varied Romance.[5]

The fact that the Spaniards were in Mexico a century before the arrival of the English on the eastern shores of North America has impressed Americans with the sense that Mexico is more tradition-laden, more intimately connected with the Old World. Stephen Crane when he was in Mexico City felt this link to the European past and expressed his sense of it in the story "The Wise Men." "The Paseo de la Reforma," he wrote, "is the famous drive of the City of Mexico, leading to the castle of Chapultepec, which last ought to be well known in the United States. It is a broad, fine avenue of macadam, with a much greater quality of dignity than anything of the kind we possess in our own land. It seems of the Old World, where to the beauty of the thing itself is added the solemnity of tradition and history, the knowledge that feet in buckskins trod the same stones, that cavalcades of steel thundered there before the coming of carriages."[6]

The flamboyant Joaquín Miller exploited to the full the "romantic" elements of the Hispanic Southwest and of Mexico. Because of the braggadocio in his own personality he emphasized not the serenities of the pastoral idyl but the high coloration, the extremes, the passion, swagger, and savagery of Mexican life. He too felt that Mexico was an extension of old Europe into the New World and expressed this concept in such poems as "The Tale of the Tall Alcide."

> Thou Italy of the Occident!
> Land of flowers and summer climes,
> Of holy priests and horrid crimes;
> Land of the cactus and sweet cocoa;
> Richer than all the Orient
> In gold and glory, in want and woe,
> In self-denial, in days misspent,
> In truth and treason, in gold and guilt,
> In ivied ruins and altars low,
> In batter'd walls and blood misspilt,
> Glorious, gory Mexico![7]

The idea persists among Americans that Mexico is the place to go for romance and adventure, and even some who know their Mexico well subscribe to it. The author of an excellent and realistic account of northern Mexico in the days of Pancho Villa admits unabashedly in the introduction to his book that he followed the revolutionary armies in search of "romantic adventure." Timothy G. Turner in *Bullets, Bottles, and Gardenias* goes on to comment on the regrettable preference among young Americans for machinery to high adventure, that older ideal which constituted a "mood which made life a delight to those who gave to it by living it, or even stayed home and dreamed it."[8]

To many American writers the epitome of all that was picturesque in Mexico could be found in the figure of the Mexican as horseman, the *vaquero,* the *charro.* In *Roughing It,* Mark Twain gave this description of the Mexican horsemen of the Southwest.

> I had never seen such wild, free, magnificent horsemanship outside of a circus as these picturesquely-clad Mexicans, Californians, and Mexicanized Americans displayed in Carson streets every day. How they rode! Leaning just gently forward out of the perpendicular, easy and nonchalant, with broad slouch-hat brim blown square up in front, and long *riata* swinging above the head, they swept through the town like the wind! The next minute they were only a sailing puff of dust on the far desert. If they trotted, they sat up gallantly and gracefully, and seemed part of the horse; did not go jiggering up and down after the silly Miss-Nancy fashion of the riding-schools.[9]

Joaquín Miller in *El Vaquero* celebrates the Mexican horseman in a poem whose first stanza, at least, rises in its freshness and sweep above the level of his usual conventional poetizing.

> His broad-brimm'd hat push'd back with careless air,
>     The proud vaquero sits his steed as free
> As winds that toss his black, abundant hair.
>     No rover ever swept a lawless sea
>     With such a fearless, heedless air as he,
> Who scorns the path and bounds with swift disdain
>     Away: a peon born, yet born to be
> A splendid king; behold him ride, and reign
> The only perfect monarch of the mottled plain.[10]

Charles Warren Stoddard yields nothing to Bret Harte when it comes to using stock characters and props for serving up an order of picturesque Californiana. In his description of the "Spanish" quarter of San Francisco, he peoples the section with types who remind him of *The Barber of Seville* and describes a "magnificent caballero," who "dashed by on a half-breed bronco" and "rode in the shade of a sombrero a yard wide, crusted with silver embroidery. His Mexican saddle was embossed with huge Mexican dollars; his jacket as gaily ornamented as a bullfighter's; his trousers open from the hip, and with a chain of silver buttons down their flapping hems; his spurs, huge wheels with murderous spikes, were fringed with little bells that jangled as he rode,—and this to the accompaniment of much strumming of guitars and the incense of cigarros."[11] Even when dismounted, the *charro* could cut a colorful figure. "Do but notice yonder Mexican in gorgeous array," wrote Sydney Lanier describing a street scene in old San Antonio, "promenading, intent upon instant subjugation of all his countrywomen in eyeshot! His black trousers with silver buttons down the seams, his jaunty hussar-jacket; his six-inch-brimmed felt *sombrero,* with marvelous silver-filigree upon all available spaces of it, save those occupied by the hat-band, which is like two silver snakes tied parallel around the crown; his red sash, serving at once to support the trousers and to inflate the full white shirt-bosom — what Mexicana can resist these things?"[12]

Frederick Remington's interest in the West went deeper than that of most of the local-color specialists. In his paintings, drawings, and descriptive writing he recorded the life of the open plains, a part of the American experience whose quality he admired and whose lifespan he knew must be short. He shared with his friend Stephen Crane an almost obsessive reverence for horses and horsemen. To both writers, the horseman in full gallop across a wide mesa represented not only mastery and adaption to a natural setting, but freedom and individuality, qualities of spirit hard to maintain in the face of the tyranny of the machine. In *Pony Tracks,* Remington describes approaching an hacienda in northern Mexico owned by an American friend, Jack.

> There lies the hacienda San José de Bavicora, gray and silent on the great plain, with the mountain standing guard against intruders, and over it the great blue dome of the sky, untroubled by clouds, except little flecks of vapor which stand, lost in immensity, burning bright like opals, as though discouraged from seeking the mountains or the sea whence they came. The marvellous color of the country beckons to the painter; its simple, natural life entrances the blond barbarian, with his fevered brain; and the gaudy *vaquero* and his trappings and his pony are the actors on this noble stage . . . . My imagination had never before pictured anything so wild as these leather-clad *vaqueros*. As they removed their hats to greet Jack, their unkept locks blew over their faces, back off their foreheads in the greatest disorder. They were clad in terracotta buckskin, elaborately trimmed with white leather, and around their lower legs wore heavy cowhide as a sort of legging. They were fully armed, and with their jingling spurs, their flapping ropes and buckskin strings, and with their gay *serapes* tied behind their saddles, they were as impressive a cavalcade of desert-scamperers as it has been my fortune to see.[13]

**By the time Hamlin Garland turned his attention to the Far West,**

the writing which produced the bitter realism of his middle-border stories was far behind him. He was ready to write to formula for money. He had a definite influence in establishing the prototype of the Western story, America's unique contribution to the "matter of romance." One of his more unlikely creations was a picturesque, half-Mexican sheriff, Delmar of Pima, who was the ancestor of a million sheriffs to follow. The improbability of this figure as a Mexican can be illustrated by the fact that he never drank anything stronger than lemonade. In fact he incorporated the virtues that Anglo-Saxons usually reserve for themselves, modesty, courage, and chastity. In the story "Delmar of Pima" he appears as the constant champion of those perennial underdogs of the old West, the sheepmen and the Mexicans. He finally forced a showdown with his enemies, the big cattlemen and their cowboy employees, as well as with the local judge and the county attorney, both in the pay of the cattle interests. They had all gathered at "Charley's Place" to celebrate their anticipated victory over "the greaser sheriff." In the midst of the celebrations, "Delmar walked in quietly, without hurry and without bluster. Every man in the room was his enemy, and every one was armed but himself. He moved straight toward the group at the table, and as he came, their faces set in surprise and fear. His approach was as sinister as the movement of a wildcat, but his smoothly-shaven face was fair as a boy's, and his broad hat sat gracefully on his head. His small hands seemed to glisten like those of a woman, and his black suit suggested priests and undertakers."[14] The crowd disbanded before the sheriff's masterful glare and abandoned plans to install a rubber stamp sheriff in place of Delmar.

Bret Harte's version of the picturesque Mexican *caballero* is his characterization of the gallant Enríquez Saltillo. Enríquez appears in several of Harte's stories, and in one of them, as will be shown later, is used by the author to make some significant observations on the character and fate of the vanishing Mexican aristocrats of the Southwest. However, in the story "'The Devotion of Enríquez" Harte simply gives an extravagantly heightened version of what the gallant, intense, passionate, pleasure-loving and volatile "Spanish" Californian was supposed to be like. All this high coloration is not without its literary intent, as it serves the author by way of contrast in his satirical treatment of an American bluestocking type, the beautiful, puritanical, "liberal," and always "interested" Miss Mannersley, daughter of a Congregational minister. Rainie Mannersley first encounters Enríquez shortly after her arrival in California when she goes to observe a dance in order to pick up some local color. Among the dancers is Enríquez Saltillo, whose antics on this occasion are later described by an American friend.

> I have a vivid recollection of him in the mysteries of the *semicuacua*, a somewhat corybantic dance which left much to the invention of the performers, and very little to the imagination of the spectator. In one of the figures a gaudy handkerchief, waved more or less gracefully by dancer and danceuse before the dazzled eyes of each other, acted as love's signal, and was used to express alternate admiration and indifference, shyness and audacity, fear and transport, coyness and coquetry, as the dance proceeded. I need not say that Enríquez's pantomimic illustration of these emotions was peculiarly extravagant; but it was always performed and accepted with a gravity that was an essential feature of the dance. At such times sighs would escape him which were supposed to portray the incipient stages of passion; snorts of jealousy burst from him at the suggestion of a rival; he was overtaken by a sort of St. Vitus's dance that expressed his timidity in making the first advances of affection; the scorn of his lady-love struck him with something like a dumb ague; and a single gesture of invitation from her produced marked delirium. All this was very like Enríquez; but on the particular occasion to which I refer I think no one was prepared to see him begin the figure with the waving of *four* handkerchiefs! Yet this he did, pirouetting, capering — brandishing his silken signals like a ballerina's kerchief in the languishment or fire of passion, until, in a final figure, where the conquered and submitting fair one usually sinks into the arms of her partner, need it be said that the ingenious Enríquez was found in the centre of the floor supporting four of the dancers!

Miss Mannersley, in spite of her determination to show a liberally appreciative interest in the customs of the natives, is somewhat aghast at this open display of eroticism. However, she manages to say to the American friend of Enríquez: " 'Do tell me — is he real?' . . . 'You know what I mean.' 'Is he quite sane? Does he do that because he likes it, or is he paid for it?' "[15] But after Enríquez serenades her, fights bulls for her, and rides wild horses for her, the intellectual, interested-in-everything, haughty and puritanical Miss Mannersley elopes with him.

The theme of Mexican style as represented by the particular elegance of the caballero is still to be found in American writing. Wallace Stevens treats the idea subtly in the poem "The Pastor Caballero." Here the *caballero* is no longer the original warrior horseman, the conquistador with his "formidable helmet." The change in headgear from helmet to broad-brimmed hat has in itself affected the very essence of the man, giving him a new style, eloquent in the ways of peace. This heightened style so affects the poet-observer that his spirit, despite awareness of human mortality in a natural world which is itself mortal (man bears poisoned laurels in a poisoned wood), soars to its "total height." The *caballero* has become pastoral.

> The importance of its hat to a form becomes
> More definite. The sweeping brim of the hat
> Makes of the form Most Merciful Capitán,
> If the observer says so: grandiloquent
> Locution of a hand in a rhapsody.
> Its line moves quickly with the genius
> Of its improvisation until, at length,
> It enfolds the head in a vital ambiance,
> A vital, linear ambiance. The flare
> In the sweeping brim becomes the origin
> Of a human evocation, so disclosed
> That, nameless, it creates an affectionate name,
> Derived from adjectives of deepest mine.
> The actual form bears outwardly this grace,
> An image of the mind, an inward mate,
> Tall and unfretted, a figure meant to bear
> Its poisoned laurels in this poisoned wood,
> High in the height that is our total height.
> The formidable helmet is nothing now.
> These two go well together, the sinuous brim
> And the green flauntings of the hours of peace.[16]

In another poem, "The Revolutionists Stop for Orangeade," Stevens treats various aspects of Mexican style and compresses a great deal into a few short verses. The "capitán profundo, capitan geloso [sic] (jealous and profound captain), though an officer in one of the Mexican revolutionary armies, nevertheless falls heir to the Castilian tradition of the warrior gentleman with his cult of honor and exaggerated sense of personal dignity. He and his fellow officers are commanding a group of street musicians to play for them. These strolling musicians, the famous *mariachis* of Mexico, take over, in this instance the role of ancient court musicians and jesters. The leader of the group of players, while clearly ready to obey the command, wheedles with and yet mocks the *capitán* in requesting not to be made to play while standing in the sun. The *mariachis* in their swagger and outlandish gear give an air of mock heroics to their singing. The big-bellied, outsized guitars (guitarrones) of the *mariachis* force the players to assume grotesque attitudes, and the songs themselves, sung in the traditional falsetto and with voices "rougher than a grinding shale," become a very parody of music. And in the seeming parody of song, the appearance and gestures of the musicians and the quality of the singing mysteriously enhance the essential pathos of music. Meanwhile, the plebian *capitán* is being serenaded not in the festive halls of a Spanish castle while drinking wine but at a roadside stand while drinking orangeade.

> Capitán profundo, capitán geloso,
> Ask us not to sing standing in the sun,
> Hairy-backed and hump-armed,
> Flat-ribbed and big-bagged.
> There is no pith in music
> Except in something false.
> Bellissimo, pomposo,
> Sing a song of serpent-kin,
> Necks among the thousand leaves,
> Tongues around the fruit.
> Sing in clownish boots
> Strapped and buckled bright.
> Wear the breeches of a mask,
> Coat half-flare and half galloon;
> Wear a helmet without reason,
> Tufted, tilted, twirled, and twisted.
> Start the singing in a voice
> Rougher than a grinding shale.
> Hang a feather by your eye,
> Nod and look a little sly.
> Thus must be the vent of pity,
> Deeper than a truer ditty
> Of the real that wrenches
> Of the quick that's wry.[17]

Paul Horgan, a man with a thorough sense of the contribution of Mexico to the feeling and tone of life in the American Southwest, sees the Mexicans as remaining picturesque figures even while adapting to American ways. The very superficiality of the adaptation, leaving so much of the original style and nature intact, seems to add a charming air of irrelevance to the way they go about their daily tasks.

> A humorous, fatalistic, and lively people, they contribute all the color to the landscape that a Latin temperament can. Their rogueries, their intrigues, their dances with guitars and brawls, their solemn marriages with white veils and enormous parties of cheering relatives and friends, their dark religious concern in the fraternity of the Penitentes, their genius for a politics that cries aloud with ingenuity and passion and irrelevance — all contribute to the astonishing spectacle of an American citizenry that preserves some antique and Southern sprightliness.
>   Even the thoroughness with which Mexican boys and girls go American is somehow irresistible. If the Indians are a tragic race in the loss of their true style, then the Mexicans (or Spanish Americans, as the more self-conscious insist on being called) — the Mexicans are irresistibly eager and droll and likable .... What makes them so engaging in spite of their masquerade as hundred

per cent Americans is the awareness they seem to have that whatever you do it can't be as important as all *that;* and this lack of intensity in the daily routine lets them laugh and dance, really dance, not shuffle around with a disguised exhaustion; it lets them make love with originality and delight; it frees their tempers and somebody gets knifed or shot and that's not so good, but hell (they say), it'll come out Aw-Kay.[18]

Aside from those American writers who have evoked the pastoral California idyl or who have felt drawn to Mexico as being closer in spirit to parental Europe or who have exploited the picturesqueness of certain Mexican types such as the horseman, there are those writers who in a more general way have responded to the color, beauty, and exoticism of Mexico. Carl Sandburg in *Smoke and Steel* uses the figure of a Mexican woman dancing to convey a sense of the exoticism and passion that Mexico has contributed to the tone of American life.

> The lady in red, she in the chile con carne red,
> Brilliant as the shine of a pepper crimson in the summer sun,
> She behind a false-face, the much sought-after dancer,
>     the most sought-after dancer of all in this masquerade,
> The lady in red sox and red hat, ankles of willow,
>     crimson arrow amidst the Spanish clashes of music,
>     I sit in a corner
>     watching her dance first with one man
>     and then another.[19]

Witter Bynner in one of the poems from the volume *Indian Earth* describes a beautiful Mexican woman as being a microcosm of the sunset of Chapala.

> There where she sips her wine, her copper brow
> Is itself the sunset. Her eyes are lifted now,
> Her eyes are evening-stars. I have seen many
> Chapala sunsets — but never before have I seen one
> Come down from the mountain to be a beautiful woman,
> To shadow a table with a dusk of light
> From a bare arm and then, alas, to rise
> And turn and go, leaving a sudden darkness.[20]

The attraction which Americans have felt toward Mexico has been similar in quality to that felt, over the centuries, by Englishmen and Germans toward Italy. Much of it is purely visual or sensual, the nostalgia of the northerner with his chilblains for the splendor and warmth of the lost Eden. Wallace Stevens, who has been characterized by Lionel Abel as being essentially the "poet of feasts and festivals" whose proper language is "the language of vacations,"[21] was drawn to celebrating in verse those places in the Western Hemisphere that North Americans seek out for their vacations. Mexico has been especially attractive to him. In a passage in "The Comedian as the Letter C," he splashes bright colors on his page taken from the tropical state of Yucatán in southern Mexico.

> In Yucatan, the Maya sonneteers
> Of the Caribbean amphitheatre,
> In spite of hawk and falcon, green toucan
> And jay, still to the night-bird made their plea,
> As if raspberry tanagers in palms,
> High up in orange air, were barbarous.[22]

Again in "Sea Surface Full of Clouds" he expresses the aesthetic exaltation he feels when experiencing the exotic hues of the southern sea off Tehuantepec, a sensation which is sharpened by the sudden and brief intrusion of the natural savagery of storm to be followed by the quick return of the cajoling sun.

> In that November off Tehuantepec
> The night-long slopping of the sea grew still.
> A mallow morning dozed upon the deck
> And made one think of musky chocolate
> And frail umbrellas. A too-fluent green
> Suggested malice in the dry machine
> Of ocean, pondering dank strategem.
> Who then beheld the figures of the clouds
> Like blooms secluded in the thick marine?
> Like blooms? Like damasks that were shaken off
> From the loosed girdles in the spangling mist.
> *C'etait ma foi, la nonchalance divine.*
> The nakedness would rise and suddenly turn
> Salt masks of beard and mouths of bellowing,
> Would — But more suddenly the heaven rolled
> Its bluest sea-clouds in the thinking green,
> And the nakedness became the broadest blooms,
> Mile-mallows that a mallow sun cajoled.[23]

The fact that the American reader had become conditioned in the "romantic" treatment of Mexico allowed writers to use this tradition to produce unexpected effects. The usual exotic image could be suddenly lifted to reveal a squalid reality beneath, or the whole "romantic" tradition could serve for purposes of satire or burlesque. John Gould Fletcher in the poem "Mexican Quarter" juxtaposes the objective reality of squalor with the subjective realities of fantasy and passionate yearning.

> By an alley with tumble-down shacks,
> And street-lamps askew, half-sputtering,
> Feebly glimmering on gutters choked with filth, and dogs
> Scratching their mangy backs.

girl dreams:

"Stars if I could reach you
(You are so very clear that it seems as if I could reach you)
I would give you all to the Madonna's image
On the gray plastered altar behind the paper flowers,
So that Juan would come back to me,
And we could live again those lazy, burning hours."

down the street a man squats, playing a guitar and humming:

"Think not that at your window I wait.
New love is better, the old is turned to hate.
Fate! Fate! All things pass away;
Life is forever, youth is but for a day.
Love again if you may."[24]

Frank Norris in *The Octopus* contrasts the California idyl with the reality of the crushing power of the railroad. The novel concerns itself with the struggle of California farmers with the railroad company at the close of the nineteenth century. The farmers, totally dependent upon the railroad to carry their crops to market, were exploited by the company which charged excessive freight rates. Any farmer who rebelled against the tyranny of the railroad found that special and ruinous rates were quoted for him. The book climaxed in a scene in which a group of farmers who had organized to defy the railroad were bloodily defeated by armed agents of the company. One of the characters of the novel was a would-be poet named Presley, who had come to California for his health and was staying on the ranch of a friend. Presley dreamed of writing the great epic of the West but felt, as he first surveyed the scene around him, that the struggle of the farmers and ranchers for a livelihood was essentially a dull matter and no material for epic poetry. There was a little town close by called Guadalajara dating back to the era before the American conquest. Presley found in the Mexican inhabitants of this town something more colorful, closer to his preconceptions of the romantic West. "These Spanish-Mexicans, decayed, picturesque, vicious, and romantic, never failed to interest Presley. A few of them still remained in Guadalajara, drifting from the saloon to the restaurant, and from the restaurant to the Plaza, relics of a former generation, standing for a different order of things, absolutely idle, living God knew how, happy with their cigarette, their guitar, their glass of mescal, and their siesta." Presley, while wandering around Guadalajara, fell in with an ancient Mexican, a centenarian, who told him about the old days when the great hacienda owned by De La Cuesta flourished. Describing a wedding at the hacienda, the centenarian told Presley that " 'for a week all the town of Guadalajara was in fete. There were bullfights in the Plaza — this very one — for five days, and to each of his tenants-in-chief, De La Cuesta gave a horse, a barrel of tallow, an ounce of silver, and half an ounce of gold dust. Ah, those were days. That was a gay life. This'— he made a comprehensive gesture with his left hand —'this is stupid.' " Presley agreed with him, feeling discouraged. The days of romance were over. He had lived too late. Getting up from where he had been sitting with the centenarian, he offered the old man a cigarette which the Mexican accepted "with the air of a grandee," offering his own snuff box in return. Presley declined saying " 'I was born too late for that . . . for that, and for many other things. Adiós.' "[25]

That evening at sunset Presley mounted a hill which overlooked an old Mexican mission church which also dated back to the early times. As he gazed at the mission he began to regain his earlier confidence that it was within his power to write the great epic of the West.

> Never had he so nearly grasped his inspiration as at that moment on the hill-top. Even now, though the sunset was fading, though the wide reach of valley was shut from sight, it still kept him company. Now the details came thronging back, the component parts of his poem, the signs and symbols of the West. It was there, close at hand, he had been in touch with it all day. It was in the centenarian's vividly coloured reminiscences — De La Cuesta, holding his grant from the Spanish crown, with his power of life and death; the romance of his marriage; the white horse with its pillion of red leather and silver bridle mountings; the bull fights in the Plaza; the gifts of gold dust, and horses and tallow . . . the sunsets behind the altar-like mesas, the banking desolation of the deserts; the strenuous, fierce life of forgotten towns, down there, far off, lost below the horizon of the southwest; the sonorous music of unfamiliar names — Quijotoa, Uintah, Sonora, Laredo, Uncompahgre. It was in the mission with its cracked bells, its decaying walls, its venerable sun dial, its fountain and old garden, and in the Mission Fathers themselves, the priests, the padres, planting the first wheat and oil and wine to produce the elements of the Sacrament — a trinity of great industries taking their rise in a religious rite.
> 
> Abruptly, as if in confirmation, Presley heard the sound of a bell from the direction of the Mission itself. It was the *de Profundis,* a note of the Old World; of the ancient regime, an echo from the hillsides of mediaeval Europe, sounding there in this new land, unfamiliar and strange at this end-of-the-century time.

But Presley was jarred out of this revery by an accident which he could witness from his hilltop. A train engine had ploughed into a flock of sheep, mangling their bodies and throwing them in all directions, soaking the railroad ties with "black blood, winking in the starlight." Presley was horror-struck. "The sweetness was gone from the evening, the sense of peace, of security, and placid contentment was stricken from the landscape. The hideous ruin in the engine's path drove all thought of his poem from his mind. The inspiration vanished like a mist. The *de Profundis* had ceased to ring." Presley rushed away, almost running across the ranch land. When he paused for breath, the night seemed to have regained its silence.

> Then, faint and prolonged, across the levels of the ranch, he heard the engine whistling for Bonneville. Again and again, at rapid intervals in its flying course, it whistled for road crossings, for sharp curves, for trestles; ominous notes, hoarse, bellowing, ringing with the accents of menace and defiance; and abruptly Presley saw again, in his imagination, the galloping monster, the terror of steel and steam, with its single eye, cyclopean, red, symbol of a vast power, huge, terrible, flinging the echo of its thunder over all the reaches of the valley, leaving blood and destruction in its path; the leviathan, with tentacles of steel clutching into the soil, the soulless Force, the iron-hearted Power, the monster, the Colossus, the Octopus.[26]

Robinson Jeffers in many of his poems establishes some kind of relationship between his principal characters, usually American, and the descendants of the darker, more earthy, more openly passionate people who once held the land. These people, Indians and Mexicans, rooted in the ancient California past, provide an important background for the action of the poems. Sometimes, rather than introducing a contemporary Mexican or Indian, Jeffers will conjure up the earlier peoples in the form of visions or dreams. In "The Coast-Range Christ," a young and passionate woman, Peace O'Farrell, has a dream which begins as the typical "romantic" vision of the old Carmel Mission as it functioned in Mexican times but which changes, as subconscious guilt feelings about advances she has made to the handsome and very religious Christian David assert themselves, into images and sequences symbolically sexual in tone. Her husband is an old man, and she has for a long time been thwarted.

> Peace dreamed marvelously all night and Carmel Mission the desolate church
> Grown much larger and more lovely and belted with a shining porch
> Of enormous pillars blazed with rozy light, the whole beauty was hers,
> All her blood went wild to feel the aisles fill up with worshippers.
> Indians and all sorts of men, and women with sheer silk bridal veils,

> Bold vaqueros with broad spurs and bandit captains out of old tales.
> Soldiers too, thousands of soldiers, bayonet-carriers, beautiful killers.
> Tall Americans and short Frenchmen shouldering the crowd in the shadow of the pillars.
> First the worshippers adored the small star-window over the door,
> While the door moved eagerly wide for the entrance of multitudes more and more.
> Then the sweet silver and terrible bells rang out wild welcome and swayed the domed steeple,
> While the sucking wings of the doorway pulsed and quivered for the entrance of people.
> Next the multitude adored the crucifix over the high stone altar,
> There a serpent for Christ was hanging, the whole crowd worshipped and did not falter.
> Wild choirs of boys' voices peeled, in unison all the roof-tiles rang,
> All the rafters gave a silver noise and all the columns sang.
> Sepulchered saints beneath the altar began to sing for Peace and to call.
> She — her vestment silks were torn and she would be shamed before them all.
> Her the crowd awaited, now it was crying her name, it howled like a wolf,
> Horrible fears ran blind through her body, a luxury of shame, what hiding, what gulf?
> Suddenly out of a smell of ferns and streams, out of the quiet hill-mist,
> David came and clasped her shoulders, "Come with me Peace, we will see Christ."
> Though her body was naked he did not see nor mind, her mouth was chill
> With sweet water and canyon streams, and death it seemed, in the sleep of the hill.
> When the gates of the east were widened, the wan stars gathered home their gleams,
> Golden-haired the gorgeous day came out of the valley to kill dreams.[27]

John Houghton Allen in the novel *Southwest* burlesqued the "romantic" treatment of things Mexican through the reactions of two of his characters, Jerry and Pete, ingenuous young men visiting the Southwest for the first time. The little Mexican-American town in Texas immediately struck them as the place for adventure and romance. They were enchanted by the crooked and cobble-stoned streets, by the haphazardly leaning houses looking like "dwellings in the land of Oz," by the windows "bellied out in the street" behind whose iron bars "and in these very United States" gazed dark-haired señoritas "like Christian slaves." These, of course, were being serenaded by caballeros strumming their guitars. Jerry and Pete fancied they saw assassins lurking in alleys, and the only time the place was dead was during the "sacred siesta" when the town "looked like something enchanted out of *La Belle au Bois Dormant*." But at four o'clock in the afternoon "citizens always awoke, they struggled alive as from the effects of drugs, and there was renewed activity in the plaza, the shouting and gregarious Mexicans carrying on their business with holiday spirit."[28]

Katherine Anne Porter, in the story "That Tree," also satirizes the "romantic" concept of Mexico. The protagonist, a young man described as being one of the "talented untalented," decides to become a poet and goes to Mexico as an obvious place for a poet to go to. He idealizes the young Mexican poets and painters he gets to know. Their poverty is virtue, their free sexuality a fine naturalism. His fiancée, a teacher from Minnesota, comes to Mexico to marry him. Shocked by his bohemianism, she ridicules his quixotic ideal of the artist and maintains that his Mexican artist friends are just looking for the main chance. Their later defection to the movies and other commercial enterprises proves her right, and her very rightness makes him hate her. Yet his American tradition of work and success, a heritage which he has tried so hard to throw off in favor of the poetic life under "that tree," rises up to take sides with her. When she leaves him, he goes in for a career, becoming a successful journalist of Latin American affairs. She, two divorces later, writes asking him to take her back. He does. After all, his whole later career has been an attempt to show her that he could achieve success on her terms.[29]

Katherine Anne Porter's satire on the bohemian life in Mexico City does not indicate that association with the artists' life in Mexico had nothing to offer a North American writer. After announcing that "I have an affinity for Latin Americans, and the Spanish language I have always loved,"[30] American black poet Langston Hughes describes a winter he spent in Mexico City among painters and writers. He got to know the Mexican muralist Diego Rivera well and also became acquainted with "the sad Orozoco [sic] and the talkative Siqueros [sic]." Miguel Covarrubias was a constant companion. Hughes found the whole experience a bracing one and one which allowed him to catch up on something that he had missed.

> I never lived in Greenwich Village in New York, so its bohemian life — in the old days when it was bohemian — was outside my orbit. Although once I lived for a year in Montmartre in Paris, I lived there as a worker, not an artist. So the nearest I've ever come to *la vie de bohème* was my winter in Mexico when my friends were almost all writers and artists like Juan de la Cabada, Maria Izquierdo, Luis Cardoza y Aragon, Manuel Bravo, Rufino Tamayo and Francesca

and Nellie Campobello. Most of my friends were almost always broke, or very nearly so. But then we didn't care.[31]

Nevertheless, recent decades have seen very specific repudiations of the "romantic" tradition which has governed the treatment in American literature of Mexico, the Southwest, and the West generally. Harvey Fergusson grumbled that what ailed "the huge and infantile body of our conventional Western romance, from Beadle's dime novels on down," was the result of its having been "sired by Sir Walter Scott and dammed by the Genteel Tradition."[32]

Mary Austin, in the autobiography *Earth Horizon,* written toward the end of her long career as a writer on things Southwestern, attacked the California myth. Referring to herself simply as Mary, she wrote concerning her first reactions to California that "Mary was frightened; at least she was never more nearly frightened in her life; frightened of the commonplaceness of intention behind the exploded [real estate] boom, the complete want of distinction in the human aspect of the country; frightened of the factitious effort of everybody to re-create a sense of the past out of sentiment for the Old Missions, out of 'Ramona,' a second-rate romance very popular at the time...."[33]

Ruth Tuck in *Not With the Fist,* a controlled but sharply indignant study of the treatment accorded to Mexican-Americans in California, is particularly contemptuous of that part of the California myth that maintains that the fine, old California families are of purely Spanish descent and not to be confused with the later, mongrelized immigrants that came up from Mexico. This myth allows "Anglos" in California to associate on equal terms with a few wealthy descendants of the old stock on the grounds that they are "Spanish," while maintaining segregationist policies toward the great majority of Mexican-Americans. Drawing upon population statistics, Ruth Tuck writes:

> By the time the colonization of the northern provinces began in earnest, racial and cultural fusion had been going on in Mexico for some three hundred years. It has been estimated that no more than 300,000 Spaniards ever came to Mexico and that most of them were men. The indigenous population of Mexico City alone was 300,000, and it was a small part of the total Indian population. The most robust Castilian gene, in such a situation, could hardly be expected to survive, unchanged, to populate Texas, New Mexico, Arizona, and California with descendants of "pure Spanish ancestry." But such is the fiction the romantic tradition likes to maintain.[34]

She then goes on to assert that the romantic tradition might better be revised to fit the facts, facts which themselves are remarkable enough to form the basis of worthy traditions. "The story would be more interesting for the re-telling. Instead of gilded artificialities about old Spain, why not the story of Rafael Bernal, the Pueblo Indian, and his heroic sons, in their fight for their riverside settlement, or the story of Dominga Valdez, the Amazon of the colonists, who drove trains of supplies through Indian ambushes? They were heroic, they were pioneers; in their time, they were the salt of the earth. They were *mestizos*. There is a cultural and genetic continuity between them and the later comers from Mexico."[35] However, she continues, stories such as these would not make such "fine escapist reading as the sentimentalized version." Furthermore, they would establish an unwanted connection between "old-Spanish" culture and the culture of present-day Mexicans in the Southwest. "It would do away with the convenient corollary . . . that any Mexican-American who is well-groomed, literate, and able must necessarily be from an 'old Spanish family,' and that the others, being of less exalted genetic origins, cannot be expected to attain literacy and/or cleanliness."[36]

In *North From Mexico,* Carey McWilliams makes a similar examination of the California myth. He has investigated the background of the revered "Spanish" founding fathers of Los Angeles and their families and has come up with some interesting facts.

> Los Angeles is merely one of the many cities in the borderlands which has fed itself on a false mythology for so long that it has become a well-fattened paradox. For example, the city boasts of the Spanish origin of its first settlers. Here are their names: Pablo Rodriguez, José Variegas, José Moreno, Felix Villavicencio, José de Lara, Antonio Mesa, Basilio Rosas, Alejandro Rosas, Antonio Navarro, and Manuel Camero. All "Spanish" names, all good "Spaniards" except — Pablo Rodríguez who was an Indian; José Variegas, first alcalde of the pueblo, also an Indian; José de Lara, also married to an Indian; Antonio Mesa, who was a Negro; Basilio Rosas, an Indian married to a mulatto; Alejandro Rosas, an Indian married to an Indian; Antonio Navarro, a mestizo with a mulatto wife; and Manuel Camero, a mulatto. The twelfth settler is merely listed as "a Chino" and was probably of Chinese descent. Thus of the original settlers of Our City the Queen of Angels, their wives included, two were Spaniards; one mestizo; two were Negroes; eight were mulattoes; and nine were Indians. None of this would really matter except that the churches in Los Angeles hold fiestas rather than bazaars and that Mexicans are still not accepted as a part of the community. When one examines how deeply this fantasy heritage has permeated the social and cultural life of the borderlands, the dichotomy begins to assume the proportion of a schizophrenic mania.[37]

There is a disgusted reference to the California myth in John Houghton Allen's novel *Southwest*. The protagonist is in one of the "dim, dirty cantinas" in a little town in southwest Texas listening to Ernesto Acuña, an old man who has been a *vaquero* all his life.

> He is an old, old man, his eyes are dim and watery and his face is wrinkled like a hide in the sun. The limed rafters and the once-white adobe walls of dame Margarita's cantina are a dirty yellow, there is a stench about the damp earth floor, and what the Mexicans call *animales* are in the thatched roof. The fat wench brings mescal and tequilla which have the flavor of wild pepper, and Ernesto and I talk until the cows come up . . . I listen to the rich raw words, and I marvel at the expression that the illiterate can have, and I feel like cheering — this is no idyll of the Californias, no besashed, singing and laughing vaqueros with long flapping toe-fenders to their stirrups or silver-mounted harness or jackets embroidered, but this is a tale of the violent and untamed, of the Old Times, told by the last of the Old Men as he spits on the dirt floor drinks tequilla — with a lick of salt and lemon to make it flavory — in the background the ruins of the walled town of San Juan, which was his *patria*, his own country.[38]

Most of the characters and objects that provided the local color material for the writers of the "romantic" tradition in Southwestern literature were associated with the Mexican big house with its feudalistic trappings. It was the revelation that a way of life existed within the continental limits of the United States — a way of life indolent, elegant, colorful, and deeply traditional that so attracted late nineteenth and early twentieth century readers to the literature of the "romantic" idyl of the Southwest. But at the very time that American readers were first becoming aware of the culture of the big house, the way of life which that culture expressed had almost totally collapsed. The defeat and dispossession of the dons, an episode that had much of poignancy in it, was a tale which remained, except for a liimited treatment of it by a few writers, untold at the time that it was happening. To be sure, the account of the life of Señora Moreno in *Ramona* gives the reader the notion that life in California for the old "Spanish" families was not to continue as it was before the American conquest. However, Señora Moreno, though she lost much of her old estate to the Americans, still was left with considerable holdings and lived out her days maintaining her aristocratic hauteur. The novel did achieve psychological realism in the description of the Señora's state of mind toward the Americans. "Any race under the sun would have been to the Señora less hateful than the American. She had scorned them in her girlhood, when they came trading to post after post. She scorned them still. The idea of being forced to wage a war with peddlers was to her too monstrous to be believed. In the outset she had no doubt that the Mexicans would win in the contest."[39] The Señora's son, Felipe, grew to hate the Americans more as he got to know them better.

> Year by year the conditions of life in California were growing more distasteful to him. The methods, aims, standards of the fast incoming Americans were to him odious. Their boasted successes, the crowding of colonies, schemes of settlement and development, — all were disagreeable and irritating. The passion for money and reckless spending of it, the great fortunes made in one hour, thrown away in another, savored to Felipe's mind more of brigandage and gambling than of the occupations of gentlemen. He loathed them. Life under the new government grew more and more intolerable to him; both his hereditary instincts and prejudices, and his temperament, revolted.[40]

Bret Harte's story "The Passing of Enríquez" is in several ways a pivotal one. It represents both the "romantic" tradition and the later realism in treating the fate of the dons. The hero of the story, a figure typical in many ways of the "romantic" approach to the "Spanish" caballero of California, is the same Enríquez who won Miss Mannersley. Yet here, as is often the case, Harte has more to say than might strike the casual reader out for a good yarn of the picturesque Southwest. Though Enriquez's Hispanicized English is made to be amusingly quaint, the story is essentially a serious one in which the author comments on the values of the Mexican landed gentry as contrasted to those of the incoming Americans. The dons were an uncommercial people, and they in fact retained something of the old Spanish chivalric code. Bret Harte's Enríquez Saltillo, for all his levity, is shown as possessing a strong sense of Spanish honor. He discovers a new vein of gold in a mine which has been on his ancestral estate for generations and brings in some Yankee capitalists to help him in the development of a large-scale mining operation. He is apparently on his way to riches when the geologist whom he has hired, Dobbs, discovers what is known among miners as a "horse," an underground obstruction in the path of the vein of metal. Sometimes the vein goes down under or around the "horse," and other times the "horse" stops the vein completely. Members of the board of the company which has been formed for the mine put great pressure on Dobbs not to mention the "horse" in preliminary reports to potential investors. Dobbs allows himself to be bought off, but Enríquez is affronted in his Spanish sense of honor. In a conversation with an American friend he recapitulates the speech he made to other members of the board.

> I say that for three hundred year my family have held the land of thees mine; that it pass from father to son, and from son to son; it pass by gift, it pass by grant but that *nevarre there pass a lie with it!* I say it was a gift by a Spanish Christian king to a Christian hidalgo for the spread of the gospel, and not for the cheat and swindler. I say that if they have struck the hoss in the mine, they have struck a hoss *in the land,* a Spanish hoss; a hoss that have no bridle worth five thousand dollar in his mouth, but a hoss to rear, and a hoss that cannot be struck out by a Yankee geologian; and that hoss is Enríquez Saltillo![41]

When it becomes apparent to the former Miss Mannersley that Enríquez is not going to accommodate the board, she leaves him. He sells out his interest in the mine and retires in relative poverty to the remaining corner of his estate where he and his infant son, while horseback riding, are swallowed into a wide crevice during an earthquake. Since Enríquez has predicted his imminent death and since one does not usually pick the time of an earthquake to go horseback riding, suicide is implied.

The story of Enríquez, for all its quixoticism, points the way toward the treatment by later American writers of the episode of the destruction of the Mexican big house and its culture by American entrepreneurs. In one of the stories in Paul Horgan's *The Return of the Weed,* a book containing a group of Southwestern tales centered on the theme of the cyclical nature of human enterprises, a pathetic portrait is given of a reduced New Mexican aristocrat, Don Elizario. The time of the story is the late eighteen hundreds. By one device or another, the Yankees have taken possession, over the course of the years, of the lands which comprised Don Elizario's estate. The Don "knew it was true, and that it was a pity, that he simply wasn't smart enough to hold his money against these newcomers, these exhausting gringos. A gentleman didn't have to be smart about money, this he knew also. They got it all, of course. He saw it go, he watched their operations with a helpless affability."[42] Here is a theme familiar to those who know the literature of the post-bellum American South, that of the reduction of a chivalric, cultured, impractical, and traditionalist aristocracy by a new element in society that is cultureless and unscrupulous but vigorous and enterprising. Several of the American characters in the Southwestern literature devoted to the theme of the destruction of the Mexican big house resemble the conquering Snopeses of the Faulkner novels treating with the downfall of the Southern landed gentry.

*In Those Days,* one of the trilogy of novels in Fergusson's *Followers of the Sun,* chronicles the career of Robert Jayson, a Connecticut Yankee who arrived in New Mexico as a young man in the eighteen eighties. Jayson, a trader and merchant, was competent but not unscrupulous. He viewed with some sympathy the plight of the former owners of the New Mexico territory. Shortly after his arrival in the area he met Diego Aragón, a young man his own age, who was the scion of an old and at that time still influential Mexican family. Robert could not look at Diego without a feeling of envy. The young Mexican had all the assurance of one to the manner born, an ease, for instance, with women and horses which Robert knew he could never duplicate. "And Diego always made him think of all that stood behind the man — of the great Aragón house he had never entered and the sheep by tens of thousands and the horses and the peons and the silver." And yet, Jayson thought, "take all that away from him and what would be left of Diego? Nothing! He didn't know how to work . . . . Looking at Diego, Robert always felt small and inadequate, but he also felt within himself an immense capacity for patient toil."[43] This capacity resulted in Jayson's becoming in time a substantial citizen of an Albuquerque that had been totally transformed by the "gringos" within a period of a few years. During the same period, Diego had been selling his lands to keep up an aristocratic and self-indulgent way of life. For a while there was a place for him in the new, bustling Albuquerque. He was elected sheriff, a role in which he could bring to bear his "caballero" qualities of fearlessness and good horsemanship. On one occasion he single-handedly broke up a riot, riding into the tumult on a big bay horse. "With a drawn gun he made the mob scatter like sheep before a thunderstorm . . . . Robert would never forget how Diego looked that day, a perfect horseman, hatless and gun in hand, smashing a riot by the sheer force of a courage nobody could match. It made Robert feel again as he had felt when he first met Diego — an envious unwilling admiration — a conviction of something lacking in himself."[44] However, Diego's days of glory came to an end when reform groups voted him out of the sheriff's post because of his Latin procedures. He "had a way, irritating to finicky persons, of usurping the functions of the judiciary." His political career was further ruined when his "gringo" wife, in divorcing him, brought to public disclosure his infidelities, "for Diego was as naturally polygamous as a buck in November."[45] From this point on Diego slipped into ruin, ending up fat, dissipated, and bewildered in the old family house, bereft of furnishings, silverware, and jewelry, which had all been sold, and surrounded by the few acres of land left of what had once been an immense estate.

> And Diego was not alone in his ruin. Almost all of the old Mexican families had lost their money and land, had fallen to pieces just as their great houses had done — those huge sprawling homesteads, with walls four feet thick, built around two and sometimes

three courtyards, covering often an acre of ground. There had been one of them every few miles along the valley from Taos to El Paso. With their wide lands about them, their great storerooms full of wheat and grain, their troops of servants and their prolific women, they had seemed as safe and permanent as anything man could build. But the railroad wiped them out. The Mexicans were no good at business and couldn't make money enough to keep them up. The hands of slaves had built them and kept them intact by incessant plastering. When they were deserted their mighty walls melted in the rain like sugar.[46]

In *The Blood of the Conquerors,* the last of the three novels in the trilogy, Fergusson describes more precisely the methods by which the Mexican landowners were dispossessed. The protagonist is young Ramón Delcasar, last in the line of a once powerful New Mexican family. He hopes to gain an inheritance from his uncle, Don Diego, and watches dismayed as the old man is systematically fleeced by his partner James MacDougall. One evening while at a dance Ramón's eye alights on the spectacle of his uncle dancing in a stiff and formal way with the wife of James MacDougall.

Don Diego was a big, paunchy Mexican with a smooth brown face, strikingly set off by fierce white whiskers. His partner was a tall, tight-lipped angular woman, who danced painfully, but with determination. The two had nothing to say to each other, but both of them smiled resolutely, and the Don visibly perspired under the effort of steering his inflexible friend.

Although he did not formulate the idea, this couple was to Ramón a symbol of the disgust with which the life of his native town inspired him. Here was the Mexican sedulously currying favour with the gringo, who robbed him for his pains. And here was the specific example of that relation which promised to rob Ramón of his heritage.

For the gringos he felt a cold hostility — a sense of antagonism and difference — but it was his senile and fatuous uncle, the type of his own defeated race, whom he despised.[47]

Later, when Don Diego finally realizes the extent to which he is being taken, he cries out to Ramón:

"But these gringos . . . They have got my money. That is all they want. My boy, all gringos are alike. They want nothing but money. They can hear the rattle of a peso as far as a burro can smell a bear. They are mean, stingy! Ah, my boy! It is not now as it was in the old days. Then money counted for nothing! Then a man could throw away his last dollar and there were always friends to give him more. But now your dollars are your only true friends, and when you have lost them, you are alone indeed. Ah, my boy! The old days were the best!" The old Don bent his head over his hands and wept.[48]

# The Passing of Enríquez    161

Fortunately for Ramón's heritage, the old man dies before the process of robbing him has been completed. James MacDougall would with comparative ease have gained possession of the remainder of Don Diego's lands, but in Ramón he has a different kind of man to deal with. MacDougall, a Snopes type, typifies the "gringo" businessman out to dispossess the Mexican. With grubbing patience, hard work, and absolute lack of scruple, he has made a fortune from nothing. Little by little he takes over land from the Mexicans. Those that will not sell their land outright to him (for an amount which seems to the simple-minded among Mexican peasants to be a staggering amount of cash, since they seldom see money, but which in fact will be "blown" in a year's time) often end up by ceding their lands to him because they cannot pay back loans he has made to them. The *ricos,* unable to adjust to the "gringo" business world and wanting to continue indolent and elegant lives, gradually sell their lands to such as MacDougall and end up impoverished, becoming submerged into the mass of poor Mexicans.

Ramón Delcasar sets out to defy MacDougall, to prevent the Mexicans from the Rio Arriba from selling out to him, to preserve his own lands, and to become a political power. Significantly, his main motive, aside from hatred of the "gringo," is his desire to win a "gringo" girl, Julia Roth, daughter of wealthy and socially prominent people. Ramón throws off his accustomed indolence, goes into the Rio Arriba country and rallies the people against the "gringo." He discovers unsuspected talents as a demagogue. He even joins the Penitentes for the political influence this action will give him among the upland Mexicans, enduring stoically the initiation lashes. However, when the girl, submitting to her parents, allows herself to be taken East in order to prevent the match, Ramón is totally deflated. Motives such as MacDougall's cannot sustain his drive. He is not acquisitive in the "gringo" sense. Gradually deteriorating, he loses himself in drink and amorous affairs, and finally buys an old hacienda which he can ranch without too much effort. There he suns himself, drinks red wine, relieves himself sexually with a peasant woman housekeeper, and concedes the victory to the gringos.

Conrad Richter in *The Lady*[49] tells a story of the last days of Hispanic feudalism as a force in New Mexico. The action of the novel takes place in Santa Fe at the turn of the century. The occasion of a murder suddenly aligns old feudalistic loyalties against the forces of the new usurping element in New Mexican society. The central figure of the book is Ellen Sessions, a descendant of an old and landed English-Mexican family, Johnson y Campo. Her husband, Judge Sessions, represents the group of early American settlers in New Mexico which had become to a considerable extent Hispanicized. Snell Beasly, a lawyer, typifies the new American element. Shrewd, ruthless, and patient, he has been acquiring wealth and property, mostly at the expense of the old families. The book is principally an analysis of that aspect of the feudal mind which claims immunity from the ordinary processes of law. Ellen Sessions in her own way is as ruthless as Beasly, but she also has, as quite genuine components of her character, generosity, graciousness, and a sense of noblesse oblige toward retainers. The ruthlessness as well as the graciousness are, to a considerable extent, the products of her aristocratic conditioning. The action of the novel begins when Ellen Sessions' prize garden is spoiled by Beasly's cattle, which have been herded through her land on a short cut. The abbreviated route is not only practical for Beasly, but it also gives him an opportunity to show his contempt for the Sessions family. Ellen, in a moment of fury, shoots, from the window of her house, one of Beasly's employees who is driving cattle through her land. The act is unwitnessed, but circumstances point strongly toward her guilt. All the chivalric and clannish instincts of the Sessions family and its sympathizers are now aroused. Though the probability of Ellen's guilt is understood, no mention of this possibility is ever made by supporters of the old order. To divert suspicion, Ellen's brother stands trial for the murder. Though he is acquitted, he has gambled his life at the trial, as the Beasly faction is known to be strong and influential. With quiet nonchalance and no comment, Ellen takes her brother's gamble as a matter of course. Shortly after the acquittal, he is killed by friends of the murdered man. The assassins are duly hanged after a verdict against them is delivered by Judge Sessions. The Beasly faction in turn kills Judge Sessions and his son. Though all the bloodshed has been precipitated by her act, Ellen Sessions maintains her equanimity throughout, even in the face of the loss of her husband and son. Eventually, however, she is forced to borrow money from Beasly and to put up the old estate as security. When Ellen defaults on the debt, Beasly is all set to take over the estate. His seemingly inevitable triumph, however, is forestalled by his death in a freak horse accident. Though Richter grants "the lady" a reprieve, he makes it clear that she represents the last flicker of the old feudal power in New Mexico.

Yet the Mexican big house, though its power had gone, survived as an anachronism in a few isolated places in New Mexico until a time within the memory of living persons. Oliver La Farge in *Behind the Mountains*[50] presents a picture of such a feudal establishment situated in the Sangre de Cristo mountains north of Taos. The large house with extensive sheep ranch attached, named Rociada (dew-covered), is presided over by Don José Baca and Doña Marguerite. Almost everyone in the region works for Don José, who is a *patrón* in the grand style. He is actuated by a spirit of noblesse oblige in his relationship with the many people who depend upon him. They on their part respond with a sense of loyalty. The sketches of life at Rociada which make up the book are the result of La Farge's having written down the reminiscences of his wife, Consuelo, daughter of Don José and Doña Marguerite. There is an aura of nostalgia for the achieved, fixed, gracious social order of old Europe which surrounds the book, a type of yearning which has periodically affected American writers from Washington Irving down through Henry James, Willa Cather, and T. S. Eliot. Though La Farge gives what are undoubtedly realistic accounts of life at Rociada, he nevertheless, because of the quality of emotion that he brings to his descriptions, presents a pastoral idyl. *Behind the Mountains* is not far removed in spirit from the earlier evocations of the California myth. Before being published in book form, the sketches that comprise the book were published serially in *The New Yorker* magazine. This suggests that the first market for these stories was, presumably, rather an urban and sophisticated one, quite different from the earlier customers for the *Ramona* variety of California myth. One can speculate upon the appeal that La Farge's Rociada sketches had for these readers. Of course, at a certain level, the immediacy of their appeal is readily understandable. They are rendered with considerable charm and grace of style; and distance, in time and place, together with insulation, lends enchantment. Also it is possible that the age of the organization man is quite as ready to respond to accounts of a life which, however, hierarchical, was anything but impersonal, as was the "Gilded Age" of the 1880's and 1890's. There may be among modern Americans, furthermore, some recognition that such establishments as Rociada, archaic as they seem in the United States, still flourish in Latin America and elsewhere. Such recognition would indicate a developing cultural awareness that the early stereotype of the great, feudally managed landed estate had considerable validity. Whatever may be the reasons for the ready reception that *Behind the Mountains* has had among contemporary readers, the treatment of the Mexican big house in American literature seems, with the publication of this book, to have swung full circle, and another example is provided of the continuing power of Mexico and its extension into the American Southwest to attract American novelists and poets in search of color and tradition.

CHAPTER SIX

# Mexican Traits — A Later Look

While modern American writers have concerned themselves increasingly with patterns of Mexican society, the way of life of the big house and, as shall be seen later, sexual and religious attitudes as well as Mexican attitudes toward death, these writers have also brought into clearer focus the individual Mexican himself, what he looks like, how he acts and feels in specific situations. Though the accounts of some of the transitional writers of the late nineteenth and early twentieth century read a good deal like the works of the early border writers, the characterizations of later writers tend to be more specific, concrete, three-dimensional. There is less over-simplification, more deference to the universal complexity of men and women.

There are, furthermore, attempts by American writers to really get inside Mexican characters they create, to register the deepest responses of individuals from another culture. This trend has reached its apogee in the remarkable books of Oscar Lewis, *Five Families,* 1959, and *The Children of Sánchez,* 1961. Referring to *The Children of Sánchez,* the literary critic Elizabeth Hardwick wrote: "In this book . . . the anthropologist Oscar Lewis has made something brilliant and of singular significance, a work of such unique concentration and sympathy that one hardly knows how to classify it."[1] Both of these books grew out of very intimate studies of Mexican families. *Five Families* takes successively one day in the lives of five Mexican families, from the time of awakening to the time of going to bed at night. In order to achieve this kind of intimate reporting, Lewis accomplished the impressive feat of so winning the confidence of the members of these families that he, a foreigner, was not only made privy to their daily acts and thoughts, but was able to win such casual acceptance that his presence in their midst throughout the day did not inhibit them from talking and acting naturally. Many of the conversations of the members of these families, families chosen as representatives of different elements in the social structure of modern Mexico, were tape-recorded. The result is a book so alive and so inward that it not only marks the plumbing of new depths in sociological analysis but successfully achieves many of the effects aimed at in serious literary fiction. *The Children of Sánchez* employs the same techniques in a more concentrated way. Here all attention is focused on one of the families studied in the previous book, the family of Jesus Sánchez, which includes several wives he is living with simultaneously, but in different establishments, and their children. In the making of this book, tape-recorded conversations have been used with remarkable effect, producing soliloquies of an unusually revealing and moving nature. We hear the voices, usually embittered and frustrated, of Sánchez, his wives, and his children, emanating from a huge slum tenement in Mexico City. The same events are often recounted to us but as they have been experienced by different people, with results similar to those achieved by Luigi Pirandello in his experimental drama, *Six Characters in Search of an Author*. As in Pirandello's play, we are impressed, in reading Lewis' book, by the different, isolated, and subjective worlds that lay in the imprisoned spirits of individuals, who scarcely can communicate even to those most close to them their individual senses of life and of reality. "One would ask, certainly," wrote Elizabeth Hardwick of Lewis' techniques, "can a work of literature be written by a taperecorder? It cannot. Lewis' books are both literally true and imaginatively presented. In the end it is his rich spirit, his depth of dedication, his sympathy that lie behind the successful recreation. Lewis' role is that of the great film director who, out of images and scenes, makes a coherent drama, giving form and meaning to the flow of reality."[2]

It is a phenomenon of American, as well as British, culture that, notwithstanding the prevalence of xenophobia among the people at large, the culture produces a considerable number of intellectuals who become deeply involved with foreign lands. In all probability there are more Francophiles among the British and Americans than there are Anglophiles or lovers of America among the French. Beyond a doubt the deep attachment for Mexico among a number of American intellectuals is generally unrequited by their Mexican opposite numbers. The explanation for this absorption in other cultures lies partly in the alienation of some modern American and British writers from their own societies and their consequent search for compensatory allegiances elsewhere. Aside from this condition, however, there is the fact that Britain and the United States, whatever their weakness, are sufficiently self-confident and flexible as societies to permit self-criticism, and, since the days of Tacitus, the allegedly superior virtues of the foreigner have served the domestic critic well. Mexico, as will be further shown, has been much resorted to by modern American writers critical of their own society

As a part of the general movement toward cultural relativism among moderns, the old ethnocentricity has been more and more replaced by a generosity of feeling on the part of Americans writing about Mexico. According to the modern canon, one must above all "understand." However, while people on the second or third rungs of intellectual awareness have been properly digesting their lessons in cultural relativism, have been reading with approval such works as Ruth Benedict's *Patterns of Culture,* a counter movement has pronounced against the tendency to exculpate people or peoples, whatever their behavior, on the grounds of cultural patterns or environmental factors. This sort of uncommitted tolerance, according to the anti-relativists, represents a weakening of the discriminatory power of the intellect and a blurring of the moral sense. Stories and novels have recently been appearing which satirize the kind of "liberal" American in Mexico who must "understand" all attitudes and actions he encounters and who therefore stifles spontaneous feelings of disaproval toward any actions, however outrageous, performed by Mexicans. Though such shifts in the direction of thought as this kind of satire, representing what David Riesman has called the "counter-cyclical" functions of the intellectual, often provide valuable correctives, the trend in recent decades toward greater appreciation in the United States of the value of Mexican culture has been all to the good. More rather than less sympathy is still needed, for the many-layered culture of Mexico has much to contribute to the entire cultural experience of the Western Hemisphere.

In spite of this greater extension of sympathies in recent years between the United States and Mexico, a good deal of the old hostility remains. This animosity, according to Texan novelist Tom Lea, still retains its virulence along the Texas border.

> The two races facing each other across the narrow water of the Rio Grande had the immemorial failing: each firmly believed that its own manners and opinions were right for the unequaled reason that its manners and opinions were its own. Men everywhere find themselves ready to resent that which they must make any effort to understand.... In their encounter, Americans were apt to feel superior and Mexicans were apt to feel abused. An ordinary American was more prosperous — because he paid more attention to "prosperity"—than an ordinary Mexican, so that an economic division generally conformed with the racial cleavage to more sharply align the border's array of old resentments and mistrusts.[3]

The image of the American as aggressively hostile to the Mexican appears continually in modern American writing. Some of the transitional writers maintain the old prejudices and display them with gusto; others simply report on the hostilities, while an increasing number of modern writers speak out against the ancient hatreds which have divided two neighboring people. Alfred Henry Lewis, a Western humorist at the turn of the century, had, in one of his stories, the following item appear in *The Wolfville Daily Coyote*: "A reckless Mexican was parading the street the other night carrying in his hand a monkey wrench. It was dark, and Mr. Daniel Boggs, a leading citizen of Wolfville, who met him, mistaking the wrench for a pistol which the Mexican was carrying for some vile purpose, very properly shot him. Mexicans are far too careless this way.' "[4] "Leading citizen" Boggs appears in another of Lewis' works. In *Wolfville* (pseudonym for Tombstone, Arizona), he is shown in a barroom with a group of friends, including a man named Enright, taking bets on whether or not a man from the neighboring town of Yallerhouse, whose face has broken out in spots, has the smallpox. Boggs opens the betting: " 'I believes in giving every gent all necessary light wherein to make up his mind; an', as I says, to open the game all logical, I ag'in moves this Yallerhouse man has the smallpox.' '*Yo también*,' yells a Mexican over near the door. 'Put that Greaser out!' shouts Enright, at the same time banging the table. 'This ain't no international incident at all, 'an nothin' but the clean-strain American wolf is eligible to howl.' The greaser goes out on his saddle-colored head, an' Enright puts Boggs's motion."[5] Lewis, thoroughly a part of his own community, is representative, in his attitudes, of the general run of Anglo-Americans in the Southwest of his day.

Bret Harte, as a transplanted Easterner, viewed the racial situation in the Southwest quite differently. In "The Story of a Mine" he commented wryly upon the psychology of Manifest Destiny. Referring to an Anglo-American swindler operating in the mine fields of California, he wrote that this man "did not scruple to cheat these Mexicans,— they were a degraded race,— and for a moment he felt almost an accredited agent of progress and civilization. We never really understand the meaning of enlightenment until we begin to use it aggressively."[6]

Bayard Taylor in *El Dorado or Adventures in the Path of Empire*, published in 1894, expressed his indignation at a situation which he heard of while visiting the California gold diggings. Shortly before his arrival, several thousand Mexicans from Sonora had established a digging and had turned over an "incredible" amount of ground. But hostility toward them on the part of American diggers mounted to the point that organized bands of American miners were formed which drove the Mexicans from the country.[7] A similar sympathy for the situation of the beleaguered Mexican in the Southwest provides the principal theme of Hamlin Garland's story "Delmar of Pima." Among the cattlemen of the Southwestern town which is the locale of the story, "to kill a Mexican was reprehensible but not criminal. . . . In the eyes of these cattle barons and their retainers the greaser was a nuisance . . . and needed to be discouraged." The Mexicans attempted ineffectually to assert their rights by political means. "Numerically they were considerably in the lead, but as the cattlemen controlled all the election machinery, numbers did not count."[8] The story is clearly in the vein of social protest writing.

Stephen Crane in his Southwestern stories is able with a few deft references to make clear to the reader the position of the Mexican in the American communities of the borderlands. In "The Bride Comes to Yellow Sky" he enumerates the customers at the Weary Gentleman saloon. "One was a drummer who talked a great deal and rapidly; three were Texans who did not care to talk at that time; and two were Mexican sheep-herders, who did not talk as a general practice in the Weary Gentleman saloon." When it seemed as though trouble were brewing, "the two Mexicans at once set down their glasses and faded out of the rear entrance of the saloon."[9] In "Moonlight on the Snow," the wild Western town of Warpost, a caricature of Tombstone, Arizona, was described as entering a reforming phase. Residents had determined to make the town over into a law-abiding community. The motive behind this decision was the desire to attract some of the Eastern development money that was being invested in many surrounding communities but was avoiding Warpost like the plague because of its terrible reputation. Leading citizens of the town held a meeting and declared that any man found guilty of a shooting, an almost daily occurrence, was to be promptly hanged. "Everybody was enthusiastic, save a few Mexicans, who did not quite understand; but as they were more than likely to be victims of any affray in which they were engaged, their silence was not considered ominous."[10]

Frank Dobie, Texan folklorist, relates an incident in the life of a well-known gunman which illustrates the situation of Mexicans in Texas in the late 1800's.

> "How many men have you killed?" a boy in Eagle Pass asked the noted bad man, King Fisher, some time before he was shot to death . . . .
> And the soft answer was, "Seven — just seven."
> "Oh, the boy exclaimed in a disappointed tone, "I thought it must be more than that."
> "I don't count Mexicans," explained King Fisher.[11]

One is not surprised to discover that some of the literature of the 1930's expressed disgust with the aggressive and contemptuous hostility that Americans have so often directed toward Mexicans. In *42nd*

*Parallel* John Dos Passos has one of his characters, Mac, a labor organizer, encounter several other Americans in a bar in Mexico City. The time is during the early stages of the Mexican Revolution. The other Americans, businessmen, are huddled together bemoaning the downfall of Porfirio Díaz, who had given so many concessions and so much protection to American business. In the United States at this time, Woodrow Wilson is in the White House. One of the Americans at the bar, an oil prospector, is complaining to Mac about the revolutionaries and about Mexicans generally. "My God, pardner, you don't know what kind of country this is! Do you know what we ought to do . . . d'you know what we'd do if we had a man in the White House instead of a yellowbellied potatomouthed reformer? We'd get up an army of a hundred thousand men and clean this place up . . . . It's a hell of a fine country but there's not one of these damn greasers worth the powder and shot to shoot 'em . . . smoke 'em out like vermin, that's what I say."[12]

Another novel of the thirties, *The Square Trap* by Irving Shulman, takes up the cause of the "pachucos," Mexican-Americans, in Los Angeles. The central figure, Tommy Cantanios, tries to break away from the restrictions and humiliations that go with being a "pachuco" in California by becoming a boxer. He has some initial successes in the ring but becomes thoroughly scared when he experiences temporary amnesia as the result of a hard blow received during a bout which he lost. He decides to quit the ring even though this means facing friends and a younger brother who have been basking vicariously in the glory of his career. After he has made this decision, he goes out for a ride with members of his club, the Cats. Though his friends are against it, he insists on their stopping at a fancy diner in a pretentious section of Los Angeles. Once inside, they are given the "water treatment." The waitress puts glasses of water before them and leaves them to cool their heels indefinitely. Finally a sign reading "We Reserve the Right to Refuse Service to Anyone" is pushed into a position on the counter where it is staring them in the face. Tommy, enraged, insists that they wait it out, much to his friends' discomfort. After a while the manager calls a policeman, who enters and politely sits down with the young men, asking them for their driver's licenses and other identification. The policeman is embarrassed when he realizes that Tommy and his friends have not been causing a disturbance as the manager had indicated over the phone. The reader gathers that this officer has some genuine compassion for the situation of the boys. One of the "Cats" shows the officer a clipping and photograph of Tommy at the height of his ring career. The policeman appears to be impressed and later demands that the restaurant serve the "pachucos," eating with them himself and paying the check. When the boys go home, all, with the exception of Tommy, feel resignedly humiliated. Tommy is deeply humiliated but not resigned. They all are convinced that what saved face for them was the clipping, which made the policeman respect Tommy as a man of importance. Policemen are so traditionally the enemy that the "Cats" cannot give this police officer credit for any real feeling for their condition. Tommy, now certain that the ring is the only way out of the "Ravine," the slum neighborhood in which he has grown up, re-enters the boxing game and is headed for a crippling and total defeat which is to leave him wrecked and in despair.[13]

Aggressive hostility is only one of several ways in which Americans have displayed toward Mexicans their sense of superiority and feelings of contempt. These attitudes have been conveyed in ways ranging from open insult to the complacent remark or action not intended to offend but clearly indicating an assumed superiority. The Mexicans in such situations have often forborne showing any outward sign of having been affronted, suppressing feelings of humiliation and rage. This psychological relationship between the peoples of the Southwest has been examined from various points of view by modern American writers.

John William De Forest, a nineteenth-century American writer, wrote one novel, *Overland,* with a Southwestern locale. The Mexican characters in the book are all stock types, the upper-class Mexicans being shown as cunning and treacherous and the lower-class as cowardly. In proclaiming the inevitable triumph of the Anglo-Saxon, he speaks with the voice of the social Darwinists. "Profound and potent sentiment of race antipathy! The contempt and hatred of white man for yellow, red, brown, and black men has worked all over the earth, is working yet, and will work for ages. It is a motive of that tremendous tragedy which Spencer has entitled 'the survival of the fittest,' and Darwin, 'natural selection.' "[14] In spite of the weakness of the book as a whole, some of the dialogue does represent quite faithfully racial attitudes in the Southwest. One of the characters, Carlos Coronado, an educated Mexican who speaks English as well as he does Spanish, plots to have his rival in love, an American army officer, assassinated. Coronado has picked a renegade named Texas Smith for the job. In one scene he upbraids Smith for not having accomplished his assignment, saying:

> "You might manage it somehow, if you had the pluck."
> "Had the pluck!" repeated Texas Smith. His shallow, haggard face turned dusky with rage, and his singularly black eyes flamed as if with hell-fire . . . . What chiefly infuriated him was that the insult should come from one whom he considered a 'greaser,' a

man of inferior race. He, Texas Smith, an American, a *white man,* was treated as if he were an 'Injun' or a 'nigger.' Coronado was thoroughly alarmed, and smoothed his ruffled feathers at once.

Smith finally calms down:

> "But you oughter be keerful how you talk that way to a white man," he said. "No white man, if he's a gentleman, can stan' being told he hain't got no pluck."
> "Certainly," assented Coronado. "Well, I have apologized. What more can I do?"
> "Square, you're all right now," said the forgiving Texan, stretching out his bony, dirty hand and grasping Coronado's. "But don't say it again. White men can't stan' sech talk . . . ."
> As Coronado rode away from this interview, he ground his teeth with rage and mortification, muttering, "A *white* man! So I am a black man. Yes, I am a greaser. Curse this whole race of English-speaking people!"[15]

Bret Harte, though he did not share — for the most part — in the racial attitudes that were being expressed all around him in California, reported them as part of the local flavor. One of the figures in his only novel, *Gabriel Conroy,* is a *mestizo* named Victor Ramírez. He has become involved with Mrs. Gabriel Conroy in a complex scheme to get control of a mine. Mrs. Conroy, who has been estranged from her husband, eventually breaks with Ramírez. In casting him off, she declares that she will win back the love of her husband as she hurls racial epithets at her former accomplice. "I will make him love me yet, if I sacrifice you, everybody, my own life, to do it! Do you hear that, Victor Ramírez, you dog! — You Spanish mongrel! — you half-breed."[16] In the story "A Pupil of Chestnut Ridge," Harte treats sardonically not only the racial prejudices of the Southwest but also the air of superiority affected by a type common to the area in Harte's time, the New England schoolmaster. A simple ranching couple, the Hoovers, knowing that they will have no children, finally in desperation adopt a little Mexican girl as the only child available for adoption. They are, however, very fearful of being criticized by their neighbors. Seeking out the local schoolmaster, Mr. Brooks, who as yet knows nothing about the girl's background, they discuss the possibility of entering her in school. Mr. Hoover, who does most of the talking, is hesitant and evasive. Finally he says:

> ". . . but thar's one thing more we oughter tell ye. She's—she's a trifle dark complected."
> The schoolmaster smiled. "Well?" he said patiently.
> "She isn't a nigger nor an Injin, ye know, but she's kinder a half-Spanish, half-Mexican Injin, what they call 'mes — mes' " —
> " 'Mestiza,' " suggested Mr. Brooks; "a half-breed or mongrel."

"I reckon. Now thar wouldn't be any objection to that, eh?" said Mr. Hoover a little uneasily.

"Not by me," returned the school master cheerfully. "And although this school is state-aided it's not a 'public school' in the eye of the law, so you have only the foolish prejudices of your neighbors to deal with." He had recognized the reason of their hesitation and knew the strong racial antagonism held toward the negro and Indian by Mr. Hoover's Southwestern compatriots, and he could not refrain from "rubbing it in."

"They kin see," interposed Mrs. Hoover, "that she's not a nigger, for her hair don't 'kink,' and a furrin Injin, of course, is different from one o' our own."[17]

O. Henry, in spite of the frequent use he makes of Spanish to spice his stories, consistently ridicules the Mexicans of the Southwest in the characters he invents. An old man is described in one of his stories as "a lineal Aztec, somewhat less than a thousand years old, who herded a hundred goats and lived in a continuous drunken dream from drinking *mescal*."[18] In the story "An Afternoon Miracle," a Mexican is mocked for his race and for his inability to fight with his fists. The heroine of the tale is Alvarita, a snake charmer, who, in spite of her assumed Spanish name, is Anglo-American. During a stopover in Texas, she goes for a swim by herself in a lonely water hole. While dressing after the swim, she loses one of her snakes and wanders around looking for it, continuing to dress.

Alvarita heard a sudden crunching of the gravel below her. Turning her head she saw a big, swarthy Mexican, with a daring and evil expression, contemplating her with an ominous, dull eye.

"What do you want?" she asked as sharply as five hairpins between her lips would permit, continuing to plait her hair, and looking him over with placid contempt. The Mexican continued to gaze at her, and showed his teeth in a white, jagged smile.

"I no hurt-y you, Señorita," he said.

"You bet you won't," answered the Queen, shaking back one finished, massive plait. "But don't you think you'd better move on?"

"Not hurt-y you — no. But maybeso take one *beso* — one li'l kees, you call him."

The man smiled again, and set his foot to ascend the slope. Alvarita leaned swiftly and picked up a stone the size of a cocoanut.

"Vamoose, quick," she ordered peremptorily, "you *coon!*"

The red of insult burned through the Mexican's dark skin.

"*Hidalgo,* Yo!" he shot between his fangs. "I am not neg-r-ro! *Diabla bonita,* for that you shall pay me."

At this point Bob Buckley, a clean-cut Saxon type, comes to the rescue. The Mexican, whose name is García, comes at him with a knife.

Buckley, grabbing the wrist of the knife-wielder, delivers "the good Saxon knock-out blow — always so pathetically disastrous to the fistless Latin races — and García [is] down and out, with his head under a clump of prickly pears."[19]

In the poem "Tamales," O. Henry manages in a few lines to hit almost all points of the Mexican stereotype from Mexican pomposity to the laziness, drunkenness, violence, political instability and lack of hygiene which make up the stock image. Don José avenges himself on the Texans for having killed his grandfather in the battle of San Jacinto by setting up a tamale stand where he serves the citizens of Austin tamales made of cats, terriers, etc.

> This is the Mexican
> Don José Calderón
> One of God's countrymen,
> Land of the buzzard,
> Cheap silver dollar, and
> Cacti and murderers.
> Why has he left his land,
> Land of the lazy man,
> Land of the pulque,
> Land of the bullfight,
> Fleas and revolution.
> This is the reason,
> Hark to the wherefore;
> Listen and tremble.
> One of his ancestors,
> Ancient and garlicky,
> Probably grandfather,
> Died with his boots on.
> Killed by the Texans,
> Texans with big guns
> At San Jacinto.
> Died without benefit
> Of priest or clergy;
> Died full of minie balls,
> Mescal and pepper.
> Dire is thy vengeance,
> Don José Calderón.
> For the slight thing we did
> Killing thy grandfather.
> What boots it if we killed
> Only one greaser,
> Don José Calderón?
> This is your deep revenge,
> You have greased all of us,
> Greased a whole nation
> With your Tamales,

Don José Calderón
Santos Espirition
Vicente Camillo
Quitana de Rios
De Rosa y Ribera.[20]

O. Henry's books were among the last to appear which presented Mexicans in such a completely stereotyped manner. As a result of early years in Texas, O. Henry had drawn his attitudes from the same Western lore that produced the frontier tales of Alfred Henry Lewis.

During the early 1900's, the period in which O. Henry's banal tales were at the height of their popularity, an important American literary artist was beginning to publish. Willa Cather's interest in Mexico was serious and lasting. In *The Song of the Lark,* one of her early novels, the Mexican community of a small Colorado town played a significant part in the early development of Thea Kronborg, the central figure of the book. Thea, who was later to become a successful concert singer, found as a young girl that there was little in her home town that she could respond to aesthetically. Her father was a minister in the kind of church which is pietistic, moralistic and totally lacking in aesthetic forms. Her brothers, sisters, and neighbors were for the most part unimaginative, materialistic small-town types. There were only two sources from which she could draw any refreshment of mind and spirit. One was the home of her piano teacher, an elderly German, a man who had become alcoholic because of the drabness and frustrations of his environment but who was capable, devoted to music, and immersed in the culture of Europe. The other was the Mexican community where she found a people who were vital, responsive to the arts, capable of enjoying life intensely, and generally indifferent to the material goals which preoccupied the rest of the town's citizens. One of Thea's Mexican friends was Johnny Tellamantez, an artist manqué. He was capable of singing with great expressiveness and was an accomplished guitarist. Periodically he went on carousals in which, combining alcohol and song, he reached for some ultimate ecstacy. His wife patiently nursed him through the after effects of these sprees. It was in the behavior of her own brother, Gunner, toward Johnny that Thea first recognized the humiliations that the Mexican encountered in the Southwest. Johnny was explaining to Thea and Gunner the custom "down in the hot country" of keeping a snake in the house to kill rats and mice. " 'They call him the house snake. They keep a little mat for him by the fire, and at night he curl up there and sit with the family, just as friendly!' Gunner sniffed with disgust. 'Well, I think that's a dirty Mexican way to keep house; so there!' Johnny shrugged his shoulders. 'Perhaps,' he muttered. A Mexican learns to dive below insults or soar above them, after he crosses the border."[21]

It is curious that this very custom in Mexico of the house snake, spoken of so contemptuously by Thea's brother, should be incorporated beautifully into a poem by the modern poet Denise Levertov.

> Xochipilli, god of spring,
>                     is sitting
> on the earth floor, gazing
> into a fire. In the fire
> a serpent is preening, uncoiling.
>
> "From thy dung
> the red flowers," says the god.
>
> By the hearth
> bodies of hares and mice,
> food for the snake.
>
> "From thy bones
> white flowers," says the god.
>
> Rain dances, many-footed
> on the thatch. Raindrops
> leap into the fire, the serpent hisses.
>
> "From this music
> seeds of the grass
> that shall sing when the wind blows."
>             The god stirs the fire.[22]

But clearly there was a wide gap between the puritan and race-proud attitudes of Thea's family and those of a poet such as Denise Levertov. An incident which was to prove decisive in bringing about Thea's estrangement from her family was the reaction of members of her family to her having gone to a Mexican dance and having sung for the Mexicans, staying out until late at night. Her brothers Charley and Gus, and her sister, Anna, expressed their disapproval while the family was at table.

> During the silence which preceded the blessing, Thea felt something uncomfortable in the air. Anna and her older brothers had lowered their eyes when she came in. Mrs. Kronborg nodded cheerfully, and after the blessing, as she began to pour the coffee, turned to her.
> "I expect you had a good time at that dance, Thea. I hope you got your sleep out."
> "High society, that," remarked Charley, giving the mashed potatoes a vicious swat. Anna's mouth and eyebrows became half-moon.
> Thea looked across the table at the uncompromising countenances of her older brothers. "Why, what's the matter with the

Mexicans?" she asked, flushing. "They don't trouble anybody, and they are kind to their families and have good manners."

"Nice clean people; got some style about them. Do you really like that kind, Thea, or do you just pretend to? That's what I'd like to know." Gus looked at her with pained inquiry. But he at least looked at her.

"They're just as clean as white people, and they have a perfect right to their own ways. Of course I like 'em. I don't pretend things."

"Everybody according to his own taste," remarked Charley bitterly.

Later Anna resumed the topic with Thea.

"I should think you would show more consideration for father's position, Thea . . . "

Thea gave her a sidelong glance. "Why, what have I done to father?"

"Everybody at Sunday-School was talking about you going over there and singing with the Mexicans all night, when you don't sing for the church. Somebody heard you, and told it all over town. Of course, we all get the blame for it."

"Anything disgraceful about singing," Thea asked with a provoking yawn.

"I must say you choose your company! You always had that streak in you, Thea . . . Of course, it reflects on father when you are scarcely polite to the nice people and make up to the rowdies."

"Oh, it's my singing with Mexicans you object to?" Thea put down a trayful of dishes. "Well, I like to sing over there, and I don't like to over here. I'll sing for them any time they ask me to. They know something about what I'm doing. They're a talented people."

"Talented!" Anna made the word sound like escaping steam. "I suppose you think it's smart to come home and throw that at your family!"[23]

Even the Mexican whose family has culture and tradition behind it does not escape the stigma which marks the members of his race in the Southwest. In *The Blood of the Conquerors,* Harvey Fergusson analyzes the ambiguous position of his protagonist, Ramón Delcasar, in New Mexico.

Whenever he felt sure of his social footing, his attitude toward women was bold and assured. But his social footing was a peculiarly uncertain thing for the reason that he was a Mexican. This meant that he faced in every social contact the possibility of a more or less covert prejudice against his blood, and that he faced it with an unduly proud and sensitive spirit concealed beneath a manner of aristocratic indifference. In the little Southwestern town where he had lived all his life . . . his social position was ostensibly the highest. He was spoken of as belonging to an old and prominent family. Yet he knew of mothers who carefully guarded their daughters from the peril of falling in love with him, and most of his boyhood fights had started when someone had called him a "damned Mexican" or a "greaser."[24]

Though the stereotype of the Mexican has disappeared largely from serious American writing, it remains in the public mind, especially in the Southwest, and constitutes a very real barrier to Mexican-Americans attempting to make their way. Ruth Tuck in *Not With the Fist* examines the rise and persistence of the stereotype in a book which is not only a sociological study but, because of its verve, personal commitment, and controlled indignation, a work which can claim its place with the literature of social protest in America. In examining the town of Descanso, California, she makes clear that a considerable amount of subconscious hypocrisy is needed to maintain the stereotype.

> If any group of citizens had risen to state, publicly, in 1910, "Now, see here, we have a dependable source of cheap labor, which we are going to need for a long time. Let's see that it stays put, without any of this nonsense about equal opportunity," such a group would have been the immediate object of community disapproval. Descanso's tradition of being casually generous, its pride in being the sort of town where one man was as good as another, would have been outraged. But, when the same thing was done without statements of public policy, without overt compulsion, or without clear definition, then Descanso considered it right and natural. Informally, on thousands of small, seemingly insignificant occasions, Descanso formed its policies. "Public education is all right, but we don't want Mexicans going to the same schools as our children." "I wouldn't hire a Mexican girl as a stenographer if she could do five hundred words a minute." "Let Mexicans in this district and you bring down property values." "They wouldn't know what to do with higher pay if they had it." "Why waste education on kids that are going to pick oranges anyway?" "A Mexican doesn't need a relief allowance like whites." "Once a Mex, always a Mex." "They can't learn like other people." "You can't have a Mexican meeting the public." Thousands — millions of these phrases, echoing down the decades, succeeded in erecting a barrier, while the people erecting it were scarcely conscious of what they did.[25]

An attitude which has probably been more difficult for Mexicans to bear than that of outright aggressiveness or the direct intent to humiliate has been that of moralistic righteousness, a compounding of the elements of Manifest Destiny and the white man's burden. Bayard Taylor from the gold fields of California complacently announced that "in speaking of us, the natives exhibited (and I say it not with any feeling of national pride) the liking which men bear to their superiors. They acknowledged our greater power and intelligence as a nation, without jealousy, and with an anticipation rather than a fear, that our rule will one day be extended over them."[26] This sort of attitude was undoubtedly widespread, but it had its critics among American writers. "It seems," wrote Ambrose Bierce commenting on a speech by President McKinley, "that we have never gone to war for conquest, for exploitation, nor for territory; we have the word of a President for that. Observe, now, how providence overrules the intention of the truly good for their advantage. We went to war with Mexico for peace, humanity and honor, yet emerged from the contest with an extension of territory beyond the dreams of political avarice."[27] Bret Harte reacted more with amusement than indignation to the patriotic fanfare that went with the expansionist spirit of his age. In *Gabriel Conroy,* the following dialogue occurs between the American, Arthur Poinsett, and the Californian-Mexican priest, Padre Felipe:

> "Honesty is the best policy," as our earliest philosopher says.
> "Pardon?" queried the padre.
> Arthur, intensely amused, made a purposely severe and literal translation of Franklin's famous apothegm, and then watched Father Felipe raise his eyes and hands to the ceiling in pious protest and mute consternation.
> "And these are your American ethics?" he said at last.
> "They are, and in conjunction with manifest destiny, and the star of empire, they have brought us here, and — have given me the honor of your acquaintance," Arthur said in English.[28]

John Houghton Allen in *Southwest* writes that because he and the rest of the Anglo-Americans had been waving the "padrone complex and carrying the white man's burden," he had never really been able to get close to the Mexicans, a situation he later regretted. Whether good or bad, the Mexicans had always attracted him as being "human to a vivid degree," and he had rather wistfully hoped to do something to improve relations between the two races. "But anybody who tried to do that in the southwest fifteen years ago was despised by his own people *and* the Mexicans."[29]

A subtle treatment of the psychological response of an American to Mexico is given in the story "Something for Bradshaw's Tombstone," by Alwyn Lee, a writer of Australian origin, now settled in the United States and writing in an American idiom. The protagonist of the story, Skinner Bradshaw, works for the State Department, is very consciously liberal, and is feeling somewhat haggard as a result of the era of the Hiss trial and of Joseph McCarthy. He is delighted to have a Point Four assignment in Mexico, something that he can really get his teeth into, and is not in the least dispirited by the fact that the location of his assignment is an obscure port town on the southern Isthmus of Tehuantepec. This place turns out to be a decadent little village gradually being reclaimed by the jungle, whose listless predominantly Indian population provides an example of the conquistadores having been passively reconquered by the natives. The only display of energy is that exhibited by the corrupt political boss, Sr. Orquienz, whose name is an Hispanicized version of Hawkins, a legacy from an English pirate ancestor of the present-day plunderer of the port town. Bradshaw has come to Tehuantepec determined not to display the least bit of condescension in his manner and thoroughly briefed in the ways of cultural relativism. He must therefore resort to various stratagems with himself to prevent the emergence in any gross form of a realization of the actual fact of his superiority.

> Skinner Bradshaw, like one magically immune from a total plague, displayed his energy to the insentient town; and, like such survivors, was touched by feelings of guilt and superiority. Such mixed, but highly creditable feelings were habitual with him; almost, with a Bradshaw of New England, a heritage. Commitment, responsibility, integrity, a job well done, or as his ancestors would have put it, grace through works — these might justify the otherwise inadmissible feeling of superiority to the sloth-stunned townspeople. The guilt of *being* superior — needed a subtler exorcism. "The siesta," he had told himself, "is a nutritional phenomenon rather than a regional institution;" and he had incorporated this remarkable phrase in the report he was engaged in composing.[30]

In the course of his mission, Bradshaw experiences, through a sudden perception of the true nature of Sr. Orquienz, a vision of evil which causes him to qualify considerably his estimation of the success of his enterprise in this report, whose original tone was one of confidence in the possibilities of redeeming Mexico through plumbing, innoculations, and fertilizers.

While American writers have expressed their attitudes toward Mexicans or commented on the attitudes of other Americans toward Mexicans since the days of the first border contacts, it has not been until comparatively recently that American writers have given their own versions of how Mexicans feel toward Americans. In *Figures in a Landscape,* Paul Horgan presents an episode whose theme is the essential cohesiveness of Mexicans by which in a crisis, whatever the issue, they will unite against even those Americans for whom they have entertained friendly feelings. The scene of the story is New Mexico in the year 1884. Patricio Melendez had been selling vegetables to Fort Banning for a long time and had developed good relationships with the soldiers there, especially with Lieutenant Dick Fielding, whom he warned of impending trouble between local Mexicans and an American named Brady who operated a mill "down the valley." Brady had been cheating his Mexican customers. When Brady shot Enrique Melendez, cousin of Patricio, in a flare-up between drunken Mexican locals and Brady – the Mexicans charged the mill, killed Brady, and continued a wild drinking party while occupying the mill. American soldiers arrived under Fielding. Patricio Melendez was one of those in the mill, and Fielding called to him saying "we must stop this terrible business." Melendez at the window of the mill "bobbed like a puppet and made sad, charming noises. He was suddenly as remote in spirit from Dick as he was in space. He seemed to deplore, vaguely; yet now that his cousin was murdered, so was Brady, and this might be a new way of life."[31] The Mexicans, including Melendez, were decimated when the American soldiers were forced to attack the mill.

John Houghton Allen put a barroom scene in the novel *Southwest* which showed the relationship between "Anglos" and Mexicans as the reverse of that pictured in such earlier Southwestern barroom scenes as the one in Alfred Henry Lewis's *Wolfville* or in Stephen Crane's "The Bride Comes to Yellow Sky." Here it is the Mexicans who treat the "gringos" with contempt. Allen's Mexicans, tough and seasoned *vaqueros,* had come into a Texas town and while drinking were surveying with disgust the citified, middle-class "gringos" at the bar. This episode was told in the novel by the old, weather-beaten *vaquero,* Ernesto Acuna, reminiscing years later. Some of the "gringos" began talking to the effect that Don Juan, the employer of the *vaqueros,* "had his greasers so spoiled ... that now they dared to drink along besides white men . . . ." For a while the Mexicans held their peace though they considered the "gringos" "a bunch of swine, who had never roped a ladino [wild steer] in their lives or ridden a wild horse, or killed an *armed* Mexican for that matter." Acuna went on to talk about the "Anglo" women in the bar.

> The gringa ladies walked wickedly about among the men, and when a man has been in the *monta* for many months, how fresh, like the turf in *lagunas* — how sweet, like huisache blossoms — how fragrant and utterably desirable they can be. We were like mariners in port, Señor. What eyes she had! What a leg on that one! Ah, *que chichis!* We felt we could use several women apiece, our limbs felt double looking at them, but after the first, not being in practice, we were through, *fregados.* We drank, and our minds were inflamed by so much beauty in those women. But they ignored us for the most part, moving about among the *white* men

on their fine, proud legs, kissing and hugging the grocer, the deputy, the clerks from the market place without shame or discrimination or passion. It made your blood boil. If *this* was being civilized, it was too tame.... There was a great contempt in our hearts for those bitches and bastards, for the men of these women in particular, who could not ride a bronc or tail a bull or stop a stampede....

After a while some of the "gringos" began singing a well-known Mexican song. The *vaqueros* were infuriated at this appropriation of something which was their own " 'as if the mirth, the deeds, the saga, the death, and the gaiety of this song' " were things the "gringos" could claim as part of their heritage. Tension finally mounted to the point that the Mexicans were openly baiting the "gringos." "El Gordo broke the kerchief at his neck and fawned on a large red-faced man; but gringos don't like cold steel. When the man saw the blade in El Gordo's hand, the bandana in his teeth, and the glint in his wheedling eyes, he turned sick and white. And El Gordo almost caressing the man with affection ... *ay, gringos.* We harried them with the foulest names in the Spanish tongue, we pleaded and spat in their faces, but all for *nothing, para nada!* I tell you they were city men."[32]

Hatred for the "gringo" is the one recognizable trait that Allen's vivacious, earthy Mexicans have in common with the Mexicans portrayed by Conrad Aiken. Here we have reptilian, totally malicious creatures for whom Americans are the natural enemies. In *A Heart for the Gods of Mexico,* three of the characters, sensitive, cultivated Bostonians, were nervously aware of the atmosphere of pure malevolence generated by the sniggering Mexicans around them as they rode through Mexico on a train.

> Derisive and demoniacal laughter, full of fierce and abandoned hatred, the pride of pridelessness, the arrogance of the self-condemned; and the often-turning reptile-lidded eyes, which slowly malevolently scrutinized the three strange Americans, the gringos — with what a loving and velvety pansy-darkness of murderousness they glowed at these natural victims! How they laughed for pure hate of this helpless and comical and so naked but nevertheless so dangerous awareness! They looked and laughed, looked and laughed again, openly, softly, mockingly, with every hope of reducing the interchange as quickly as possible to that level of frank enmity in which the more quickly and absorbedly animal of the two natures would have all the advantage.[33]

Gilbert Neiman in *There Is a Tyrant in Every Country* produced a shrewd and fantastic novel about Mexico which, in some of its more macabre passages, is reminiscent of another powerful novel set in Mexico, *Under the Volcano* by the British novelist Malcolm Lowry. Proclaimed by Neiman's friend Henry Miller as the best work on Mexico ever produced by an American, it is in fact an uneven performance, combining elements of the spy thriller with a perceptive analysis of the way Mexicans affect Americans and vice versa. Neiman, despite a certain amount of juvenile swagger, is a colorful, imaginative writer with a sure feel for Mexico. In one scene he has a Mexican woman deliver a speech on the American character, an oration which might well have been a device on Neiman's part to allow him to get off his own chest some of his principal "gripes" about the United States. And yet this critique could well represent the attitudes of a cultivated Mexican toward the colossus of the north.

> For twelve years I was married to an American. I know all about them. I learned their language and the way they think. They are very ambitious, filled with self-love, proud of their property, and above all of their opinions. Those they love most. Their opinions are their most precious property. They call them ideals. Rarely do they kill out of passion, but often they kill for their opinions. Look at all their ridiculous wars. Give them a vague idea, something they picked up as children, words they heard in a song, a story their father told them, and they will expand it until it hardens their arteries. Any trivial thing can be the cause. They secrete it like an oyster does a pearl. To make money for loved ones, an idea like "nothing succeeds like success," the virtues of keeping up insurance installments, the necessity of converting the heathen, or the sanctity of democracy.

When the narrator, to whom this speech has been delivered, begins to bristle, the elderly and love-craving Mexican woman goes on to say: "'Don't spit at me like a young tiger, because I'd like to help you. You're so dumb. So charmingly American, innocent and rash. That's the only beautiful thing they have in their country, the youth there.'"[34]

Aside from recording the racial tension between Mexican and American and the views that each have held of the national character of the other, modern American writers have displayed an interest in the racial situation of Mexico as such. There has been a fascination with the spectacle of a country in which the indigenous American stock is still so strong and where pre-European culture still exerts its influence. In contrast with the attitude of the old border writer, the modern American writer looks upon the *mestizo* with both interest and favor as a man who in his person represents the continuity of the American experience. The hero of Jack London's story "The Mexican," Felipe Rivera, is a man, who, though he despises boxing, becomes a boxer in California in order to raise money for the cause of the Mexican Revolution. He represents the coming people of Mexico, the men of the earth, and his fierce stoic strength is accredited to the fact that he draws his blood from two strong and warlike races. Amid the din of fight night in the arena, he is pictured as a figure whose ominous immobility, as he sits in his corner, portends the strength, energy, and ferocity to be unleashed later. "Indian blood, as well as Spanish, was in his veins, and he sat back in a corner, silent, immobile, only his black eyes passing from face to face and noting everything."[35] The *mestizo* as a figure who carries the culture of two worlds is acclaimed by Carey McWilliams in *North from Mexico*. One of the principal theses of the book is that Mexican culture in the Southwest has something important and permanent to offer the entire region. This culture, he reminds the reader, owes a great deal to the Indian as well as to the Spaniard. In discussing the Spanish-speaking people of New Mexico he writes that "probably as much of their inheritance is Indian as Spanish: Spanish their language — a baroque sixteenth century Spanish — and their religion; but Indian their knowledge of hunting, farming, and the ways of the land. Their attitude toward land tenure, for example, is quite similar to that of the Indians. These are the real peasants, the *paisanos,* the men of the country. And it is through them that Spanish-Mexican influences have survived in New Mexico."[36]

One American writer develops a scene in which Mexicans argue among themselves about the future role of the *mestizo* in Mexico. Josephina Niggli in *Step Down Elder Brother* has written a novel about the Mexican industrial city of Monterrey emphasizing the class conflict which has arisen between the old families and the new middle-class *mestizo* group. In one scene the aristocratic Don Rafael is discussing the situation of the *mestizo* with members of his family: his daughter Brunhilda, whose name reflects Don Rafael's admiration for German culture, Tito, her fiance, and Cardito, her younger brother.

> Don Rafael pyramided his hands, rested his face against them. He spoke with the deliberation of a man who knows his pronouncements mean the difference between light and dark in the minds of his family. "I was lately reading an essay by Vasconcelos." He paused to give weight to the name of the famous Mexican philosopher. "He contends that we have produced a new race in the Republic, the *mestizo* who will inherit Mexico. It is his by right. Mexico produced him and must return to him."
> Brunhilda said coldly, "Nuevo León is a creole state, father. We have no place for the *mestizo* here."
> "It will not stay creole long, my daughter. As long as we possessed our broad grazing lands there was no reason for the

*mestizo* to leave the wealth of the south. But when Colonel Robertson built our railroad, when industry absorbed us, the *mestizo* came, lured by our money. Now that he is here, he will stay."

Brunhilda said violently, "He cannot conquer us. We are the great families still."

Tito laughed, "Ay, little cat, open your eyes. Ten years ago Nuevo León was a creole state, but not anymore. The *mestizo* is everywhere."

Cardito's dry young voice said abruptly, "The *mestizo* is the middle class. Without him there can be no democracy."

"Words," said Brunhilda. "Fine words that mean nothing."

"Listen," said Cardito, his eyes filling with fire, the orator's tone coming into his voice. "In the rest of South America the creole still holds the whip hand. Look at Peru. Lima is a creole city with processions to honor the arrival of the Spanish ambassadors, the Afternoon of Mantón to open the season's bullfight, and a snap of the fingers for the Indian starving in the mountains. Peru today is the Mexico of eighteen forty. We are the only Latin-American republic that has evolved a middle class, and that middle class is *mestizo*."[37]

One of Don Rafael's daughters eventually marries a bustling and enterprising *mestizo*.

Witter Bynner in the poem "In Mescala," expresses the idea that Mexico's Indians have reconquered Mexico from the Spanish conquerors by the weight of their impassive endurance.

Above a floating edge of hyacinths,
Lantanas and zinnias interrupt the streets;
Weeds hung with blossom crowd to the roofless church
Where priests from Spain built better than their bones;
And in the humbled plaza, two old sages
With Asian faces and with Indian hats
Play — on a drum and a morning-glory pipe —
A jolly requiem for the Spanish dead.[38]

And yet, in spite of the enthusiasm of the Indianists within Mexico and without, Mexico has not solved her racial problems. Though the *mestizo* has certainly come into his own, the pure-blooded Indian, who numbers in the millions in Mexico, still lives on the outskirts of Mexican society. One of the best of modern American novels to deal with this situation is *Crazy February* by Carter Wilson. The scene is Chiapas in southern Mexico, and most of the characters are Indians. The book presents a study of the relationships of the Indian communities with general Mexican officialdom. There is no oversimplification here. The Indians are not the heroes and the officials the villains, nor vice versa. What is presented to us is the complexity of Mexican society and the fact that

Mexico is by no means racially or culturally unified. The pure Indian is shown as living much apart from general, mestizo Mexican society. Between the two groups there exists much prejudice and misunderstanding, with a few sensitive people on both sides with the capacity and good will to bridge the gap. This book is not a sociological tract in the guise of a novel but is genuinely a work of literary art. Aesthetically and thematically it is firmly conceived and developed.

One of the interesting aspects of the Indian scene in Mexico, which Carter Wilson touches upon, is that Indian identity might be a cultural not a racial matter. Of two brothers in the novel, Miguel and Juan Lopez Oso, Miguel had left the Indian village and become a worker on a large Mexican ranch. He adopted general Mexican clothing and ways and no longer considered himself an Indian. This change in identity caused considerable strain between the two brothers during the few periods in which they still associated with each other. Once when Miguel had spent the night in Juan's house, during which there had been considerable drinking, Juan was suffering from a hangover the next day.

> "A little crudo, huh, Juan?" Miguel put his hand on his brother's shoulder. "Well, they say Indians shouldn't drink."
> Juan shrugged, and his brother's hand fell away. He thought of the other saying — Mexicans shouldn't drink with Indians.[39]

Selden Rodman in *Mexican Journal* expressed his sense of this situation, observing that it is a phenomenon of "still class-ridden Mexico" that the Indian with his *serape* cannot be seen in a theater or in a restaurant. Rodman described experiencing an "uncomfortable feeling of class" as he emerges from the plush lobby of a theater into a street that "was romantically illuminated by clusters of cast-iron *quetzal* birds with bulbs hanging from their distended tongues" and saw "Indians along the wall, blankets held over mouths" eyeing him sullenly.[40]

The extent to which racism is perceived in Mexico does, to some extent, depend upon the eye of the beholder. Langston Hughes, whose father had settled in Mexico in order to escape the color line in Oklahoma, felt general relief from racial pressure in Mexico. In *I Wonder as I Wander,* he described his meeting with Diego Rivera.

> It was Covarrubias who introduced me to Diego Rivera, that mountain of a man, darker than I am in complexion. When I told Diego he looked more like an American Negro than a Mexican Indian, Rivera said, "One of my grandmothers was a Negro."
> Then he and Covarrubias told me about the African strains to be found in Mexican blood, particularly in the Vera Cruz section of the coast where many of the people are dark indeed. Certainly, Diego

Rivera had large and quite Negroid features and a deep bronze complexion. But fortunately in Mexico color did not matter as it does in the United States.[41]

Undoubtedly color in Mexico does not have that sense of untouchability that it does in the United States, but even the people in the slums of Mexico City are not without their sense of race. In *Five Families,* Oscar Lewis reports of the children of Antonia, daughter of Jesus Sánchez, that "both children were light-skinned like their father, and Antonia kept them indoors much of the time to prevent their skin growing dark."[42] A half-brother of Antonia was a young man named Roberto, who had a dark complexion. The people in the Casa Grande, a large slum tenement in the heart of Mexico City, frequently taunted Roberto with the epithet "negro cambujo," which could be freely translated as "lousy black." In *The Children of Sánchez,* Roberto bitterly describes a boyhood experience in which he was rebuffed because of his appearance. Once, with his brother Manuel and a friend, Alberto, the Donkey, Roberto was accosting people outside of a public swimming pool for the additional money which the boys needed in order to get into the pool. A passing drunk gave Manuel and Alberto the money they needed. When Roberto asked for some money, the man said: " 'No, you little son-of-a-bitch. Get out of here. You're too black.' " In reporting this incident, Roberto said, "That hurt me very much. My brother and Alberto went in without me, leaving me desperate and humiliated."[43] Roberto's deeply ingrained sense of inferiority may have stemmed from his consciousness of racial difference. He only felt free when alone and on the open road.

The expression of this awareness that some of Mexico's ancient ills continue under the new order provides a contrapuntal theme to the general enthusiasm expressed by American writers for the Mexican Revolution. "Along the street," wrote John Dos Passos in "Land of Great Volcanos," "shuffles an Indian in old wornout sandals, a dusty silent man in whitish rags, bowed under a crate he carries by a strap across his forehead. He walks with his eyes on the ground and says nothing. Politicians of all colors go by, in pink limousines, purple roadsters, monogrammed speed cars."[44] The principal difference between these politicians and the pre-revolutionary breed may be, indeed, that the present crop is "of all colors," showing at least some movement upward from the bottom.

Along with the politicians, another perennial class still carries on in much the same way in Mexico, the caste of military officers. Gomez, the impresario of a small-town bull ring in Tom Lea's *The Brave Bulls,* knew that he could have no redress against the arrogance of a colonel. Realistically he adjusted to it. Though much harried as the day of the big *corrida* approached, he had the additional worry of seeing about getting a new head usher. "Since the trouble with the colonel last time who took eight seats without tickets and threw the head usher in jail for protesting, Gomez had to be careful about ushers. The colonel was still mad; it was bad to have a mad colonel around. A new head usher."[45] Selden Rodman, again in *Mexican Journal,* expressed his feeling of embarrassment for his friend, Don Paco, who did not dare stand up for him before a bullying official. "I looked at Don Paco. His eyes were lowered. In Mexico, with the Revolution become official, a pervasive fear of soldiers and federal officialdom remains. The resignation on Don Paco's face, his obvious fear of running afoul of the higher unseen powers with their seals, revenue stamps, and interminable forms, reminded me unpleasantly of Germany."[46]

The question of authority as it affects individuals and as it is passed on from one regime to another is taken up in a subtle novel about modern Mexico, *Fiesta,* by Robert Ramsey. Two of the principal figures of the book are Don Hipolito and his father General Yanez, who were once peons on the hacienda they now operate. Don Hipolito tries to conceal his Indian origin by wearing English clothes. Yet, in spite of the obvious spuriousness of their claims, General Yanez and Don Hipolito are presented as being in a certain way authentic as representing the inevitable principle of authority, a necessary myth. Ramsey develops this idea in a scene in which Dr. Horstelman, a German living in Mexico, discusses General Yanez with a movie director who is planning a film designed to glorify the Revolution with General Yanez as the central figure, a legendary hero. The speciousness of taking an illiterate Indian, who managed without doing much to emerge from the Revolution as a general, and of blowing him up to heroic proportions is, of course, apparent to the doctor, but nevertheless he sees a certain fitness to the procedure. Mexico, as Horstelman explains it, is a land in which the drama of the conquest repeats itself periodically with the Indians as the perennial victims. " 'Although the Indian part of the country seems simple at first,' " says the doctor, " 'in reality it is not, but is a complicated mixture of pride, arrogance, resentment, fear of authority, resignation to a hopeless condition, uncertainty, a feeling of having no identity, of being rejected and belonging nowhere, and out of this uncertainty needing authority, requiring strong leaders.' " Though these leaders have always turned out to be pillagers, they have seemed to the Indians to be "a means of escape, at least a hope of escape . . . ." Such need and expectation would be directed, says Horstelman to the movie maker, even to " 'this mythical one you intend for the country. He is true then, this myth; for it is necessary to have some myth to believe.' "[47]

Mexican officialdom has been viewed by modern American writers not only in terms of power but also in terms of corruption. The theme of corrupt practices in office has been handled much as it was by the early writers, probably because the facts of the situation have not changed much. Sidney Lanier in the essay "San Antonio de Bexar" goes back to the early history of Texas under Mexico to illustrate why he is pessimistic about Mexican politics. He tells the story of Sandoval, a late eighteenth century governor of Texas and an honorable man, who was accused by a rival, Franquis, of irregularities in office.

> The testimony being taken and returned, the Attorney General in November, 1741, entirely acquits Sandoval. But alas for the stout old soldier! this is in Mexico, where from of old, if one is asked who rules now, one must reply with the circumspection of that Georgia judge, who, being asked the politics of his son, made answer that he knew not, not having seen the creature since breakfast. Vizzarón has gone out; the Duke de la Conquista has come into the Viceroyalty; and Sandoval has hardly had time to taste his hard-earned triumph before, through the machinations of Franquis, he finds himself in prison by order of the new viceroy.[48]

The subject of Mexican corruption, on a humbler governmental level, is treated in a section of Robert Herrick's novel *Waste*. Gordie Lane, the very spoiled son of a rich American woman, has shot, with practically no provocation, a Mexican-American boy, Tranquilino. The sheriff handling the case is Mexican-American himself, but the boy is acquitted. Not long after, the sheriff appears in a big, red, new car which becomes known as "the Lane boy's price." Also the sheriff's two-story adobe dwelling in Santa Anna "grew a new corrugated iron roof in the spring when his term ended; he did not run for re-election, his people being against him."[49] Mexican graft even gets notice in modern American verse. In William Carlos Williams' "The Desert Music," the poet is wandering through Ciudad Juárez, across the border from El Paso, Texas, in the role of a typical American tourist. He repeats to himself some recent gossip and adds his own comment as he ambles wearily toward a night club.

> They had the mayor up last month for taking $3000 a week from the whore houses of the city. Not much left for the girls.[50]

In Oscar Lewis' *The Children of Sánchez*, Roberto, one of the sons of Sánchez, claims that he spent six months in a Mexico City jail because of mistaken identity. According to his report, he was beaten three times a day, tortured by electric shocks and dunkings in a barrel of water, to force him to confess a robbery which he did not commit.[51] Roberto's brother Manuel makes the following comments on the Mexican police:

> In my opinion, the Mexican police system is the best system of organized gangsters in the world. It is a disaster, a filthy thing. I might as well come right out with it, the justice here in Mexico turns my stomach. Why? Because justice is for the one who has the money. When a rich man gets killed, the police don't let grass grow under their feet, because there is money around. But how many poor guys are found drowned in the canal, stabbed in the back, or lying in the gutter in a dark street, and the police never, but never, solve the crime. And there are people who do two or three years in jail, because they have no one to stand up for them, or because they don't have fifty pesos for a payoff.[52]

Thievery as practiced by Mexicans generally continues to be a subject in American writing. The attitudes taken by the authors, however, have changed markedly from the tone of outrage and contempt employed by the early border writers. In some cases the modern writer protests against the stereotype by which Mexicans are automatically assumed to be thieves. One of the villains, a cowhand, in Walter van Tilburg Clark's *The Ox-Bow Incident* urges that a group of men, including a Mexican, suspected of cattle rustling be hanged immediately. The presence of a Mexican among the men seems to this cowhand to confirm their guilt. Urging on his fellows, he claims that if they wait for the law to take a hand, they will "have every thieving Mex and Indian and runaway Reb in the whole territory" eating off their own plates. "I say stretch the bastards. . . ."[53] The suspected men, who in fact are innocent, are lynched. The act of theft on the part of Robinson Jeffers' old Mexican, Escobar, showing as it does a contempt for the work-a-day world, is invested with an aura of almost druidical sacredness.

> Old Escobar had a cunning trick when he
>    stole beef. He and his grandsons
> Would drive the cow up here to a starlight death and
>    hoist the carcass into the tree's hollow,
> Then let them search his cabin, he could smile for
>    pleasure, to think of his meat hanging secure
> Exalted over the earth and the ocean, a theft like
>    a star, secret against the supreme sky.[54]

Robbery is treated by some writers as simply part of the quaint folkways south of the border, which must be taken in stride. MacKinley Helm in the collection of short stories, *A Matter of Love,* a group of sketches about Mexican life told in the first person, writes about a friend, Pepe Mantillo, who "made his living by robbing the churches — although we did not, when we spoke of it, refer to his calling by its actual name."[55] The song writers, MacGregor and Horter, in Wright Morris' novel *Love Among the Cannibals*[56] have their car stripped down during a trip to

Acapulco and then have to pay for it to be reassembled, undoubtedly by the same Mexicans who had stripped it down. The situation is taken as a matter of course and with a certain resigned amusement. These sophisticated attitudes toward Mexican stealing of necessity contain an element of condescension. Frederick Conner, the protagonist of Gilbert Neiman's *There's a Tyrant in Every Country,* loses his original attitude of contempt for Mexicans as a thieving people when he gets to know some of the hordes of totally homeless children who sleep in doorways in Mexico City. He suddenly realizes what it must be like "to have to sleep with no shoes and little clothing in one of these huge doorways, everything inside bolted against you. One would grow up a thief and a murderer."[57]

The whole subject of murder, savagery, and violence continues to feature prominently in the report on Mexico by American writers. Bayard Taylor wrote of the "disgusting class" of *leperos,* the threadbare vagabonds who have always abounded in the cities of Mexico, that "if it be an object with any one to have you removed from this sphere of being, they will murder you for a small consideration."[58] Frederic Remington described having been fascinated by the inherent savagery expressed in the face of an old Mexican fiddler performing at a hacienda in northern Mexico. The weather-beaten, crumbled ruin of a face seemed to the writer to be something from the pre-history of man. Remington guessed that if this man from Sonora had never committed murder it was simply that he had never had the opportunity. And, on the subject of opportunities for murder, Remington rather smugly added that "Sonora is a long travel from Plymouth Rock."[59]

The age-old story of the brutal persecution of witches has its counterpart in Mexico, where witches can be men as well as women. In Wilson's *Crazy February,* a young Indian, Mario, thinks back on how his father, the elder of the village, failed in his efforts to prevent the slaughtering of people as witches.

> He remembered evenings when he was younger, and men would come together at his father's house, since his father was an elder of the hamlet. At first only five or six men, claiming that someone was a witch, and they wanted to take him to the village. Mario's father, speaking from the doorway, would spread his smooth calmness over them, and they would go away. But later Mario might see them talking among themselves on the road, or at another's house, and there would be a larger pack of men, some of them with their hunting guns. Sometime in the night the boy would hear feet on the road, like horses going by, and then a single shot, and his father would sigh, as though in his dream. The next morning the news of the witch's death would run around the circle of women drawing water, and

Mario would know when he came home from school that the man was dead. And at the same time, the whole event would be over. That night no one would hum on the road and everything would be quiet again. These things were like a storm. Terrible because no one knew exactly what would happen when the storm broke. And more terrible because the land was always the same, unmarked, when the storm was over.[60]

Even in American novels where there are no Mexicans present, the Mexican reputation for violence can find its echoes. In one of the first of the American naturalistic novels, *McTeague* by Frank Norris, the bitterly jealous Marcus Schouler, in a barroom scene, hurls a knife at the huge dentist, McTeague, to the stupefaction of the other customers. "What a — what a devil!" shouts one of them, "What treachery! A regular greaser trick!"[61] In Kate Chopin's novel, *The Awakening,* which has its locale in New Orleans and environs, a young Creole, Robert Lebrun, is about to leave Louisiana in order to take up a business career in Mexico. A woman friend was bent on giving him advice about Mexico:

> Madame Ratignolle hoped that Robert would exercise extreme caution in dealing with the Mexicans, who, she considered, were a treacherous people, unscrupulous and revengeful. She trusted she did them no injustice in thus condemning them as a race. She had known personally but one Mexican, who made and sold excellent tamales, and whom she would have trusted implicitly, so soft-spoken was he. One day he was arrested for stabbing his wife. She never knew whether he had been hanged or not.[62]

The almost hysterical fear that some Americans felt toward "violent" Mexicans became a source of amusement to Sherwood Anderson. He was spending the night in a small hotel in northern Mexico, and, because he could not sleep, he went out to smoke on the balcony. He was seated near the window of the Americans in the next room. Down below, an elderly Mexican night watchman was pacing his rounds. The woman of the couple in the next room became panicky, convinced that the two figures, that on the balcony and the one pacing below, were both Mexicans closing in on them. She awakened her husband and whispered of possible kidnapping or murder. When Anderson overheard them, he "became malicious." A cock had begun to crow and was being answered by others in the town. Anderson started crowing lustily himself, and kept it up.[63]

However, the humorous approach remains the exception. Frederic Remington's contemporary and friend, Stephen Crane, also had an eye for that which was savage, animal-like in the Mexicans he reported on. In the story "Moonlight on the Snow," he wrote that the chief function of the Southwestern town of Warpost was to prey upon the cowboys who "when they were paid, rode gaily into town to look for fun. To this end there were in Warpost many thugs and thieves. There was treachery and obscenity and merciless greed in every direction. Even Mexico was levied upon to furnish a kind of ruffian which appears infrequently in the northern races."[64] Crane's conception of a ruffian, Mexican style, is described elsewhere.

In "Horses — One Dash," written in that spare and very specific language which has left its mark on American fiction, Crane gives his portrayal of Mexican bandits. The American, Richardson, while riding through rural Mexico with a Mexican attendant, secured lodgings for the night in a small adobe house in a remote town. All was quiet when the two men settled down, but some hours later Richardson became aware of a disturbance in the other room. There had been arrivals since he and his servant had entered the house. A drinking party was obviously in session, and the noise of it had an ominous undertone of savagery. In a little while, "he heard two men quarreling in short, sharp words like pistol-shots; they were calling each other worse names than common people know in other countries." Suddenly the blanket which separated Richardson's room from the other "was flung aside, and the red light of a torch flared into the room. It was held high by a fat, round-faced Mexican, whose little snake-like moustache was as black as his eyes, and whose eyes were black as jet. He was insane with the wild rage of a man whose liquor is dully burning at his brain." Several other equally savage-looking men gathered behind him. "The fat one," as he glared at Richardson, "posed in the manner of a grandee. Presently his hand dropped to his belt, and from his lips there spun an epithet — a hideous word which often foreshadows knife-blows, a word peculiarly of Mexico, where people have to dig deep to find an insult that has not lost its savour." The Mexicans urged each other to the attack. Aside from the pleasure of the kill, there would be booty in the form of an expensive saddle and beautifully worked boots as well as in the always acceptable form of whatever money Richardson might have in his possession. Yet, for all their drunken rage, as the American held a gun on them and stared coldly in their direction, they kept back. Not one of them was quite drunk enough to want to be the sacrificial victim that would be required if the American was to be overpowered. The deadlock was finally broken with the sound of giggling girls. These had obviously been sent for some time ago and were just arriving. The Mexicans turned to other pursuits.[65]

Robinson Jeffers in *Tamar* uses the theme of Mexican violence to set the tone for violent actions to come, reminding the reader by his choice of Mexican figures of the pre-American heritage of California.

>     Sylvia Vierra and her man had lived in
>         the little white-washed farm-hut
> Under the surf-reverberant blue-gums; two years ago
>         they had had much wine in the house, their friend
> Verdugo came avisiting, he being drunk on the raw
>         plenty of wine they thought abused
> Nine-year-old Mary, Sylvia's daughter, they struck him
>         from behind and when he was down unmanned him
> With the kitchen knife, then plotted drunkenly — for he
>         seemed to be dead — where to dispose the body.
> That evening Tamar Cauldwell riding her white pony
>         along the coast-road saw a great bonfire
> Periling the gum-tree grove, and riding under the
>         smoke met evil odors, turning in there
> Saw by the firelight a man's feet hang out of the fire;
>         then Tamar never having suffered
> Fear in her life, knocked at the hut's door and un-
>         answered entered, and found the Vierras asleep
> Steaming away their wine, but little Mary weeping,
>         She had taken the child and ridden homeward.[66]

A crime of violence is put in the context of the religious and political conflicts of modern Mexico in one of the stories in MacKinley Helm's *A Matter of Love*. José and Lupita have argued about what to name their baby boy. José wants to name him Revolución, and Lupita insists on a Christian name. The couple are taken before Abadesa (Abbess), Doña Belica, and the priest, Padre Orlando. Faced with these representatives of clerical authority, José experiences rising up within him the deeply ingrained fear of the Church, a fear which is more profoundly a part of his nature than his recently acquired revolutionary sentiments. Though he quails before the Abadesa and the priest, he snatches the child, to save face, from Lupita's arms and runs. She shouts at him to stop or she will "make shame" of his name. José fears the "one shame that can shame a Mexican man." Rather than be publicly called a cuckold, he returns the infant. However, the doubt, having entered his mind, fixes itself there. The child is dutifully christened Juan María Navidad de Jesús. After the ceremony, José goes out and gets drunk. He returns home, strangles the infant, stabs Lupita to death, and flees never to be heard from again. The dead child is dressed in pure white, and the nuns rejoice that he has gone to heaven spotlessly innocent.[67]

In another story in the same collection, Helm again turns to a study of crime in Mexico. Unlike the early border writers with their blanket indictment of Mexican violence, Helm is prepared to consider the situation in its relation to conventions, strongly ascribed to, which have been violated. Yet the conclusion that the author comes to is not a completely relativistic one. The scene of most of the action is San Rafael de Aldama, an imaginary town modeled upon San Miguel Allende. Luke Bustamente is married to Maruca Ugarte. She is looking forward to celebrating the occasion of her fourth anniversary at the mayor's fiesta wearing a new dress which has been ordered in Mexico City. However, Luke does not come home on that night nor for several nights to come, since his return has been prevented by a mistress jealous of Maruca's new dress. Maruca, of the proud and rich Ugartes, ceases from this time forward, to regard Luke as her husband. She takes up with a young American painter, Jonathan Wells, a good friend of the narrator, and, in open defiance of Mexican convention, she flaunts her affair publicly. Jonathan is invited to go swimming by Luke's two brothers and a cousin. The fact that the American unguardedly accepts the invitation marks his ignorance of Mexican ways. His body is later found at the bottom of the pool. At the time of this occurrence, the narrator of the story is not in San Rafael but in Oaxaca, considerably to the south He comes across Luke's two brothers and cousin, and, not having been appraised of events in San Rafael, is most surprised to see them so far from their usual haunts. However, he invites them for some beers in a cafe. They respond gracefully and are politely evasive about things in San Rafael. The next day, the narrator gets a letter from an American friend in San Rafael, describing the death of Jonathan. The narrator then accosts the three Mexican youths and charges them with complicity in the murder of his friend. They blandly and politely disclaim any knowledge of the drowning and, furthermore, explain that they are preparing to embark on a tour of study abroad — made possible by a loan from the lawyer Ugarte, Maruca's father. In considering this and other experiences in San Rafael, the narrator has a mental conversation with Dr. Margrove, a long-time American resident of the town, who told him when he first arrived that he would have to learn to accept the ways of San Rafael and not pass judgement. In the course of this mental conversation, the narrator thinks: "I must tell you now, after observing the ways of the town for some years, that I cannot ignore them. I am under a spell. And in my mind, I can't leave the place, for I love it — though work keeps me absent. As for liking the ways of the people, let me say more correctly, that they fill me with wonder — like eagles in air, like serpents on rocks, like ships on the sea, like young men with maidens. San Rafael de Aldama is an adulterous woman: she eateth, and wipeth her mouth, and saith, I have done no wrong." [68]

In the slum areas of Mexico City, according to Oscar Lewis' informants, a person is wise to look the other way if he chances upon a scene in which a crime is being committed. A woman named Rosa Gomez repeats a tale told to her by her husband, Beto, who works for a bus company in Mexico City. "Last night Beto told me that a collector on the Tzotzil line was murdered. They got him when he went to check in. This guy couldn't keep quiet and when he saw someone about to take a man's wallet he said, 'Watch out for thieves.' They didn't try anything more but just looked at him mad-like and that night on the last run this guy got down off the bus to check in and the other guy, without making any noise, hit him on the head with a piece of iron and whistled like the collectors do and the driver started off. Later they found him there all covered with blood." [69]

Witter Bynner's poem, "Volcano," equating land and people, can serve as a coda to the subject of Mexican violence.

> Once were these mountains a vast volcano-rim?
> Are these September clouds, that hang the peaks
> With rain and in canyons drift downward like snow,
> All that remains in the plaza, how eyes that were laughing
> With sun go suddenly hot with lava, like Garifo's —
> Who has had to leave Chapala for a while
> Because there was too much fire in his knife. [70]

Often allied to violence, but not necessarily so, is the characteristic of cruelty, a quality which has been an age-old ingredient in the legend of Spain, whether on the Peninsula or in the New World. Spaniards have complained bitterly about the *leyenda negra* (black legend) and have blamed their former arch-enemies the English, especially English historians, for having so firmly established this image of Spain in the minds of the rest of Europe and of North America. However, when Americans first encountered in the Southwest a people who bore the impress of Spanish culture, these Americans were, as has been shown, repelled by what seemed to them to be a strong strain of cruelty in the nature of the people. The American frontiersmen in the Southwest, to be sure, were not in the least prone to give the Mexican the benefit of the doubt, nor were they inclined to search deeply for the explanation of Mexican conduct. But the report of Mexican cruelty has persisted in American letters, sometimes being explained as a combination of Spanish and Indian elements in Mexican culture. Stephen Crane wrote a piece for the *Philadelphia Press,* which appeared on May 19, 1895, entitled "Mexican Sights and Street Scenes," which illustrated the cruelty shown by Mexicans to animals.

> When a burdened donkey falls down, a half a dozen Indians gather around it and brace themselves. Then they take clubs and hammer the everlasting daylight out of the donkey. They also swear in Mexican. Mexican is a very capable language for pur-

poses of profanity. A good swearer here can bring rain in thirty minutes.

It is a great thing to hear the thump, thump of the clubs and the howling of the natives, and to see the little legs of the donkey quiver and to see him roll his eyes. Finally, after they have hammered him out as flat as a drum head it flashes upon them suddenly that the burro cannot get up until they remove the load. Well, then, at last they remove his load and the donkey, not much larger than a kitten at best, and now disheveled, weak, and tottering, struggles gratefully to his feet.

Further in the article, Crane takes up the subject of street vendors in Mexico City, in the course of which he relates this incident.

It is never just to condemn a class, in returning to the street vendors, it is but fair to record an extraordinary instance of the gentleness, humanity, and fine capability of pity in one of their number. An American lady was strolling in the public park one afternoon when she observed a vendor with four little plum-colored birds seated quietly and peacefully upon his brown hand.

"Oh, look at those dear little birds, she cried to her escort. How tame they are!"

Her escort too was struck with admiration and astonishment and they went close to the little birds. They saw their happy, restful countenances and with what wealth of love they looked up into the face of their owner.

The lady bought two of these birds, although she hated to wound their little hearts by tearing them away from their master.

When she got to her room she closed the door and the windows, and then reached into the wicker cage and brought out one of the pets, for she wished to gain their affection too, and teach them to sit upon her finger.

The little bird which she brought out made a desperate attempt to perch upon her finger, but suddenly toppled off and fell to the floor with a sound like that made by a water-soaked bean bag.

The loving vendor had filled his birds full of shot. This accounted for their happy, restful countenances and their very apparent resolution never to desert the adored finger of their master.

In an hour, both the little birds died. You would die too if your stomach was full of shot.

Thus ended the Mexican counterpart of "The Jumping Frog of Calaveras County."

One of the memorable scenes in Frank Norris's *The Octopus,* was a description of a huge roundup of jack rabbits. A number of farmers and ranchers had gotten together to rid themselves of these crop-damaging pests. The men started in a very wide circle, and as they moved forward, shrinking the circumference, they made a great deal of noise driving the frightened rabbits toward the center. Finally, as the circle closed, the rabbits were driven into a prearranged corral where they were clubbed to death.

> Armed with a club in each hand, the young fellows from Guadalajara and Bonneville, and the farm boys from the ranches, leaped over the rails of the corral. They walked unsteadily upon the myriad of crowding bodies underfoot, or, as space was cleared, sank almost waist-deep into the mass that leaped and squirmed about them. The Anglo-Saxon spectators round about drew back in disgust, but the hot, degenerated blood of Portuguese, Mexican, and mixed Spaniard boiled up in excitement at this wholesale slaughter.[71]

The theme of Hispanic cruelty appeared elsewhere in the book. The California-Mexican priest, Fr. Sarria, a well-liked man, devoted to works of charity, stopped by at the ranch of his friend, Annixter. While Annixter and Fr. Sarria were enjoying a drink together, Annixter's Irish setter nosed over the wicker basket which the priest had brought with him. The top fell off, and out came two game cocks, fitted out with "enormous, cruel-looking spurs." Annixter was at first astonished and then amused.

> "Oh, you old rat! You'll be a dry nurse to a burro, and keep a hospital for infirm puppies, but you will fight game cocks. Oh, Lord! Why Sarria, this is as good a grind as I ever heard. There's the Spanish cropping out, after all."
>
> Speechless with chagrin, the priest bundled the cocks into the basket and catching up the valise, took himself abruptly away, almost running till he had put himself out of hearing of Annixter's raillery.[72]

Anita Brenner in *Idols Behind Altars* recalls early scenes in the neighborhood of her father's house in Mexico when soldiers of the Revolution would gather in nearby fields to amuse themselves. "I'd see a circle of men around a plunging, bellowing calf, with ropes tied to its hoofs and a soldier hanging on each, in a tug-of-war to split a haunch first. Live meat ripped open glints rose and blue in the sun."[73] Callous indifference to suffering, squalor, and an attendant sense of evil are the oppressive elements that go into one of Conrad Aiken's Mexican street scenes. Blomberg, a sensitive Bostonian in the novel *A Heart for the Gods of Mexico,* looks with pity and revulsion upon the living refuse of Mexico City.

> A blind beggar, with white slits for eyes, and as evil a face as he ever had seen, was led into the cafe, and out again, by a frightened little girl. A starved dog with a broken back, the hind quarters twisted, dragged itself crookedly to the little parapet of flowerpots by the entrance, and lay there, mutely begging. No attention

was paid to it. The eyes, tender and trusting, beseeching, were enough to break one's heart; and when at last it gave up hope, and began to drag itself away, it heaved such a sigh of pure and beaten despair as ought rightly to have ended the world. He watched its pitifully slow progress all along the side of the darkening square, towards the palace, and then out of sight round a corner. He felt quite sure that it was going away to die; that sigh could have meant nothing else. And it was an indictment of mankind.[74]

The plight of dogs in Mexico is used by poet Denise Levertov to provide a basic image for her poem "As It Happens."

> Like dogs in Mexico,
> furless, sore, misshapen,
>
> arrives from laborious nowhere
> agony. And proves
>
> to have eyes of kindness,
> a pitiful tail; wants
>
> love. Give it some, in form of
> dry tortilla, . . .[75]

In Tennessee Williams' *The Night of the Iguana,* the torturing of the great lizard reenforces general themes of brutality. In a hotel in tropical Mexico, Shannon, the renegade minister, is talking to Hannah, New England spinster.

> SHANNON: It's a kind of lizard — a big one, a giant one. The Mexican kids caught it and tied it up.
>
> HANNAH: Why did they tie it up?
>
> SHANNON: Because that's what they do. They tie them up and fatten them up and then eat them up, when they're ready for eating. They're a delicacy. Taste like white meat of chicken. At least the Mexicans think so. And also the kids, the Mexican kids, have a lot of fun with them, poking out their eyes with sticks and burning their tails with matches. You know? Fun? Like that?[76]

The Beat Poets felt the lure of Mexico and responded to its vividness and intensity, but along with fascination, they sometimes felt a degree of repulsion. In "Impressions of Mexico," Gregory Corso accuses Mexican reality of being worse than nightmare.

> I tell you, Mexico —
> I think miles and miles of dead full-bodied horses —

Thoroughbreds and work horses, flat on their sides
Stiffened with straight legs and lipless mouths,
It is the stiff leg, Mexico, the jutted tooth,
That wrecks my equestrian dream of nightmare.[77]

The success of a bullfighter, Gitanillo, in Josephina Niggli's *Mexican Village,* is attributed to the fact that "Mexico loved the streak of cruelty in him that gave him a dangerous, sinister glamour."[78]

In *Behind the Mountains,* Oliver La Farge tells of an aristocratic Mexican boy who becomes repelled by the cruelty of a Mexican man he once admired. Young Pino Baca, son of the *patron,* Don José, had always felt a great inner excitement when he met Pascual Orozco, a professional horse thief, who periodically stole horses from the big ranches of the Rio Grande Valley and drove them by forced marches into the inaccessible regions of the Sangre de Cristo mountains north of Santa Fe and Taos. Orozco was famous for cunning, daring, and inexhaustible physical endurance. To Pino Baca the horse thief was an object of hero worship, and the boy was very flattered when Orozco began addressing him using the familiar form in Spanish. On one occasion, Orozco was giving Pino a lift into town in a Model T Ford. A dog, which had frequently made a nuisance of itself, came racing up to the car barking furiously. While continuing to drive, Orozco, with one hand, looped his lariat around the dog's neck and dragged the animal along the road until its head separated from its body. The boy was horrified. "This was the thing inside Pascual. You knew he was deadly, and that fascinated you, but you never dreamed what it would be like to have him let you see it." Pino Baca, after that occasion, never felt the same about Orozco. "At moments when he thought of the horse thief, or when he met him, first would come the old familiar admiration, then, the remembering. And if Pasqual was physically present, Pino would assume the graceful politeness that is the ancient Spanish mask. At this time Pasqual stopped addressing him as 'thou'.[79] The story serves as a reminder of the danger of generalizing about the nature of a people, as in this case both reprover and reproved are Mexicans, though undoubtedly to the author the difference in class is an important factor.

That age in the history of Europe which approved the baiting of animals (and there are those who see in the Spanish bullfight evidence of a culture's arrested sensibility) also considered the tormenting of the insane to be a form of sport. Skinner Bradshaw, in Alwyn Lee's story of the Point Four official in Mexico, was treated to the daily spectacle of an aged and insane woman being tormented by street urchins. " 'Apart from the cruelty of it,' " Bradshaw thought to himself, " 'all children, of course, are cruel . . . the appalling thing is that nobody sees anything wrong in it. Here it is perfectly O.K. to make fun of insane people. Medieval. . . .' "⁸⁰ The fetid atmosphere, a combination of physical decay and moral corruption, which hangs over Alwyn Lee's Mexican port town has its counterparts in other accounts of Mexico. In Aiken's *A Heart for the Gods of Mexico* one character, summing up his total impression of the country, exclaims: " 'My God, *everything* here seems poisonous!' "⁸¹ Callous indifference, in Ernest Hemingway's story "The Mother of a Queen," is made to seem the more corrupt because of the ornateness of the excuse. Paco, a Mexican matador and a homosexual, a "queen," has been informed by the management of the graveyard in which his mother has been buried that if he doesn't keep up his rent on the plot, the body will be dug up and the bones thrown on the common heap. Paco has been doing very well in appearances throughout Mexico and can well afford to pay the rent. His American manager reminds him each time a notice comes from the cemetery, and each time Paco claims that he will attend to the matter soon. Finally, when the body is dug up and tossed away, Paco's manager, in an explosion of rage and loathing, expresses his complete disgust. Paco shows no signs of offense at the insults that have been thrown at him and answers simperingly: " 'It is my mother, now she is so much dearer to me. Now I don't have to think of her buried in one place and be sad. Now she is all about me in the air, like the birds and the flowers. Now she will always be with me.' "⁸² A stronger dose of corrupt callousness and cruelty goes into Neiman's portrait of El General País in *There Is A Tyrant in Every Country*. The general is an actual person, but his portrait also serves symbolically as one of the faces of Mexico. The protagonist first comes across the general in a photograph on the cover of a popular magazine picked up at a Chicago newsstand.

> A toad if ever there was one. His skin was dark and hard as an alligator's, with an assortment of pimples and moles that would have made a decorative, serviceable leather for women's shoes. The bulge of his several chins made a billowing flare that folded over his collar. His hyperthyroid eyes were the shiny, fat, moist ones of a tropical reptile. You could see him clambering up on a rank, mossy bank through the putrescent scum of a stagnant marsh. . . . At one and the same time he was greedy yet complacent, powerful yet soft. The outer coating was padded, but the clench of his jaw was deadly as steel. Although his smile was smug and idiotic, the voracious dark of his scheming eyes gave off sparks that spat brighter than metals. . . . From what I'd read about Mexico, he was the essence of the country.⁸³

When the narrator finally encounters the General in Mexico, that sinister man, who "had a grandeur about his thousand diseases," lived up to expectations. Prominent among his characteristics was a total cruelty.

The belief in Mexican cruelty has been a fixed part of the folklore of Texas since the Alamo and the massacre of Fannin's men at Goliad. Though modern Texas writers have been, by and large, appreciative of Mexican culture, they have made their contributions to the legend. Tom Lea in *The Wonderful Country,* a novel of the Texas border region in the 1880's, had a General Castro give an order to a captain known as "El Verdugo," the hangman, to bury six captives from the opposing forces of General Salcido up to their chins and then ride horses over their heads. The order was carried out, after which "the troopers rode their horses through the water several times."[84] John Houghton Allen in *Southwest* included a portrait of General Fierro, a man who was in fact Pancho Villa's right-hand man and a celebrated sadist. " 'Fierro was our General,' " reminisces a Mexican character in the novel, " 'a good companion, but very brutal. He used to kill Obregón's men with his bare hands, and he was strong as a horse. He shot all the sentries who slept at their posts, muttering *"Pobrecito! Pobrecito!"* when he did, for he was not a man without sentiment. When he took a town he sometimes tied the Chinese together by their pigtails and burned them alive, because he hated Chinamen, and he would not have you consider him a man without humor.' "[85] Frank Dobie, as is his way, vivified an idea by re-telling a legend of the border region. The old Hacienda de Las Cinco Llagas (Hacienda of the Five Wounds) in northern Mexico was owned in Spanish times by the Marqués de Aguayo. The Marques, a powerful man in middle age, suspected that his young wife was having an affair with his handsome nephew. He had horses posted at intervals from the hacienda at Los Patos to the distant town of Mazapil. At Mazapil he engaged in a game of monte after dark with some friends. After a while he casually excused himself, got on a horse and rode like fury to the first post, where the horse dropped dead from exhaustion. He took the fresh mount waiting for him and rode like the wind to the next post, where the horse died as he took another mount. And so it went from post to post until he reached the hacienda where he surprised his wife and nephew in bed and stabbed them in such a way as to make the act seem to have been a joint suicide. He then rode back in the same manner but this time killing his *mozo,* servant, at each stop to eliminate witnesses. When he reached Mazapil, the monte game was still in progress and he rejoined it. Though he was tried for murder, he was acquitted on the ground that no one could have covered the distance from Mazapil to Los Patos and back again in such short time. This story, Dobie tells us, is still celebrated in a borderland ballad.[86]

The stereotype of the Mexican as a coward, usually contrasted to a bold American hero, so common in the early border chronicles, has by and large disappeared from serious American writing about Mexico. A version of this theme does, however, survive in the work of two transitionary writers, Bret Harte and Stephen Crane. The gambler, Jack Hamlin, in Harte's *Gabriel Conroy,* by a show of nerve and self-assurance, got the better of a group of Mexicans. Conroy had accused Victor Ramírez of cheating at monte. Ramírez rallied a group of fellow Mexicans to avenge this insult upon him and upon the Mexican race. However, the "allies" turned irresolute and were "wholesomely restrained by something in Mr. Hamlin's eye which was visible, and probably a suspicion of something in Mr. Hamlin's pocket which was not." Seeing the Mexicans were losing their nerve, the American pushed his advantage. "Under the pretense of hearing more distinctly, Jack Hamlin approached the nearest man, who, I grieve to say, instantly and somewhat undignifiedly retreated. Mr. Hamlin laughed. But already a crowd of loungers had gathered, and he felt it was time to end this badinage, grateful as it was to his sense of humor. So he lifted his hat gravely to Victor and his friends, replaced it perhaps aggressively tilted a trifle over his straight nose, and lounged slowly back to his hotel, leaving his late adversaries in secure but unsatisfactory and dishonorable possession of the field."[87]

Stephen Crane gives the theme a more developed and less complacent treatment. Yet in depicting the brave and stoic white American in contention with a morally inferior, lesser and darker breed of natives, he does maintain a somewhat Kiplingesque attitude. The protagonist of the story "A Man and — Some Others" is an American named Bill, a once successful mine owner who lost his fortune in cards and became successively a gambler, cowboy, rancher, and, after having killed his ranch foreman, an itinerant hobo and shepherd. At the opening of the story he had worked his way to the Southwest and was camping on a range used by Mexican sheepherders who had come to resent his presence. One of them, José, informed Bill that they had decided to kill him if he did not vacate. Bill answered that he intended to fight for his right to stay. The Mexican simply "waved his hand in a consummate expression of indifference. 'Oh, all right,' he said. Then in a tone of deep menace and glee, he added. 'We will keel you eef you no geet. They have decide.'" Bill settled down to waiting for the inevitable attack. A young "tenderfoot" from the East rode up and wanted to camp with Bill for the night. In trying to dissuade him Bill said, "'Well, you see, mister . . . I'd like your company well enough, but — you see, some of these here greasers are goin' to chase me off the range tonight;

and while I might like a man's company all right, I couldn't let him in for no such game when he ain't got nothing to do with the trouble.'"
When asked if the Mexicans would kill him, Bill answered,

> "Don't know. Can't tell till afterward. You see, they take some feller that's alone like me, and then they rush his camp when he ain't quite ready for em, and ginerally plug-im with a sawed-off shotgun load before he has a chance to get at 'em. They lay around and wait for their chance, and it comes soon enough. Of course, a feller alone like me has got to let up watching some time. Maybe they catch'im asleep. Maybe the feller gets tired waiting and goes out in broad day, and kills two or three just to make the whole crowd pile on him and settle the thing. I heard of a case like that once. It's awful hard on a man's mind to get a gang after him."

The young man decided to stick it out with Bill, who proceeded to pile up his sleeping bag by the fire to create the illusion of a sleeping figure. Later at night the dummy was riddled with bullets, and the Mexicans, confident they had got their man, walked forward jubilantly to be met by curses and gun fire. One of them was killed, and the others fled in terror. "The silence returned to the wilderness. The tired flames faintly illuminated the blanketed thing and the flung corpse of the marauder, and sang the fire chorus, the ancient melody which bears the message of the inconsequence of human tragedy." Later the Mexicans crept up again and blasted the camp with a volley that inflicted a mortal wound on Bill, who with his companion fired away killing other Mexicans and dispersing the rest. The young man noted as the Mexicans staggered off in defeat "that one who still possessed a serape had from it none of the grandeur of the cloaked Spaniard, but that against the sky the silhouette resembled a cornucopia of childhood's Christmas." While the story contrasted Mexican treachery and cowardice with the stoic bravery of an American, the author's main concern was not the depicting of racial types. Both Bill and his adversaries were men with ferocious, elemental natures. The story served to present a view of human conflicts as being similar to the grapplings of savage animal forces, struggles in which death is inflicted against the background of a nature which is totally unconcerned and which after all is over will swing "again into stillness and the peace of wilderness." Only in terms of stoically humanistic value can these events be invested with any significance. The young Easterner, when he realized that the other man was fatally wounded, "suddenly felt for Bill, this grimy sheepherder, some deep form of idolatry. Bill was dying, and the dignity of last defeat, the superiority of him who stands in his grave, was in the pose of the lost sheepherder."[88]

In "Horses — One Dash," another Crane story, the contrast of racial types is a primary consideration. Not only is the cool self-possession of Richardson contrasted with the animality and essential cowardice of the drunken Mexican bandits, it is also contrasted to the quaking fear displayed by his Mexican man servant, José. Though Richardson and his attendant managed to get out of the adobe house which lodged the bandits, Richardson knew that he had not seen the last of them, that, because he had fled, "their valor would grow like weeds in the spring, and upon discovering his escape they would ride forth dauntless warriors." Richardson tried to get as much distance behind him as he could before the discovery was made.

> Riding with José was like riding with a corpse. His face resembled a cast in lead. Sometimes he swung forward and almost pitched from his seat. Richardson was too frightened to do anything but hate this man for his fear. Finally he issued a mandate which nearly caused José's eyes to slide out of his head and fall to the ground like two silver coins.
> "Ride behind me — about fifty paces."
> "Señor — — — " stuttered the servant.
> "Go!" cried the American, furiously. He glared at the other and laid his hand on his revolver. José looked at his master wildly. He made a piteous gesture. Then slowly he fell back, watching the hard face of the American for a sign of mercy.
> Richardson had resolved in his rage that at any rate he was going to use the eyes and ears of extreme fear to detect the approach of danger; and so he established his servant as a sort of outpost.
> As they proceeded he was obliged to watch sharply to see that the servant did not slink forward and join him. When José made beseeching circles in the air with his arm he replied by menacingly gripping his revolver.
> José had a revolver, too; nevertheless it was very clear in his mind that the revolver was distinctly an American weapon. He had been educated in the Rio Grande country.[89]

American courage confronts Mexican cowardice again in Crane's story, "The Five White Mice." Three Americans were walking along the streets of Mexico City at night. Only one, the New York Kid, was sober. When another of them, Benson, drunkenly jostled a passing Mexican, that man, moved to "a rage made by vanity" prepared to pull a knife as an evil expression settled on his face. "The sober Kid saw this face as if he and it were alone in space — a yellow mask, smiling in eager cruelty, in satisfaction, and, above all, it was lit with sinister decision."[90] However, when the Mexican realized that one of the Americans was sober and capable of putting up a fight, he backed off.

To the charge of cowardice and treachery as elements in the Mexican character, Charles F. Lummis, that redoubtable defender of Mexico, makes an indignant rebuttal.

> The Mexican is popularly listed — thanks to the safely remote pens of those who know him from a car window, and who would run from his gray wrath — as cowardly and treacherous. He is neither. The sixth generation is too soon to turn coward the blood which made the noblest record of lonely heroism that time ever read. As for treachery, it is merely a question of philosophy whether, in exterminating a rattle-snake, we shall invite it to strike us first, that it may have "a fair show." The Latin method is not to allow that and the foe the privilege of the first bite....[91]

In the short story "A New Mexico David," presumably based upon historical material, Lummis presents the citizens of early Santa Fe as formidable Indian fighters. He traces their skirmishes with the Navajos and recounts instances of heroism. There is Doña Antonia Romero, a woman who saved the town by hitting a Navajo over the head with a *metate* (hand mill), as the warrior, who had climbed the gate of the outer wall, was about to remove the bar and let all his fellow tribesmen into the city. There is also Don Domingo Baca, who, during a Navajo raid, "was pierced by seven lances, and his abdomen was so torn that his bowels fell out. He caught up a pillow, lashed it around his belly, and continued loading and firing for several hours, until the fury of the attack was spent. He then replaced his dangling entrails and sewed up the wound himself. He lived for many years." After giving several more examples of bravery, Lummis concludes with the statement that "despite its fearful besetments the little colony kept alive, and became famous throughout the Territory for its heroic warriors. They were the flower of New Mexico."[92]

Felipe Rivera, the prize fighter in Jack London's "The Mexican," is characterized as a man of tremendous courage. Though relatively inexperienced in the ring, he eagerly accepted the opportunity to take the place of a fighter who had become ill and go into the ring against a celebrated boxer, Danny Ward. The California crowd was all against him, simply because he was a Mexican, and the referee cheated in Ward's favor. Nevertheless Rivera won. "There were no congratulations for Rivera. He walked to his corner unattended, where his seconds had not yet placed his stool. He leaned backward on the ropes and looked his hatred at them, till the whole ten thousand Gringos were included. His knees trembled under him, and he was sobbing from exhaustion."[93]

One of the components of the Mexican ideal of *machismo* is courage.

Manuel in *The Children of Sánchez,* a young man who is struggling for survival in the slums of Mexico City, has this to say:

> I have learned to hide my fear and to show only courage because from what I have observed a person is treated according to the impression he makes. That's why when I am really very afraid inside, outwardly I am calm. It has helped me too, because I didn't suffer as much as some of my friends who trembled when they were grabbed by the police. If a guy shows weakness and has tears in his eyes, and begs for mercy, that is when the others pile on him. In my neighborhood, you are either a *picudo,* a tough guy, or a *pendejo,* a fool.
>
> Mexicans, and I think everyone in the world, admire the person "with balls," as we say. The character who throws punches and kicks, without stopping to think, is the one who comes out on top. The one who has guts enough to stand up against an older, stronger guy, is more respected. If someone shouts, you've got to shout louder. If any so-and-so comes to me and says, "Fuck your mother," I answer, "Fuck your mother a thousand times." And if he gives one step forward and I take one step back, I lose prestige. But if I go forward too, and pile on and make a fool out of him, then the others will treat me with respect. In a fight, I would never give up or say "Enough," even though the other was killing me. I would try to go to my death, smiling. That is what we mean by being "macho," by being manly.[94]

It is undeniably an important part of the Hispanic code that a man who faces death must die not only bravely but with style. Timothy Turner in *Bullets, Bottles, and Gardenias* describes an execution which he witnessed in northern Mexico. A civilian, during the Revolution, was sentenced to die before a firing squad for having leaked information to a faction opposed to the group in control of the area. Turner, as a newspaperman, arrived at the place of execution at dawn. It was still so dark that all he could see of the man standing before the soldiers was his white shirt. Nevertheless, even by the lines of the shirt, Turner could see that the man was controlled, poised. "The officer ordered his men to throw in the shells, and to aim, and then for the first time the prisoner spoke. His voice was calm, even, and terrible. 'Capitán, capitán, apunta bien el corazón.'" (Captain, Captain, aim well at the heart.)[95] The same book contains a photograph of General Santiago Ramírez, one of Villa's officers, standing before a firing squad a moment before his death. He is handsomely attired, not in his uniform, but in his Sunday best. His taut, angular face is expressive of an immense pride. After discoursing on Mexican bravery, Turner states that the Mexican is the most warlike of the Latin Americans and adds, gratuitously, that he is "also the most individualistic, a poet, a musician, a humorist."[96]

The ambivalence of the report on Mexican courage which appears in modern American writing is symptomatic of the difficulties which American authors have had in coming to grips with the subtle, complex, and illusive society to the south. Writers generally must deal with the apparent paradox in the human make-up of contrasting qualities going hand in hand, but in the case of the image of the Mexican as fashioned by American writers the composite portrait is remarkably *chiaroscuro*. However, in respect to one aspect of the Mexican personality, both early and modern American writers seem to have agreed. With considerable regularity they have reported upon the good manners displayed by Mexicans. Owen Wister wrote in his journals:

> I notice always how civil and courteous the humblest Mexican is in his manners. One came to our camp and sat on his horse and held a conversation with us consisting of four words and five minutes, during which he smiled with continual gaiety. He was a patch of rags but perfectly happy — and when he bade us good-bye and rode away, we all commented upon the pleasant manner he had. It is certainly something we of the north could not achieve, and it renders genial the unimportant — which are the most numerous — moments of life.[97]

A similar report comes from Bayard Taylor in his account of California before the old Mexican culture had become submerged. "In spite of the lack of cultivation, except such instruction as the priests were competent to give, the native population possesses a native refinement of manner which would grace the most polished society. They acknowledge their want of education; they tell you they grow as the trees, with the form and character that nature gives them; but even uncultured nature in California wears all the ripeness and maturity of older lands."[98]

Mary Austin, by way of illustrating the excellence of Mexican manners, tells a charming tale about a little town in New Mexico in a short story entitled "The Politeness of Cuesta La Plata." A government dietitian comes to the town of Cuesta La Plata during World War I on an assignment to teach the people about methods of preserving food as well as about means of economizing while shopping and other aspects of the home economist's science. She cautions the people, who can only occasionally afford meat, to eat meat only once a day. One of the important items on her agenda is acquainting the townspeople with a special government formula for making cheese out of goat's milk. The town has prided itself for centuries on its fame as a producer of goat's milk cheese, yet the townspeople give the young lady a most cordial reception and listen to her lecture with utmost gravity and respect. Just before she leaves, a dance is held in her honor. "It is not for nothing" concludes Mary Austin, "that Cuesta La Plata is known as the politest town in New Mexico."[99]

In spite of the insistence of some modern American writers on the fact of Mexican cruelty, there are others who picture the Mexicans as essentially kind. Eugene Manlove Rhodes, a novelist who grew up in the West and was a cowhand in the Southwest in his youth, invariably depicted Mexicans as courteous and helpful. Undersheriff Anastasio Barela in *The Desire of the Moth*[100] and Joe Benevides in *Copper Streak Trail*[101] both played prominent roles assisting the major figures, isolated cowhands beset by intrigues who were badly in need of help. Fr. Vaillant in Willa Cather's *Death Comes for the Archbishop* counted upon the generosity of the poor Mexicans. "When he left Denver, he told his congregation there that he was going to the Mexicans to beg for money. The church in Denver was under a roof, but the windows had been boarded up for months because nobody would buy glass for them. In his Denver congregation there were men who owned mines and sawmills and flourishing businesses, but they needed all their money to push their enterprises. Down among the Mexicans, who owned nothing but a mud house and a burro, he could always raise money. If they had anything at all, they gave."[102]

In Paul Horgan's novel *Main Line West,* there is a scene which conveys the author's sense of Mexican kindness. A young boy, Danny, is riding on a train through Arizona with his widowed mother, an evangelist who has recently been stoned while leading an outdoor revivalist meeting. Her pleas for peace were considered treasonous to an audience caught in the patriotic fever of World War I. The conductor of the train is one of the mob that stoned her, though she does not recognize him when he collects her ticket. Everyone in the car ignores the fact that she is obviously in serious condition except a Mexican couple who try vainly to get help from the conductor. She dies on the train, and the Mexicans do what they can to comfort Danny.[103] In Robinson Jeffers' poem, "The Living Shepherdess," the only people who are kind to the mad Claire Walker, doomed in her pregnancy, are a "Spanish-Indian boy," who comforts her while the Saxon boys torment her, and the seer of strange visions, Onorio Vasquez.[104]

John Houghton Allen's version of the way Mexicans treat the insane contrasts interestingly with Skinner Bradshaw's experience in Alwyn Lee's story.

> You see, the Mexicans can be children, and sometimes the Mexicans can be nice children, especially when they take care of their halfwits at home, the Mexicans would never be so inhuman to

send anybody away from his *patria*, his home. They tease these halfwits, they are amused by their antics, but they are good to them. In fact they treat them something like sacred lunatics at times, and are superstitious about them. We had a couple of these unfortunates in the village, nor would anybody think of sending them to an asylum. That would be a disgrace to the Jesús Maria [the name of an hacienda], even though one of the idiots was not properly ours.[105]

Timothy Turner recalls an event which occurred shortly after he first arrived in the Southwest and which left a lasting impression. He was walking along a railroad track when he met a Mexican peon. "It was noon and he asked me if I were hungry and, not realizing why he asked, I replied I was. Thereupon he pulled out an old blue handkerchief, unslung a little canvas bag and laid out some limp tortillas and from a little can a miserable pile of beans. With great circumspection he divided this meal into two parts, and, waving his hand, invited me, with many a formal phrase, to accept of his hospitality. I ate the food, though I did not want it, and I have never forgotten the incident. It was the first impression on my mind of the innate gentleness and goodness of the Mexican, who is so much maligned and misunderstood, even by himself."[106]

Clearly there is much opportunity for misunderstanding in dealing with a culture as complex, decentralized, and regionalistic as that of Mexico. The "many Mexicos" account in part for the fluctuations of the image of the Mexican in modern American writing. The people in the Isthmus of Tehuantepec who furnish the characters for Alwyn Lee's story are in fact a vastly different people from the open-natured *rancheros* of the north Mexican states who people the novels of John Houghton Allen, and Tom Lea and the tales of Frank Dobie. Furthermore, the preconceptions, preoccupations, and generally the "axes to grind" of the American writers who have sought out Mexico or the Hispanic Southwest for material have also definitely colored the portrait of Mexico in American letters. The next three chapters will deal with American writers, often directly or implicitly critical of their own society, who have felt that Mexican culture can provide a salutary example in important areas of human experience.

*CHAPTER SEVEN*

## Children of the Earth

The modern era has tended to view the inner resources of man as a fixed economy in which advances in one direction entail sacrifices in another. As human life has become increasingly organized along rational, scientific, and technological lines, the primitive component in man, the source of impulse and spontaneous emotion, has become correspondingly underprivileged. Sigmund Freud, though working in the interest of civilized behavior in society, viewed with a comprehending, if somewhat abstract, compassion the thwarted primitive who is the alter ego of civilized man. The modern artist, whether influenced by Freud or simply reacting naturally to environmental pressures, has often felt a strong sense of kinship with humanity in its more primitive expressions. The emotional spontaneity so often blighted in modern industrial society is one of the sources from which the artist draws his creative energies. In very self-defense, therefore, he may feel impelled to align himself with primitive values in an increasingly mechanized society. One such artist was D. H. Lawrence, who in his search for the primitive turned to Mexico and the Hispanic Southwest of the United States. Though he vacillated a good deal as to the relevance of Mexico to his own vision of a new religion and social order, he saw in Mexico, when he was most pleased with it, a country whose people had not lost the primitive élan, who were closer to the earth and the rhythm of nature than were the people in his own industrialized England or in most of Western Europe and North America. The Lawrencian view of Mexico has had its influence on American writers. Poets and novelists such as Witter Bynner, Hart Crane, Conrad Aiken, Selden Rodman, Katherine Anne Porter, and even the strongly Catholic Paul Horgan have been impressed by Lawrence's interpretation of Mexican culture, though they have maintained their own, sometimes strong, reservations. Much of what originally attracted Lawrence to Mexico has drawn a number of modern American writers, whether within the sphere of his influence or not, southward in search of antidotes to the ills of their own society. These, some of them exulting like converts to a new faith, have advertised the tonic effects of their experience in a land whose people live in close harmony with nature.

Allen Ginsberg, as he approaches the United States border, feels that his trip to Mexico has "armed" him.

> — Returning
>         armed with New Testament,
> critic of horse and mule, [rather than of cars]
>         tanned and bearded
> satisfying Whitman, concerned
>         with a few traditions.[1]

The Mexicans, these enthusiasts have pronounced, are a vivid, passionate, and spontaneous people, not acquisitive but endowed with a great capacity to enjoy the moment, communal in their use of the land, responsive to the arts, and devoted to gracious customs and impressive rituals which derive from ancient tradition. In all such assertions, these moderns could not, in their attitudes, be farther removed from the disdain expressed by the early border novelists and chroniclers for backward, unmechanical, dirty, lazy, savage, and superstitious Mexico.

Waldo Frank felt as he traveled through the Southwest that the Mexicans were the only people who had really left a cultural impress upon the land. All else seemed to him to have the flimsy impermanence which he considered to be the mark of the transient "gringo" with his materialistic and exploitative ambition. Not having this kind of ambition, the Mexican, according to Frank, was not "an ideal pioneer," for he was not the kind who "must for ever be ready to move on." Instead "he became attached to his soil and loved it and drew pleasure and drew beauty from it." The Mexican's adobe house "gives us his inner life. Here a man has settled down and sought happiness in harmony with his surroundings: sought life by cultivation, rather than exploitation."[2] Harvey Fergusson has elaborated this concept in his discussion of the villagers of Chimayo, Cordova, Truchas, Trampas, Chamisal, and Peñasco, small communities in the Sangre de Cristo mountains between Santa Fe and Taos.

> The wide-hatted men and the black-shawled women are figures little changed. And here is an atmosphere, too, that belongs unmistakably to another age, before hurry began or machinery was invented. It is profoundly quiet but with a quiet that never seems dead. One gets from the faces and movements of the people and from their voices an impression of indolent vitality — of life that is never driven or frantic as it is wherever machines set the pace and the hope of progress is an ever-receding goal.
>
> These owners of tiny farms were sometimes called paisanos — men of the country, men of the soil. And true peasants they are,

perhaps the only ones that ever existed within our borders. For the peasant is a lover of the earth who asks nothing better than to live his whole life on one patch of soil, scratching it for a living, laying his bones in it at last. And there has never been much of this resigned sedentary spirit in the American farmer of the Anglo-Saxon breed. He was originally a wanderer and always an exploiter. He settles down only when there is no place else to go. He does not cherish the earth, he loves to conquer it. Always he tends to exhaust the soil and move on, whether in a few years or a few generations, as did the tobacco planters in Virginia, the cotton planters farther south. His interest is always in a "money crop." He believes in progress and longs for change.

No wonder he has always despised these men in whom the blood of an ancient European peasantry mingles with that of sedentary Indians. They ask of the earth only a living and imitate the past because it has seemed good. For men who accept life as it is progress must be a meaningless word and it has never meant anything to the paisano, at least as long as he could cling to his patch of land.[3]

Frank Waters in *People of the Valley,* a novel about Mexican-Americans in New Mexico, gives a similar account of Mexican passion for the land and suspicion of progress. In this work of fiction, whose effectiveness lies in its clear simplicity of style and in its restrained lyricism, we are introduced to an old Mexican matriarch, Maria del Valle. She has become increasingly suspicious and disgruntled at plans to build a dam which would flood the immediate vicinity of the valley but would, it has been pointed out to her, provide a steady water supply for the surrounding area. The valley has for centuries been subject to periodic droughts, disastrous to the people. In order for this dam to be built, however, the people would have to sell their lands to the American government, at a good price, and move elsewhere. This is the "catch," and it catches at the throats of the people, who are torn between their desire for the immediate cash, as well as their sense of the benefits the dam would bring, and the ancient sense of their own "tierra." Maria explains to a local judge her feeling about the situation. "I do not oppose the dam, new customs, a new vision of life; I oppose nothing. But I uphold the old ways for they are good too. I awaken in men their love for their land for they are a people of the land. It is their faith. And so I place their faith above all the lesser benefits they might derive from that which would oppose it."[4]

Certainly the Indian element in the Mexican people accounts in part for their passionate devotion to the land. In Neil Claremon's *Borderland,* a novel whose locale is northern Sonora, we are given a situation similar to the one described above. The people in this case are the Opata Indians. They continue to live in the mountains despite the fact that their water supply has been cut off by a dam. Brito, an enlightened Mexican rancher, tries to persuade them to leave their old lands and with his help settle in the fertile valley below. The Opatas, however, resist moving and express sentiments similar to those spoken by Frank Waters' Maria del Valle.

Robert Herrick in the novel *Waste* (1924) used the primitive virtues of the Indians and Mexicans in a community in northern New Mexico to further point up the moral deficit of the "dollar civilization" prevailing in the rest of the United States. The device is similar to one used by Willa Cather in *The Professor's House,* published a year later. In Cather's novel the discovery of the ruins of an ancient Pueblo Indian city in the Southwest with its evidence of a past life which was peaceful, communal, and non-acquisitive provided a contrasting background to the events of the plot in which an invention produced in the interest of pure science was later commercialized and exploited, upon the death of the young and idealistic inventor, by those who had inherited the patent. In Herrick's novel, the protagonist Thornton had been fighting his private battle to maintain self-respect and a sense of purpose in an environment in which no one seemed to be motivated by anything but the desire for money. As an engineer he had worked for a private power company tapping the resources of the West and had become disgusted with the policy of the company which had an eye only to profits and was totally disinterested in his own project for developing the area in terms of the public good. The women he had been interested in, whatever their virtues, bore the marks of the corruption that follows upon the irresponsible use of private wealth. His professional advancement, despite a high degree of competence, was always frustrated by his own nonconformity and social idealism. In New Mexico, which he was visiting for the first time, he licked his wounds and tried to think his position through.

> He liked this country immensely. Something in its stark indifference to man soothed him like the touch of a large, firm hand. The Indians blended with the background whether cultivating their fields along the river bed, or living their family life in the pueblo, or driving their little horse teams through the winding cañons. The Mexicans, living much the same sort of life as their Indian predecessors, even mixed with them in blood, in the same sort of indistinguishable mud houses, clustered in unobtrusive hamlets harmonized with nature, the strange practices of the Penitentes seeming but a natural barbaric rite in this primitive arid land...

Only the "tourist" crossing the plains for his beloved heaven of California brought the smell and the ugliness of dollar civilization, and for the most part, luckily, the tourists passed by the great highway to the south through Santa Fe, only stray specimens of the tribe occasionally venturing into the Santa Cruz district in search of "color . . . ." There were few human beings in this immense area of land and sky, untouched by the hand of man save along the river bottoms, or by a road blasted indistinguishably from the sandstone cliffs of a cañon. So few! and so impotent! With irony Thornton thus summed up the fascination of this mountain region — Man had been able to do little harm in it, to spoil it! . . ."[5]

Thornton eventually joined the staff of the institute where he had received his professional training, accepting, as a teacher, a salary which was a fraction of what he had been making in private industry.

Joseph Wood Krutch, too, made his pilgrimage to an unspoiled land and recorded his experiences in Baja California in *The Forgotten Peninsula*. This starkly beautiful desert area was, Krutch correctly surmised, on the very eve of an invasion by tourists. This sense of things accounts for the elegaic tone of the book. Already, Krutch notes, things are in a state of transition, but south of La Paz "neither Coca-Cola nor Pepsi-Cola is available at the one general store, and there is no surer sign that contact with the great world has been lost."[6] Los Angeles Bay, some three hundred and thirty miles from the United States border seemed "idyllically simple" to Krutch. It had the benefit of some, but very little, contact with the outside world through battered cars and trucks, occasional planes landing on a small strip, and contact with tuna boats equipped with radios. But nevertheless, the unspoiled life was still lived there with its "wider margin of leisure."[7] This admittedly transitional stage, on the way to the horrors of touristy San Felipe toward the border, seemed perfect to Joseph Wood Krutch.

Of the Mexican inhabitant of lower Baja, Krutch writes: "As an individual he is neat and with him it is a case of individual enterprise, analagous perhaps to his love of colorful costume and gay mood. In any event, from whatever the cause, it gives to even small Baja villages something of the charm of the little old towns in the hills above the sea in southern France. Isolation, poverty, and primitive facilities take on a certain dignity. To come upon such a village after traversing mountain or desert is to feel that it belongs. It may not be progressive but it has character and individuality."[8]

As a Texan from the cattle country, Tom Lea likes his Mexicans best when they are close to the land. Though in his novels he treats Mexican politicians and army officers with considerable contempt, the former for their corruptness, the latter for their arrogance and cruelty, he has great affection for the Mexican *ranchero*. It has been said by those who knew the West several decades ago, before the American cattle industry had become as mechanized as it is today, that the Anglo-American cattlemen of the Southwest were remarkably like their opposite numbers in the north Mexican states, that despite differences in language and ethnic origin the two peoples in fact shared the same culture. Whereas the contemporary American cattleman has become more like an ordinary businessman, the *ranchero* of Sonora or Chihuahua, still carrying on his work very much through the exertion of his body and the skill of his hands and his legs, retains much of the character shaped by the old cattle culture, the grace, the courtesy, the hospitality, the openness, the relaxed attitude toward life, the love of the work as such, the closeness to the land — not that these characteristics have been totally lost by the American cattleman but they have been considerably muted in the general standardizing of types that seems to be in process throughout the country. Don Santiago Santos of Sonora in Tom Lea's *The Wonderful Country* represents the sense of tradition and the love of the land characteristic of the *rancheros* of the north Mexican states. Don Santiago says of himself, "We Santos . . . we live where we belong, I think. We have lived in Bavinuchi since the times of the King Carlos III. He granted us the land. A Santos was *Marqués* of Sonora. We do not produce any *marqueses* in these times, nor any damned politicians either. My grandfather said it was better to own land than to govern it. We Santos produce *rancheros*. I wish there were more of us. By the time there is fuzz on our cheeks we have learned the music of the bull pens, we know horses and firearms and these sierras."[9]

John Steinbeck, whatever his later failures, moved the divining rod of an early talent across the California earth, and in the best stories in *The Long Valley* and *The Pastures of Heaven* struck spring water with the taste of the land in it. In *The Long Valley* he tells a story which illustrates the feeling a Mexican has for his *tierra,* the region in which he was born and raised. An aged Mexican appeared at Carl Tifflin's California ranch and announced: "I am Gitano, and I have come back." The old man, it developed, had been born near the ranch before it was built and had spent his early youth in the area. Now he had come back to die. In order to be allowed to stay on the ranch while he awaited death, he volunteered to work for room and board. Tifflin felt that he could not take on anyone else, even under such terms. Being the kind of man who was ashamed of any trace of compassion in his nature, he fought down a surge of sympathy and grossly replied to the Mexican that if ham and eggs could be grown on the hillside the ranch might be able to feed another mouth. At this point the mechanism in Tifflin's make-up by which incipient feelings of compassion were habitually supplanted by an urge to be cruel went into full operation. Tifflin turned to someone standing next to him and, pointing out an ancient horse, Old Easter, said, within full earshot of Gitano, that the horse had gotten too old to be any good and ought to be shot. Gitano was later led to the bunkhouse and told that he could have one meal and spend the night. The next morning the Mexican, determined not to be thwarted in the appointment he had made with death, took up a handsome sword which had been in his family for generations, went out into the pasture, mounted Old Easter, and rode up into the mountains which he had known so well in his youth. Tifflin's comment: "They never get too old to steal."[10]

Those Americans in Robinson Jeffers' narrative poems who are shown to have a strong kinship with the land are often provided with a link to the Hispanic past of California. The primitive, earth-drawn Cawdor takes as his mistress the Mexican Indian, Concha Rosas. When he later marries Fera, an Anglo-American woman, Concha Rosas still remains as a servant in the house though her dark presence is a constant irritation to Fera. Cawdor, though he has ceased to have a physical relationship with Concha Rosas, seems still to value the sight of her as a symbol of the ancient California earth to which he is strongly attached. In one of the poems in *Californians,* Ruth Allison is in love with Paul Hayworth, product of many generations on the California land. His mother is an Alera, a member of an old Mexican-Californian family. She warns Ruth Allison that there has always been a streak of wildness in the Alera men, that they are hard to keep, and so it turns out, as Paul deserts Ruth for the glamorous wife of a rich rancher, a parvenue to the area from San Francisco. Ruth dies of a broken heart.

Blomberg in Conrad Aiken's *A Heart for the Gods of Mexico* muses, as he travels across the United States en route to Mexico, about the failure of Americans to have established any spirit-nourishing relationship with the land. He feels that others before them on the American continent have done better and that the Mexico to which he is traveling will offer something different. Contemplating the Mississippi as it pours into the Gulf, Blomberg thinks:

> A whole continent pouring itself out lavishly to the sea, in superb, everlasting waste, an immense creative giving, power that could afford to be careless both of means and end — and mankind beside

it became as spiritually empty as the locust, and as parasitic. Surely the Indians had been better than this, and the Frenchmen, too, who had first explored these savage waters: in either had been a dignity, a virtue, now lost. And the Mexican Indians, to whom they were going — what of those? Lawrence said — and all the psycho-analysts said — and the guide books said —

It was as if he had heard a bell, suddenly, from a deep valley, a jungle valley, inviting to the sacrifice, whether pagan or Christian: there, there were still gods. But here, in this melancholy wreckage of a meagre past, in this sloven street, spangled with tin beer-caps, which they were climbing slowly again, past stinking cellars and boarded windows, here there was no longer even a true love of earth. This people was lost. . . .[11]

In extolling the Mexican as a fine, primitive type, the modern American writer is likely to depict him as being more immediately responsive emotionally than the sallow Saxon, more passionate, intense, vivid in personality. In *One Flew Over the Cuckoo's Nest*, Ken Kesey gives this concept an effectively impressionistic treatment. In the psychiatric ward, which is the novel's locale, one of the inmates, old Colonel Matterson, whose "face is sixty years of southwest army camps," is talking to the narrator, the Indian "Chief" Bromden who is himself an inmate. Matterson says:

"Now . . . The cross is . . . Mex-i-co." He looks up to see if I'm paying attention, and when he sees I am he smiles at me and goes on. "Mexico is . . . the wal-nut. The hazelnut. The ay-corn. Mexico is . . . the rain-bow. The rain-bow is . . . wooden. Mexico is . . . woo-den."

I can see what he's driving at. He's been saying this sort of thing for the whole six years he's been here, but I never paid him any mind, figured he was no more than a talking statue, a thing made out of bone and arthritis, rambling on and on with these goofy definitions of his that didn't make a lick of sense. Now, at last, I see what he's saying. I'm trying to hold him for one last look to remember him, and that's what makes me look hard enough to understand. He pauses and peers up at me again to make sure I'm getting it, and I want to yell out to him Yes, I see: Mexico *is* like the walnut; it's brown and hard and you feel it with your eye and it *feels* like the walnut! You're making sense, old man, a sense of your own. You're not crazy the way they think. Yes . . . I see . . .[12]

Unlike the early writers who deplored Mexican demonstrativeness, the moderns, living in a society increasingly inclined to repudiate the puritan ideal of restraint, look with some envy on a people who seem to be so lacking in inhibition. Mark Twain tells of a court case in San Francisco in which a Spaniard was being tried for murdering a Mexican. The Mexican's wife was present during the trial and throughout the proceedings, glared fiercely at the defendant "because you know how they love and they hate, and this one had loved her husband with all her might, and now she had boiled it all down into hate, and stood here spitting it at that Spaniard with her eyes." When the Spaniard was acquitted, the woman pulled out a pistol and shot him dead in the courtroom. The judge adjourned the court, and the spectators took up a collection for the widow and orphans. The judge's final comment: "Ah, she was a spirited wench!"[13]

This sort of admiration for Mexican ferocity as an evidence of an unspoiled primitivism became a frequent theme in modern American writing about Mexico. In some hands it was crudely worked and in others managed with a degree of subtlety. Katherine Anne Porter was undoubtedly attracted to an element of earthy vitality in Mexico's people, but she reported her Mexico straight with a fine sense of the realities of the human situation. Not distorting or exaggerating in her own writing, she satirized those Americans who went to Mexico to revel in the primitive, who saw evidence on all sides of a magnificent instinctualism and tried their hardest to go elemental themselves. However, when she turned to the theme of Mexican primitivism herself, she handled it convincingly, as can be seen in several of the stories in the collection *Flowering Judas,* especially in "María Concepción," a story of vengeance and the repose that followed its successful accomplishment. The scene was rural Mexico and the characters Mexican Indians. María Concepción, diligent and thrifty housewife, became aware that her husband, Juan Villegas, was having an affair with a woman of her acquaintance, María Rosa. Rage against her husband was short-lived. What could one expect of men? But for María Rosa she felt an enduring hatred which was a physical presence. Later Juan went off to join the revolutionary armies, taking with him not his wife but María Rosa, who became one of the *soldaderas,* the women who served the soldiers of the Revolution both as lovers and as the nearest thing to a supply corps the revolutionary armies ever had. María Concepción, meanwhile, maintained her house and went to church daily. Finally Juan and María Rosa returned to the village. Immediately after their arrival, María Rosa gave birth to a son. At first Juan did not even think of María Concepción, but having gotten drunk he returned to his old home purely out of force of habit. There he confronted María Concepción, beat her, and fell into a drunken sleep. She slipped out of the house. Not knowing at first where she was going, she suddenly realized her purpose, and, feeling for the first time a loosening of the constriction of her innards which had been a continual affliction since her discovery of Juan's infidelity, she gave full consent to the action which she had proposed to herself. Later she returned to her home. Juan was just waking up, and, crawling to him on knees and elbows, writhing and moaning, she confessed murder. At the moment of her confession, Juan suddenly saw her as an exalted personage, precious in her superior quality, someone to be guarded. He immediately became intensely alert. Thoroughly scrubbing the bloody knife which she had presented to him, he carefully rehearsed her in what she was to say at the arrival of the rural police. The expected knock at the door occurred after a short period of waiting, and Juan and María Concepción were taken to the house of María Rosa. In the presence of the corpse, the inquest was carried out. Neighbors had been rounded up for questioning and were already at the house. Several of these had no liking for María Concepción, but the police and anyone else who pried into the affairs of the community were natural enemies. The villagers united to form a shield of silence and evasion to protect María Concepción, who quietly repeated the lines she had rehearsed with Juan, denying that she had ever left the house that day.

> María Concepción suddenly felt herself guarded, surrounded upborne by her faithful friends. They were around her, speaking for her, defending her, the forces of life were ranged invincibly with her against the beaten dead. María Rosa had thrown away her share of strength in them, she lay forfeited among them. María Concepción looked from one to the other of the circling, intent faces. Their eyes gave back reassurance, understanding, a secret and mighty sympathy.
>
> The gendarmes were at a loss. They, too, felt that sheltering wall cast impenetrably around her. They were certain she had done it, and yet they could not accuse her. Nobody could be accused; there was not a shred of true evidence. They shrugged their shoulders, snapped their fingers and shuffled their feet. Well, then, good night to everybody. Many pardons for having intruded.
>
> A small bundle lying against the wall at the head of the coffin squirmed like an eel. A wail, a mere sliver of sound, issued. María Concepción took the son of María Rosa in her arms.
>
> "He is mine," she said clearly, "I will take him with me."
>
> No one assented in words, but an approving nod, a bare breath of complete agreement, stirred among them as they made way for her.

As they walked home, Juan felt empty and exhausted. He wondered why he had taken all that trouble to save María Concepción, who now looked utterly unattractive to him. He thought back on adventures in the army and sessions of love with María Rosa. "Their days of marching, of eating, of quarreling and making love between battles were over.

Tomorrow he must go back to dull and endless labor. . . ." As soon as he arrived home, he stretched on the floor and fell into a deep sleep. His wife remained awake for a while.

> María Concepción could hear Juan's breathing. The sound vapored from the low doorway, calmly; the house seemed to be resting after a burdensome day. She breathed, too, very slowly and quietly, each inspiration saturating her with repose. The child's light, faint breath was a mere shadowy moth of sound in the silver air. The night, the earth under her, seemed to swell and recede together with a limitless, unhurried, benign breathing. She drooped and closed her eyes, feeling the slow rise and fall within her own body. She did not know what it was, but it eased her all through. Even as she was falling asleep, head bowed over the child, she was still aware of a strange, wakeful happiness.[14]

One may surmise that the author's principal interest was not in telling a tale of violence but rather in presenting an analysis of an individual whose psychological organization was more elementary, more immediately connected with organic needs than is the case of most people in the more elaborated societies in which all kinds of abstract ideals and rationalizations interpose between basic urges and what is admitted to the self.

When Hart Crane first arrived in Mexico, his reaction was one of exultation in a gorgeous primitivism far removed from the drab, mechanized money-culture of his native land. In time he underwent considerable disillusion, finally writing a poem addressed to "my country, O my land, my friends," in which he confessed a sharp nostalgia for the "too-keen cider — the too-soft snow" while he remained disconsolately in a purgatory-like exile amid "the scents of Eden."[9] Encounters with pompous officialdom and acquaintance with members of the new, post-revolutionary bourgeoisie, as well as the repeated experience of being stood up by people who did not honor their appointments all contributed to produce an ambivalent view of the country. His own behavior in Mexico, furthermore, undoubtedly did not endear him to the people, thus engendering a mutual souring of relations. However, Crane maintained to the end a conviction that Mexico had a powerful and original contribution to make to the culture of the world. His letters, furthermore, do not show a steady decline in his regard for Mexico but rather a fluctuation in attitudes. For the people of rural Mexico, those close to the land, his appreciation was constant. On April 12, 1931, he wrote to Samuel Loveman that "the peons are the marvel of the place, just as Lawrence said. So lovable, and although picturesque, not in any way consciously so. What faces, and the suffering in them — but so little evidence of bitterness."[16] The next year he wrote at greater length of his reaction to rural Mexico, in a letter to Caresse Crosby dated March 31, 1932.

> Mexico with its volcanoes, endless ranges, countless flowers, dances, villages, lovely brown-skinned Indians with simple courtesies, and constant sunlight— it enthralls me more than any other spot I've ever known. It *is* and isn't an easy place to live. Altogether more strange to us than even the orient... But it would take volumes to even hint at all I have seen and felt. Have rung bells and beaten pre-Conquistadorial drums in firelight circles at ancient ceremonies, while rockets went zooming up into the dawn over Tepotzlan; have picked up obsidian arrows and terracotta idols from the furrows of corn-fields in far valleys; bathed with creatures more beautiful than the inhabitants of Bali in mountain streams and been in the friendliest jails that ever man got thrown in. There is never an end to dancing, singing, rockets and the rather lurking and suave dangers that give the same edge to life here that the mountains give to the horizon.[17]

The opinion of what Mexico offers the literary artist that Crane expressed to Waldo Frank in a letter written on June 13, 1931, is one that he never repudiated. "In contrast to their general directions and preoccupations, however, I still (to date, at any rate) harbor the illusion that there is a soil, a mythology, a people and a spirit here that are capable of unique and magnificent utterance."[18]

The poetic imagination of Wallace Stevens responded most to Mexicans when they could be viewed as primitives. In *Poetry and the Age,* Randall Jarrell reminds us that Stevens, in *Harmonium,* "still loves America best when he can think of it as wilderness, naturalness, pure potentiality (he treats with especial sympathy Negroes, Mexican Indians, and anybody else he can consider wild)...."[19] Something of this same feeling carries over into *Transport to Summer.* In the poem "Jouga" in that volume, it is the feral quality that gives the Mexican "Ha-ee-me" (Jaime) his style. He is united erotically with his guitar and its beats and by extension with all nature itself, including the "great jaguar running," this last image reminding one of Hart Crane's reference to the "lurking and suave dangers of Mexico."

> The physical world is meaningless tonight
> And there is no other. There is Ha-ee-me, who sits
> And plays his guitar. Ha-ee-me is a beast.
> Or perhaps his guitar is a beast or perhaps they are
> Two beasts. But of the same kind — two conjural beasts.
> Ha-ee-me is the male beast ... an imbecile,
> Who knocks out a noise. The guitar is another beast
> Beneath his tip-tap-tap. It is she that responds.

> Two beasts but two of a kind and then not beasts.
> Yet two not quite of a kind. It is like that here.
> There are many of these beasts that one never sees,
> Moving so that the foot-falls are slight and almost nothing.
> This afternoon the wind and the sea were like that —
> And after a while, when Ha-ee-me has gone to sleep,
> A great jaguar running will make a little sound.[20]

In one of his early poems, "The Quarrel," Robinson Jeffers uses the *cholo* (mestizo) of California as an example of the man whose savage simplicities are to be envied.

> When I left you I wandered at will
>    Where our modern city has a
> Slight air of antiquity still —
>    Down by the Mexican Plaza.
> And the bell of Our Lady with no low
>    Tones, but with confident voice,
> Struck ten, and a drunken cholo
>    Was calling the girl of his choice.
> "Carajo," he cursed her, with other
>    Words to be spoken less lightly
> Discussing her morals and mother
>    More fluently than politely.
> And I thought, as I heard his solo,
>    "How simple were life — how human —
> If I were a drunken cholo
>    And you my dark-skinned woman!"[21]

The futility and aimlessness of a group of hard-drinking, much-divorcing, self-centered, and self-indulging group of Americans in Santa Fe are contrasted in Paul Horgan's novel *No Quarter Given* with the simplicity and dignity of Mexicans and Indians finding fulfillment in adherence to ancient cultural patterns. Among the Americans, but not really of them, are several sensitive people, Edmund Abbey, composer; Maggie Michaelis, actress and Abbey's lover — later his wife; David Abbey, stepson of Edmund, an aspiring writer; and the wealthy and cultivated Mrs. Manning, very much to the manner born and attuned to that which is indigenous in the culture of the Southwest. These people, in protest against the vulgarities of the other Americans, label themselves "the Mexicans." After Edmund Abbey first declares his love to Maggie Michaelis, he adds, "Well, I feel primitive," to which she answers, "We're all Mexicans. You and I and David. I suppose we all have the same simplicity. Nothing is without its solution. For the Mexicans it's living as you must, and talking about it afterward to God. The grandest wisdom in the world." Some time after this scene, Abbey discovers that a musical composition that he is working on is being influenced by his acquaintance with an ancient, simple, and extremely vigorous Mexican woman. He explains the influence by saying that it is "related to her astonishing vitality, her travel toward death with all the fury and liveliness of a child."[22]

The concept that the Mexicans in their poverty and apparent tedium are in fact more really alive than Americans hurrying around vast modern cities can be found in several variants in modern American writing, perhaps most freshly expressed by Gilbert Neiman in *There is a Tyrant in Every Country*.

> Their air was that of a people who exulted in hardship, who found life in poverty less tedious than it appeared on the surface. Amidst the plenty of Chicago, the throngs there made you feel, inside, like nothing. To watch them was to be wrung through a wringer; you came out a tattered dishrag, a shredded sponge. Here the people had a vibrant tension that teemed with potential miracles, as though they always expected the maximum could be conjured out of nothing. The air was threaded with their expectations, no two intentions the same, but all marvelous. In our cities we seem directed, led on by the same purpose, a visible similarity of pursuit. Here you felt each pair of eyes — young, old, or in-between — had a different screw missing behind them, a peculiar twist which gave them a strictly personal slant on the world.[23]

Elizabeth Hardwick in her review of *The Children of Sánchez* comments upon the intensity of the lives of the impoverished and really superfluous people living in a slum tenement in Mexico City. "The lives in the Casa Grande tenement are not torpid, but violent and high-pitched. The economy, the nation have no real use for these people, and yet the useless are persons of strongly marked temperament who must fully experience, day in and day out, the terrible unfolding of their destiny. The story truly inspires pity and terror; with fear we gaze upon these unjust accidents of birth, nationality, of time."[24]

Mexico, especially in its Indian component, has been viewed as being, despite its primitiveness, seeped in an ancient wisdom which could serve to upbraid the upstart, saucy, essentially shallow technologized societies of the north. Jack Kerouac in *On The Road* makes some observations along these lines, the sensitivity of which makes one regret that he never reached his full literary potential. Sal Paradise (for which read Jack Kerouac) and his friends have just crossed the Mexican border for the first time. Sal registers his initial impression of the people.

> Not like driving across Carolina, or Texas, or Arizona, or Illinois; but like driving across the world and into places where we would finally learn ourselves among the Fellahin Indians of the world,

the essential strain of the basic primitive, wailing humanity that stretches in a belt around the equatorial belly of the world from Malaya (the long fingernail of China) to India the great subcontinent to Arabia to Morocco to the selfsame deserts and jungles of Mexico and over the waves to Polynesia to mystic Siam of the Yellow Robe and on around, on around, so that you hear the same mournful wail by the rooted walls of Cadiz, Spain, that you hear 12,000 miles around in the depths of Benares the Capital of the World. These people [the Mexicans] were unmistakably Indians and were not at all like the Pedros and Panchos of silly, civilized American lore — they had high cheekbones and slanted eyes, and soft ways; they were not fools, they were not clowns; they were great, grave Indians and they were the source of mankind and the fathers of it. The waves are Chinese, but the earth is an Indian thing. As essential as rocks in the desert are they in the desert of "history." And they knew this when we passed, ostensibly self-important moneybag Americans on a lark in their land; they knew who was the father and who was the son of antique life on earth, and made no comment. For when destruction comes to the world of "history" and the Apocalypse of the Fellahin returns once more as so many times before, people will still stare with the same eyes from the caves of Mexico as well as from the caves of Bali, where it all began and where Adam was suckled and taught to know.[25]

Sherwood Anderson, writing as long ago as 1939, described the Mexican Indian and related him so uncannily to current world concerns that his observations deserve to be quoted in full:

In his own person he is of the earth, so that, when he walks, always half running, with the curious dancing step, you feel him away and apart from your own complex, modern self. He is like the leaves you see dancing along roads, when the wind blows. He dances and his dancing is like the dancing of tree tops in a wind. You feel even his cruelty as something akin to the cruelty of nature. You think of cruelty and treachery that is not in the Indian hypocritical. Why, I dare say that the men of the so-called "upper classes," in Mexico, the Spaniards and the *mestizos* (the half breeds), having read our books, read the speeches of our statesmen, seen our movies, listened to our radios, have become as mealy-mouthed as we have.

Such continual lying always going on. But you can't lie to the earth.

What is in my head at the moment is not a question of superiority, of inferiority. I have a sudden conviction that this Southern land belongs to the Indian for the very simple reason that his hands have touched the land. He has plowed and planted it and that simple fact has made it his land.

In Mexico, the enslavement of a whole people has gone on for many generations, and, oddly enough, this enslavement seems to have ground into the Mexicans a kind of dignity, making them, to the visitor from the North, from the United States, something new in his experience. I use the word "dignity." It is because there is, apparently, in the Mexican Indian some of the dignity of his mountains. It is like the dignity of great trees. It is something that we, in our own complex civilization have lost. It may be that it has been paid for, by the Mexican, at a terrible price, but he seems to have got it.

Is it a thing on which a new kind of civilization can be built? If it can be done, such a civilization will be new. If it can be done, the new culture will be based upon the ability of the Mexican to do without. It is possible that, in enslaving a whole people, keeping them, for generations there close to earth, always without, there has been ground into them a great lesson. It is possible that, in grinding this people, for so long, down and down into earth, we, from the outside, the exploiters, have taught them the way. It would certainly be interesting, if in the end, these Indians, toward whom we sons of old Europe have been so cruel, should have got out of our cruelty the sort of education we may all need before a new civilization can really be born.[26]

All this praise for the Mexican as a noble savage, on the part of modern American writers, carries with it at least an implicit criticism of the mechanized and commercialized society of the United States. A number of American writers have used the Mexican very specifically as a foil by which to emphasize the demoralizing and dehumanizing effects of industrialism and commercialism. Frederick Remington felt a happy release from modernity as he shared the life of the wild *vaqueros* on his friend's hacienda in northern Mexico. Squatting among them and tearing at mounds of beef with his fingers or with a hunting knife, he felt that it was "all so beautifully primitive" to be among men in whom ran "the wildest blood of Spain, Morocco, and the American Indian," men who were "untainted by the enfeebling influence of luxury and modern life." Remington enjoyed watching the Mexican mule teamsters getting their animals lined up for the morning's work. He marveled at how well these men had their mules trained, "as bankers do their depositors in our land," and was delighted at the way the teamsters spoke to their beasts "in that easy, familiar way and with that mutual comprehension which is lost to those of the human race who have progressed beyond the natural state."[27] Charles F. Lummis announced what was to be the principal theme of his book *The Land of Poco Tiempo* by inviting his reader to enter into this land of "pretty soon." "Why hurry with the hurrying world? The 'Pretty Soon' of New Spain is better than the

'Now! Now!' of the haggard States."[28] And Carl Sandburg, reproducing the tempo of the "Now! Now!", rushes his American tourists through Santa Fe.

> "The fast travelers with extra tires come in a hurry and solve me and pass on to say all their lives, 'Santa Fe? O yes, Santa Fe, I have seen Santa Fe.' 'Hurry up,' is their first and last word on my zigzag streets, my lazy 'dobe corners.'"

And as for the ancient cultures

> The six-cylinder go-getters ask:
>   What time is it?
>   Who were the Aztecs and the
>     Zunis anyhow?
>   What do I care about Cahokia?
>   Where do we go from here?
>   What are the facts?"[29]

It was precisely the lack of "hurry up" that attracted Joseph Wood Krutch to San Ignacio, which he claimed to be "the most charming town in Baja." "Banish a few small motorized trucks and you could hardly know whether you were in the eighteenth century or the twentieth . . . Bustle is certainly the last word one would apply to San Ignacio, but bustle is almost everywhere in the modern world and tranquility is rare."[30]

Lummis, continuing his discourse on the psychology of the "pretty soon," goes on to say, "I would not be understood that it is idleness. There is work; but such unfatal work! The *paisano* has learned to live even while he works — wherein he is more wise than we, who slave away our youth (which is life) in chasing that which we are past enjoyment of when we overtake it. He tills his fields and tends his herds; but there is no unseemingly haste, no self-tripping race for wealth. *Lo que puede* — that which can be — is enough," and, by way of illustrating the Mexican attitude toward commercialism, Lummis tells a story of two old men of New Mexico.

> Cristobal Nuñez and Transito Baca are two venerable residents of Llanito, brothers-in-law, and equally addicted to legitimately obtained hiccoughs. Having amassed a few round *pesos* by labor at sheep-shearing, they formed a partnership, bought ten gallons of whiskey in Santa Fe, and started over the mountainous roads to retail it in outlying *plazas* from a small cart. Each knowing the other's failing, they swore a solemn oath that neither would give the other a drop during the trip; and thus forearmed, they set out. They had spent every cent, save a nickel which Cristobal had accidentally retained.

"*Válgame Diós,*" groaned Cristobal, after they had gone a few miles, "but it is very long without to drink. For the love of the Virgin, *cuñado,* give a little to me."

"But how! That thou not rememberest our compromise," asked the virtuous Transito.

Cristobal groaned again, and rode a few miles in silence. Then an idea percolated through his shaggy locks — the nickel in his pocket.

It is truth, *compadre,* that we compromised not to give us one drop. But of the *to sell* was nothing said. See! That I have *cinco centavos!* Sell-me a drinklet to me."

"'*Sta bueno!*" said Transito, pocketing the nickel and pouring his companion a small dose. "The saints are witness that I kept my oath. I give not, but sell."

Everything takes its time in New Mexico, but in half an hour the inspiration got across the wagon to Transito.

"*Carrambas!* How buy I not a drinklet *también?* I have *cinco centavos* now. Sell-me a little to me *compadre.*" And Cristobal did so, thereby regaining his nickel.

"But wait-me a so-little, and I will buy a drinklet from thee also that we may drink joined."

Back went the nickel to Transito; and in a moment the two old men were clinking glasses mutually "*á la vuestra salud, compadre.*" This seemed more social, till a disturbing thought occurred to Transito.

*Pero hombre!* Though hast had two drinks and I only one. Go, sell-me to me another, that we are equals."

This logic was not to be gainsaid; and Cristobal doled out the whiskey and resumed the nimble coin. Just then a trace broke.

"Ill-said horses! And of ill-said fathers and mothers! That now we have to go to camp here. Tomorrow we will fix the harness."

But they did not fix it tomorrow, nor the next day, nor the next. They just stayed in camp and tended strictly to business — which was remarkably good. Now Cristobal was merchant, and Transito customer; and *al contrario.* No one else came along to disturb the routine of trade, until the third day, when a sheep-herder found two white-headed men sleeping beside an empty ten-gallon keg. A much worn nickel lay in one half-closed fist, and the wool-propeller took it along for luck.

"And how to you went the journey? people asked in Llanito.

"*Mala suerta,*" sighed Cristobal sadly." We sold all our whiskey; but some *ladrón* robbed to us asleep of all we had taken in."[31]

Mary Austin gives an idyllic picture of the good life lived close to the earth by the people in the New Mexican town of El Pueblo de las Uvas (the town of the grapes), where life is a continual round of fiestas. Of the people in the town she writes: "There is not much villainy among them. What incentive to thieving or killing can there be when there is little wealth and that to be had for the borrowing! If they love too hotly, as we say 'take their meat before grace,' so do their betters. Eh, what! shall a man be a saint before he is dead? and besides, Holy Church takes it out of you one way or another before all is done." Then, in a sweeping gesture, Mary Austin extends her invitation to the harassed "gringos." "Come away, you who are obsessed with your own importance in the scheme of things, and have got nothing you did not sweat for, come away by the brown valleys and full-bosomed hills to the even-breathing days, to the kindliness, earthiness, ease of El Pueblo de las Uvas."[32]

Robert Herrick in *Waste* is much more acrid as he develops his critique of American society at large by comparing it with life in a small New Mexican community, the village of Tia, Mexican and Indian, the one shading indistinguishably into the other. Thornton, the novel's protagonist, studied with interest and appreciation the Mexican woman, María, who was his cook while he was in Tia. This woman, "half pure pueblo Indian and half Spanish, dark-skinned and fine-featured like her Indian father, with a certain communicability and grace inherited from her Latin mother," was a refreshing change from the people he had been used to. Though she perforce lived a life of the utmost simplicity, she struck Thornton as being "half-mystic, invariably happy and contented." One day Thornton was discussing her with his friend Cynthia Lane, a wealthy woman who, though she possessed a good deal of charm and a degree of sensitivity, maintained toward those whom she considered inferiors the habitual hauteur of one conscious that wealth brings considerable immunity. Thornton, while agreeing with Cynthia that María was an excellent cook, said that, quite apart from her skill, he would keep her on for her temperament alone, adding, pointedly, "I suspect she is nearer the mysteries than either you or I, Cynthia."[33] When Cynthia's spoiled son Gordie, in a fit of pique and with no real provocation, shot and killed María's son, Tranquilino, Cynthia, against Thornton's advice, sought to placate María by buying her off. To Cynthia it was inconceivable that a woman of María's class would not settle for money. Thornton reluctantly accompanied Cynthia on her mission to María's house, where María was standing vigil over the body of her son.

> The place was clean and orderly. María had finished her housework, spread a white sheet over the boy's form in the inner room, and was sitting near the bed with folded hands, an inscrutable look on her fine face. She rose when Cynthia entered and recognized her with a slow movement of the head. Cynthia crossed the outer

room, went straight to the figure on the bed, drew back the sheet a little way, let it fall. María replaced it above the lad's face.

"Terrible, terrible!" Cynthia murmured . . . .

Thornton turned away and did not see what happened next, but he heard María's low, clear, slightly guttural voice say distinctly:

"No, lady! I do not take blood money!"

Cynthia evidently persisted and as Thornton, too miserable to stay, turned to leave the house, he caught the look of cold scorn on the fine Indian features of María as she pushed away the proffered money. . . ." [34]

Cynthia, however, still managed to make money talk by bribing the Mexican sheriff of the area. For her, wealth still meant immunity. Apart from the comparison that Thornton could not avoid drawing between the characters of Cynthia and María, he made other, more generalized comparisons between life in the little village of Tia and society in the vast industrial and commercial America beyond it. "Thornton felt that Tia, including María and Tranquilino, was in many essentials the most urbane, the most civilized American community in which he had ever lived, poor and primitive as it was by the ordinary standards. In sacrificing all the comforts and prestige of life, the Indians had retained their civility, their inner selves." Thornton admired the attitude by which "property was for use, not for possession." The inhabitants of Tia seemed "uncaring, almost uncomprehending" when it came to money. Instead, "their minds were alive to things, useful or ornamental things, like their blankets, their vessels and skins, but not to the abstraction of possessions. Just as they were sensitive to the moods and the ways of nature, the clouds and the seasons, the habits of wild animals. They ignored or discarded so much that the white man had cumbered his life with. . . ." [35]

In a more easy-going way, Frank Dobie handles somewhat similar themes. The almost mediaeval isolation of the old Hacienda de las Cinco Llagas, in Dobie's *The Mexico I Like,* cast a spell upon the American traveler, who felt himself relieved, if only temporarily, of the burdens of modern society. "No newspapers came here, except an occasional one from Torreón, and so far as the problems of society were concerned the industrial age had barely been inaugurated. The peons distrusted an imported plow because 'steel makes the ground cold,' and corn and beans require warm earth. The mule too has a 'cold hoof,' and therefore in land to be sown in *frijoles* the plow had better be pulled by an ox. The man who guided the one-handled wooden plow, moving as slow as the finger of destiny writes, watched to see if the ox dragged his foot at the turn of the furrow — for, if so, it was a 'sign of rain.' " [36] In

*Coronado's Children,* Dobie develops an idea comparable to one expressed by Herrick in *Waste.* Herrick had interrupted his narrative at one point to comment bitterly that while the American "prided himself that he had escaped squalor and looked down upon all 'dirty peoples,' " he had, in fact, only "taken squalor into his soul and was sick with spiritual corruption."[37] Dobie's tale, though much milder in tone, nevertheless points up the same situation. A Texan named Dee Devis was greatly looked down upon as being "the second sorriest white man in Sabinal." The only thing that kept him from being "the sorriest white man" in the region was that, though living with a "pelada," a contemptuous term for a low-class Mexican woman, he had been respectable enough to actually marry her. Davis's hygienic Texan acquaintances would have nothing to do with him for having so lost caste as to live in a shack with a Mexican woman. Yet, muses Dobie, "it seemed to me then, and it seems to me still, that there are many ways of living worse than the way of this village scavenger with a soft goatskin to sit on, and aromatic Black Horse tobacco to inhale leisurely through a clean white shuck, and bright zinnias and blue morning-glories in the dooryard, and long siestas while the shadows of evening lengthen to soften the light of day, and an easy-going Mexican wife, and playing around a patient burro out in the corral an urchin that will be twelve mañana, as it were. . . ."[38] A juxtaposition of two ways of looking at life, the Anglo-American and the Mexican, was made by Paul Horgan in *The Return of the Weed.* Don Elizário, aristocrat and former great landowner, had been reduced to living in the Elks Club in Albuquerque. Though much gone to seed, his graciousness was still intact, and, on one occasion, he offered to share his precious bottle of whiskey with two young American businessmen who had come into the club. These, while accepting his liquor, amused themselves by baiting the old man. " 'You're a right busy man, Don Elizário,' said the laundryman with a gleam of his eye across his thin nose at the insurance man. 'Sittin' here all day and workin' at your likker.' The Don leaned back and rolled a gurgling laugh deep down in his contented throat. The insurance man said: 'Well, it's a job you can do better than most, Don Elizário, eh?—You just better keep at it, we'd never get anything done in this town if we waited on the earliest settlers, now would we.' 'No, no,' said the old man. 'My people have no gift for business. They are too fond of life. —Your glass.' "[39]

Tom Lea in *The Brave Bulls* has his version of the theme of the greater virtue of the life lived close to the land. One of the most attractive figures in the novel is Tiburcio Balbuena, the operator of Las Astas, where fighting bulls are raised. Balbuena enjoys hard work in an ancient profession; he likes the country with its communal traditions rather than the city with its feral individualism and sterile manipulations. One afternoon he was talking to Eládio Gomez, the impresario of a small-town bull ring, who had come to Las Astas to see about some bulls. The two were remarking on the strange fact that the ferocious bulls, bred especially for the ring, were so calm and manageable on the open range when they ran in herds. However, after an individual bull had been weeded out of the herd, lured by oxen especially trained in the job of separating the bulls, he would become almost unmanageable.

> "It is strange," said Eládio Gomez, "how the herd instinct makes it possible to husband such beasts. The herd makes the tranquillity, the feeling of well-being. Take a bull suddenly from that divided responsibility of herd thinking, make him an individual and he tries to kill you."
> "Exactly!" said Balbuena. The old man winked. "The symbolism there may be why I prefer the country life!"
> "The most symbolical part," said Gomez, is the ox. Our castrated friend. Our servant with the empty sac, who is traitor to his kind. We use him to trap the savage bull from freedom, to manipulate him by deceit to where he would not go."
> "Clearly symbolical!" said Balbuena.[40]

The ordinary Mexican has been seen by some modern American writers as possessing a natural majesty in the dignity of his bearing and a sort of sanctity in the very simplicity of his wants. Witter Bynner's "Countryman" is a naturally regal figure.

> Swinging a blanket over his left shoulder,
> Wearing its bright-colored heart upon his sleeve,
> He takes up his bed and walks. It serves him well
> For warmth at night on his mat, or in the evening
> Against a wind that pours along the lake.
> Even at noon it hangs from his neck to his ankle,
> Unneeded in the sun except as a king
> Always has need to be wearing majesty.[41]

Hart Crane in a letter to Waldo Frank, June 13, 1931, after expressing grave doubts about some aspects of Mexico's situation ("You were right, it's a sick country; and God knows if it ever has been, or will be otherwise. I doubt if I will ever be able to fathom the Indian really. It may be a dangerous quest, also. I'm pretty sure it is, in fact.") goes on to assert that "humanity is so unmechanized here still, so immediate and really dignified (I'm speaking of the Indians, peons, country people

—not the average mestizo) that it is giving me an entirely fresh perspective."[42]

Denise Levertov, in a poem called simply "Corazón" (Heart), expresses her sense of the peasant heart of Mexico.

> When in bushy hollows between
> moonround and moonround of hill, white clouds
> loiter arm-in-arm, out of curl,
> and sheep in the ravines
> vaguely congregate, the heart
> of Mexico sits in the rain
> not caring to seek shelter,
> a blanket of geranium pink drawn up
> over his silent mouth.[43]

Father Vaillant in Willa Cather's *Death Comes for the Archbishop* exclaimed that the more he worked with Mexicans, the more he thought that Christ had in mind people such as they when he said "unless ye become like little children." Christ was thinking, Fr. Vaillant explained, of "people who are not clever in the things of this world, whose minds are not upon gain and worldly advancement."[44] Henry Miller attributed a Christ-like character to a Mexican worker who was sent over one day to weed the garden of Miller's house in California. Something about the simple gravity of the man was enough to send Miller into a pastoral extravaganza. Miller's conviction that he was in the presence of a saintly figure was perhaps aided by the fact that there was no distracting communication through the medium of language, as Miller had no Spanish and the worker no English. "If we were suddenly faced with overwhelming calamity," wrote Miller, "if I had to choose just one man with whom I would share the rest of my life in the midst of chaos and destruction, I would pick that unknown Mexican peon." The worker's behavior, indicating complete selflessness, and the spirituality of his good looks made him appear to be the Christ returned to earth. "He was a gem, of the human realm, for which we have ceased to search. A gem we tread upon unthinkingly, as we would a weed or a stone, whilst hunting for uranium or some other currently 'rare' mineral which will give us, idiots that we are, priority over the rest of the human race in the race toward annihilation."[45] Steinbeck's California Mexicans in *Tortilla Flat,* bibulous and much given to fornication, are clearly not candidates for canonization, and yet Steinbeck endows them with a certain holy innocence. Danny and his genial friends, who live gaily for the moment and make no plans that will commit them beyond sundown, are meant to be a living rebuke to the sordidly ambitious, repressed, materialistic and compulsively hard-working American bourgeoise. "The paisanos," Steinbeck writes of Danny and his friends, "are clean of commercialism, free of the complicated systems of American business, and, having nothing that can be stolen, exploited or mortgaged, that system has not attacked them vigorously."[46]

A middle-western businessman, McKee, in Wright Morris's novel *The Field of Vision,* was very much of that system. McKee sought escape in the abstractions of business from having to confront in himself the fact of fundamental emotional inadequacies. The world of business was his comfortable provincialism. Outside of it he tended to be anxious, easily alarmed. The very remoteness of Mexicans from the assumptions and techniques of the age of technology was to McKee unsettling. Once when seated high in the bullfight arena in Mexico City he noticed a group of men, "who looked like midgets," scurrying out to pick up a Pepsi Cola bottle which had been thrown into the ring.

> They looked like circus dwarfs with that bottle, and confirmed McKee's feeling of some basic disorder. Some disproportion that made him feel a little unbalanced, unsure of himself. The way he'd feel if he landed on the moon, or felt drawn to it. He watched the men, all of them so many midgets, and it crossed his mind what was wrong with it. Back in the States they'd have a truck or some machine, to take care of that. But people — pretty little ones at that — still did the work in Mexico. On the little highway coming down they'd crossed an iron bridge that looked like it was crawling with hundreds of insects, but on closer inspection they turned out to be Indians. Full grown ones. What were they up to? They were chipping the rust off that fool bridge with sharp pointed rocks. Coming on them like that McKee had had the feeling that his eyes were slipping, or that liquid in his ear drums, since the scale of the thing, like the men with the bottle, threw him off.[47]

It is toward that America populated with types such as McKee, emotionally impotent products of a mechanized society, that Robinson Jeffers directs his scorn. In "The Dead Men's Child," an allegorical poem, he makes use of Mexicans conceived of as people of the earth to express his sense of the value of the changeless, and the peril inherent in the Promethean ideal of progress. The scene of the poem is a place in the California desert where once a group of escaping Mexican smugglers had died of thirst.

> A good while later, men found
> A vein of silver in the cliff and opened the mine, A little encampment grew up, Mexican laborers

> Came with their wives and black-eyed children. One saint's day
>   evening some of the younger people of the camp
> Made fire on the mound of half forgotten dead men, opposite the
>   ironwood tree. They ate and drank there
> In a circle about the flame, under the desert stars.
>   Rosaria Rivas was one of the girls
> In that company; after some months she was found pregnant. She
>   told her parents that when the fire
> Died down and the others departed she had remained on the place.
>   In the night chill she had drawn her skirt
> (Being all alone) above her knees to warm them at the red embers,
>   then suddenly a swirl of wind
> From the east blew dust and ashes into her unsheltered body. So
>   by mere ignorant accident Rosaria
> Conceived a child, neither for pleasure nor kindness, only by the
>   innocent malice of the dark wind
> Driving the dust of the dead. Her story was easily
> Believed; the more because she had little reason for lying. Morality
>   was not so enviously strict
> Among them that love had to go masked. Her child was born the
>   due tenth moon after that saint's day,
> And she was much pitied, having the pain without the pleasure.
>   But people soon perceived that her son
> Was only a little different from other children; they all are mon-
>   grels between the present and the past,
> Their natures drawing as much from men and beasts long dead as
>   from either parent. Yet in time this child
> Of the dust of dead men proved his quality. He throve in fortune;
>   he was never duped nor reckless; his life
> Ran smooth because he had nothing *future* about him. Men do not
>   stumble on bones mostly but on seeds,
> And this young man was not of the sad race of Prometheus, to
>   waste himself in favor of the future.[48]

A culture which, in its pure form, rejects the future and reveres the past is the subject of Virginia Sorensen's novel *The Proper Gods*. Here again, a modern American writer, critical of the commercialization of life in the United States, turns to a society which is primitive, cohesive, traditional, communal and non-acquisitive. The book is about the Yaqui Indians of Sonora, a people who comprise one of the many subcultures of Mexico. The Yaquis, for all their separatism, are definitely Mexicans. Their culture, though still grounded in the pre-Columbian past, contains many Hispanic influences. During the Revolution, some of the most effective troops marshalled by such northern generals as Alvaro Obregón were Yaquis, and many a northern leader has attributed his prowess to the Yaqui blood in his veins. Throughout the long tyranny of Porfirio Díaz, the Yaquis, because of their proud insistence upon maintaining tribal authority, were much persecuted so that many of them fled Sonora, establishing themselves in villages of their own making in Arizona, where some of these colonies flourish today. The novel opened with the arrival of Adan Savala, a young Yaqui who had been born and raised in Arizona, at the village of Potam in Sonora. Adan, who had fought in Europe during World War II, had recently received his discharge from the army and was still dressed in a United States Army uniform, carrying all his possessions in a barracks bag. Having been long removed from tribal influences and exposed to many things which most Yaqui Indians never experience in the course of a lifetime, Adan approached Potam with misgivings. His family, consisting of his grandfather and grandmother, his father, mother, and two sisters, had moved to Potam because of his grandfather's nostalgic longing for the community of his birth and early years. Achai, the grandfather, a great traditionalist, steeped in Yaqui ritual and lore, had insisted upon the move to Potam because of the disgust with which he had observed the increasing neglect of many of the old customs and ceremonies by the people in the Yaqui community of Pascua Village, now totally surrounded by the city of Tucson, Arizona. In Potam the ritualized life of the Yaqui culture was observed with the purity of its ancient forms intact. By the time of Adan's arrival in Potam, Achai had already become a recognized leader in the village. At first there were frequent arguments between Adan and Achai, with Adan expressing his skepticism openly, sometimes holding up the Americans or non-Yaqui Mexicans (known as "Yoris" in the Yaqui tongue) as examples of progressive peoples, and Achai trying to win Adan back to the ancient ways. During one such argument Achai said:

> "Do you think you would be happy, Adan? If you were Americano, do you think so? I have seen plenty of those people in my time! They were never happy very long, I could see it in their faces. And once a priest came, who told me many truths about his people. Priests often came to La Gloria [a Yaqui religious ceremony], and they always spoke to me because I had much authority in Pascua [Arizona] . . . The priest told me, Adan, that many Americanos are not happy at all — even those who are most rich. They are rivals, and this never ends with them. They are never free. They must have more and more, they must become more and more and more, he said; they are never satisfied in their lives. Always there is more in the stores in the towns, more of everything no matter what is bought and carried away." Adan nodded and smiled. He had seen that himself. But if for Yoris and Americanos it was always in possessions they conformed, what of Yaquis? It was another way with them: to be monarca in the

center line, to be captain from the Day of Ashes until the Resurrection. To be a pueblo mayor —."[49]

Throughout the novel Adan was torn between the forces of tradition and revolt, the former represented not only by Achai but by most of his immediate family and by the woman he loved and her family. Those who influenced him toward revolt were principally his *mestizo* cousin, Sixto, and an energetic young Mexican captain both of whom felt that the Yaquis should become less stiff-necked and tradition-bound and should participate more in general Mexican life. Sixto was one of the new group of *mestizo* business entrepreneurs thrown up by the Revolution, a group which had moved in to take the place, in terms of power and influence, of the dispossessed *criollos*. For all his materialism, Sixto was hardly a stock villain, being portrayed as an ingenious, witty, worldly, charming and compulsively generous young man. But the final triumph in the struggle for the protagonist's allegiance went to the forces of tradition. Adan had become increasingly influenced by Achai's total unworldliness and absolute devotion to the impressive cycle of ritualized drama that made up the life of the Yaquis. He had also been drawn toward the formal patterns of the life of Potam by his passionate involvement with a woman who was in no way a rebel, an involvement which was to end in a formal Yaqui wedding. The manner of Achai's death, stoic, dignified, surrounded by prescribed ritual, confirmed Adan in his decision to assume the position of leadership, his father being an ineffectual man, which would inevitably be conferred upon him should he stay in Potam. In one of the final scenes of the novel, Sixto and the Mexican captain, over a few whiskeys, shrugged off Adan's defection from the cause of modernity with a few jokes about the incurable backwardness of the Indians. *Mestizos* such as themselves were, after all, Mexico's only hope.

*The Proper Gods* is a skillfully developed work of fiction. Its characters are not noble savages but individualized and believable humans. Passages describing, with impressive mastery of detail, the ceremonial life of the Yaquis are aesthetically effective. The author had, in fact, spent only two weeks living among the Yaquis in Sonora. The actual experience among the people was supplemented by intensive study of research notes on the life of the Yaquis taken by Professor Edward Spicer, cultural anthropologist and expert on the Indian cultures of North and Latin America. The denouement of the novel in which the principal figure resolves his problems by returning to pure orthodoxy is not really warranted, according to Professor Spicer, in terms of the actual situation of the Yaquis, many of whose young people are defecting from the sub-culture and becoming absorbed into general Mexican life. Another social scientist, Charles J. Erasmus, takes a thoroughly unsentimental view of the Yaquis and their culture. "By suppressing the felt needs and aspirations of the larger society in which they feel rejected or inadequate, they can continue to satisfy their need for self-esteem by taking part in the activities of a group made up of others like themselves. Together they can play their own prestige game until enough dissenters break away."[50] The resolution of the novel, therefore, must be one which has subjective value for the author. Quite possibly the book provides another example of an American writer's seeking in Mexico, and not necessarily the Mexico which *is* but the Mexico which is wanted, a setting through which to sublimate a frustrating discontent with the materialism and spiritual flatness surrounding the American life of the author's experience.

This championing of the basic Mexican peasant, whether Indian or *mestizo,* against the forces that have produced modern industrial society has been a continuing tradition in modern American writing about Mexico. The early John Dos Passos, speaking in the passionate voice of the 'thirties, took up the cause of Juan Sin Tierra (John Without Land). "Ten million Mexican peasants and workmen, disunited, confused by political rows, sleeping on a straw mat on the floor, eating off a few tortillas a day and a speck of chili to take away the raw taste of the corn, standing up in their fields against the Catholic Church, against the two world groups of petroleum interests, against the inconceivably powerful financial bloody juggernaut of the Colossus of the North. Which side are you on, on the side of the dollar, omnipotent god, or on the side of the silent dark man (he has lice, he drinks too much when he can get it, he has spasms of sudden ferocious cruelty), Juan Sin Tierra, with his eyes on the ground?"[51] Approximately a decade later Ruth Tuck was saying of Juan Perez, her generic term for the Mexican peon who has crossed into the United States, that he "has a phrase to sum up his experience. He says, 'Yes, in coming to the United States, I have gained much. But I have also lost much. I have exchanged the spiritual for the material.' He reverts to his old figure of the money-changer: 'I am like the man who went to the *cambiador,* but could not count. I do not precisely know what I got in return. I live better, I have more things, but I do not feel at home in the world.'"[52] And Henry Miller, writing in 1957, reminds his readers that the Mexican migrant worker who comes to the United States often does not get even the tangible advantage for which he came.

And how did my good friend, who was a "wet-back," naturally, come off after three years of backbreaking labor and little pay in this glorious state of California? Did he accumulate a small fortune (the bait we hold out to them) to bring back to his family below the Rio Grande? Did he save enough, at least, to permit himself a month's holiday with his loved ones?

He returned as he came, with a torn shirt and a ragged coat, his pockets empty, his shoes busted, his skin tanned a little deeper from exposure to wind and sun, his spirit unquenchable but bruised, grateful, let us proudly assume, for the poor food he had been handed and for the lousy mattress he had been privileged to sleep on. He had one treasure which he could produce as evidence of the rewards of sweat and toil: a certificate for a cemetery plot which some smart aleck had sold him. How would he return to occupy this plot at the appointed time, nobody had explained to him. Nobody could. He will never occupy it, we who sold it to him know. His place, gem that he is, is not in the Monterey Cemetery but in the bed of a fevered river, in the ruins of an ancient civilization, in the waste of a scorched earth.[53]

Those Mexicans who stayed within the boundaries of the United States have, according to some writers, vitiated themselves through their imitation of standard American ways, thus ending up in a cultural no-man's land. John Houghton Allen mourned what he called "the sad decay of Americanization" which overtook the once-primitive *vaqueros* of Southwest Texas. They have become "schizophrenic, modern peasants," caught up in American gadgetry. Their women have taken to dressing like "gringos" or "as the parents, spitting in disgust would say, like whores." All of them have moved into "ugly galvanized towns like Pena and now like the gringos these people affect to scorn any remote connection with the soil. And now they sit in these gringo towns like Indians off a reservation, having lost the last shreds of their nobility, not knowing what ails them really."[54] A group of "pachucos," in Irving Shulman's *The Square Trap,* reveals the cultural situation of young Mexican-Americans in California, as they talk things over. One of them, Benny, begins to talk admiringly of his Uncle Leo, a carefree bachelor who never works for any more money than is necessary for his immediate needs, who lives in a shack, never strains himself, and is completely generous about sharing whatever he happens to have in the icebox. " 'He travels and lives real light, my Uncle Leo,' " says Benny. " 'And that's why he's rich. He's got what he wants and he don't want no more.' " Another of "The Cats," Go-Go, snorts with disgust. " 'Your uncle . . . livin' in a shack with no clothes and stealin' chickens and only with one shirt. And then you wonder why the Anglos think we're all a bunch of lazy bastards who like to live here,' he pointed at the Ravine, 'and don't wanna do nothin' but lay around in the sun. Guys like your uncle give me a real pain in the ass.' "[55] Shulman, who realistically recognizes the social and economic problems of the "pachucos" in California, does not prescribe a simple primitivism as the way out. The loss of the old culture, whatever its virtues, he sees as inevitable for the Mexican-Americans who have to cope with life in Los Angeles.

Frank Goodwyn in *The Magic of Limping John*[56] uses the superstitions of the Mexican folk culture in Southwest Texas to present what is in effect an anti-primitivistic parable. Limping John Luna, an itinerant fiddler in the town of Los Puentes, suddenly, because of a series of accidents by which he seemed to have demonstrated supernatural powers, acquires the reputation of being a wizard. Luna, an essentially tough-minded type, does his best to pooh-pooh all talk of wizardry, but the more he denies having extraordinary powers, the greater his reputation as a wizard grows. As his scoundrelly friend Don Fabian assures him, there is no escape; it is simply his destiny to be a wizard. One day a distraught father brings him a dead infant and implores him to bring it back to life. While Luna is outside of his hut, a friend switches a live baby for the dead one. On returning, Luna believes that he has revived the child. From then on, he actually thinks himself to be possessed of magical power. With his friend Don Fabian to handle the financial arrangements, he goes into business as a *curandero,* making money hand-over-fist dispensing cures. Later Luna finds out about the baby-switch. However, he has grown soft and corrupt and cannot give up the new life. Natalia Rodríguez, the girl who has loved him, dies of grief because of the change in him. Luna, plagued by his conscience, breaks his fiddle while playing at his own wedding party where he was to be married to the voluptuous and ambitious Clara. The book ends with Luna back in the hut, trying to use his wizardry to repair his smashed fiddle. He has gone mad. This novel makes very skillful use of folkloric material, reporting in pungent detail on the diet, drinking habits, amours, superstitions, violence, sense of destiny of the Mexicans of southwest Texas. Despite this grounding in folklore, however, the book does not deal in pastoral quaintness, nor does it uphold as superior wisdom the peasant otherworldliness of the superstitious people of Los Puentes, but rather, for all its robust humor, the novel works out its theme — amid scenes of death and violence — of the tragedy of human ignorance and the greed by which this ignorance is exploited.

The cult of primitivism which has brought Americans to Mexico in a self-conscious search for the elemental, within themselves and without, as well as the practice of this cult by Mexicans themselves, the Indianists who since the Revolution have exalted all things Indian and thoroughly depreciated Spain's contribution to the culture of Mexico, all this has come in for some satirical treatment. Carter Wilson's young Mexican doctor, who was required by Mexican law to put in a term of medical practice among the Indians of Chiapas, did not share in this cult.

> He thought all Mexicans who made beautiful pronouncements about the Indians were foolish. Sentimental. The Indians were men and they suffered like everyone else. He saw their suffering close up, and it was not beautiful or pure. Indians died like everyone else, he said. They were a little tougher, that was true, but they were also dirty and more stupid. That was also true. The intellectuals in Mexico City could fawn over the Indian, but the Doctor didn't see any intellectuals in the plaza of Chomtik that morning. None of them would help him wash the instruments after the autopsy.[57]

Katherine Anne Porter also contributed to the satirical treatment of this theme. "The journalist" in the story "That Tree," who first went to Mexico to be a poet and had gone native with much deliberation, took his midwestern, school-teacher wife, Miriam, to a cafe in Mexico City one evening. While they were dancing, one of four quarreling generals got to his feet and grabbed for his gun. Immediately the Mexican girls on the dance floor, in a gesture which seemed to "the journalist" to display a magnificently primitive instinct for self-preservation, swung their partners' backs to the generals as shields. Miriam simply dove under the table. This action struck "the journalist" as "the most utterly humiliating moment of his whole, blighted life." Later he accused her of having "instincts out of tune." She glared at him, and "when she tightened her mouth to bite her lip and say 'instincts!' she could make it sound like the most obscene word in the language." Katherine Anne Porter in the same story ridicules the self-conscious Indianism of the post-revolutionary painters in Mexico. The simple Indian girl who had been living with "the journalist" had to be moved along, with the arrival of Miriam in Mexico City. The girl was later taken up by a Mexican who was one of the "more famous and successful painters." In time she grew to be "very sophisticated" and became "a character." "She took, later on, to wearing native art-jewelry and doing native dances in costume, and learned to paint almost as well as a seven-year-old child. 'You know, [said the painter] the primitive style.' "[58] The American archeologist, Givens, in the story "María Concepción," is described as liking "his Indians best when he could feel a fatherly indulgence for their primitive childish ways." He used to enjoy regaling his American friends with stories about how he had often saved Juan Villegas, his Indian digger, from scrapes which the Indian had gotten into because of his irresponsible nature. After Juan married María Concepción, Givens "used to twit him, with exactly the right shade of condescension, on his many infidelities . . ."[59]

Mexican primitivism as it expresses itself in the tendency to let things go to seed has seemed less than enchanting to some modern American writers. Saul Bellow in *The Adventures of Augie March* wrote of the town of Chilpanzingo: "Here was the *zocalo*. White filthy walls sunk toward the ground and rat-gnawed Spanish charm molded from the balconies, a horrible street like Seville rotting, and falling down to flowering garbage heaps . . . decay in the town, the spiky, twisted patch of grave iron on the slope, bleeding bougainvillea bubbles on the walls, vines shrieky green. . . ."[60] Selden Rodman in *Mexican Journal* found it hard to maintain the familiar delight in Mexican concern for the aesthetic at the expense of the practical. Of the house he and his family had rented in Mexico City he wrote:

> Is this house we're living in a symbol of Mexico? Or is it we who read into it our own anxieties? Here am I, a lifelong lover of the arts who ofttimes deplores "American materialism," finding myself in the position of resenting the peon who spends all day weeding the flowerbeds. Why, I find myself asking, is he being asked to do all this "useless" prettifying — and the gardens that surround us are undeniably pretty — when the suggestion that he make our toilet work elicits nothing more than an offended shake of the head? The two incompetent females who "run" this establishment — that is, collect rent and wash their hands of service — hate us for making our utilitarian demands. And in self-defense we are coming to hate them for ignoring our comforts. And, by extension, for their willingness to provide for the esthetic.[61]

At the hands of Lawrence Ferlinghetti, the theme of Mexican innocence comes off quite differently from the way in which it has been treated by such purveyors of Mexican innocent merriment as John Steinbeck and Richard Summers. The passengers on Ferlinghetti's bus, rolling through northern Mexico, seem to be the victims of the radio announcer, whose loud voice is projected at them from the driver's radio.

> It is *innocence,* it is their seeming *innocence* which presents itself incessantly, as you see the *camion* passengers so gravely taking in everything the hotrod announcer throws at them (The announcer himself knowing just whom he's talking to, in fact can see them all in every country backstreet in dustbin Mexico). He's talking to them in person, and they are listening, laughing, smiling, gawking out windows, peering ahead thru Madonna fringe as radio blasts on with rock-and-roll played by nothing but trumpets borrowed from hock-

shops in Mexico City (*monte de piedads* of leftover life). And the whole absurd Gestalt of the *camion* bowling along like some flippy total caravanserai-symbol, wheeling into space with all the ancient trappings, shawls & superstitions, hunger & flocked beauty (the young dark girl's eyes on the road) carrying along with it all the claptraps and fandanglements of microphones, phonographs, plastic madonnas.

 All sit there still groping on into the falling dusk. Innocence persists, insanely intarissable, in spite of all. The road does not end. It is as if the radio were not playing at all. There is a stillness in the air, in the light of the dusk, in the eyes fixed forward, in the still end of life, an intolerable sweetness. . . .[62]

Ferlinghetti, as one of the earlier Beat Poets, had a hand in fostering the neo-primitivism which Leslie Fiedler was later to analyze in some detail, the sort of primitivism in which sophisticated and somewhat spoiled modern urbanites play at being Indian. In *Mexican Night,* Ferlinghetti records an experience in which the real and the neo-primitivism momentarily come in contact and reveal to the poet the common ground between them. The poet, in Mexico, is groping his way at night toward his lodgings after a particularly bad drug trip.

 A *pulque* drunk lurches against
me, white corn teeth gleaming under broken
sombrero, Indian eyes blind, glazed, primitive night
upon us, he in his dark world, I, mine; lurching past
each other, *almost* like lost humanoids, awful, beasts
abroad.[63]

Denise Levertov also considers the Mexican countryman, *campesino,* in terms of his drinking, but in her poem, "Canticle" — the title itself suggestive — there is a curious mixture of the sordid and the religious, as though to suggest that the hard-pressed Mexican peasant seeks in the cantina, the "death-in-life temple," some form of ecstasy of escape which is comparable to a religious experience.

Flies, acolytes
of the death-in-life temple
buzz their prayers

and from the altar
of excrement arises
an incense

of orange and purple
petals. Drink
campesino,

stain with ferment
the blinding white that clothes
your dark body.[64]

In this consideration of American reactions to that which is primitive or thought to be primitive in Mexican life, there has not as yet been mention of a rather specialized form of Mexican primitivism which has received its share of attention in American writing, Mexican banditry. Even a superficial contact with Mexican culture is likely to impress one with the unique position of the bandit in the folk culture of Mexico. As a type, the bandit is most prominent in the lore of the borderlands, as the north Mexican states seem to have produced the most formidable specimens of this breed, and, furthermore, the Mexican bandit of the borderlands has had an opportunity to tweak the nose of the "gringo," thus adding considerably to his laurels. The prominence of the bandit in the lore of Mexico is directly related to the historical experience of the Mexicans, who as a people have known a continual series of oppressors. There is a racial aspect to the heroic proportions that the figure of the bandit has assumed. Almost invariably the bandit has been a *mestizo* or an Indian. In either case he has represented the great mass of the people, the dispossessed, against hated overlords: first the despised *gachupines,* the Spanish bureaucrats of colonial times, then their successors the *criollos*. Finally, during the Revolution, the bandit took on the new, respectable role of patriot, of general of the army. In assuming this role he treated the people to the edifying sight of the dark-visaged man wearing the epaulettes formerly reserved for the sons of gentlemen, the *criollos* boasting their Spanish blood. To the American writer encountering the bandit in Mexican folklore, this figure still had something of the smell of the liberator about him. As a picaresque figure he promised a degree of liberation from the psychological oppressions resulting from the growing mechanization and mass conformity of life in the United States. The Mexican bandit was to some American writers so freshly a symbol of the protesting individualist that he retained much of the aura of glory with which he had been invested by his own people and was forgiven such pecadillos as whimsical throat-cuttings and other similar manifestations of his uninhibited nature. Those American writers who have made the culture of the borderlands their business have stated well the role played by the bandit in the folklore of the region. Of the Rio Grande country in the 1850's, Paul Horgan wrote: "When out of the welter of torture, murder, burning, and theft there merged an occasional Mexican virtuoso of remorseless savagery, he was celebrated in folk songs, for mingled with the terror that greeted his sudden appearances was a sigh of admiration. His type, with few variations, was the reigning folk hero along the boundary river for a century." [65]
And of the same region Frank Dobie wrote that "here, indeed, history

was the 'prolongated shadow' of an individual" in a land "in which with hardly half a dozen exceptions unnumbered monuments are to men of blood and violence and in which the ballads sung nightly on a thousand plazas heroize the bandit always mounted." [66]

Mary Austin in the story "The Bandit's Prayer," recounts an old folk legend of New Mexico in which a bandit gets the better of a representative of what, in the eyes of many Mexicans, has been one of the historic oppressors, the Church. The bandit Pedro de Urdemanas, known as "the gypsy," was aware that Padre Eleguius had on his person, as he rode through the desert country of New Mexico, money which had been donated to the Church. When Pedro and his fellow brigand, Juan, rode up beside the priest, the following conversation ensued:

> "I was much struck, Padre," said the gypsy, "with your saying that God has all gifts in His hand and that if a man lacks anything, he has but to ask it faithfully and it will be his, even though it were that filthy necessity, money?"
> "It is true," said the Padre, "that all things are in His hand."
> "Why then, " said Urdemanas with a sigh, "it must be that God does not hear the prayers of a poor man, for there is nothing I lack so much as money and yet I swear to you that all I have in the world is two pesos"— and he showed them to the priest in his hand.
> "It must be," said the priest, "that you do not pray aright."
> "Why, then, Padre, you shall teach me. And when so excellent a time as the present!" Dismounting, he laid hand on the priest's bridle rein in such a manner that there was no gainsaying it. "Just to make sure," said the gypsy to his companion, "what money have you, Juan?"
> "I have four reales."
> "And you, Padre?"
> "I have five pesos," said the priest, and that was no falsehood, since he allowed so much for his expenses, and the other two hundred and ninety-five in his bag he considered the property of the Church.
> "Now that we know where we stand," said Urdemanas, "let us pray, Padre."
> So they knelt down and the Padre prayed, and it may be with one eye on his black bag, with the gypsy and his rogue repeating the words behind him. When the priest could think of nothing more to say, they stood up.
> "And now," said Pedro, "let us see how God has used us." So he looked in his hand and there were still but two pesos. Then he looked at the *compañero* who showed him four reales. "And you, Padre?" But the priest being somewhat slow, Urdemanas opened his black bag for him and there beheld the offering. "Ah, Padre,

it is easy to see that you are in favor with God. And since it is so easy for you to pray five pesos into three hundred and so impossible for us, we will take these for our necessities."[67]

The bandit of historical fact when he passed into folklore often became endowed by the popular imagination with elements of the humorously grotesque, and something of this transformation was carried over into the treatment of the Mexican bandit by American writers. It did not take much alteration to make Villa's right-hand man, General Fierro, a thoroughly bandit type, into a grotesque, and one of the tales in John Houghton Allen's loosely constructed novel *Southwest* shows Fierro in a light which has that peculiarly folkloric humorous-grotesque quality. A *vaquero*, Javier, is reminiscing about days spent with Fierro during the Revolution. On one occasion one of Fierro's men rode up to him to deliver the tidings of "the defeat of Obregón by the glorious arms of Pancho Villa." The man dismounted, gave a salute, and shouted, as Javier tells the story, " ' "Good news, my General, good news, my General! Long live the Revolution! The Federals are conquered, and their asses are dragging from every lamppost in the town." ' " So overjoyed was Fierro at this announcement that

> "he too dismounted and threw himself upon the trooper, giving many *gritos,* long-lives to Pancho Villa, vivas for the Revolution, and like a man, ending with the *abrazo,* saying, 'Embrace me, *companero!* Embrace me, my brave!' but such a stretch was that, and so strong was the embrace of my *compadre* Fierro that the soldier gave one cry, '*Ay!*' and fell doubled at his feet, mouthing a torrent of blood. Fierro had been a little embarrassed – he who in hand-to-hand fighting used to kill not with the pistol or machete but with his hands, rolling up his sleeves with gusto and hugging men to death like a bear – he had forgotten in his enthusiasm how strong he was."

The incident resulted in an inquest conducted by Pancho Villa himself

> "Pancho Villa absolved his General of all blame, of course, because Fierro in this case had been an involuntary murderer, and Pancho Villa had a large genial way of looking on misdemeanors of this sort, but he positively prohibited in the future, under pain of death, that his General Fierro, his own right hand and his brother in the Dorados – and how it hurt Don Pancho to issue such an order we can never know – *embrace anyone, friend or enemy, woman or child.* I was a sentinel at headquarters that day," Javier said, "and I remember Fierro stood at attention with the sweat beading his face that looked like the relief maps on the walls, and he took his injunction very seriously. It was even said that this depriving our General of the right to embrace embittered Fierro, he was such a

sensitive man, and that was the reason he was uncongenial, and why he burnt the Chinamen, until that too was forbidden him, and shot all the dogs in the plaza, for he had a big heart and he wanted to enjoy himself when he took a town, and it was very tame to just shoot civilians."[68]

Frank Dobie describes listening to a popular singer in northern Mexico as he sang *corridos* about Villa and other famous bandits. He gives the reader some concept of the effect produced by these songs upon the listener and also a sense of the powerful influence such figures as Villa have had upon the emotional and imaginative life of the people of Mexico.

> I cannot describe the liberating and refreshing effect the opening bars of the song had upon me. The song was one of the several popular *corridos* about Villa. At the end of the first verse I yelled "Viva Pancho Villa!" and then the troubadour sang on "as if his song could have no ending." There were between thirty-five and forty verses to it — all about the "terror of the North," "the man who laughs and kills," "a prophet like Mohamet," "this Bonaparte of the sierras," sitting on "his sorrel horse, pistol in hand, teeth gleaming," the "feline pupils of his eyes dilating," shouting, "We are born to die," the "very god of his Dorados," "rude but great of heart," making "formidable explosions of steam engines," dynamiting bridges, amid *"una gran confusion,"* burning caboose and passenger cars, now sacking Torreon, now in the town of Columbus leaving "as a little remembrance only sixteen dead gringos." But alas for *"pobre* Pancho Villa." In Parral traitors and ingrates waylaid and murdered him . . . That night the *músico* sang ballads about Heraclio Bernal, who gave five hundred pesos to a poor family in the sierras, who killed ten *gachupines* in the mountains of Durango and ordered their skins tanned for boot leather, and who even when dead and in his coffin made all the mounted police and soldiers shake with fear. The *músico* sang about nearly all the other famous *bandidos* of his *país*. In fact, *tragedias* of desperate deeds and men made up most of his repertoire. It was the old, old story of the *valiente* on horseback.[69]

One of the latest books about Villa by an American writer is Haldeen Braddy's *Cock of the Walk*.[70] The writer, a professor of English, can no more resist the legend of Villa than can the illiterate Mexicans in the mountains and on the deserts of Villa's native state of Chihuahua. Here we see Villa hiding a treasure in the fastnesses of the Sierra Madres with the help of forty workmen who, as the story goes, were shot for their pains, falling into self-prepared graves, thus leaving no witnesses to the treasure's site. Villa is shown perpetuating ghastly murders and tortures. "He could kill man upon man. . . . Always afterwards he felt unworried, calm — relaxed. Always afterwards he slept like a baby. He shot somebody just like that, and a little time afterwards he began to get sleepy, began to dream his wonderful dream."[71] This is the Villa to whom "the gift of song" came naturally, the "bold and terrible man, full of ambivalences and contradictions, delighted with children and fond of slitting throats. . . ."[72] Whatever his savageries, Villa to Braddy is still Robin Hood. Casting a colder eye upon the figure of Pancho Villa, Anita Brenner summed up his career with the statement that "when Villa was peacefully assassinated in the fall of 1924, his epitaph was a universal sigh of regret and relief. He left behind him stories to find in the bottles of old people whose guerrilla day is past, and stories that flow from the fountain pens of the poets who rather hoped but never quite believed Villa would save whatever it was they wanted saved; songs, many songs, and a scattering of wives who harvest the only material crops of that fame which is now legend."[73]

The great fame enjoyed by Mexico's legendary men on horseback rests upon the continued vigor of the oral tradition as it expresses itself in folk tales and ballads, a vigor which is maintained because of the great responsiveness of the Mexican people to the folk arts, which have not yet in Mexico been destroyed by the standardization and commercialism of popular culture which so characterize life in the United States. The same temper which makes the common people delight in the folk arts has resulted, among the educated people of Mexico, in a high degree of sensibility to the arts generally. This aspect of the Mexican character, it will be recalled, was noted by the early border writers. It has been emphasized by modern American writers, often for purposes of contrast with cultural conditions prevailing in the United States. In discussing the translation of "lower-class Mexican Spanish," Oscar Lewis says in the introduction to *The Children of Sánchez:* "The English translation gives a surprisingly high level of language and vocabulary to relatively unlettered people. The fluency of language and the vocabulary of Mexicans, be they peasants or slum dwellers, have always impressed me."[74] One of the slum dwellers, Manuel, son of Jesús Sánchez, is capable of expressing himself in a manner which reveals considerable sensibility, as in the following passage. "It sounds laughable, but if I could find the appropriate word, I would like to write poetry someday. I have always tried to see beauty, even among all the evils I have experienced, so that I wouldn't be completely disillusioned by life. I would like to sing the poetry of life . . . great emotions, sublime love, to express the lowest passions in the most beautiful way. Men who can write of these things make the world more habitable; they raise life to a different level."[75]

Edward Larocque Tinker in *The Horsemen of the Americas and the Literature They Inspired* gives the following account of how a *corrido* (ballad recounting events of the day) gets started in Mexico.

> I shall never forget the first time I heard one. It was while Pancho Villa was attacking General Alvaro Obregón in Celaya. One night, walking along the troops' boxcars, I heard singing and the strumming of guitars. Following my ears, I came to a campfire, where a group of ragged soldiers were gathered with some of their *soldaderas* — those incredible Amazons who cooked for their men and, with pots and pans and often a baby on their back, kept up with them on gruelling marches; or if need arose, snatched a rifle from a corpse and fought as fiercely as any male. This picturesque crew was listening in the moonlight like fascinated children, to the singing of three men. One of them was a thin, hatchet-faced mestizo with the sly look of a coyote, another, a young Indio, with the rapt expression of a choirboy; while between the two, twanging his guitar, was a man with a harelip, one of the ugliest human beings I ever saw.
>
> As I listened to the assonances of their voices, I too was fascinated. Verse after verse took the same melodic pattern and I suddenly realized that this was no epic of ancient exploits, but a fresh-minted account of the battle of the day before, celebrating the conduct of every general and each act of individual heroism. It was a corrido — hot from the oven of their vivid memory of the struggle between Villa and Obregón. These singers were in almost every essential the lineal descendants of the troubadours who performed at the Court of Eleanor of Aquitaine, in the middle of the twelfth century; and their song was the Creole counterpart of the early Spanish *romances*, those Iberian *Chansons de Geste*, in which countless mediaeval bards sang of the fabulous exploits of the *lira mendicorum* — *romances*, the first of which must have come to America with the Conquistadores, for Bernal Diaz wrote that one of Cortez' soldiers, named Ortiz, was a *tocador de bihuela* (a guitar-like instrument of Moorish design) and taught dancing.[76]

The continued existence in Mexico of folk tales relating ancient events in the history of Spain amazed Timothy Turner. In *Bullets, Bottles, and Gardenias* he described chatting with an elderly policeman in Ciudad Juárez. "We used to sit out under the stars in the patio of the comandancia while he told me tales of Good King Boabdil, the last ruler of the Spanish Moors, tales that had come down to him by word of mouth, over the seas and up over the mountains and plains of Mexico up through the ages; tales with which I was already familiar from my Washington Irving. An illiterate Mexican mestizo, a humble policeman, telling me grand tales of Boabdil, that elegant and virtuous monarch of those glorious days!"[77]

The quality of Mexican folk music and of the voices of popular singers impressed American writers as having a greater immediacy of emotion than is found in the more industrialized societies. "It is the rhythm, if you insist on explicitness," wrote Mary Austin, "which has not yet lost the sense of right- and left-handedness, of male and female, all the plain distinctions with which life marked us before we gave ourselves to the god of machines."[78] Hart Crane wrote of the Mexican singing voice that it was "capable of heart-wringing vibrations." He enjoyed hearing singers who during the day were "masons, plumbers, or pickslingers" drop in of an evening and sing endless *corridos* "about 'poor Pancho Villa,' Zapata, and other dead revolutionaries." And comparing these singers to popular entertainers he had known in the United States, Crane declared these Mexicans to be "preferable to all the trained and professional whoopers-up I've ever heard."[79] Witter Bynner in the poem "Street Musicians" pays his compliment to the folk musicians of Mexico.

> Serenely the men of music play and sing,
> Oftentimes to a wave that likewise breaks
> In music, their faces remaining aloof, poised
> As a violin, contained as the strings of a harp.
> When tomatoes have been planted, Carlos comes,
> And when he sings or when he speaks, conjures
> Such gentle kingliness that his guitar
> Is the feathered mantle of Montezuma, gleaming.[80]

The vitality of the folk arts, so associated with what American writers have considered to be the primitive élan of rural Mexico, expresses itself in the workmanship that goes into all kinds of artifacts and pieces of furniture. These objects have come in for much admiring comment by American writers. Father Vaillant in Willa Cather's *Death Comes for the Archbishop* was very pleased with the primitive furnishings he had inherited from the Mexican priest who had formerly occupied his house in Santa Fe. Since "there was not at that time a turning-lathe or a saw-mill in all northern New Mexico," all the wood work was either ax-hewn or carved by knife. "The native carpenters whittled out chair rungs and table legs, and fitted them together with wooden pins instead of iron nails. Wooden chests were used instead of dressers with drawers, and sometimes these were beautifully carved, or covered with decorated leather."[81] Carey McWilliams remarked upon the aesthetic effectiveness of the craft work in this same area of New Mexico, calling it "Indian in feeling, Spanish in plan." The Mexican craftsmen were on the one hand "under a heavy debt to the Indians," but these in turn "borrowed freely" from that which was Hispanic in Mexican culture.[82] The result of this intermingling of cultural influences was a remarkably fresh and vital native art. Robert Ramsey in the novel *Fiesta* worked in a deft touch when in a brief description he managed to say so much about the Mexican temper. He described a heavy-set Mexican man as "walking with difficulty over the large cobblestones on a wooden leg, finely carpentered as a piece of cabinetwork, with the craftsmanship of an artist lavished upon it, but somehow a little ill-fitting or poorly designed."[83] It is this very aspect of Mexican culture by which the aesthetic has been emphasized above the practical which has so attracted modern American writers, reacting against the mechanized pragmatism of the United States, to Mexico. As F. S. C. Northrop has put it: "The Mexicans . . . have a culture extending to the humblest Indian of the villages, rich in things aesthetic and in the religion of passion, beauty, and worship. With respect to these values there is no doubt that their culture is superior to that of the United States."[84] However, these values in Mexico, as elsewhere, face the danger of extinction. Poet Gregory Corso catches a glimpse of a Mexican scene which in his poem speaks for itself.

> Through a moving window
> I see a glimpse of burros
>    a Pepsi Cola stand,
> an old Indian sitting
>    smiling toothless by a hut.[85]

Oliver La Farge writes in the introduction to *Five Families* by Oscar Lewis that "all of the families in this book consist of people whose culture is what we usually call 'in transition,' meaning that it is going to hell in a handbasket before the onslaught of the Age of Technology. Here is the greatest export of the Euro-North American family of nations— a new material culture that shatters the non-material cultures of the people it reaches, and that today is reaching them all. All over the world people are hating the light-skinned machine-age nations, and busily aping them. One of the first returns they get is a cultural desolation."[86]

## CHAPTER EIGHT

## Love, Fate, and Death

The "optative mood" of American society, eloquently stated by Emerson and automatically acted upon without conscious definition by the great mass of Americans, is one which has clearly produced results. Despite all current criticism of the idea of progress, the characteristic response by which Americans tell themselves that "things *can* be done" is still a vital impulse in American life and one to be valued. Yet a society which is to have an important development must be one which can criticize its most fundamental attitudes. Much of the current literature critical of the striving aspect of American life has shown the American as attenuating himself in the pursuit of abstractions. The man caught up in various schemes of amelioration, whether for himself or for society at large, is likely to form a self-image which is somewhat in the nature of a blueprint, a projection of plans and goals, a concept of self in which the primal man of flesh and bone and capacity for strong feeling is lost sight of, repressed. Furthermore, to the mind constantly projecting itself into worthwhile tomorrows, death is hardly credible and if momentarily sighted is rapidly shunted off as a clearly unprogressive intruder. Thus, as has been seen, when the Americans pushed westward to the point of colliding with Mexico, they looked with contempt upon a people who seemed to have absolutely no concept of self-improvement, who were animalistically passionate, and morbid in their continual consciousness of death, characteristics which are the very ones which modern American writers have seized upon in order to use Mexico as a foil by which to criticize their own society. To some of these moderns, the attitude of acceptance with which the Mexican approaches life has seemed to be in salutary contrast to the tendency of Americans, in several major areas of life, to refuse to accept things as they are. The Mexicans, these critics have noted with approval, seem to value life as such, not simply as a God-given opportunity to *do* something. More specifically, recent American writers have contrasted the natural acceptance of sexuality in Mexico with the puritanical denial of the body still claimed to be a force in American life. The American idea that one can plan for or insure against almost anything has been contrasted to the profound fatalism of Mexico, an attitude of resignation before an existence which is seen as essentially unpredictable, uncontrollable. Finally, the various subterfuges and euphemisms by which Americans so often try to evade any real confrontation with the fact of death have been compared with the almost passionate embracing of death in Mexico, a stark recognition which has been seen as a necessary complement to an intense, palpable sense of life.

It must be said that some of the Mexicans conjured up by American writers to shame us with their spontaneous naturalism have been creatures who have been tailored to fit the assigned role. When it comes to sex, the Spaniard and the Latin American are considerably more complex than the donjuanesque figures of popular legend. The Spanish historian, Gregorio Marañon, in an excellent discussion of Don Juan as he relates to Spanish culture, wrote that "far from being characteristically and originally Spanish, Don Juan's type of love is an exotic importation into Spain [from France through Francophile members of the Spanish court], without national roots or tradition. The form of love which is most typically Spanish is . . . that of the Castilian home: Monogamous, austere to the point of mysticism. Usually there are a large number of children, who were conceived almost without sin; and the bedroom has the severe dignity of a cell." There are, Marañon continued, other cultural influences in Spain which affect ways of sexual expression. There is the powerful gypsy influence in the south. But gypsy love, for all its tempestuousness, is "deep, enduring, ardently monogamous, almost mystical, incapable of deserting the beloved,"[1] in short very different from casual donjuanism. The results of the Moorish influence in Andalusia, however, do conform more with the popular conception of sexuality among Spanish-speaking people. According to Marañon:

> It is true that there have always been, and still are, Andalusians who dream of being sultans, and quite a few of them enact a parody of this dream, while keeping within the laws of contemporary society. They will have a legitimate wife who represents the Sultana, shares the responsibility of the home, is the mother of their children, and in the long run the mistress of their deepest affection. Behind her back they enjoy a host of paramours with whom they satisfy their more ephemeral passions. In fact this sort of shamefaced harem is by no means exclusively Andalusian, even though its origins may be traced to Andalusia. It exists more or less openly all over the Latin world, and beyond. So firmly is it established, that often the legitimate wife, like the Sultana of the harem, is aware of and condones her husband's polygamous affairs.[2]

Thus Spanish sexual customs have spread to Latin America, and it might well be that the Andalusian influence is stronger in the Americas than the austere Castilian. The Spaniards are fond of saying of their Latin American offspring that these have inherited all of the Spanish vices and none of the Spanish virtues. Individuals among cultivated Latin Americans, however, undoubtedly experience conflicts in sexual matters, arising from the combination of Christian mysticism and Arabic sensuality in the Hispanic tradition. Thus to depict all Mexicans as having a sunny naturalism in matters of sex is an oversimplification.

The view of the Mexicans as conforming more with the natural rhythms of organic life, of being a more accepting people in terms of the biological realities, while being generally valid, can be questioned on at least one score. Human beings seem to have the curious urge, expressed differently in different societies, to make themselves uncomfortable by fighting down some basic, functional aspect of their instinctual nature. If among Anglo-Saxons this urge has shown itself in the effort to overcome the base promptings of carnal desire, among the Spaniards and those who have inherited their tradition, the effort has been to overcome the instinct of self-preservation by establishing a rather unrealistic cult of bravery, such as that which is exhibited at the bullfight. In this connection it has been argued that man's genius for making himself uncomfortable has been responsible for many of his most impressive achievements.

Yet, whatever these demurrers, much of the contrast that has been developed by modern American writers between life in the United States and life in Mexico has been to the point and valid, if not in the letter, in some instances, at least in the spirit. In the story "A Pupil of Chestnut Ridge," Bret Harte deals with the rapid physical maturing and the natural sexual precocity of the Mexican woman, a precocity which in this case throws her American mentors somewhat for a loss. The good and simple pioneer family, Mr. and Mrs. Hoover, devout Free Will Baptists, have adopted a twelve-year-old California-Mexican girl, Concha, and have sent her to the local school, where she is the only Mexican. The young schoolmaster, Mr. Brooks, is somewhat ill at ease and unable to cope with her precocity, as she from the first carries on a subtle but unmistakable flirtation with him. One day, during recess, he leaves the school house to investigate the strange quiet and finds none of the students in the school yard. Hearing faint sounds of music coming from a nearby glen, he decides to investigate and finds all his pupils gathered in a circle and in a state of rapture while within the enclosure Concha is dancing the suggestive "semicuacua" to the accompaniment of an accordion played by one of the boys. Not long after that occasion,

Concha elopes with the Hoovers' ranch hand Pedro, a dispossessed and impoverished *hidalgo*. Mr. Hoover sums up the situation to the schoolmaster. "She wasn't no child, Mr. Brooks. We were deceived.... She was a grown woman — accordin to these folks' ways and ages — when she kem here. And that's what bothered me."[3]

Writing in quite another key, Robinson Jeffers makes use of the Mexican woman as a devotee for his god of elemental, passionate force. The girl California, in "Roan Stallion," is half-Mexican.

> a Scottish sailor
> had planted her in young native earth,
> Spanish and Indian, twenty-one years before.[4]

It is she who worships the stallion as a symbol of primal force. The powerful, sleek, clean virility of the stallion is contrasted to the blurred, drunken passion of her Anglo-American husband, Johnny, who represents modern man debauched by what little of modern technological civilization he is able in his dullness to acquire. In *Women at Point Sur,* Jeffers again uses an Indian-Mexican woman, the servant girl Maruca, to be a sort of Mother Earth in microcosm, all passion, ferocity, and fertility. The Reverend Doctor Barclay has left his Christian church to seek the true, fierce god. The reader may be advised at this point to exercise a temporary suspension of the sense of humor in order to receive the message which follows in all its stern import. The Reverend Barclay, having given Maruca eight dollars for the privilege of lying with her, exults, "I have bought salvation! I lay in a woman's lap uniting myself with the infinite God."[5] Onorio Vasquez, the Mexican seer of visions, assumes the role of prophet for the Reverend Barclay, the master, who proclaims the religion of the supremacy of desire and the falsehood of all ethics of restraint.

John Steinbeck's Mexicans are totally sinless in their happy naturalism. In *Tortilla Flat,* Teresina was regularly becoming a mother, and her large brood of children had an assortment of fathers. The question of paternity sometimes confused her, but when it "became too. complicated for her mind to unravel, she usually laid that problem in the arms of the Mother of Jesús, who, she knew, had more knowledge of, interest in and time for such things than she." When Danny and his friends became aware, on one occasion, that she had no more food in the house, the happy *paisanos* stole some crates of food and presented them to her. The presentation was the occasion of a fiesta. In due time, "Teresina discovered, by a method she had found to be infallible, that she was going to have a baby. As she poured a quart of the new beans into the kettle, she wondered idly which one of Danny's friends was responsible."[6]

In one of the episodes in Steinbeck's *The Pastures of Heaven*,[7] the two sisters López, María and Rosa, opened a little restaurant, after the death of their father, in their California home, putting out a sign which read "Spanish Cookings." Business, however, was very slow, and the economic situation of these two good-natured women became critical. One day Rosa, rather impulsively, gave herself along with the enchiladas to one of the customers. As she explained the incident to her sister: " 'Do not make a mistake . . . I did not take money. The man had eaten three enchiladas — three!' " And the enchiladas had been duly paid for. María, taking the cue, decided to go in for a similar encouragement of the customers. Business picked up markedly until "gringo" rigidities in such matters blighted the whole harmonious arrangement. One day one of the sisters kindly offered a ride in her wagon to a man whom she knew, who was walking along the road toward the bus station. This man was "the ugliest, shyest man in the valley," and his wife, in order to hide her shame in him, used to boast that he was something of a Don Juan, a claim which could not have been farther from the truth. When, however, word reached the wife that her husband had been seen riding along side of one of the López women, she became infuriated. Shortly after, the sheriff came to the López restaurant and told the sisters that they were running a disorderly house and would have to close down. In despair, the sisters decided to go to San Francisco to become out-and-out prostitutes.

A lively novel about the Mexican *colonia* in Tucson, Arizona, *Dark Madonna*,[8] by Richard Summers, also depicts the Mexicans as Nature's children. The heroine, Lupe, is seduced on several occasions and ends up with an illegitimate child, which she cares for tenderly. Her brother, Mucio, himself the result of his mother's having cuckolded his supposed father, takes turns with a rival in visiting the bed of the torrid Yoya. Another character, María Delgado, like Steinbeck's Teresina, is always becoming pregnant by a different man. The prevailing mood is one of innocent merriment among a people whose vividness contrasts with the work-a-day sobriety of the other citizens of the city.

The poor and dispossessed in the slum of Mexico City manage, despite their marginal existence, to have sexual lives of considerable range and intensity. Manuel, in *The Children of Sánchez*, lived in free union (the poor seldom married) with Paula by whom he had children. She was devoted to him. Though they had almost daily union, there was a certain quiet passivity in her nature. Manuel simultaneously carried on an affair with Graciela. She was rich-natured, intense, and highly charged erotically. They went to hotels after she finished her work as a waitress. Manuel felt himself to be deeply in love with each woman, but in different ways.[9]

In *The Mexico I Like,* Frank Dobie presents a dialogue between the narrator, presumably Dobie himself, who takes the Christian-chivalric view of the love relationship, and a Mexican named Inocencio, who argues for the blamelessness of nature.

> "When you use that word love, Inocencio, you use a word that you do not know the meaning of. Perhaps no Mexican knows it."
> "Excuse me, *patrón*. I am but of the *gente* uninstructed. I never looked inside a dictionary."
> "Probably the dictionary would not help," I replied.
> "I only know," my commentator went on, "that according to nature this man, that man, says, 'I am bound to pluck this flower no matter how many thorns prick my hand.' And then, the flower plucked, he is like the buck that sheds his horns."
> "Yes, but while the buck wears them, how proud, how bounding in life he is!"
> "You know best, *patrón*. There is no blame for nature. As our fathers said, 'A pair of *chiches* [breasts] pulls stronger than a yoke of oxen."
> Here Inocencio put himself in the attitude of a vaquero who with heels braced into the ground and body-stiffened back is being pulled by a rope wrapped around his waist.
> "What if the man forces his will against the pull?" I asked.
> "Why should he? When the fruit is ripe, unless someone pulls it, it will fall anyhow."
> "With proverbs you can prove the devil both white and black."
> "Yes, the devil is a chameleon."
> "As regards fruit, I was going to say," I went on, "that the owner of a garden has a right to what is in it."
> "Yes, but there are wild fruits. Remember the *dicho*. 'All meat is to be eaten, all women sampled.' Come, my friend. Molest your mind no further on this matter . . . ."[10]

In the novel *The Black Bull,* Frank Goodwyn writes of the ranching people, Mexican and Anglo, of southwestern Texas. What Goodwyn admires in the Mexican ranchers and their women is their natural vitality. These people enjoy the pleasures of the body keenly, but their lives are also set in a pattern of hard work and the raising of families. A typical *vaquero,* in the novel, is Timoteo Nieto, a man in his early forties.

> He could work all day in the dust and sun, dance all night with little in his stomach except wine and a few bites of highly spiced beef, and work all the next day with practically no signs of weariness. He ate sparingly and spasmodically but dearly enjoyed what he did eat. Being gifted with high sensitivity, he felt his pleasures keenly and lingered long over the thought of them . . . . His wife,

Cristina, was the principal source of pleasant memories. She had a beautiful body built for copious enjoyment and the production of numerous babies. In addition to much delight she had given Timoteo six children.[11]

His daughter, Josepha, grown to womanhood, was of much the same constitution. She combined a capacity for vibrant emotion with a general tranquility of spirit. All the sights, smells, and cadences of ranch life in southwest Texas, "the strong odor from the land's exotic shrubbery and from the fresh meat roasting in the scattered homes, the tumbling of life-oak foliage in the boisterous breeze, and the steady, metallic clanging and pumping of the windmill on the western rim of the sandbowl," combined to give Josepha an enveloping sense of well-being and identification with the land. The night she became engaged to Robelin Alegría, during a dance at the ranch, she "almost ached for the experience of being completely possessed by him."[12]

The earthy, functional sexuality of Frank Goodwyn's Mexican characters contrasts with the feverishness of the "subterranean" world of Jack Kerouac, in which dark-skinned people, be they Mexican or Negro, are valued for that extra jounce of passion they are supposed to be able to deliver to the initiates taking the new road to nirvana. Sal Paradise in *On The Road* has a meteoric affair with a Mexican-American girl named Terry, whom he picked up on a bus bound for Los Angeles. When their money runs out, they leave Los Angeles and proceed to Terry's home town of Sabinal, California, where Sal, together with Terry's brother Freddy and another Mexican, daily considers the prospect of looking for a job but puts the effort off until *mañana,* while everybody gets drunk. Sal spends his nights with Terry and the baby she has had by a man who has since walked out on her. For a while Sal feels like assuming the responsibilities of a father, but eventually, broke, bored, and jittery, he calls it quits after one final session of "sweet old love." The lovers part company with no regrets.[13]

A more complex treatment of the sexual relations of a North American man and a Mexican woman is undertaken by Tennessee Williams in the short story "Rubio y Morena" — Blond and Brunette. The man is Kamrowski, a writer, who suffers from a psychological block in his relationship with women that renders him impotent. Once, while he was staying in a hotel in Laredo, Texas, a tall Mexican woman simply moved into his room and attached herself to him. The two stayed and traveled together. "Morena. That's all she was. Something dark. Dark of skin, dark of hair, dark of eyes. But mystery can be loved as well as knowledge and there could be little doubt that Kamrowski loved her."[14] Because of her easy naturalness in bed, of her not insisting upon an intellectual confrontation as others had, Amada, the *Morena,* restored Kamrowski's sexual self-confidence. "That nervous block described in the beginning was now so thoroughly dissolved by virtue of the effortless association with Amada, that his libido had now begun to ask for an extended field of play. The mind of a woman no longer emasculated him. The simple, half-Indian girl had restored his male dominance."[15] The condition described by Williams, though some women might deny it, has afflicted certain men since long before Oliver Goldsmith wrote *She Stoops To Conquer*. Once restored to his virility, Kamrowski repaid Amada by engaging in a number of infidelities. He had by now gained some reknown as a writer; women began to flatter him, and his vanity expanded. In time Amada (whose name in Spanish means beloved) left Kamrowski and returned to Laredo. Her absence revealed to him that he still loved her, and finally he goes in search of her. When he found her, dying, in her mother's impoverished shack, he discovered that she had another, a more important gift to give him. "Instantly the long boney arms flung about him an embrace which took his breath. She pressed their faces painfully together, her Indian cheekbones bruising his softer flesh. Scalding tears and the pressure of those gaunt arms broke finally all the way through the encrusted shell of his ego, which had never before been broken all the way through, and he was released. He was let out of the small but apparently rather light and comfortable room of his known self into a space that lacked the comfort of limits. He entered into a space of bewildering dark and immensity, and yet not dark, of which light is really the darker side of the sphere. He was not at home in it."[16]

The Mexican, seen as passionate and unburdened by scruples, appears in the works of some American writers to add to the discomfort of guilt-ridden American characters who must walk, unrelieved of inhibitions, through a land in which love, on all sides, is for the taking. The American girl, Laura, in Katherine Ann Porter's story "Flowering Judas" is a case in point. Though of a conventional, puritanical background, she has become a Communist party worker in Mexico City. Her work brings her in contact with a Mexican party leader, Braggioni, a highly-sexed, shrewd, fierce, and totally opportunistic man, who exploits the Communist cause for his own advantage. Braggioni stalks her hungrily, and Laura, a woman who recoils compulsively from sex, dreads the inevitable sexual demand. Avoiding him as much as possible, she devotes her time to teaching school to Mexican youngsters, whom she loves but cannot come close to, and giving herself unstintingly to party work. When a friend, Eugenio, an agitator who has been imprisoned, dies from an overdose of sleeping pills which Laura has given him to be taken sparingly, the event registers itself in her dream the following night. Eugenio, in the dream, offers her the ripe blossoms of the Judas tree to eat. When she greedily swallows them, he accuses her of eating his own flesh and blood, crying "murderer! cannibal!" She awakens shouting "no! no!" Though the interpretation is left to the reader, the dream apparently represents Laura's subconscious awareness that in her own way she, as much as Braggioni, has been exploiting the political cause for which she works, seeking in it a substitute for the sexual expression she cannot permit herself and for the love she craves.[17]

In a similar fashion, a hotel in the lush tropics of southern Mexico and a background of Mexican servants casually indulgent in sex form an effective contrast against which to play the conflicts and agonies of the Reverend Shannon in Tennessee Williams' play *The Night of the Iguana*. Shannon is a renegade minister, guilt-ridden, talking periodically of returning to his church. But the thwarted mysticism and the ascetic strain in his nature are countered by a strong sexual drive and a tendency toward unorthodox thinking. Shannon, as we see him in the play, has been reduced to being a tour guide working for a rather shabby travel agency that specializes in organizing tours for ladies. He has brought a group of them to the Costa Verde Hotel, whose proprietress, the lusty Maxine, wants him to stay behind as her permanent lover. At one point in the play, Shannon gives his version to Hannah, sensitive, young New England spinster, of why he has gone to seed in the tropics.

> I think I first *faced* it in that nameless country. The gradual, rapid, natural, unnatural — predestined, accidental — cracking up and going to pieces of young Mr. T. Lawrence Shannon, yes, still *young* Mr. T. Lawrence Shannon, by which rapid-slow process . . . his final tour of ladies through tropical countries. . . . Why did I say "tropical?" Hell! Yes! It's always been tropical countries I took ladies through. Does that, does that — huh? — signify something, I wonder? Maybe. Fast decay is a thing of hot climates, steamy, hot, wet climates, and I run back to them like a. . . . Incomplete sentence. . . . Always seducing a lady or two, or three or four or five ladies in the party, but really ravaging her first by pointing out to her the — what — horrors? Yes, horrors! — of the tropical country being conducted a tour through.[18]

Two American woman poets use the jungles of southern Mexico to evoke the sense of a released voluptuousness. To Denise Levertov, in "Tomatlan," it is the climate itself which is the agent of desire.

> At the touch
> of the sea wind
>     the palms
> shake their green breasts, their

>                     rustling fingers —
> flames of desire and pleasure.
> The sea wind that
>
>                     moves like a panther
> blows the spray inland.
>                     Voluptuous
> and simple — the world is
> larger than one thought. . . .[19]

Muriel Rukeyser, who gained earlier fame as a writer of poems which revealed a stern social consciousness, turns to the theme of personal love and release in the poem "Cries From Chiapas." She uses not only the geography and animals but the women of that state in southern Mexico to provide her background chorus of desire.

> Women of Chiapas!
>                     Dream-borne voices of women
> Splinters of mountains,
>                     broken obsidian,
>                                         silver.
> White tigers
>                     haunting
>                                         your forehead here
> black hungers of women,
>                     confusion
>                                         turning like tigers
> And your voice —
> I am
> almost asleep
>                     almost awake
>                                         in your arms.[20]

Paul Horgan in the novel *No Quarter Given* contrasts American and Mexican sexual attitudes. Edmund Abbey, composer, and Maggie Michaelis, actress, he already married, are faced with all the complexities of sophisticated and sensitive northerners trying to handle a love situation gracefully. One evening, walking through the streets of Santa Fe, they pass a Mexican dance hall and feel a surge of envy as they catch a glimpse of the animated scene within where the Mexicans are dancing "to the sound of aching violin, thumped guitar" and where there are "reckless bodily promises inspired by music and society" and "hints of lusty living and thoughtless grace in that people."[21]

However, freedom and the denial of it wear different forms in different societies. To match the inhibitions in the area of sexuality to be found in the United States are the taboos, rather rigidly enforced from without, in respect to the sexual conduct of Mexican women. Here we encounter the famed double standard, an inevitable component of the code of *machismo*. A society which on the one hand puts a premium on masculine virility and masculine sexual virtuosity and on the other hand encourages attitudes of jealous possessiveness on the part of the men toward their women forces a division upon the women of such a society into two marked classifications, the respectable and the unrespectable, with little grey area between. Joseph Wood Krutch in *The Forgotten Peninsula* has this to say about a small village in Baja California: "El Marmol I had visited several times and met the caretaker for the now closed quarries as an old friend. But I have never 'met' his wife though I have glimpsed her several times."[22] Perhaps such a code of male dominance is not unnatural in a land and nature-attached people whose precarious economies demand the reliability and stability of the woman of the house but whose men, in order to maintain their economy and at the same time endure — and even enjoy — life, might well erect a paradoxical set of mores. A revealing comparison might be made, in this respect, between the cultures of rural Mexico and some of the agricultural societies of the Orient.

The sexual code of the Mexicans in the border region provided some of the most interesting commentary in John Houghton Allen's novel *Southwest*. Of a Mexican named Lazaro, a man who had been a bootlegger and had served several terms in prison for robbery, Allen wrote that

> few of these things discredited Lazaro as a man — the only reason he was held in contempt by the Mexicans, though he was a liar and *sinverguenza* [a without — shame] among other things, was because of the fact that Lazaro wore the horns. The Mexicans are very sensitive about having the horns put on them, or at least, in a manner so that it shows.
>
> And that stallion Luro had done it unfairly, while Lazaro was doing a stretch on the prison farm. The Mexicans thought he should put a knife in Luro's ribs, or at least dry-gulch him, but Lazaro acted in this matter in a strangely civilized manner, very unlike a Mexican — it might be he had not dared avenge this insult to his questionable honor because he was fresh out of prison and always rather a stranger in a strange land. This the Mexicans could understand, but what they could never understand or forgive in Lazaro was the fact that he took the woman back. *Because he loved her*, he said — and they would listen, and spit eloquently on the floor. That wasn't any reason, that was no way for a man to act.[23]

Elsewhere in the novel, Allen commented that the "respectable" single woman in Mexico is ruined if she is known to have had an affair. Of one such woman he wrote that "you knew, even if it were regretfully, and she knew . . . that she might go with you to the ends of the earth, she might even love you a while in return, but in the end she would despise you for the sacrifice you made, and because you had violated her bitter pride."[24] Another episode was labeled by the author "a footnote to their Mexican morality." General Fierro and his Dorados staged a raid on the hacienda of Don Santiago during the Revolution. All members of the household were herded into the courtyard. Fierro addressed them, saying that those men would be spared whose women agreed to sleep with his Dorados. Though the women began to weep, no one made a move until finally the wife of Don Santiago's son, Antonio, begged for the life of her husband "whom she liked better than honor," agreeing to Fierro's terms. But Fierro had only been amusing himself. He had all the men of the hacienda, including Antonio, lined up against the wall and gave the order to his Dorados to fire. "It was only then that there had been tears in Antonio's eyes, but they were tears of rage and shame. . . . And he spoke for the first time, and he shouted as the fusillade rang out, and the bullets buried in the soft bodies and *caliche* walls, 'You slut . . . you dirty slut!' "[25]

A contrast to the intensity that Mexicans bring to their sexual lives is the passivity with which they have been said to regard their destinies. American writers have found this acceptance and resignation a soothing relief from the din of battle as carried on by the unquiet conquistadores of the north. Some of these writers have commented upon the unquestioning acceptance by young Mexicans of the authority of parents. However important sex as such may be to Mexicans, the formal avenue of its expression in marriage is a road along which they often allow themselves to be led with a fatalistic sense of inevitability. Should a road desired by the young be declared off bounds by parental decree, it is usually not entered. In Josephina Niggli's *Mexican Village,* young Antonio, son of the aristocratic Don Saturnino, was in love with Maria, a *mestiza* from an ordinary family. Don Saturnino would never countenance Antonio's marrying a woman of Maria's background. Maria and Antonio understood without discussion that their courses would diverge, "because in their respective blood, Indian and Spanish, there was a fatalism which recognized and accepted the events binding them to action."[26] In the novel *Step Down Elder Brother* by the same author, young Domingo Vasquez de Anda of Monterey knew in February that, though he loved another woman, he would in all probability marry Veronica, daughter of a family close to his own and of equal social status, the following December. "His acceptance of Veronica was in the plane of his training. For generations, the men and women of his family

*Love, Fate, and Death* 263

had married according to the dictates of the family. He merely slipped into the groove that was already worn smooth for him. And December was very far from February. Too much could happen in the intervening months for him to worry much about it. This, too, was a part of his training, incorporated in the texture of air and earth."[27] A similar theme is treated by Gilbert Neiman in *There is a Tyrant in Every Country.* The American, Frederick Conner, has been told by the daughter of Don Calixto, a tough *ranchero,* that she will have to marry one of the three men whom her father has picked out for her. When Conner asked if she were in love with any of them, she replied, as if the American were a child, " 'When I marry one of these three, naturally I will love him.' "

Conner's commentary upon this conversation was that "she knew the way the world was. I didn't. The slow beat of her voice said that if I knew the way the world was, I would never have wanted to change it for her sake. Her knowledge was deeper than mine. She had century-old knowledge. Mine was of the time I was born in. She knew how many centuries it takes to make the least change in human nature. One can be destroyed but he cannot be changed."[28]

This pattern of arranged marriages does not apply, however, among Mexico's urban poor. The people of the large Casa Grande tenement in Mexico City whom Oscar Lewis presents in *The Children of Sánchez* almost never marry but live in free union, switching partners quite regularly. Jesús Sánchez himself was something of an exception in that, although he maintained several households simultaneously, he supported his wives and various children from the meager salary he made as a buyer for a restaurant. This type of responsibility was not shown by most of the inhabitants of the tenement, including the grown children of Sánchez. More commonly, women with their children would be deserted as new alliances were formed.

Frank Dobie takes a look at other aspects of Mexican fatalism. In *Apache Gold and Yaqui Silver,* a book concerned with the folklore that has developed around the mines of the Southwest and northern Mexico, he tells of a very poor Mexican, Ignacio, who refuses to accompany an Indian friend who offers to show him a cave full of treasure which the Indians looted from the Spaniards many generations past. In refusing, Ignacio says that he and his wife are poor "because God wills it." Tipped off by Ignacio's wife, a team of American explorers find the cave with all its treasure.[29] In *The Mexico I Like,* Dobie views Mexican fatalism humorously. Don Marcelo of the Hacienda de las Cinco Llagas, a portly man, complained once to the narrator of the inconvenience of weight. The narrator replied that if Don Marcelo would grow some grapes and eat them instead of tortillas and *piloncillo,* cubes of brown sugar, he would lose weight. To this Don Marcelo replied. "If a man is destined to be fat, belts will not reduce his thickness."[30]

Adan Savala in Virginia Sorensen's *The Proper Gods,* fresh out of the American army and imbued with American ideas of progress, argues with his grandfather, Achai, that the people of the Yaqui village of Potam should develop means of making money and use the money for health and improvements. Looking at the naked children running through the dusty roads of the village and remembering the high infant mortality rate, Adan says "children do not grow strong on fiestas." Turning to practical solutions, he suggests that the strong *carrizo* cane which grows in the neighborhood of the village be sold. Adan's cousin Sixto has assured him that there is a market for this cane and has offered to go into partnership with Adan in cutting and selling the cane. Achai is completely hostile to this idea, insisting upon the evil of money. The cane, he says, has for generations been for the communal use of the village of Potam and has never been sold. As for the children, "Our children are strong, Adan. If they are meant to remain, they are strong."[31] On the cultural level of the Yaqui village and its many counterparts throughout the Indian subcultures of Mexico, Mexican fatalism does not budge easily. A similar fatalism is to be found among the urban poor in Mexico. Manuel in *The Children of Sánchez* says: "To me, one's destiny is controlled by a mysterious hand that moves all things. Only for the select, do things turn out as planned; to those of us who are born to be *tamale* eaters, heaven sends only *tamales.*"[32]

The famous conversations between Carlos Castañeda and his Yaqui mentor, Don Juan Matus, touch on the subject of fate at various points and with differing positions revealed. At one meeting, Don Juan holds forth for the position that a warrior, a man who has achieved certain spiritual powers, must not resign himself in terms of possible future events: " 'All I can say to you,' Don Juan said, 'is that a warrior is never available; never is he standing on the road waiting to be clobbered. Thus he cuts to the minimum his chances of the unforeseen. What you call accidents are, most of the time, very easy to avoid, except for fools who are living helter-skelter.' "[33] However, at a later meeting Don Juan talks about death in deterministic terms. Castañeda had caught a rabbit in a trap, and, as was so often the case with any happening that occurred between the two men, the event led to a discussion. Castañeda reports Don Juan's remarks: "He said that the powers that guided men or animals had led that particular rabbit to me, in the same way that they will lead me to my own death. He said the rabbit's death had been a gift for me in exactly the same way my own death will be a gift for something or someone else."[34] Of course, there may not be, ultimately, a contradiction here. Perhaps Don Juan thinks that many things can be "accidents" but that death is never an accident.

Somewhere between the themes of fate and death, in terms of Mexican life, comes the ritual of the bullfight, that quintessentially Spanish spectacle which Mexico, for all its self-conscious rejection of Spain, has kept. That Mexico should have retained the bullfight when many Latin American countries have rejected it is a curious fact and one which has brought forth several explanations, including the assertion that the bullfight with its ritualistic bloodiness appeals not only to that which is Spanish in the Mexican make-up but also, in other areas of the cultural personality, to that which is Indian. To the growing number of "gringo" *aficionados,* many of them nurtured on Ernest Hemingway's *Death in the Afternoon,* the significance of Mexico's having stayed with the bullfight is essentially a practical one. Many cannot afford to go to Spain; Mexico brings the bullfight to America's back door. There are now almost as many elaborate mystiques of the bullfight as there are American intellectuals who have become *aficionados,* but there is one strain common to the thought of much of the American writing which holds up the bullfight as the fitting morality play for our times. The bullfight allows the American, protected from reality all his life by the palliations of modern American society, to face up to the real thing. This is not ketchup; it is blood! And though the squeamish American may end up by vomiting on the polaroid glasses which have slipped from the bridge of his nose, he must hold his ground and receive the catharsis he so badly needs. Aside from this central theme, there are numerous treatments, some of them good, of the bullfight as tradition, art, drama.

John Houghton Allen describes the bullfight as being essentially a spectacle, not a sport, as being "a little raw perhaps, but beautiful and stylized as some Catholic ceremony — and once you get over your gringo prejudices, it seems nothing but a rather rude and healthy holiday, bread and circus to these people." The *corrida de toros,* furthermore, contains a degree of suspense to be found no place else, as it is "the last drama of our times that has death as an immediate object."[35] Tom Lea presents a scene in *The Brave Bulls* which elaborates similar concepts. Though the conversation is between Mexican citizens of the little town of Cuenca, the theoretical nature of these explanations of the essential meaning of the bullfight sounds more like the talk one hears from American converts than like anything one is likely to hear from Mexicans who take their *fiesta brava* as a matter of course.

> "It is of course necessary," old Iriarte put in, "to understand our festival is not a sport but a spectacle. It is a form of drama as certainly as the works of Sophocles. But what a difference between the happenings on a stage or in a poem, and the happenings in a plaza!"
>
> "Exactly," the Engineer said. "The festival of the bulls is the only art form in which violence, bloodshed and death are palpable and unfeigned. It is the only art in which the artist deals actual death and risks actual death, as if a poet were called upon to scan his lines with his life. It is the contemplation of this visible violence and actual death that gives the art its particular power, gentlemen."
>
> It is also that actuality which confuses the art with the sport and confounds foreigners who find real blood a revulsion — or a morbid thrill," Santana said.
>
> "All arts, even the most abstract," Don Alberto broke in again, "are essentially creations to thrill. To allow man to participate in God's designs at one step removed from the anguish of living them. Sitting safely in a chair."
>
> "The heart of the matter is this," said the Engineer. "There is enormous difference between the thrill given by art and the thrill given by watching merely exciting forms of peril. The difference, let us say, between a corrida de toros and a motorcycle race. Peril moves us simply as witnesses to a gripping body sensation. Violence, or peril, made significant by art amplifies the sensation beyond the body, distills it, lifts it beyond the realm of mere incident. A corrida de toros, by that token of art, presents us with a moving image and symbol of our own hearts grappling with violence and death. Can this be a sport? Unless, indeed, man facing his destiny in sport, combat between equals. No! In the plaza the man lives by his bravery, and the bull dies. Sometimes it is another case, but that is not the plan of our festival which is designed to show the glory of courage over the power of death. Each of us reads into this theme our private response. It is that meaning of man face to face with the inner and outer brute force of living, and man's tragedy in dealing death while subject to it himself, which has gripped the mind and emotion of the Latin race."[36]

Tiburcio Balbuena, breeder of brave bulls at Las Astas, talks of the symbolic nature of the life of a fighting bull, who is never to know old age and never to reproduce.

> "The festival has symbolisms that sometimes strike me, gentlemen. I love the brave bulls. For them there is no coming of old age and weakness and dying fire. No servitude, no toil. Yet we deny them the benignity of reproducing their kind. Certain of their male relations will stay home to take care of the cows and carry on the breed with those formidable sacs that swing between their legs. But not our fighters to the death. They are virgins. It is a curious thing, our festival."[37]

Some of the best bullfight scenes in modern American writing about Mexico appear in Robert Ramsey's novel *Fiesta*, and yet the author is not primarily interested in the bullfight as a cultural phenomenon nor as a form of therapy for the ailing American character. Rather, he uses the bullfight as he does the entire Mexican setting of the book, for his own purpose as a novelist, which is to examine the role of authority in human life. Though the novel does have this ultimate concern with a universal problem, on a more immediate level it is a very authentic presentation of life in modern Mexico. Antonio, the protagonist, is a young man who works for Don Hipólito, the *patrón* of a modernized Mexican hacienda. Antonio's position is somewhere between that of a chauffeur and secretary. Though he is intrusted with a good deal of responsibility, he feels that he is essentially a servant, a menial denied the opportunity to properly develop his abilities. A further humiliation of his job is that once a week he is expected to assume the role of matador and fight bulls for the amusement of Don Hipólito, General Yanez, the *patrón's* father, and any guests who might be visiting the hacienda. Antonio has a fear of the bulls which he cannot overcome, yet every week, with the terror rising within him, he must step into the ring. The author uses the black bull as a concentrated symbol of the fears that beset a man and that must be fought. For Antonio, the experience of the bull ring stirred up "a fear that never quite left him, and that encompassed others too indefinite for him to understand clearly or even name: a fear of authority, of the powerful, the patron, the power of the Church, and of the mysterious things of the past, the ancient cruel gods of the Indians not quite forgotten. In the bull ring all these mysterious and instinctive fears out of the past became merged in the one ancient antagonist, the great black bull. From week to week he faced this fear; he believed that if he could escape this, he would escape all the rest."[38] Antonio thinks that he sees a way of delivering himself from the suave tyranny of Don Hipólito when a movie actress, Consuelo, visiting the hacienda, becomes attracted to him and invites him to accompany her to Mexico City where, she promises, she will use her influence to promote his career as a matador. In Mexico City he finds that he has exchanged one form of tyranny for another, this time at the hands of the arrogant and capricious Consuelo. However, in a finely executed scene in the *Plaza de Toros* in Mexico City, Antonio steps into the role as first matador when an aging torero, whose nerves are shot, pays with his life for a moment of indecision. Rising to the occasion, Antonio overcomes his fear and, feeling that he has banished it forever, puts in a masterful performance. This triumph over fear shows Antonio how he can gain a measure of release from the authority of Don Hipólito

— not by escape, as with the actress Consuelo, but by mastery of himself in the dangerous art of the *corrida,* symbolizing the art of life. In any case, freedom from authority can only be a partial thing. Men must accept much with resignation. Antonio returns to the hacienda.

Of the many American writers who have expended paper on the theme of the bullfight, Wright Morris, in *The Field of Vision,* has given the subject one of its freshest looks. Gordon Boyd, hero of the novel, grasps, while he is watching a bullfight in Mexico, the idea that the matador gains mastery by his cunning awareness of the power of the absence of movement.

> What did it? What charm, craft or cunning dominated the bull? In his mind's eye — if he turned the flow backward, bull and cloth flowing away from one another — Boyd could see the still point where the dance was. The man rooted to it. From this point hung the cloth that blew in the draft, or quivered like flesh. The bull could understand movement, but not its absence, and the man could understand both movement and its absence, and in controlling this impulse to move, the still point, he dominated the bull. Except for the still point, there would be no dance. The cloth, not the sword, brought the bull to heel. The moment of truth was at that moment, and not at the kill.[39]

Having given the reader a sense of the bullfight as a sort of frieze, Morris suddenly switches field and shows the *Plaza de Toros* as a scene of animated emotion comparable to the passionate life of children. Here we have the old theme of Mexican primitivism again. Gordon Boyd, while watching the *corrida,* is suddenly reminded of children and his long-standing conviction that "children and only children, led passionate lives." Children were the ones who "struck out blindly," who "laughed and cried," who "cheated, hooted, looted and lied to one another, were cruel and loving, heartless and generous, at the same time. They represented the forces he felt submerged in life. All the powers that convention concealed, the way the paving concealed the wires in the street, the sewage and the waste, were made visible. The flow of current that kept the city going, the wheels turning, the lights burning, and the desires that made peace impossible in this world." Boyd recognized that much in the action of children was vulgar and cruel, and yet he saw an element of beauty in it which he could not comprehend until he saw a bullfight. Then came the recognition. "There he saw that the running of the small fry was the first running of the bulls. Every day a fresh collection of gorings, heroes, and the burial of the dead."[40]

The philosopher, F. S. C. Northrop, after paying his respects to Hemingway's *Death in the Afternoon,* compares the bullfight to sports as practiced in the United States and England and finds the "passionately pursued sport of the Spanish and Indian Mexicans" in which "death is very real" to be a significant expression of the human spirit besides which those other sports seem trifling. "For the aim is not, as in games in the United States, upon the end of the contest — the victory, the killing of the bull; nor is it, as in Great Britain, upon the utilitarian exercise and building of character for some later triumph at Waterloo which one is supposed to achieve in the process. Instead, it is upon living dangerously (and let anyone master the rules within which the matador must operate before he concludes that this sport is not dangerous), and upon the artistry with which the aesthetic ritual is pursued."[41]

The reaction of American writers to the bullfight, however, has not been all cheers and *ole*'s. Critical treatments of the *fiesta brava* have ranged from James M. Cain's irreverent "there's nothing as much like one dead bull as another dead bull"[42] to Lysander Kemp's carefully worked out critique, "The Only Beast," subtitled "Reflections on Not Attending the Bullfights." In between there are varying degrees of demurrers and disavowals. Langston Hughes, because he recognized the brutality involved, would periodically swear off bullfights, but another Sunday would find him back at the bullring. In *I Wonder as I Wander,* he gives an account of this inner conflict.

> Every Sunday there were the bullfights. After the regular season in the big ring, young fighters at Vista Alegre were pitted by unscrupulous promoters against enormous bulls, their bodies tossed, trampled and gored with frequency by animals too swift and tricky for beginners. I watched two boys killed. Every week after such a spectacle, I would swear each Sunday night never to attend another bullfight. But the next Sunday afternoon I'd be there before the gates opened. From the days of my adolescence when I first saw the famous Mexican matador, Rudolfo Gaona,, and the great Spaniard, Sanchez Mejias (of Lorca's *Five O'Clock in the Afternoon*), I have been fascinated with bullfights — to my mind the most beautiful and dangerous of sports in the world.[43]

Witter Bynner in *Journey with Genius,* a book of recollections of times spent with D. H. Lawrence in Mexico, gave an affecting account of Lawrence and his wife Frieda at the bullfight, in a passage whose tone implies sympathy with Lawrence's reaction. Lawrence on his part effectively satirized Bynner as Owen Rhys in the novel *The Plumed Serpent.* Owen Rhys, as Lawrence depicted him, was the victim of that peculiarly American depravity, the cult of experience. For Owen, in his "American logic," " 'never having seen [a bullfight] meant having to go.' "[44] Once he got there, he was shocked to the point of being "nearly in hysterics," yet "he was seeing LIFE, and what can an American do more!"[45] Bynner in *Journey with Genius* somewhat half-heartedly defended his attendance at bullfights, but in his description of Lawrence at the *corrida* he was enough of an artist to make a convincing statement against the spectacle. Lawrence had watched the performance with a mounting agony which reached its climax as the bull — " 'He's not the brute; they're the brutes.' " — turned to gore the aged horse upon which the picador was mounted.

> The lance was futile. The horse tumbled against the fence and sheepishly found his feet, the bull shoved and gored and ripped; and while the crowd gave a sigh of relief, Lawrence groaned and shook. By the time the toreros had again drawn their prey toward the cloaks and the picador had remounted and forced his steed into motion toward the exit, the horse's bowels were bulging almost to the ground, like vines and gourds. But the bull had not had enough. "Stop it!" cried Lawrence to the bull, jumping out of his seat. But just before the picador reached the gate, horns were lowered again for another snorting plunge, and this time the entire covering of the horse's belly was ripped off. He fell dead, his contents out on the ground, with earth being shoveled over them by attendants. Lawrence had sat down again, dazed and dark with anger and shame. Frieda was watching him. The proud front of the bull — head, neck, chest, leg, hoof — shone crimson in a moment of sun. The crowd was throatily satisfied![46]

This last point, the effect of the spectacle upon the crowd, has given the critics their most telling argument. In *Mexican Journal* Selden Rodman wrote that "the torture of the beast in the ring — the last *matador* yesterday struck his bull fifteen times with the sword before it finally crumpled — is not the real point. The real point, for me, is the degradation of those who watch."[47] This idea, carefully developed, forms the core of the argument presented by Lysander Kemp in his essay "The Only Beast." In submitting what he calls "a minority opinion" on a sport which he believes to be "nearly indefensible," he takes up in turn most of the classical apologias for the bullfight. The title of the essay, taken from the statement of Blasco-Ibanez that the only beast in the *Plaza de Toros* is the crowd, contains in itself the key to the argument. But before getting to this point, Kemp works rapidly through "the two most persuasive arguments," the aesthetic and the emotional — that the bullfight is great art and that it is exciting and significant drama. As to the contention that the bullfight is "spectacular ballet," he replies that if one should suggest that the death be taken out of the spectacle by putting a button on the sword and knobs on the bull's horns — while retaining all the aesthetics of the many stances and passes — the grounds of the argument would immediately shift. The bullfight, the apologist would then say, is no mere ballet; it is a great drama which differs from the theatre in not being make-believe "but the real thing." To this assertion

Kemp replies that the bullfight is neither drama, tragedy, nor "moral entertainment." He admits the bravery of the good matador, "but bravery is moral only when the circumstances which occasion it are moral also." Therefore, the bullfight is not tragedy, which involves a moral choice, nor in any real sense drama. It is, in short, "not a moral occasion when performed for an audience for money, however beautiful and exciting the performance may be, for the simple reason that there is no initial moral obligation for the man to enter the arena in the first place." As to the humanitarian argument, Kemp says that it is usually avoided or dismissed. Sometimes, however, the apologist will assert that bullfighting is no more essentially cruel than fox hunting, *paté de fois gras,* or zoos in which animals intended for the wilderness serve life sentences. To all of this the author replies, "I cannot understand how one form of cruelty is excused by a list of other forms of cruelty that are inexcusable." At this point, Kemp moves into the heart of his argument.

> However, I cannot wholly sympathize with those who base their objections to the bullfight solely on the fact that a few animals must suffer. The suffering is deplorable, but the harm to the human beings who watch it is even more deplorable. It is not good, it is not healthy, even though it may in some sense be "normal" or "natural," to enjoy the sight of suffering and death, or to ignore or tolerate it for the sake of enjoying other emotions. It has been argued that in all of us there is an appetite for raw violence, and if we are deprived of satisfying it vicariously, in some such innocent form as the bullfight, we end up by satisfying it directly, in rioting, beating up our wives and neighbors, or, at the extreme, lynching Negroes or shoveling Jews into ovens.
>
> This is half-true. The appetite exists, and to a point it does need to be satisfied and will somehow find satisfaction as do our other appetites. But it can be satisfied less grossly than in the *Plaza de Toros.* One of the functions of civilization is to direct the expression of our desires, by early training and social pressures, so that, ideally, we will receive the minimum harm and the maximum value and pleasure from that expression.

Kemp, for all of his knowledge of the literature of the bullfight, admits that he has never been to a *corrida* and never intends to go to one. The nearest thing he has had to the actual experience of the bullfight is the visit he once made to a bullfight museum, the *Museo Taurino,* in Guadalajara, Mexico. This museum contained all kinds of souvenirs, posters, *momento mori,* relating to the careers of the great bullfighters, Spanish and Mexican. However, "the real attractions" were the waxworks, which were life-sized. One was a set of three showing the three stages of the killing of the matador Manuel Granero. The first two showed him being lifted up by the bull's horns, looking a bit surprised, but still ungored. In the third, Granero was on the ground with the bull's horn thrust into his eye-socket. "The amount of blood depicted was eminently satisfactory." There was also a scene showing the goring in the abdomen of the famous Gallito. Finally, "the masterpiece of the collection," was a little cubicle made up like a hospital room. Stretched out on a bed was a figure representing the dead Manolete with a huge crucifix in his hands. The face was long, thin, and arrogant, and "the sculptor fashioned it in such a way that it looked not merely dead but extremely dead, very, very arrogantly dead, much deader than you ever dreamed dead could be. The image was shocking, that dead yellowish-white waxen face against the dead-white pillow." At this point Kemp was glad to get out of the place. "When I saw this last morbid item, and then stepped outside into the clean sunlight of a Mexican afternoon, I felt like a Lazarus returned from the dead. I had seen death in the afternoon and I, for one, had not liked it."[48]

But the Spanish spectacle is only one of the forms through which Mexico makes its obeisance to death, nor did Mexico need the instruction of Spain to tell it what death was about. When the conquistadores arrived in Mexico they found a people who "laid death as a wafer on their tongues."[49] It is this virtually sacramental approach to death, inherited from the ancient cultures and reinforced by the infusion of Spanish tradition, that has made the culture of Mexico seem significant to a number of modern American writers. Of the literary descendants of Walt Whitman — Whitman who was so remarkably a microcosm of America's cultural possibilities — those who have turned with appreciation to Mexico are not the ideological heirs of the hearty, progressive, public Whitman but rather those writers who share the sensibility of the self-concealing Whitman who wooed death "in the moonlight by Paumonok's grey beach." These have found the chill death-wind of Mexico a relieving contrast to the Chamber of Commerce sunshine back home.

William Carlos Williams was stirred by the religious art of the Aztecs with its dark concerns. Of the rooms in which the ancient priests carried out their rituals he wrote:

> Decorated with curious imagery in stone, the woodwork carved in relief and painted with figures of monsters and other things, unpaved, darkened and bloodstained, it was in these chapels that the religious practices which so shocked the Christian were performed. Here it was that the tribe's deep feeling for a reality that stems back into the permanence of remote origins had its firm

*Love, Fate, and Death* 273

hold. It was the earthward thrust of their logic; blood and earth; the realization of their primal and continuous identity with the ground itself, where everything is fixed in darkness.[50]

Among the Maya Indians too was a death art "half a thousand years old" which a modern poet could contemplate. Allen Ginsberg finds images for his own concepts of death in a deathshead and other statuary and friezes in the pyramids of Chichen Itza.

> but deathshead's here
> on portal still and thinks its way
>     through centuries the thought
> of the same night in which I sit
>     in skully meditation
>       \*   \*   \*
> and only the crude skull figurement's
>     gaunt insensible glare is left,
>       \*   \*   \*
> over the holy ruin of the world
> dissolving into the sunless wall of a blackened room
> on a time-rude pyramid rebuilt
> in the bleak flat night of Yucatan
> where I come with my own mad mind to study
>     alien hieroglyphs of Eternity.[51]

Anita Brenner noted that the concern with death is "an organic part of Mexican thought." As an art motif, she continued, it predated the Conquest, carried through the colonial period, and is constantly seen today in various forms. "There are skulls in monolith of lava, miniature of gold and crystal, mask of obsidian and jade; skulls carved on walls, moulded upon pots, traced on scrolls, woven into garments; formalized into hieroglyphs, given a skeleton and an occupation in figurines; filled out around whistles, savings-banks, rattles, bells, holiday masks and jewels; woodcut and etched on ballads; strung into drinking-shop decorations; made into candies and toys. The skull has many meanings in Mexican argot. It trails gods, clowns, devils and subsidiary bogies in Mexican lore. There is a national holiday for it."[52] In Saul Bellow's novel *The Adventures of Augie March*, the hero, fresh from Chicago and making his first visit to Mexico, concluded, upon seeing evidence on all sides of a different attitude toward death, that the ancient Aztec death-attraction survived in Mexico in various transformations. Instead of the old racks of skulls there were now "corpses of dogs, rats, horses, asses, by the road." Furthermore, "the bones dug out of the rented graves are thrown on a pile when the lease is up; and there are coffins looking like such a rough joke on the female form, sold in the open shops, black, white, gray, and in all sizes, with their heavy death fringes daubed in

Sapolio silver on the black. Beggars in dog voices on the church steps enacted the last feebleness for you with ancient Church Spanish, and show their old flails of stump and their sores." All this did not displease the young Chicagoan. It simply emphasized to him "how openly death is received everywhere, in the beauty of the place, and how it is acknowledged that anyone may be roughly handled. . . ."[53]

Allen Ginsberg made it a point to go to Guanajuato because he "longed to see" the mummies there

> grasping their bodies
> with stiff arms, in soiled
> funeral clothes;
> \*   \*   \*
> one death-man had
> raised up his arms
> to cover his eyes [54]

According to Manuel, in *The Children of Sánchez,* death in the slums of Mexico City is a frequent and easily observed visitor and is taken in stride. "Life around here," he says, "is raw, it is more real, than among people with money. Here, a boy often isn't scared off at the sight of the female sexual organ. Nor is he shocked when he sees a guy lifting someone's wallet, or using a knife on a man. Just having seen so much evil at close range makes him face reality. After a while, even death itself doesn't frighten us."[55]

The cult of death in Mexico has a festive as well as a somber side. There are numerous references to the air of gaiety surrounding Mexican funerals to be found in the works of modern American writers, who, in contrast to the early border writers, have looked with a benevolent eye upon the proceedings. The Mexican view of death as being as natural as birth and as much an occasion for fiesta has pleased modern American observers, who have sometimes compared the naturalness of the Mexican attitude with the fake, professional lugubriousness of the American funeral parlor. Especially singled out for attention have been the celebrations on the occasion of the Day of the Dead, All Souls' Day, in Mexico. Frank Dobie writes:

> Now it was the Day of the Dead — that day when all of Mexico toasts Death herself and, familiarly, without fear, because she is seen so often, makes her a comrade. In pulque shops men were drinking out of goblets carved into skulls; in humble homes women were setting out, for those who have "ceased to be," the big-loafed "bread of the dead;" in the market booths vendors were

eagerly offering toy hearses, jumping-jack skeletons, and doll corpses that leapt out of coffins at the pull of a string. Into the graveyards throngs were carrying the yellow "flower of the dead," there to spend the day burning candles and drinking wine in honor of the silent host beneath the sod, spreading over tombs picnic lunches from which the children would merrily devour sweets cut in the form of urns, cross-bones, and death's-heads, while balladists sang and peddled broadsides displaying the skull as both clown and king.[56]

Hart Crane in a letter to Charlotte and Richard Rychtarik (November 4, 1931) enthused about the festivities of the Day of the Dead. "All over the country, and right here in this metropolitan city, you will find the cemeteries full of dark-skinned men and women, whole families in fact, sitting on tombstones day and night holding lighted candles to the dead. They bring their food and drink with them. Far from being sad, it's very merry. They drink and eat much — and it all ends up by setting off firecrackers made in the image of Judas."[57] In *Mexican Journal,* Selden Rodman describes the crowds dispersing after having celebrated the Day of the Dead in Toluca. "Climbing one of the pine-covered mountains beyond Toluca, we passed a crowd wearing masks, brandishing black parasols, and carrying a mock coffin. They would drop the coffin from time to time and, as it crashed to the ground, laugh uproariously. How healthy is the Mexican attitude toward death, and how remote from our lugubrious solemnity.[58]

The Mexican mystique of death has stimulated the talents of modern American writers of story and verse. Frank Dobie beautifully recounts an old Mexican legend of a man who set out to find a suitable *madrina,* godmother, for his infant son. One person after another whom the father asked turned out to be either unwilling or unsuitable. Finally on the Day of the Dead he met Death herself and knew that he had found the *madrina* for his child. " 'Dark one,' " he said to her, " 'I thought I should encounter you on this Day of the Dead. Yet every day is your day. I know you well and you I accept for my son's godmother. I accept because you alone are impartial and treat all equally, the rich and the poor, the young and the old, the high and the low, the ugly and the beautiful, the valiant and the cowardly, the weak and the strong. You take them all with you. When there is no other to relieve wretchedness, you end it. You grant to toiling slaves release and rest. You dry tears and stop hunger. In your ways of justice and mercy you are the only friend of the poor, and you are most powerful of all powers. You, then, I choose as *madrina* for my child.' "[59]

Don Juan Matus, Yaqui spiritual mentor to Carlos Castañeda, also sees death as counselor and companion. " 'The thing to do when you're impatient,' " he says to Castañeda, " 'is to turn to your left and ask advice from your death. An immense amount of pettiness is dropped if your death makes a gesture to you, or if you catch a glimpse of it, or if you just have the feeling that your companion is there watching you . . . Death is the only wise adviser that we have.' "[60] On another occasion Don Juan says that a man who is going to have spiritual power will reach a point in his life when he "realizes that death is the irreplaceable partner that sits next to him on the mat. Every bit of knowledge that becomes power has death as its central force. Death lends the ultimate touch, and whatever is touched by death indeed becomes power."[61]

Witter Bynner in the poem "A Boatman" conveys the Mexican Indian's sense that affinity for death is part of the attraction felt for the earth, in which lie the bodies of his ancestors with whose lives he feels his own to be in unbroken continuity.

> In a pool of shadow floating cool on the sand,
> As if for a fish to lean in motionless,
> The boatman lies asleep, hands under head,
> Dreaming of death; and close to him as a weed
> Is to a fish, his hat is sleeping too. . . .
> How intimate he is with the good earth,
> As if, long buried, he were still alive
> Among the many other mounds of sand.[62]

In the long poem "The Desert Music," by William Carlos Williams, the poet, as tourist, was shocked as he crossed the bridge separating El Paso, Texas from Ciudad Juárez, Chihuahua, Mexico, to see the headless, truncated body of a man wedged into the structure of the bridge and totally ignored by passers-by. The day was spent in Ciudad Juárez acting like any other American tourist, buying things and going to bars, restaurants, night clubs, where the continual banging of the *mariachi* music, put out for the American tourists, assailed the poet's ears. But crossing back into the United States in the late afternoon, the poet suddenly knew that it was not the *mariachis* who made Mexico's real music; the real music of Mexico was death, a universal music but one more readily accessible to the ear in a land where death was so casually exposed.

> But what's THAT?
> the music! the
> *music!* as when Casals struck
> and held a deep cello tone
> and I am speechless

> There it sat
> in the projecting angle of the bridge flange
> as I stood aghast and looked at it —
> in the half light: shapeless or rather returned
> to its original shape, armless, legless,
> headless, packed like the pit of a fruit into
> that obscure corner — or
> a fish to swim against the stream — or
> a child in the womb prepared to imitate life,
> warding its life against
> a birth of awful promise. The music
> guards it, a mucus, a film surrounds it,
> a benumbing ink that stains the
> sea of our minds — to hold us off — shed
> of a shape close as it can get to no shape,
> a music! a protecting music.[63]

Noni, the heroine of Conrad Aiken's *A Heart for the Gods of Mexico,* has been told by her doctor that she has one more year to live. She chooses to leave Boston and go to Mexico, where she has never been, because Mexico, as the land which has worshipped death fittingly, seems to her to be the proper place in which to meet a rendezvous with death. While walking the streets of Mexico City she thinks of the ancient capital of Tenochtitlan, of the names the Aztecs gave to months, and of the festivals designated for those months.

> "In the month of diminishing waters! Isn't that nice? The month of the diminishing of waters. A procession of priests with music of flutes and trumpets, carrying on plumed litters infants with painted faces, in gay clothing, with coloured paper wings, to be sacrificed on the mountains or in a whirlpool in the lake. It is said that the people wept as they passed by; but if so — "
> "Mounted the stairs, breaking an earthenware flute against each step — "
> "Then seized by the priests, his heart torn out, and held up to the sun, his head spitted on the tzompantli — "
> "Tzompantli?"
> "Tzompantli. My God, what a people; the whole land bathed in blood — !"[64]

And Noni's friend Blomberg, who has suspended his business activities to stand vigil with Noni in Mexico, thinks as he listens to the clacking of the wheels of the train taking him through the United States towards the border: . . . "well, we're off to Clixl Claxl, Ixl Oxl, and Popocatepetl —that's where Hart Crane went, just before he drowned himself in the Caribbean — they say it's a death-country, a murder country, and the buzzards—"[65]

Waldo Frank, too, thought of the connections between Hart Crane, Mexico, and Death. He wrote in the introduction to *The Collected Poems of Hart Crane*: "Nor was it accidental that Crane now chose to go to Mexico, where for a thousand years a cult of Death — personal immolation in a Nature ruthless and terrible as the Sea — has been practiced by a folk of genius . . . Crane fought death in Mexico. But on his return to New York, to the modern chaos, there was the Sea: and he could not resist it."[66] In the same introductory essay, Frank reflected that at the time that Crane sailed for Mexico he himself was writing in his book *America Hispana*:

> Perhaps the earth of Mexico conspired to create the tragic mood of the Aztec, and to fulfill it in the Conquest from which modern Mexico was born. It is an earth unwieldy to man's pleasure. Titantic and volcanic mountains, mesetas of thin air, exuberant valleys, burning deserts, encourage a culture not smiling but extreme, from tears to frenzied laughter. This earth is a tyrant; it exiles valley from valley, it begrudges loam for corn or overwhelms it with torrential rains. Man is a stranger within it, and yet he loves it like a goddess, radiant, cruel, suddenly indulgent, in whose house he must serve forever. It is no mystery that in such an earth man should have built temples of blood or possessed his life in contemplation of a loveliness deadly as fire and distant as the stars. But this man was still man. In a hostile and adorable world, man's and woman's love of life breathed on. . . .[67]

The idea suggested by Frank that there is a relationship between the Mexican's sense of death and his love of life is one that has been developed by Anita Brenner. "Ever recurrent in Mexican thought," she wrote in *Idols Behind Altars*, "is this concern for the sheer fact of life. Life shifting from one form to another, and all still the same . . . plants and people of necessity dying, at a definite fixed point, to be reborn. Hence the constant considering of death. . . ."[68] To prove the antiquity of this concept of death, the great renewer of life, Anita Brenner quotes from a verse by the venerable Aztec poet-statesman, Nezahualcoyotl: " 'The darkness of the sepulchre is but a strengthening couch for the glorious sun, and the obscurity of the night but serves to reveal the brilliance of the stars. . . .' "[69] Anita Brenner, referring to the many death images made to celebrate the Day of the Dead, credits the Mexicans as a people with a quality of perception and sensibility usually reserved for artists.

> It is no mood of futility that broods in this way over death, but rather a concern with death because of the passion for life. It is an artist's mood, his sense of limitation, his struggle with limitation, and his great assertion, the purpose of making — by his own

strength — life. The control is achieved in the artist's way, by giving a physical place to a physical fact, making an image of it. The skull is the symbol of the thing which like the rain, the trees, the colors and the moving birds is caught, controlled, and made into lasting visible life. And it is the artist's way, as it is the Mexican way, to disregard other things for the sake of making images.[70]

F..S. C. Northrup also relates the Mexican sense of death to the concepts of the artist, especially to the work of the Mexican painter Orozco. This sense of tragedy and death, characteristic of the culture of Mexico, provides an important and salutary contrast, according to Northrop, to that strain of puritanism, innocuous idealism, and opportunistic pragmatism which makes for so much of the cultural climate of the United States.

> At no point do the values of the Indian and the Spanish spirit stand in greater contrast to those of the Anglo-American people to their north than in these frescos of Orozco: Spanish America with its conviction that tragedy, brutality, chaos, failure, and death, as well as triumph and compassion, aim at order, and earthly life are an essential part of the glory of man; Anglo-America with its pollyannic tendency, its Christian Science, its life under the elms as if there were no desire there also, its worship of the successful businessman, its formal Kantian idealism empty of empirical content, and its pragmatism making even truth itself dependent upon a successful reward at the end. This opposition must be understood and reconciled if Pan-Americanism is ever to become a spontaneous movement of the spirit.[71]

CHAPTER NINE

## Idols and Altars

Nowhere has the contrast between the treatment of Mexican culture by early American writers and those of modern times been greater than in the area of religion. Gone is the early contempt for Mexican Catholicism as pagan, and in its place is a feeling for the special coloration of religion in Mexico, with its infusion of Indian elements, as not only aesthetically stimulating but culturally significant — a bridge between pre-Columbian and Europeanized America. The folk mythology of rural Mexico, peopled with witches and supernatural beings, so derided by the early writers as childish superstition, has also come in for some recent appreciation. Such manifestations of the popular imagination, often counterpoised to formalized religion, have been valued by modern American writers ruefully aware of the disappearance of the rich life of fancy in their own technological society, where the level of taste has descended to that of the mass media which have overwhelmed the old folkloric culture and anesthetized the sensibilities of the people.

The chill of personal isolation in the culturally fragmented United States has caused some sensitive individuals to look with envy upon the society to the south where each Mexican seems sure of his cultural identification within the rich fabric of ancient and binding traditions. At the turn of the century, discontent with industrialized and no-longer homogeneous America found one avenue of expression in a sort of cult of the old missions, a nostalgia which contributed to the growth of the California myth. The old mission culture with its serenity and gentle paternalism found a number of devotees among the readers of *Ramona,* which gave an admiring portrait of the Franciscan missionaries in California. Another book of the period, much more openly nostalgic in tone, was *In the Footprints of the Padres* by Charles Warren Stoddard, a convert to Roman Catholicism. This informal treatment of California life in the late 1800's combined personal reminiscences with backward glances into California history. By way of introduction, Stoddard presented one of his poems, "The Litany of the Shrines," which took up each of the California missions in turn, ending with the verse:

> 'Twas thus the missions rose and thus they fell —
> Perchance a solitary boy-soprano,
> Last of his race, was left the tale to tell.
> Ring, gentle Angelus! ring in my dream,
> But wake me not, for I would rather seem
> To live the life they lived who've slumbered long
> Beneath their fallen altars, than to waken
> And find their sanctuaries thus forsaken:
> God grant their memory may survive in song![1]

Elsewhere in the book, Stoddard wrote of the mission church of San Carlos de Carmelo, outside of Monterey, California, which was the church of the famed leader of the Franciscan missionary enterprise in California, Fray Junipero Serra.

> What a beautiful church it must have been, with its quaint carvings, its star-window that seems to have been blown out of shape in some wintry wind, and all its lines hardened again in the sunshine of the long, long summer; with its Saracenic door! — what memories the Padres must have brought with them from Spain — and the Moorish seal that is set upon it! Here we have evidence of it painfully wrought out by the hands of rude Indian artisans. The ancient bells have been carried away into unknown parts; the owl hoots in the belfry; the hills are shorn of their conventual tenements; while the wind and the rain and a whole heartless company of iconoclasts have it all their own way.[2]

In 1927 a book appeared which dealt much more competently with religion in the Hispanic Southwest than did these earlier nostalgic evocations, Willa Cather's *Death Comes for the Archbishop,* a novel based upon the life of Archbishop Jean Batiste Lamy, who entered New Mexico in 1850 and died in Santa Fe in 1888. When Mary Austin first read *Death Comes for the Archbishop* — Mary Austin who was almost obsessive in her involvement with the Spanish-Indian culture of the Southwest and never so happy as when she could corner somebody and "talk Indian" — she complained petulantly that here was no proper treatment of the Southwest but a book about French priests. She had a point. *Death Comes for the Archbishop* transcends the boundaries of regionalist fiction. Among the several cultural confrontations presented in the novel is the familiar one of Europe vis-a-vis America — but with a difference. Here we do not have upper-class New Yorkers or Bostonians coping with their English opposite numbers but two Frenchmen, one of them definitely a sophisticate, making their way in pioneer America. This was an America, however, which the cultivated Bishop Latour of the novel, despite the vast gulf between a crude society and the ancient, achieved culture of his homeland, could appreciate, an America, the author seems to imply, which the bishop could approve more than he could have approved the America which came later. When Bishop Latour met the frontiersman Kit Carson, an immediate respect and liking sprang up between them. Each recognized in the other a man who lived by standards. The bishop's relations with his friend the Navajo chieftain were based upon similar feelings of mutual respect. With the Mexicans, however, especially the native Mexican clergy, Bishop Latour had a more complex relationship. Here the intellectually refined, rather rationalistic Catholicism of France confronted Mexican Catholicism, rooted in the soil and compounded with Indian elements. Some of the best scenes in the book are those in which the bishop takes on a formidable adversary, Father Martínez of Taos, *mestizo,* passionate, unruly, and profoundly a product of his native New Mexico. Yet for all its differences, the Mexican Catholicism of the area was still Catholicism, and Bishop Latour adjusted to many of its regional peculiarities, though he combatted others. In all essentials he could claim it for his own. Shortly after his arrival in Santa Fe as vicar apostolic to take charge of Catholic affairs over an extensive area of the Southwest, he had to make a long journey into the north Mexican state of Durango to have his credentials confirmed by the Bishop there, who had formerly been in charge of the area now assigned to Father Latour. This arduous and solitary journey on horseback through cactus-studded desert country was not displeasing to Latour as it gave him a chance to gather his thoughts and get the feel of the land. At one point of the journey he came across a poor Mexican family settled in an oasis in the desert, and he was given a night's lodging. Seated in a room in this remote and primitive mud adobe house he breathed the accustomed air of Christian culture.

> From the moment he entered this room with its thick whitewashed adobe walls, Father Latour had felt a kind of peace about it. In its barrenness and simplicity there was something comely, as there was about the serious girl who had placed their food before them and who now stood in the shadows against the wall, her eager eyes fixed upon his face. He found himself very much at home with the four dark-headed men who sat beside him in the candlelight. Their manners were gentle, their voices low and agreeable. When he said grace before meat, the men had knelt on the floor beside the table.[3]

Into this short scene Willa Cather has compressed much of her sense of religion as a civilizing force. Here were people who lived barely at the level of subsistance but who were in no way brutalized because through their religion they participated in an ancient and refining culture.

One of the appeals of Catholicism to modern American intellectuals has been its sophistication. This attraction has been especially strong to Americans who have emerged from religious backgrounds which have been puritanical and naïvely fundamentalistic. The opening scene of *Death Comes for the Archbishop* takes place in Rome where Father Latour has gone to be briefed on his mission to the American Southwest, to which he has just been assigned. Here Father Latour sits among witty and cultivated European churchmen in an atmosphere of intellectual grace combined with a certain worldly shrewdness, marks of a time-nurtured, developed, self-confident culture, which the author herself obviously relishes. From a technical point of view, the scene is a masterpiece. The almost oriental splendor, luxury, and refinement which surround the lives of high churchmen in Rome most effectively emphasizes the primitiveness of the world which Father Latour then enters, in America's new frontier in the Hispanic Southwest.

The idea that Catholicism, especially Mediterranean Catholicism, has brought to the New World a certain sophisticated moral realism has appeared in the work of other American writers dealing with the Southwest or Mexico. In Paul Horgan's novel *The Common Heart,* an old-timer, Don Hilario Ascarate, reminisces to Doctor Rush, the protagonist, about the old days in Albuquerque. The aged Mexican recalls Doña Catalina, who ran a sumptuous brothel situated immediately next to the church of San Felipe de Neri. The priests used to excoriate Doña Catalina and her enterprise from the pulpit while often she herself would be attending Mass, with her black rebosa over her face, sometimes seeming to nod in agreement. "Out of church, she was generous and friendly with the priests, sent them fine foods across the Plaza, and curtsied and crossed herself when she met them in open air; and they bowed to her, blessing her and thanking her for the offerings she made, and in general recognizing her humanity without condoning the expression of its failures."[4] Paul Horgan, who has evidently been influenced by Latin Catholicism with its somewhat laissez-faire attitude in matters of sex, so different from the Irish austerity which has impressed itself upon most of the Catholic Church in North America, has several of his characters in the novel *No Quarter Given* vouch for God's lenience in dealing with sins of the flesh. In one scene the sculptress, Maggie Michaelis, is chatting with an ancient Mexican woman, Concepción, who is modeling for the young artist in a studio in Santa Fe. The old woman is encouraging Maggie in her love affair with the already-married composer, Edmund Abbey. Concepción says that "if she had to live her life all over again ... she would give much less attention to the matter of sin, because in the end God forgave it all anyway ...; if they weren't married, they must go to confession afterwards."[5] Another character in the novel, Mrs. Manning, says of the Mexicans: "They are a race that take passions for granted, and cope with them as best they can ... and if their emotional troubles go past their own talents, why then: what: why, they tell everything to God, and God's priest brings both punishment and solace. The Church is a great realist, you know."[6] Among the people whom the reader becomes acquainted with in Oscar Lewis' *Five Families* is Augustin Gómez, a man of forty-two who has four children by his wife. He has taken up with a young girl, Alicia, by whom he has had a child and whom he continues to see twice a week. Nevertheless, he prays daily before a picture of the Virgin of Guadalupe and criticizes his wife Rosa for insufficient attention to her religious duties.[7] Another view of Catholic realism is given by MacKinley Helm in *A Matter of Love*. An American Protestant couple, living in Mexico, invited a Mexican bishop to lunch. The reverend gentleman turned out to be a most entertaining guest, whom the Americans admired for his love of good food and drink, his urbanity, culture, and Rabelaisian humor. "The bishop put us at ease, as we sat in the garden sipping cognac and cocktails with a story as droll as some of the tales in the Bible, and in language likewise ingenuous: for like the best raconteurs in the Scriptures, he spoke of pissing and screwing in the very same words and with the same organs that we use in real life."[8]

Yet for all the plaudits, a critical undertone in the treatment of Mexican Catholicism by American writers is still audible. Bret Harte took a decidedly unsentimental attitude toward the California missions, referring to them with an irreverence reminiscent of the mockery in the narrative of James Ohio Pattie. In "Friar Pedro's Ride," a doggerel piece written for *The Overland Monthly,* a mission padre was shown as using the military to force conversion or "reconversion" upon the Indians.

> It was the morning season of the year;
>    It was the morning era of the land;
> The water-courses rang full loud and clear;
>    Portala's cross stood where Portala's hand
> Had planted it when Faith was taught by Fear;
>    When Monks and Missions held the sole command
> Of all that shore beside the peaceful sea
>    Where spring-tides beat their long-drawn reveille.
> Out of the Mission of San Luis Rey,
>    All in that brisk, tumultuous spring weather,
> Rode Friar Pedro, in a pious way,
>    With six dragoons in cuirasses of leather,

> Each armed alike for either prayer or fray,
>     Handcuffs and missals they had slung together;
> And as an aid the gospel truths to scatter
>     Each swung a lasso — *alias* a 'riata.'
> In sooth, that year the harvest had been slack,
>     The crop of converts scarce worth computation;
> Some souls were lost, whose owners had turned back
>     To save their bodies frequent flagellation,
> And some preferred the songs of birds, alack,
>     To Latin matins and their soul's salvation,
> And thought their own wild whoopings were less dreary
>     Than Father Pedro's droning *miserere*.
> To bring them back to matins and to prime,
>     To pious works and secular submission,
> To prove to them that liberty was crime,
>     This was in fact the Padre's present mission;
> To get new souls perchance at the same time
>     And bring them to a "sense of their condition" —
> That easy phrase which in the past and present
>     Means making that condition most unpleasant.[9]

In the verses that followed, the dragoons with "pious fervor" raided an Indian camp, lassoing the savages, while Father Pedro, surveying the conflict from a knoll, cheered on the soldiers with church-Latin phrases. In the short story "The Adventure of Padre Vicentio," Harte insinuated the transgression of clerical vows in his treatment of another mission padre. "For the Padre was a man of notable reputation and character; his ministration at the mission of San Jose had been marked with cordiality and unction; he was adored by the simple-minded savages, and had succeeded in impressing his individuality so strongly upon them that the very children were said to have miraculously resembled him in feature."[10] Padre José in "The Legend of Monte del Diablo" was condescendingly portrayed as a man charming in his superstitious naïvete. The Padre had ascended a mountain in California and, looking over the beauty of the country, became exhilarated by the reflection that a New Spain could be transplanted on this land, all under the sway of gentle Mother Church. Absorbed in these pious reflections, he suddenly became aware that he was not alone. Seated beside him was a "grave and decorous figure." This man was dressed in the manner of an elderly Spanish *hidalgo* of a century past, yet Padre José was not surprised. The friar's "adventurous life and poetic imagination, continually on the lookout for the marvelous, gave him a certain advantage over the practical and material-minded. He instantly detected the diabolical nature of his visitant. . . ."[11] The Devil showed the padre two visions, one of the stately forces of Spain retreating from America, the other of the boisterous and swaggering Anglo-Americans, leveling all that stood in their path so that "the bowels of the earth were torn and rent as with a convulsion. And Father José looked in vain for holy cross or Christian symbol. . . ."[12] The Devil then proposed a bargain. Since Spain was to lose out anyway, he urged that the padre abandon his mission work in return for the wherewithal to live in comfortable retirement in Spain. The padre resisted the temptation and grappled with the Devil — only to awaken to find himself being carried down the mountain on a litter, the victim of an attack by a grizzly bear.

Harvey Fergusson views the Mexican church as oppressively authoritarian and terroristic in the pursuit of its aims. He admires Padre Antonio José Martínez of Taos as a sort of latter-day Protestant. Describing him as a liberal in his own way, despite his power obsession, Fergusson praises Padre Martínez for running an excellent school and starting the area's first newspaper, *El Crepúsculo*. When, after much tension between them, Martínez was excommunicated by Bishop Lamy (whom Fergusson labels a puritan) for open defiance, Martínez continued saying Mass and preaching in schism. "At any rate," comments Fergusson, "Padre Martínez was officially denied communion with God through the Church of Rome and he went right on to the end of his life communicating with God through the church of Padre Martínez. Nothing but death could break this man's spirit, nor his personal power, and he apparently feared neither the Pope nor the devil."[13] In the novel *The Blood of the Conquerors,* Fergusson writes of a priest in Albuquerque that "Father Lugaria was a man of imagination, and the special home of his imagination was hell. He was a veritable artist of hell. He loved hell. Again and again he digressed from the strict line of his argument to speak of hell. With all the vividness of a thing seen, he described its flames, its fiends, the terrible stink of burning flesh and the vast chorus of agony that filled it. . . ."[14]

In the short novel *The Pearl*,[15] John Steinbeck puts the priest in the role of exploiter of the people, the position he held in most of the early border accounts. The parable-like method chosen by Steinbeck lends itself well to a theme that is essentially "proletarian." The abstract and allegorical nature of the figures gives them a poetic effectiveness and makes the oversimplification of human character and of society seem fitting in terms of the literary form. Kino, a poor fisherman in a little village on the coast of Vera Cruz, finds a pearl of unusual size and beauty. Immediately the cupidity of all the regular exploiters of the fishermen, the doctor, the pearl merchants, and the priest, is aroused. Though Kino and his wife, Juana, have been living in a common-law relationship because they could not afford the marriage fee demanded by the Church, the priest now comes by to see them, unctuously professing concern for their welfare and offering to marry them free, hoping thereby to get a large donation for the Church. The offer is not accepted. Eventually Kino, harassed to despair by having had to cope with guile and to ward off the constant threat of murder, and having finally had to flee to the mountains after killing in self-defense, returns to the village to accept with resignation the fate that awaits him and throws the great pearl, which has become the symbol of the evil attached to riches, into the sea.

In those areas of Europe and the Americas where folk culture survives, there exists a sort of people's religion, subterranean but very pervasive, which, though it may borrow much from formal religion, lives its own secretive life, sometimes in opposition to the organized faiths. Rural Mexico is especially rich in this kind of folk culture because, added to the usual superstitions inherited from a European peasantry there are many concepts relating to the supernatural which derive from the Indian side of *mestizo* Mexico. Frank Dobie, no great friend of organized religion, delights in the people's religion of Mexico for its exuberance of fancy. *Coronado's Children*[16] is full of Mexican tales about apparitions and evil forces surrounding sites of buried treasure and the graves of travelers murdered for money. The *Mexico I Like* also contains a good deal of this sort of lore. Among the tales of the marvelous in this book is a story about a *nagual*. According to Dobie, the concept of the *nagual* comes from the Indian side of Mexico's heritage. It was often a custom among Indians to name a son after an animal. The son, it was believed, would then grow up in great rapport with that animal, sometimes to the extent of being able to assume at will the animal's form. A person who had this power of transformation was a *nagual*. In the book, old Don Encarnación, known as Chon to his friends, tells the narrator of an encounter he had with a *nagual* in his youth. When it was reported by a terrified *vaquero* that there was a *nagual* in the neighborhood, Chon's girl friend dared Chon to catch the *nagual* and bring it to her. Chon set out with three *vaqueros* to find the creature and at night discovered a huge goat taking the bells off other goats which were sleeping, then arousing them and herding them away from the *rancho*. Chon knew that this was the *nagual*. He roped it, and one of the *vaqueros* hit it over the head with a machete. As blood poured out of the back of the head the *nagual* said: " 'Chon, you have killed your own grandfather.' " When Chon returned home he found his family seated around the body of his grandfather who had apparently fallen and knocked his head.[17]

The concept of the *nagual* which Dobie presents as an Indian belief to be found in northern Mexico must in-fact be widespread among Mexico's Indians because Carter Wilson in *Crazy February,* with its locale in Chiapas in the extreme south of Mexico, presents a scene very reminiscent of Dobie's tale. The village teacher, the Maestro, is talking to a young Indian, Mario, about Juan Lopez Oso, a sinister and physically powerful man with strong political ambitions among the Indians.

"You don't like this Juan Lopez Oso, do you?" the Maestro asked Mario.
"There's nothing wrong with him."
"But why don't you like him?"
Mario thought a moment, pressing his folded hands together between his knees. "Do you know what our word *chanul* means?" he said finally.
"Of course," the Maestro said. "That's your word for soul."
"But I don't think it's the same thing," Mario said. "A man's *chanul* is the animal he has. Some men have sheep and others have cows or pigs. A man told me once my soul is a rabbit, but who knows if that's true."
Mario breathed and looked into the fire. He found it difficult and dangerous to say what he had to say now to the Maestro. "And some men, when they're drunk, they tell you what animal they have. This Juan Lopez Oso was drunk once, and he told me his animal is a tiger." Mario laughed. "I don't know whether to believe it. But a man knows best about himself."[18]

In his first book, *The Teaching of Don Juan: a Yaqui Way of Knowledge,* Carlos Castañeda described his early researches, as a young anthropology student, in the state of Sonora. He questioned the country folk about their belief in *diableros,* people who could transform themselves into animals. One woman told him a story which closely paralleled Frank Dobie's tale of the *nagual.* It was about a woman she knew who "used to turn into a female dog. And one night a dog went into the house of a white man to steal cheese. The white man killed the dog with a shotgun, and at the very moment the dog died in the house of the white man the woman died in her own hut."[19]

Don Juan himself strongly asserted to Castañeda his belief in the strong affinity between spiritually powerful human beings and animals: "To achieve the mood of a warrior is not a simple matter. It is a revolution. To regard the lion and the water rats and our fellow men as equals is a magnificent act of the warrior's spirit. It takes power to do that."[20]

Much of the refreshing quality of John Houghton Allen's novel *Southwest* is due to its canny mixture of the contemporary with elements of fantasy taken from Mexico's folkloric heritage. At one point in the discursive narrative, Allen wanders into a tale about a carousel in a village square.

It was said that one night a dozen years before, when this little carousel had been bright and painted and turned to a lively tune, a drunken vaquero from the unknown ends of this weird land had climbed on the blue horse — it is still a blue horse, they say, but faded like old denim — and had roared around in glee, roweling with the huge Mexican spurs, taking slugs from his bottle of mescal and waving the bottle in the air, spoiling all the children's fun and bringing the *policía* down the street, until even in his drunken condition he realized he was out of order. He realized this, or at last he tired of the silly diversion, but when he stepped down from that same wooden horse, he had not gone three steps in the plaza, until he disappeared. All the people in the square saw it, and the *policía*.

He just blinked out, and he never was heard of, he was not seen again. And the Mexicans, being the charming and superstitious people they are, had deserted that little square, and its tiny carousel had been abandoned like an accursed thing. Old crones said that anyone who rode the blue horse, who stepped down from that ramshackle merry-go-round in the deserted square, would not get to the street corner before he was gone, just like that, and nobody would hear of him again. Even the old man hurried by the place at night.[21]

Richard Summer's novel *Dark Madonna*,[22] dealing with the Mexican quarter in Tucson, Arizona, is full of elements of popular religion. In one scene, shamans from the Papago Indian tribe dance in the house of a Mexican woman, María Delgado, to cure her of an illness. Lupe Salcido goes to the witch Señora Anaya to get her lover back, and she also goes to the Yaqui Indian village of Pascua to implore the image of Santa Rosa to kill a rival. Candles are burnt at the shrine of El Tiradito, whose origins and raison d'être are obscure but clearly not Christian. Lupe's mother, Concepción, distrusts all American doctors and relies on witchcraft and burning candles. Lupe herself is in cultural midpassage. She will resort to witchcraft and will hope for miraculous cures, but she also advises her friend, María Delgado, to see an American doctor. Concepción uses money, badly needed for family food, to buy candles to light at the shrine of El Tiradito to change the family luck.

The position of the *curandera,* a witch who dispenses cures, charms, and curses, continues to be strong in much of rural Mexico. MacKinley Helm in *A Matter of Love* turns his attention to her art. Though he can treat the subject with amused condescension ("The Señora Amelia brewed troublesome spells for a price, while Elisa, also for money, removed them. Between them they did quite a nice little business."), he also appears, on occasion, to take the matter seriously. One of the episodes of the book deals with a curse placed upon a rival in love. Rosita went to the *curandera* Amelia in order to avenge herself on

Isaura, who had taken Rosita's young man, Augustín. "Isaura, a pretty young girl of fifteen, in no time at all became an old hag.... I can't quite describe how she struck me, the first time I noticed the change Her complexion was spotted, her eyes were obtrusive, and her teeth had lost their virginal luster. I remember thinking how young she was to be aging, for most of us will have had ten years or so to add to our childhood before the decay." Later the houseboy, Pedro, says to the author: " 'You ought to take a look at Isaura, Señor. She looks like a toad.... Her face is all yellow and warty. She has lost all her teeth, and her eyes pop right out of her head. I saw her one day through the window of her grandmother's house. They say she never goes out on the street any more. Augustín has come back to Rosita.' "[23] The author at least affects to be reporting an actual experience. Elsewhere in the book he recounts a conversation he had with a local doctor about witchcraft among the Indians. " 'Do you know,' [the doctor] informed me, 'that when I deliver a baby in an Indian family the father makes a cut with his knife in the mouth of the child and draws out blood with his lips? He professes to protect it from witchcraft. They live out their lives in ungodly terror. The witches are Indians and their clients must be of prevailingly Indian blood — but their victims can easily be you or I.' "[24]

Dr. Méndez in *Crazy February* finds that, despite considerable intimacy, there are still barriers in his relationship with Mario, his young Indian assistant. This becomes evident to Méndez in a scene in which he questions Mario about a *curandero,* an Indian curer:

>"Mario, come here."
>Mario came to the door.
>"What are those people doing there? Those going to the church."
>"They're going to pray to the saints."
>"That man in the black tunic — is he a Curer?"
>"Which one?"
>The Doctor was irritated. There was only one man in a black tunic. The Doctor pointed. "There. Is he a curer?"
>"What curer?"
>"Is that man a doctor?"
>"No." Mario risked a smile. "You are the doctor here in Chomtik." He returned to his pail and mop, and the Doctor could hear him giggling to himself.
>So the barrier was still there, the Doctor thought. Mario was his friend in everything. They shared experiences, they shared bottles. The Doctor shared in Mario's life. But still he wouldn't tell about the curers.[25]

In *The Forgotten Village,*[26] John Steinbeck again as in *The Pearl* uses rural Mexico to present a morality tale. The *curandera* is portrayed here not as a picturesquely folkloric figure but as a potent and reactionary force in rural Mexico's struggle against backwardness. Juan Diego, an Indian boy in a mountain village in Mexico, arouses the hostility of the village and is ostracized from his family when he sides with the local school teacher in favoring modern medicine against the cures of the *curandera,* Trini. A polluted well causes mortal illness among many of the townspeople. Juan's little brother dies, and his little sister is near death. Trini's snakeskin cure proves powerless, but she is cunning and maintains her prestige by subtly undermining and ridiculing the school teacher as well as the doctors whom Juan, as the result of a journey of desperation, has persuaded to come to the village from Mexico City. These doctors purify the well and try to innoculate the people with horse-blood serum. The people are incensed by the fancied insult of having horse blood put into them. Egged on by Trini, they drive the doctors out of the village. Juan leaves with the doctors bound for medical school in Mexico City, where he is told that the forces represented by people like Trini will not prevail, that Mexico is moving toward the light.

From the surface evidence of the fusion of Indian and Spanish elements in Mexico's folklore, those interested in the culture of Mexico have gone on to probe the extent to which pre-Christian civilization is still influencing the country on the profoundest conceptual and aesthetic levels. This question of the interaction of indigenous and European cultural impulses in Mexico is a significant one and one that has been argued about heatedly, especially among Mexico's own intellectuals. But to scholars and writers in the United States also, the question has been meaningful. There has been a persistent feeling among North Americans, more articulated in modern times, that in loosening their ties with Europe by settling in the New World, they incurred a certain spiritual deficit which could be removed by laying claim to some of the cultural treasure of indigenous America. Furthermore, if such a claim could be made to seem plausible, the new Americans could establish, at least spiritually, an ancient lineal connection with the American earth. Hart Crane, calling upon Pocahontas to "dance us back the tribal morn," was making a contact, part of the mythical "bridge" that was the subject of his poem, between modern and pristine, indigenous America. In search of this contact, writers such as Archibald McLeish, William Carlos Williams, Hart Crane and others have turned to Mexico where there has been a significant fusion between the culture of Indian America and that of Europe in America. The question of the degree of fusion remains, however. Witter Bynner maintains that the real Mexico, Indian Mexico, has never and will never accept the effete "foreign god" of Europe but will stay with the vitally real earth god which has been its own through the ages of pre-Columbian America. This concept forms the theme of his poem, "Indian Earth."

> 1
> They think they have won you to their foreign god.
> They put you in their churches. On your necks
> They hang their little symbols of remorse.
> And all the while your hearts go up a hill
> To other priests of whom you never speak
> In your confessional. You sin your sins,
> Your little sins, and weep. But oh, the sin
> Of tearing your heart out to the perfect sun!
>
> 2
> It is the earth itself that hems you round
> Against intruders alien to the earth,
> That brings you heaven under a shadowy tree,
> Curves heaven to your arm and lets you lie
> Close to its living thorn. The crown is yours,
> Not theirs. You know the one divinity,
> The only death, the offering of the heart
> To the cruel earth, the love, the consummation.
>
> 3
> Your houses are made of it. They come and go,
> Arise from it and crumble back to it.
> In your old graves your intimate images
> Are made of it, mother and sire and son,
> Infant in arms, each with his earthen face.
> Anyone who has taken once a handful
> Of Indian earth out from among your bones
> Feels in his hand the fusing of your will.
>
> 4
> No need of priests with knives for trespassers.
> Let come who may with an estranging hand.
> Let touch who will this earth so deeply yours,
> None of it ever goes away from you.
> Your gods are here, deeper than any spade;
> And when you lie on the earth under the sun,
> They whisper up to you ancestral spells
> From your own roots, to rot these foreign hearts.[27]

The continued vitality in Mexico of Indian systems of belief has been dramatically demonstrated by the works of Carlos Castañeda, which in the early 1970s became, it would almost seem, the holy scriptures of a new cult. These books became a rallying cause for Chicanos, hallucinatory drug enthusiasts, and seekers — particularly in cult-prone California — after new forms of religion in a period in which literal, scientific rationalism had become, in some intellectual and artistic quarters, discredited.

But amid the din caused by both the true believers and the snorting refuters it is well to be reminded that Carlos Castañeda is a professionally trained anthropologist. His first book, *The Teachings of Don Juan: A Yaqui Way of Knowledge,* was in fact his doctoral dissertation for the University of California at Los Angeles. If the work of an anthropologist is to study and publish findings on values and systems of belief as they interrelate to form a cultural whole, then it must be said that Castañeda's publications are anthropological works.

The great excitement which these books have engendered, however, must be ascribed to the fact that they undertake considerably more than do typical anthropological papers. A reader of any sensibility who encounters Castañeda's work must be struck by its literary quality. The man has the mind, heart, and imagination of a good novelist. The Yaqui "sorcerer" from Sonora, Don Juan Matus, and his apprentice, Carlos Castañeda himself, emerge as characters with a great deal of dramatic vitality. The persona of Carlos Castañeda which is projected in the works is that of an appealingly humble young man devotedly undergoing, while bearing up under many rebukes, the severe and sometimes frightening and even dangerous spiritual assignments of a stern and fractious taskmaster, who is, from another side of his nature, an earthy, humorous, and delightful old man.

The effectiveness of the persona that Casteñada has given himself in his books is enhanced by the mystery in which he has enshrouded himself in his personal life. He has enjoyed being secretive or vague about his origins. Apparently he is a South American. Though he has been known to say that his home was Brazil, *Time* magazine's researchers claim that in fact he was born in Catamarca, Peru.[28] More interesting, however, is the question of what value to put upon reports of marvelous happenings issuing from a man who has been quoted as calling himself a great "bullshitter" but who more often takes on the air of a serious devotee. In other words, how close are Castañeda the anthropologist, Casteñada the literary man, and Casteñada the disciple who appears in the books? However one might answer this question, the fact remains that the works themselves are of considerable interest and literary value, and as such they are worthy of analysis.

When Carlos Castañeda first met the old Yaqui, Juan Matus, in an Arizona bus station in 1960, Castañeda, as he depicts himself in his first book, was a typical graduate student in anthropology. He began to interview the old man about aspects of Yaqui belief, taking down notes and generally treating Juan Matus with a degree of intellectual condescension. Instead of being affronted by this patronizing attitude, Juan Matus was amused by the pretensions of the young man, who must have seemed "green" indeed to the venerable Don Juan. Castañeda, in his turn, began to realize that Matus was in no way impressed or honored by a young intellectual's attentions, and shortly it began to dawn on Castañeda that it was Juan Matus not himself who possessed the real store of knowledge. Thus began a close personal relationship and an apprenticeship which lasted for ten years, with Castañeda making periodic trips from Los Angeles to northern Sonora, where he would stay in Don Juan's house as the teaching and learning progressed.

Castañeda soon recognized that Don Juan's philosophical and religious ideas were anything but primitive but were in fact concepts that were interrelated into a sophisticated system. "My apprenticeship . . . and the strenuous experiences I had undergone . . . were but a very small fragment of a system of logical thought from which Don Juan drew meaningful inferences for his day-to-day life, a vastly complex system of beliefs in which inquiry was an experience leading to exultation."[29] The word *logical* is important here, because Castañeda increasingly accepted the idea that what the Western world has called sorcery is built upon a respectable logic of its own. "For the American Indian, perhaps for thousands of years, the vague phenomenon we call sorcery has been a serious, bona fide practice, comparable to that of our science. Our difficulty in understanding it stems, no doubt, from the alien units of meaning with which it deals."[30]

Apart from the element of belief, Don Juan advocated an ethic of will through which, by the following of very specific procedures, one acquired not only knowledge but various powers. One who has attained to such acquisitions has become a "warrior." "For me the real accomplishment," Carlos Castañeda said, "is the art of being a warrior, which, as don Juan says, is the only way to balance the terror of being a man with the wonder of being a man."[31] This coupling of the notion of terror with that of will has led to this system's being called a form of existential stoicism.

At various points in the books, Carlos Castañeda, at first by means of drugs prepared by Don Juan, "meets" various powers, some of which the drugs have conjured up but which seem to have personhood of their own. There is peyote, "Mescalito," and a mushroom compound, "Humito" — the Little Smoke. The appearance of these forces raises several questions in the reader's mind. Are these and other apparitions to be taken as transcendent, other worldly beings? At one point, Don Juan is talking about "diableros," sorcerers of a kind. "There is a crack between the two worlds, the world of the diableros and the world of living men. There is a place where the two worlds overlap. The crack is there. It opens and closes like a door in the wind. To get there, a man must exercise his will."[32] Here we are definitely told about "two worlds." This idea seems to be strengthened by Castañeda's insistence that the appearance of personalized forces identified with certain drugs are not merely hallucinations resulting from having taken the drugs but have an objective reality apart from the drug taker. For example, talking about his experiences with "Mescalito," peyote, Castañeda writes: "It had taken me three years to realize, or rather to find out, that whatever is contained in the cactus *Lophophora williansii* had nothing to do with me in order to exist as an entity; it existed by itself out there, at large. I knew it then."[33] "Mescalito" was a powerful protector and his presence constituted an experience of "nonordinary reality." "The meetings with the allies or with Mescalito took place in a realm that was not illusory."[34]

Don Juan makes a distinction between the powers and functions of "Mescalito" and "Humito." " 'Mescalito is a protector because he talks to you and can guide your acts. . . . Mescalito teaches the right way to live. And you can see him because he is outside you. The smoke [Humito], on the other hand, is an ally. It transforms you and gives you power without ever showing its presence. You can't talk to it. But you know it exists because it takes your body away and makes you as light as air. Yet you never see it. But it is there giving you power to accomplish unimaginable things, such as when it takes your body away.' " However, when Castañeda pursues this idea, Don Juan answers in a manner which suggests a definite degree of subjectivity in these experiences:

> "I really felt I had lost my body, don Juan."
> "You did."
> "You mean, I really didn't have a body?"
> "What do *you* think yourself?"
> "Well, I don't know. All I can tell you is what I felt."
> "That is all there is in reality — what you felt."[35]

In an interview which appeared in the magazine *Psychology Today,* Castañeda took the position that there was nothing transcendent in his view of the world. "It has been this element of engagement in the world that has kept me following the path which Don Juan showed me. There is no need to transcend the world. Everything we need to know is right in front of us, if we pay attention. If you enter a state of nonordinary reality, as you do when you use psychotropic plants, it is only to draw from it what you need in order to see the miraculous character of ordinary reality. For me the way to live — the path with heart — is not introspection or mystical transcendence but presence in the world. This world is the warrior's hunting ground. . . ."[36] There seem to be some contradictory elements here, but perhaps their resolution lies in the concept of "nonordinary reality." Thus instead of two worlds or two realities, there is only one reality, but ordinarily only part of this reality is perceived. It is only in certain states, perhaps at first drug induced, but not necessarily so, that one can perceive that extended reality that Castañeda has called "nonordinary reality."

Castañeda's statement in the interview in which he said that under certain states one can "see the miraculous character of ordinary reality" would seem to place him in an affinity with such American writers as Emerson, Thoreau, and Whitman who have emphasized the miraculous qualities of the ordinary, which only the prepared spirit can perceive. One also feels something strongly akin to the spirit of Thoreau in Don Juan's comments about the power of place. Castañeda asks:

> "But what can I do with this hill, Don Juan?"
> "Fix every feature of it in your memory. This is the place where you will come in *dreaming*. This is the place where you will meet with powers, where secrets will someday be revealed to you."[37]

One is reminded too, in the relationship of Don Juan and his disciple, Carlos Castañeda, of the similar relationship in William Faulkner's "The Bear" between Sam Fathers and Ike McCaslin. Sam Fathers, half Indian and heir to the lore of the vanishing wilderness, takes on young Ike as a disciple, almost as in a laying on of hands. Ike is instructed by the last man left to do it into the rites and mysteries that make one powerful in the wilderness.

The American writers mentioned above sought the experience of the miraculous in the ordinary without recourse to drugs. In the early part of Castañeda's apprenticeship, he was given, under Don Juan's careful supervision, drugs concocted from desert plants. These drugs were to become the "allies" of a "man of knowledge." According to Don Juan, these drugs and their emanations "are forces, neither good nor bad, just forces that a brujo [sorcerer] learns to harness."[38] However, after an apprentice has gotten to a certain point in his training, he should no longer have to rely on drugs. " 'Power plants are only an aid,' Don Juan said. 'The real thing is when the body realizes it can *see*.' "[39]

The distinction between "looking" and "seeing" becomes the subject of several dialogues between master and apprentice. At one point Castañeda says: "Then, Don Juan, you don't see the world in the usual way anymore." The answer is: "I see both ways. When I want to *look* at the world I see it the way you do. Then when I want to *see* it I look at it the way I know and I perceive it in a different way."[40] Don Juan tries to teach Castañeda the technique involved in *seeing*. "The trick is to feel with your eyes. . . . Your problem now is that you don't know what to feel. It'll come to you, though, with practice." He goes on to say that one must learn to see two images and then focus on the area between the images. "Any change worthy of notice would take place there, in that area."[41]

Another interesting distinction that Don Juan makes is between "doing" and "not-doing." He centers his discussion on a pebble. *"Doing* would be to leave the pebble lying around because it is merely a small rock. *Not-doing* would be to proceed with that pebble as if it were something far beyond a mere rock. In this case, that pebble has soaked in you for a long time and now it is you."[42] This concept of creatively passive receptivity in contemplating a natural object again reminds one of Thoreau. " 'When one is *not-doing,*' " says Don Juan, " 'one is feeling the world, and one feels the world through its lines.' "[43]

There is an earthy humor, particularly on the part of Don Juan himself, that runs throughout Castañeda's books and contrasts refreshingly with philosophical and magical elements. Like Plato reporting on Socrates, Castañeda laces his dialogues with humorous bursts on the part of the master or his sorcerer friends. At one point Castañeda, in a very earnest manner, is asking Don Juan and Don Juan's sorcerer friend Don Genaro what a warrior can do when an "ally" appears suddenly and menacingly.

> "All right!" I said. "What can a warrior do?"
> Don Genaro blinked and made smacking sounds with his lips, as if he were searching for a right word. He looked at me fixedly, holding his chin.
> "A warrior wets his pants," he said with Indian solemnity. Don Juan covered his face and Don Genaro slapped the ground, exploding in a howling laughter.[44]

The downgrading of an experience which had shaken Castañeda takes on a humorous twist. After taking the "humito," Castañeda sees a huge, scaly beast with wings who takes bull-like passes at him. Castañeda soars out of range. Before smoking the plant, he had been told by Don Juan that he would encounter a "guardian." When he recovered from the drug and found himself in Don Juan's house, he said to Don Juan with some pride: "I really thought I had overpowered the guardian." The master's answer was: "You must be kidding."[45] On another occasion, Don Juan reports to Castañeda on his conversation with a magical deer. According to Castañeda: "I said that his dialogue with the deer had been sort of dumb. 'What did you expect?' he asked, still laughing. 'I'm an Indian.' "[46] Perhaps this mixture of the humorous with the seriously religious can be associated with a general tendency in Indian religious expression.

Several Indian groups, the Yaquis themselves and the Hopis for example, traditionally introduce clowns into some of their most sacred dances and other ceremonies. In performing their ritualistic roles, these clowns carry on uproariously and sometimes even obscenely to the delight of participants and Indian onlookers. Although to White observers these procedures have sometimes seemed sacrilegious, they might well be taken as indications of a kind of psychological vigor which takes into account the life process in its entirety.

Carlos Castañeda's books have dramatized, to a wide American reading public, the mysteries of the "separate reality" in which Indian life in the borderlands has been grounded. Because of the great interest that these books have generated, they can be expected to have an influence upon further literary treatments of the area, and in fact such an influence can already be detected. In Neil Claremon's novel *Borderland,* a young White man, J. P., is coached in the mysteries of Indian practice, lore, and belief by a young Opata woman, Tsari, in a manner reminiscent of the relationship of Castañeda and Don Juan. Here, however, the theme of sexual attraction has been added. The scene again is northern Sonora. Tsari is in the process of becoming a *curandera,* curer, through her tutelage to an older and full-fledged *curandera,* Teresa. Tsari's love for J. P. at first seems to pose for her a problem of cultural choice, but the problem is resolved by J. P.'s willingness, even eagerness, to become initiated into Opata beliefs and practices. He proves himself by the skill and intuition by which he successfully plays midwife to Tsari in delivering, in a complicated birth, their twins.

The ideas propounded by Don Juan and by Claremon's Tsari seem to be of purely Indian origin unfused with Christian elements. However, much of the religious practice of Indians in northern Mexico has been fused with Christian concepts and ceremonial, as any witness to the dramatic Yaqui Easter ceremonies can attest. Anita Brenner in *Idols Behind Altars,* a book whose title indicates its principal theme, held that there has been a considerable degree of fusion, with Indian elements pervading many forms nominally Christian. Though the religious statues in churches throughout Mexico are "images of the official deities," they have been "remade in forms that were their origin," namely Indian forms. "The set of beliefs of which these things are symbols, is hardly a system, and not always articulate. It underlies all Mexican religions which have had a priesthood, including Christianity. It is not everywhere accompanied by rite; but always by the constant Indian attitude, which is the participation of the same stuff of being, with other lives not human."[47] One is reminded here of Frank Dobie's treatment of the folkloric concept of the *nagual,* the human who can assume the form of an animal. Dobie emphasizes that those elements in Mexican folklore in which animals are invested with human characteristic and vice versa come from the Indian heritage of Mexico. Selden Rodman reports seeing, in the state of Chiapas in the south of Mexico, groups of life-size images of the saints ranged across the transept of a church. Some of them had, beneath the silken gowns they were wearing, small images of jaguars. The jaguar, he was told, was an original Indian god, now being worshipped "under protective cover" as the Saint of the Witch Doctors.[48]

If the blending of cultures has been most complex in those areas of Mexico where the great Indian cultures once flourished, such as in the valley of Mexico around Mexico City and in the southern states of Yucatan and Chiapas, it has also come about in the most northerly reaches of Mexican culture in what is now the American Southwest. Charles F. Lummis wrote of the brotherhood of the Penitentes in New Mexico that "the society was from an early date as much Indian as Spanish, as much pagan as Christian. It is of a piece with the faith of all Mexicans of the mixed blood. Everywhere they have substituted Christian images for those of their native idolatry and made over Jesus into a symbol of their own sacrifices of blood. That is why Mexico can fight the Church and expel its ministers and still remain a devoutly religious country."[49] This conflict between the native elements in Mexico's religion and the formal organization of the Catholic Church is one which Willa Cather dramatized in *Death Comes for the Archbishop.* In the course of disciplining the native clergy of New Mexico, Bishop Latour rode into Taos to confront the powerful Fr. Martínez. At that first meeting, while the amenities were just barely preserved, the elements of the conflict were brought out into the open. " 'If you try to introduce European civilization here and change our old ways,' " said Martínez to Latour, " 'to interfere with the secret dances of the Indians, let us say, or abolish the bloody rites of the Penitentes, I foretell an early death for you. I advise you to study our native traditions before you begin your reforms. You are among barbarous people, my Frenchman, between two savage races. The dark things forbidden by your Church are a part of Indian religion. You cannot introduce French fashions here.' "[50] That Bishop Lamy of Santa Fe did largely succeed in introducing "French fashions" may be attributed in part to the fact that the area was now under American rule and taking on increasingly the orderly pattern of North American society. In Mexico proper the ambivalence in the religious life of the people continues. Hart Crane, in a letter to William Wright (September 21, 1931), describes attending a ceremony in honor of Tepozteco, the ancient Aztec god of pulque, which took place in the town of Tepoztlan. Of the people taking an active part in the proceedings he wrote:

> These, divided into several groups around lanterns (of all places!) on the roof of the Cathedral and Monastery which dominates the town, made a wonderful sight with their dark faces, white "pyjama" suits and enormous white hats. A drummer and a flute player standing facing the dark temple on the heights, alternated their barbaric service at ten-minute intervals with loud ringing of all the church bells by the sextons of the church. Two voices, still in conflict here in Mexico, the idol's and the cross. Yet there really did not seem to be a real conflict that amazing night. Nearly all of these "elders" I have been describing go to mass.[51]

Lawrence Ferlinghetti also witnesses a scene in which Indian rites are carried on in front of a cathedral:

> The Aztec dancers with armadillo mandolins under the Indian laurels in the late dusk in front of the cathedral. . . . A tall young Indian prince, very bronze and very beautiful, with long bronze legs, dancing with an Indian maid in feathered headband, her eyes bloodshot. He plays his armadillo guitar as he dances, shellbells on his ankles. . . . A circle of older dancers surrounds them. They look in each others' eyes as they dance, unsmiling. A feather blows out of her headband into the center of the dancing circle where it lies on the cobbles. They dance around it, hooking their ankles together, slowly. They are smiling in each others' eyes, very beautiful. . . . The faint rattle and whir of their ankle bells, echoing hollowly, fills the sweet air.[52]

Two modern American writers think of the relationships of the great Indian civilizations of the Americas to the classical world. Allen Ginsberg contemplated ruins of Chichen Itza, Palenque, and Xbalba:

> Yet these ruins so much
>     woke me to nostalgia
> for the classic stations
>     of the earth,
> the ancient continent
>     I have not seen.[53]

Henry Miller in *The Colossus of Maroussi,* thought by several Miller scholars to be his greatest work, experienced a sense of proximity between the passionate and expressive Crete of the ancient King Minos and the Mexico of the Aztecs and Mayas. In this creative and highly imaginative book, based upon his stay in Greece, Miller expresses his sense of the fatuity of thinking of the Americas as the new world and as primarily belonging to the Western world:

## Idols and Altars 301

The Western world, we say, never once thinking to include those other great social experiments which were made in South America and Central America, passing them over always in our rapid historical surveys as if they were accidents, jumping from the Middle Ages to the discovery of America, as if this bastard bloom on the North American continent marked the continuation of the line of true development of man's evolution. Seated on King Minos' throne I felt closer to Montezuma than to Homer or Praxiteles or Caesar or Dante. Looking at the Minoan scripts I thought of the Mayan legends which I had once glimpsed in the British Museum and which stand out in my memory as the most wonderful, the most natural, the most artistic specimens of calligraphy in the long history of letters.[54]

In a lighter vein, the practice among poor Mexicans of reprimanding sacred statues for not granting requests, a practice noted with disgust by the early border writers as evidence of a blasphemous idolatry, also receives attention from a number of modern American writers. The modern attitude is usually a somewhat condescending expression of delight at the quaintness of a peasant folk. Scenes in which statues or images are punished for having failed to perform appear in Helen Hunt Jackson's *Ramona,* in John Steinbeck's *Tortilla Flat,* in Richard Summer's *Dark Madonna,* and in Frank Goodwyn's *The Magic of Limping John.* Frank Dobie gives the subject of the Mexican familiarity with the divine his usual savory treatment. In *The Mexico I Like,* Don Marcelo, *patrón* of the Hacienda de Las Cinco Llagas, tells a story about praying for rain.

> "This was some years ago. The custom then was to get a priest to bless the seeds of the corn and the *frijol* on Candelmas Day. Then followed the planting. The year I am talking about the seed rain did not fall until close to the day of San Isidro, the fifteenth of May. It was not much of a rain, but it sprouted the corn. For ten days the corn grew; then it stood still. Then it began to twist and wither. Unless rain came it would surely die. The *gente* were taking the images and pictures of San Isidro outside and imploring him to make it rain. Some whipped San Isidro. Day after day passed and not one cloud drifted into sight.
>
> "Well, as everybody knows, the time for the rainy season to begin is the day of San Juan, the twenty-four of June. This day was at hand, and it still was dry. Then one morning the *peones,* all of them, came in a group and one of them said to me, '*Patrón,* we want to borrow *La Virgen María* from the Church.' "
>
> " 'Why do you want the Holy Virgin?' I asked."
>
> " 'We want to have a procession and pray for rain.' "
>
> " 'Very well.' "
>
> "They took her, the wooden image, and carried her on a platform and went up to the *capilla* [chapel] and over the fields, stopping at crosses to pray. Then they brought her back to her place."

"The next day the rain started and it did not stop for two days and two nights. The clouds poured themselves out. It hailed. The wind blew. It was a barbarity. When the sky was clean again, there was no corn. What had not died from drouth had been beaten down and washed away. Then once more the *peones* came.

" 'What is it now,' I asked."

" 'Why *Patrón*,' the spokesman said, 'we want to borrow *El Señor* from the church.' "

" 'And why do you want *El Señor* at this time,' I asked."

" 'We want to have a procession — ' "

" '*Válgame Dios!*' I said, 'You don't mean to tell me you are going to bring *El Señor* out to pray for another rain right now?' "

" 'No, *Patrón*. We want to take him out and show him what kind of mother he has. Just look at the fields and see what she has done!' "[55]

The Virgin, however, is not usually in bad repute in Mexico. In her role as benefactress, she is a powerful force in the emotional life of the nation. Dobie, again in *The Mexico I Like,* tells a Mexican legend which is in direct line of descent from the mediaeval tales of the miracles of the Virgin — but with a Mexican flavoring, perhaps, in the kind of succor chosen for the Virgin to dispense. A married woman, who was a devotee of "La Virgen de las Margaritas," the Virgin of the Daisies, had a lover to whom she used to bring tortillas, rice, frijoles, and other good things to eat when her husband, at noontime, was presumably at the mines. One time at noon her suspicious husband went home and found his wife leaving the house with a basket covered by a cloth embroidered with patterns of daisies. The husband asked what was in the basket. She replied, daisies to bring to the chapel of Our Lady of the Daisies. He ripped off the cloth and in fact discovered marvelously fresh daisies in the basket, which had a moment before been loaded with food.[56]

Frank Goodwyn in *The Magic of Limping John* explains why one of the characters in the book is especially devoted to the Virgin. "A most reverent worshipper of Mary was Don Gavino Rodriguez of the Black Horse Saloon. To Don Gavino, the Virgin had many advantages over her son Jesús and her husband, Dios. Dios was too distant and vague; Jesús too easy-going and gentle to get much done. But Mary combined two supreme virtues: virginity and motherhood. All the love and respect which he had learned as a boy to lavish on his earthly mother was turned in manhood to the Virgin, spiritual mother of all men."[57]

When a Mexican thinks of the Virgin, he almost invariably thinks of the Virgin of Guadalupe, the special patroness of Mexico, who, it is said, appeared in early colonial times to the poor Indian, Juan Diego, and has ever since, though considered to be the special protector of the Indians, been the object of adoration by the whole nation. Modern

American writers, unlike the early border writers who summarily dismissed the Virgin of Guadalupe as a prime example of priestly craftiness in exploiting the Indians, have marveled at the immense force of the Virgin of Guadalupe in the culture of Mexico and have considered it generally to be beneficient. "The figure of the Virgin of Guadalupe," wrote Hart Crane to his stepmother (December 12, 1931), "miraculously unites the teachings of the early Catholic missionaries with many survivals of the old Indian myths and pagan cults. She is a typical Mexican product, a strange blend of Christian and pagan strains. What a country and people! The most illogical and baffling on earth; but how appealing! I enclose the authoritative portrait of this Virgin, who, I think, is quite beautiful. She is really the Goddess of the Mexican masses, and you will find her image or picture everywhere. . . ."[58] Selden Rodman in *Mexican Journal* also attests to the ubiquitousness of the image of the Virgin of Guadalupe throughout Mexico and claims her to be the one unifying force in a decentralized country of many subcultures. He credits her alone with the survival of Catholicism in a land where it has suffered more persecution than in any area outside of Communist countries. "And that it *more* than survives, what visitor like myself, an unbeliever, familiar with the half-hearted Sunday lip-service prevailing in the States among Catholics no more than Protestants, can doubt? The crowds in the innumerable churches, even on weekdays, testify to it. The solitary Indian before his tiny shrine along the loneliest road, his arms stretched out in the sign of the cross, bears witness."[59] F. S. C. Northrop gives his explanation of the power of the Virgin of Guadalupe in the culture of Mexico.

> The fact is, this image of the Virgin conveys in some direct and effective way a basic, intuitively felt element in the nature of things and in the human experience which is spontaneously natural and convincing to the native Mexicans. In some way, the Virgin of Guadalupe and the story of her revelation, directed especially to the Indians, call forth from the Mexican spirit a devotion and sweeping response not equaled by any other influence in Mexico even today.
> 
> The truth is that it is the Virgin representing what Plato termed the female *eros* (the emotional, passionate, metaphysical principle in the nature of things) and not the Christ representing the male *logos* (the rational, doctrinal principal, formalized explicitly for orthodox Catholicism by St. Thomas Aquinas) who has for the most part caught the imagination and devotion of the Mexicans.
> 
> This fact shows in countless ways. Anyone who has walked among the mountains or through the fields and orchards of Switzerland, Bavaria, Austria, or France, will recall coming again and again, even in out-of-the-way places, upon little shrines of the

Christ hanging upon the Cross. This is the true and natural symbol for orthodox Catholicism. Nevertheless, in journeys covering hundreds of miles radiating from Mexico City in every direction no such image of the Christ located in the countryside or even made very conspicuous in the churches comes to mind; in its place appears instead the Madonna of Guadalupe.[60]

It is, then, the aesthetic, intuitive aspect of religion which appeals to the Mexican spirit, and it is this strongly aesthetic emphasis in Mexican Catholicism, so derided as empty pomp and show by the puritanical early chroniclers and novelists of the borderlands, which has strongly attracted a number of modern American writers, most of whom have no formal religious commitments. Mary Austin, considering the poverty and illiteracy of the people in the small communities of New Mexico, saw that their religion was the "one source they had of art and drama and mystery, of spiritual energization and culture. . . ."[61] And yet this one source was enough, as Mary Austin saw it, to endow these people with an aesthetic and spiritual life considerably superior to that led by most people in modern, industrialized society. A sensitively written book, *The Silver Cradle,* by Julia Nott Waugh, about the Mexican *colónia* in San Antonio, Texas, makes much the same point. The focus of the life of the people of this poor quarter of the city is the church of Jesús y María. "For these Latin-Americans whose lives are hard, who feel not seldom that every man's hand is against them, find in the climate of religion food for their essential needs: beauty and drama and a sense of refuge." These people "against a backdrop of factories and x-rays and automobiles and airplanes, imbue with life their Spanish and their Indian past. It is they who are forever bringing fruits from their fields, flowers from their gardens, offering those little plays and songs and dances that delight their inmost soul." These offerings, brought to the church, "eternally repeated," are the offerings of people who, "accepting faith, living with a sense of continuity, out of poverty and piety create the poetry of the poor."[62]

The ritual, art, drama, and emotional intensity of Mexican Catholicism has been contrasted by modern American writers with the austerity, "preachifying" moralism, and aesthetic barrenness of much of American Protestantism. Bret Harte, for all his jibes at the California mission padres, felt the attraction of the aesthetic aspect of Catholicism in the Hispanic Southwest. In the story "A Pupil of Chestnut Ridge," Mr. Brooks, the schoolmaster, went to the home of the Hoovers, Free-Will Baptists, to discuss the education of Conchita, the Mexican girl the Hoovers had adopted. "He was ushered into a well-furnished sitting room, whose glaring freshness was subdued and repressed by black-framed engravings of scriptural subjects. As Mr. Brooks glanced at them and recalled the schoolrooms of the old missions, with their monastic shadows which half hid the gaudy, tinseled saints and flaming or ensanguined hearts upon the walls, he feared that the little waif of Mother Church had not gained any cheerfulness in the exchange."[63] Hart treats a similar theme in the story, "Convert of the Mission." The Rev. Stephen Masterton was a fire-breathing, flesh-hating evangelical preacher in California. Because of a nervous breakdown, he was advised by his doctor, Doctor Duchesne, to go to a quiet Mexican-California adobe town and rest. Following this advice, he goes to such a town, gets a small adobe house, hires a wrinkled Indian servant, and starts resting. At first he is scandalized by the indolence and frivolity of the Mexicans and the evidence of accursed papistry on all sides. However, he meets by chance a beautiful Mexican teenage girl, Pepita Ramírez, whom he encountered while she was strumming her guitar and singing in her garden at night. The clergyman was much affected by her and conceived the plan of converting her from idolatry and saving her soul. Accordingly, he sent a message to her, asking her to meet him in the garden at night. Naturally Pepita construed the note to be a request for an assignation and gleefully complied. After much coquetry on her part and confusion on his, he says:

> "I want to talk to you ... on far more serious matters. I wished to" — but he stopped. He could not address this quaint child-woman, staring at him in black-eyed wonder, in either the measured or the impetuous terms with which he could have exhorted a maturer, responsible being. He made a step towards her; she drew back, striking at his extended hand half impatiently, half mischievously with her fan.
> He flushed — and then burst out bluntly, "I want to talk with you about your soul."
> "My what?"
> "Your immortal soul, unhappy girl."
> "What have you to make with that? Are you a devil?"
> Her eyes grew rounder, though she faced him boldly.
> "I am a minister of the Gospel," he said in hurried entreaty.
> "My immortal soul lif with the Padre at the Mission — You moost seek her there! My mortal *body*," she added with a mischievous smile, "say to you, 'good a' night, Don Esteban.'" She dropped him a little courtesy [sic] and — ran away.[64]

Some time later, Doctor Duchesne was talking to one of Rev. Masterton's colleagues, a Deacon Sanderson.

> "And what has become of Mr. Masterton, who used to be in your — vocation?" A long groan from the deacon. "Hallo! I hope

he has not had a relapse," said the Doctor, earnestly. "I thought I'd knocked all that nonsense out of him — I beg your pardon — I mean," he added, hurriedly, "he wrote to me only a few weeks ago that he was picking up his strength again and doing well!"

"In his weak, gross, sinful flesh — yes, no doubt," returned the Deacon, scornfully, "and, perhaps, even in a worldly sense, for those who value the vanities of life; but he is lost to us, for all time, and lost to eternal life forever. Not," he continued in sanctimonious vindictiveness, "but that I often had my doubts of Brother Masterton's steadfastness. He was too much given to imagery and song."

"But what has he done?" persisted Doctor Duchesne.

"Done! He has embraced the Scarlet Woman!"

"Dear me!" said the Doctor, "so soon? Is it anybody you know here? — not anybody's wife? Eh?"

"He has entered the Church of Rome," said the Deacon indignantly.

Furthermore, the Rev. Masterson had been seen playing the organ in an " 'idolatrous chapel' " with a " 'foreign female Papist for a teacher,' " and worst of all " 'this miserable backslider was to take to himself a wife — in one of these strange women — that very Jezebel who seduced him? What do you call that?' " " 'It looks a good deal like human nature,' said the Doctor, musingly, " 'but *I* call it a cure!' " [65]

Mary Austin also compared the drama of Mexican Catholicism with what she considered to be the dullness of American Protestantism. She accused the Protestant missionaries and the Indian Bureau in New Mexico of trying to smother the aesthetic aspects of the life of the Pueblo Indians and the Mexicans. "The Franciscans, at least, for the beauty they destroyed, left such beauty as they had, and a type of architecture destined to prevail throughout the Southwest." [66] Remarking on the lack of significant ritual in North American life, she added that anyone who had seen a religious procession in the streets of Santa Fe would have "the key to much in our English-speaking life that is mortifying and confusing. For what do our Kiwanis and Ku-Kluxers seek, with their made-up school-boy titles and their pillowcases, but to recapture the lost art of expressing dramatically the fundamental life relations which, here in our Southwest, flow naturally into forms born of the great age of Dante and Lope de Vega?" [67] As indicated previously, the matter of the difference in emotional climate between North American Protestantism and Mexican Catholicism engaged the attention of F. S. C. Northrop as well. In discussing the aesthetic richness of Mexican Catholicism in contrast to the blandness of American Protestantism, he summed up the situation as definitively as he had the conditions of other major areas of culture in which the two societies were compared. In *The Meeting of East and West* he wrote:

> With respect to art, the Protestant Church is scared. At its worst its art is crude; at its best neutral, preferring a pure white in the New England Congregational churches or a dull grey in the Episcopal chapels, which does not commit itself. A church with the diversity of vivid colors which the Indian aesthetic imagination demands would shock a Protestant congregation. But imagine, conversely, how the Protestant religion must appear to the religious Mexicans. Its exceedingly verbal preaching, its aesthetic color-blindness, and its emotional tepidity and coldness must make it look to them like no religion at all.[68]

CHAPTER TEN

## Chicano Literature

While, in the course of the twentieth century, North American writers have been dealing with Mexico in a more sophisticated manner than did their predecessors of the nineteenth, they have discovered, beginning in the 1960s that they have had to share the field with a new breed of writers, the Chicano authors. These Southwestern writers of Mexican-American descent have claimed that the literary images that they have created of themselves have a truer ring of authenticity than have any portraitures created by outsiders. Chicano literature, in fact, has roots dating back to the mid-nineteenth century, but the literature created by Mexican-American authors beginning in the nineteen-sixties has been distinguished by the fact that it is related, to a greater or lesser extent, to a political and social movement.

The Chicano movement is a complex one, and one that moves from one phase into another. The very term Chicano is a matter of controversy. Its origin is debated among the Chicanos themselves. One creditable version is that it originated among Indian groups in Chihuahua as an elision of the word *Mexicano*. From there, allegedly, it was taken up by Anglos in the border region and used toward Mexican-Americans in an abusive or patronizing manner. But, as in the history of the word "black," young militants seized upon a derogatory term and defiantly inscribed it upon their banners. Originally many Mexican-Americans spurned the word as having too radical a connotation, but it is gaining more and more general acceptance among them.

Attitudes among the Chicanos range from an assertive separatism, as in the programs of the Black Panthers and other Black nationalists, to an ideal of cultural identification with the Mexican-American heritage within the general framework of American society. The meaning of the term Aztlán, the word used to express the concept of the land of the Chicanos, will vary according to where a given Chicano stands within this range of attitudes. The more militant Chicanos identify themselves with the "third world," seeing their plight as being the same as that of the darker peoples of the underdeveloped nations whom they describe as being victims of "imperialism." The phrase "cultural rape" has been used to describe the Chicano's sense of the effect of Anglo attempts to impose Anglo-American values upon the Mexican-American community. There has been much emphasis upon the revitalizing of the Spanish language in the Chicano community. The name Reis Tijerina invokes the whole mystique of *la tierra* and the important issue of who rightfully owns it, and the name Cesar Chávez connotes much more than grapes or lettuce. The man has been the living example of success in the struggle for *la causa,* a cause seen as having a much broader range than simply better pay and working conditions for agricultural workers. It has been the cause of the renewed self-identity, racial and cultural pride, and accomplishment of *la raza,* the Mexican-American "race."

Chicano literature has been the most intense expression of the creative spirit of the movement. Much of the earlier writing first saw the light of print in "angry" journals or newspapers: in the Chicano magazine *El Grito* or in Chicano newspapers such as *La Raza, El Gallo,* or *Bronce.* The writing was often unabashedly cause writing, whose aim was not primarily literary but inspirational. As such, a good deal of it is of an ephemeral nature headed for, as was the case of the proletarian literature of the 1930s, oblivion. But even in this early period, literature of a lasting quality was being written. A case in point is the work of the poet Alurista, an activist in the movement. Admittedly, he has produced a good deal of writing more hortatory than literary, but he is a poet of very considerable talents.

As do other Chicano poets, Alurista weaves strands of English and Spanish in his poems, with sometimes striking effects:[1]

>   dust gathers on the shoulders
>       of dignitaries
>   y de dignidad
>       no saben nada
>   muertos en el polvo
>       they bite the earth
>   and return
>       to dust

Mexican-Americans in the past have tended to assert their Spanishness and deny their Indianness, often in an effort to secure acceptance by the Anglos, to become "agringados," as the Chicanos put it. In reaction to this attitude, the Chicanos stress the Indian part of their heritage, and much of this emphasis has found its way into Chicano writing. Alurista in his poems often invokes the Aztec past and tellingly juxtaposes the ancient and mythic with images of contemporary Chicano life in the barrios.

out the alley our soul awaits us
to meet on pebbled streets the breeze
the bongo rhythm of our thumping heart
to catch the wind the odor and the flesh
to launch our gaze on once lost hopes
a candle
sitting in lonely stare
a tear
irrigating our cheekbone high lands
pyramids, feathers and rituals of love
people in the dusk afternoon of a cloudy horizon
love
Quetzalcoatl in life rejoices
and we walk down age carved alleys
running to find alma, sangre y aliento
feathers in stomach gnaw melancholic ulcers
and Huitzilopochtli drinks our blood
raza rain in Tlaloc's agony
raza run to the sun and sing
of the barrio
and the soft winds that flagellate our skeleton[2]

The futility and cultural treason involved when Mexican-Americans deny their culture and imitate Anglo ways has drawn a lot of fire from the Chicanos. Such people have been disdainfully referred to as *Malinches,* from the name of Cortez's Indian mistress; *vendidos,* sell-outs; or *agringados,* gringo-fied ones. But the creative writer, among the Chicanos, sometimes expresses the other side of this situation, the wistfulness and pain involved in being culturally divided. The poet Nephtalí de Leon uses an Anglo girl as a metaphor for all of Anglo-America, which, though perhaps finding the Chicano exotic, romantic, interesting, wants to remake him to its own image.

how sad it was to know you —
    oh White Dream of America!
to know that you would love me
    if I were not myself . . .

She told me that she liked me
    that she would know my life,
  but . . . she confessed —
    she feared my ways, my looks, my gaze,
      my simple love and my unworded thoughts . . .
i met her once
  i met her twice
  She said that i was strange
    and fascinating too . . .
      and . . .
       . . . Odd.[3]

Sometimes a Chicano poem, though not written with the sophisticated skill of an Alurista, might impress one through its simplicity and clarity of statement, as in the case of "I Too, America" by Leo Romero, in which the word "American" is conceived of in its broader, hemispheric sense:

> I too am an American
> and my eyes are brown and my hair
> obsidian black
> America from Spain
> Catholic America
> conquistadores
> Sur América
> mestizo Méjico
> Simón Bolivar los Incas
> los Aztecas
> Juárez y Villa y Zapata[4]

In prose, too, the Chicanos have been prolific, and in all the prose genres: the essay, the memoir, the drama, the short story, and the novel. Of the various memoirs and autobiographical accounts that exist, one of the most impressive is *Barrio Boy* by Ernesto Galarza. At the outbreak of the great revolution in Mexico that ousted Portfirio Díaz, beginning in 1910, Galarza was taken, as a small boy, from a little village in the state of Nayarit to Sacramento, California, where he had to make his way through the Anglo school system. He was, in fact, a brilliant student and has since become a distinguished professor of history in the United States. Though of an older generation, he understands and responds to the Chicano movement. The Chicanos, in their turn, think of him as an elder statesman, admire him, and turn to him for advice and inspiration. *Barrio Boy* is Galarza's account of his life from childhood through junior high school.

The epigraph to *Barrio Boy,* that Galarza has chosen from the writings of Henry Adams, reminds us that Galarza is a professional historian: "This was the journey he remembered. The actual journey may have been quite different . . . The memory was all that mattered." However, despite this disclaimer as to accuracy, Galarza has marshalled forth a wealth of detail and presented it in a style so lucid that one is convinced that the book is the work of a man with a highly retentive memory. Though, from a sociological point of view, the North American reader might find the latter part of the book, in which young Ernesto struggles with the problems of acculturation in Sacramento, the more engrossing, it is the first part of the book, "In A Mountain Village," that is the literary tour de force.

This part deals with the experience of growing up in Jalcocotán, a small and inaccessible village surrounded by jungle in a remote area of the Sierra Madres. The compression of life into a small and isolated village area resulted in an intensively interacting social microcosm. Almost nothing could occur out-of-doors that was not generally observed:

> Whatever happened in Jalcocotán had to happen on our street because there was no other place for it to happen. Two men, drunk with tequila, fought with machetes on the upper edge of the village until they were separated and led away by the neighbors. A hundred faces peered around doorways watching the fight. When someone died people joined the funeral procession as it passed by their doors. If a stranger arrived on horseback, the clopping of horseshoes on the rocks of the trail announced his arrival before he could turn into the street. Arriving in Jalco was like stepping on a stage. The spectators were already in the doorways, watching.[5]

Despite his youth and the isolation of his life experience, young Ernesto Galarza began to piece together in his own mind what was wrong with his Mexico. He was able to view, and to at least intuitively understand, the elements in microcosm which in macrocosm were gathering force and were to cause the greatest upheaval in Mexico's history, the revolution which was to destroy the Porfiriato, the thirty years of dictatorial reign by President Porfirio Díaz. The boy Ernesto was deferential, as befitted a *bién educado* youth in Jalcocotán, but, without intruding himself, he listened carefully to what the older people were saying:

> Old men in the village talked of the time they had worked on a hacienda as if they had served a sentence in prison or on a chain gang. They remembered capataces who had whipped them or cursed them fifty years before, and they still murmured a phrase: "Algún día me la pagan." There were a hundred blood debts of this kind in Jalcocotán, Doña Esther said, thousands of them in all the villages of the Sierra Madre, and millions in all the pueblos of Mexico.
> "Algún día me la pagan."
> "Tía, what does that mean?" I asked her more than once. She always sent me to my mother with the question. Her answer was: "It means that somebody owes him something."
> "But what does somebody owe him?"
> The anger and the foreboding in "algún día me la pagan" was in my mother's voice: "Something that hurts." She did not explain, just as she would not tell me why Catalino the bandit hated the *rurales* and shot so many of them.
> Guessing at what people meant, I came to *feel* certain words rather than to *know* them. They were words which came from the lips of the *jalcocotecanos* with an accent of suspicion, of fear, and of hatred. These words were *los rurales*, the *jefe político*, the *señor gobernador, las autoridades, el gobierno*. When a stranger rode into Jalco, people stopped talking. Every detail about him and his horse was observed for a clue to to whether he was one of the *autoridades*.

> It was the same with all outsiders. They always came asking questions, which the *jalcocotecanos* answered politely but roundabout. For me the world began to divide itself into two kinds of people — the men on horseback and the men who walked.[6]

In his introduction to *Barrio Boy,* Ernesto Galarza declares that the book had its beginnings in the anecdotes that he told his wife and daughters about his early life. The finished work still retains something of the intimacy of the anecdotal manner, but in its clarity and sureness of style and in the reflections that accompany the narration of events the book bespeaks the life of intellectual exercise and discipline which lies behind it.

In contrast to the calmly reminiscent mood of such personal accounts as *Barrio Boy,* there emerged another genre of Chicano literature which was literally forged, during the 1960s, in the heat of social battles, particularly during the critical and now famous strike organized by the United Farm Workers under the leadership of Cesar Chávez against the grape ranchers in Delano, California. The Teatro Campesino (Peasant's Theater), founded by the young playwright Luis Miguel Valdez, saw itself as being engaged primarily not in dramaturgy but in social action. It was viewed as a form of communication to the oppressed — not about them.

At first the short skits, actos, were matters of spontaneous improvisations, sometimes performed in the back of an open truck which acted as a moving stage. The director would suggest a basic situation which needed explanation to the strikers and their sympathizers. Signs explaining a person's role would be hung on anyone who would take one. There would be *Esquirol,* strikebreaker; *Patroncito,* the boss; *Huelgista,* striker; and *Contratista,* labor contractor. The volunteers with their signs hanging on them would then move into their act, thinking up their lines as they went along. The dialogue fluctuated between English and Spanish, and there was much use of gesticulation to overcome language problems. Though much of the rhetoric was impassioned, there was also a good deal of slapstick humor. Farm workers would laugh at the images of a harsh reality which were being presented to them through the medium of a comic exaggeration. This was drama as social instrument. At Delano it had the immediate purpose of organizing the farm workers. Such theater is not, in the more conventional sense, dramatic literature, but it has ancient precedent in the medieval morality plays by which the church sought to bring its message to the people.

Although the actos performed at Delano were at first spontaneous, later a small group of workers under the direction of Miguel Valdez would meet at night, after picketing all day, and work at developing scripts for the acts. In this way began the repertoire of the Teatro Campesino, which now began to move about, giving performances not only to workers' groups but at the universities.

The example of the Teatro Campesino soon gave rise to other Chicano theater groups which took names like Teatro del Pueblo or Teatro Libertad. Valdez has been helpful in assisting some of these groups in their early stages and in sharing script material with them. Most of the groups were soon on their own, however, developing their own materials.

In time, the teatros began to broaden their subject matter to cover the wider range of Chicano social and cultural interests. While some of the plays remained strictly didactic, others began to put more emphasis upon entertainment, particularly through humor — although the didactic element, at least by implication, usually remained. A brief examination of some of the plays developed and produced by the Teatro de la Esperanza (Theater of Hope) of Santa Barbara, one of the more ingenious of the groups, will serve to exemplify the directions being taken by Chicano theater. This teatro has its own theater building and plays to general audiences, including many students.

*La Bolsa Negra,* The Black Briefcase, by Frank Ramírez, is an essentially didactic play. It is something of a Chicano version of Chaucer's "Pardoner's Tale," although the ending is different. A group of Chicanos, wandering through a desolate area of the barrio, find — amidst the ashcans — a black briefcase full of money. In the first flush of joy, they agree to share the money equally. However, "El Espíritu Deseoso," The Spirit of Greed, appears and appeals to their individual avarice. They soon fall out and begin to fight among themselves. At the last minute, their sense of "Chicanismo" rallies them. They come to their senses and fall upon "El Espíritu Deseoso." They then turn to the audience and address it on the necessity of being unselfish, of uniting, and, for those Chicanos who achieve professional success, the necessity of coming back to the barrio and of using their skills for the needs and the advancement of La Raza.

*Brujerías,* Bewitchings, by Roderigo Duarte-Clark, also has a didactic purpose, but the play is, at the same time, heavily laced with humor. It is basically a satire aimed at the superstitions of the barrio. "El Espíritu de la Superstición," The Spirit of Superstition, rises up behind the bed of the old couple, Don Rafael and Doña Petra. The Spirit begins to address the audience in Spanish, but suddenly breaks off: "Oh! But how stupid of me! I forgot that there are some in the audience who do not speak Spanish: The Culturally Deprived!!! Ha! Ha! Ha! Bueno pues, como dicen los Gavachos [Anglos]: "Sorry Charlie! . . ."[7] Then follows a thoroughly comical treatment of belief in witches and in the Church's dealing in holy water for sale. The dialogue is in a mixture of Spanish and mispronounced, ungrammatical English, and in the course of the action the idiosyncracies of the barrio Chicanos are good-humoredly satirized.

In another play, *Pánfila La Curandera,* the dealer in folk or magic cures, la curandera, is not satirized as an example of superstition, but rather lauded as a figure embodying the authentic culture of the barrio, as against the artificialities of Middle Class American life. In this play, based on an idea by Antonio López, we are taken into the middle class household of Mr. and Mrs. Fatcat, who have a little girl who is very ill and who has not been responding to the treatment of the family doctor. Rosita, the Chicano maid, while not liking her employers, is fond of the little girl and worried about her. She brings Pánfila, the curandera, into the house while the family is away at the doctor's. There is a highly amusing scene in which Pánfila, in rich Chicano dialect, exclaims over the sumptuous furnishings of the apartment. Rosita informs Pánfila that, though the Fatcats are rich, they are also extremely stingy — as exemplified by the salary they pay her. The Fatcats arrive, even more discouraged over the condition of their daughter. Though Rosita tries to hide Pánfila, she is discovered at length — much to the horror of the Fatcats. There follow a number of demeaning remarks on their part about barrio customs, but it finally occurs to Mr. Fatcat that a curandera is considerably cheaper than an American doctor. Why not give Pánfila a try! The curandera summons up the wisdom of her folk medicine, and the child is cured — much to the vindication of barrio culture.

While Chicano drama, though it has been broadening its range in theme and technique, continues to put considerable emphasis upon its role as teacher of social awareness, the short story in Chicano literature has been, from the beginning, a freer form. Though it has not escaped some of the literary liabilities of "cause writing," it has, as a genre, been much more responsive to the aesthetic criteria of literary art. An example of a well-realized story about Chicano life in California is *The Visit* by Nick Vaca. It centers about a visit made by a young man, Ralph, to his sick father. On his way, Ralph congratulates himself on being the only one of twelve children who still sees the old man. He reflects, in a maudlin way, on how he would like an opportunity to give his right arm for his father, Don Pedro. During the visit they drink and talk about the Mexican revolution. After several drinks, the father, who has for years boasted about his role in the revolution, admits that he, after one year, ran out on the revolution and escaped to the States. Later, the father, who has been ill for some time and is incapacitated, urges Ralph to take him to the doctor. The son is evasive but finally says he will. In vain the father tries to get Ralph to commit himself on a day and time. Ralph finally leaves, somewhat drunk, still wondering if he will ever have the opportunity to give his right arm for his father. The author appears to be making an implied parallel between Don Pedro's having run out on a revolution, which he then glorified consistently in terms of his own role, and Ralph's refusing to extend real assistance to his father while indulging in glory dreams of giving his right arm for the old man. The story combines good psychological analysis with effective narrative writing. There is no effort at prettying up the face of La Raza.

In quite a different vein is a superbly written story by Miguel Méndez. "Tata Casehua" has nothing to do with the Chicano movement in the United States but rather is centered in the life of the Yaqui Indians of Sonora. The story has been published in the original Spanish together with an English translation by Octavio Romano in *El Espejo, Selected Mexican-American Literature*. It makes effective use of stream of consciousness techniques and of fantasy and conjures up an ancient mythic world. Yet at the same time there are elements of modern race consciousness and of class conflict. Ironically, the enemy in this case is the Mexican of Sonora, who regards the Yaqui as an inferior, exploits him, and makes no effort to understand his culture.

Texas, where tensions between Chicanos and Anglos are perhaps most acute, has been the locale for a good deal of Chicano writing. A story by Daniel Garza from Sequin, Texas, deals with the subject of haircuts. In subtlety "Everybody Knows Tobie" ranks with Ring Lardner's famous story on the same theme. Indeed, Garza makes a similar use of point of view in his story. The first person narrator, Joey, is unaware, in his boyish innocence, of the deeper and more sinister implications of the events he tells us about, implications which we as readers are intended to comprehend. The thirteen-year-old Joey is the younger brother of Tobie, an energetic and appealing young Chicano who has won the approval of the Anglos in their Texas town by delivering newspapers with efficiency and extra service. Tobie can even get his hair cut by Mr. Brewer, the Anglo town barber, who will usually not cut the hair of Mexicans, especially of the Mexicans and Chicanos who flock to the town in September and October to work in the cotton harvest. Tobie convinces Joey that he too should go to Mr. Brewer for his haircut. All he needs to do is to tell Mr. Brewer that he is Tobie's brother. Joey finally acts on this suggestion. He takes a seat in the barbershop and starts waiting. The Anglo customers look at him and begin leaving, muttering excuses. When it is his turn to take the chair, Joey is told, not unkindly but definitely, that he will have to go to Mr. López's barbershop for his haircut. Joey is so upset that he forgets to tell Mr. Brewer that he is Tobie's brother. He slinks out, utterly humiliated.

While he is sitting on a curb in an alley where he has left his bike, a middle-aged cotton picker, noticing his dejection, comes up to him:

> He asked, "Que pasó, Chamaco?"
> "Nada," I answered.
> "Maybe the cotton has not been good for you this year."
> "No, *señor*. I live here in town."
> And then the Chicano said, "Chico, I mistook you for one of us."
> Suddenly the Chicano became less interested in me and walked away unconcerned.
> I could not have told him that I had tried for a haircut at the Gringo's because he would have laughed at me and called me a *pocho*, a Chicano who prefers Gringo ways.[8]

By early November all of the cotton pickers have left for South Texas or Mexico. Tobie decides to quit his newspaper route for a better paying job, and Joey takes over the route. When he delivers the paper to Mr. Brewer, the barber, Brewer finds out that Joey is Tobie's brother and apologizes for the earlier incident. From now on, Joey is assured, he can go to Brewer's for his haircuts. Joey is now in high spirits and reflects upon the past in a very different mood:

> Those incidents which had happened to me during the cotton harvest in my town: Mr. Brewer sending me to Mr. López's for the haircut, and the Chicano cotton picker avoiding me after discovering that I was not one of his people, and the Gringo customers leaving Mr. Brewer's barbershop because of me; all seemed so insignificant. And now I felt that delivering the *Daily News* to the businessmen had given me a place among them, and all because of the fact that everybody in my town knew Tobie.[9]

At first reading, this story, written with admirable clarity and with persuasive dialogue, might seem to be a simple recounting of a humiliating experience and of its happy aftermath. But in fact the story effectively reenacts typical events which reveal the complexity of the life situation of a Mexican-American living in a small, Anglo-dominated community. Not only is this situation complex, it is basically untenable. What gives the story its poignant twist is that young Joey has not yet faced up to the facts of his life. It has not yet dawned on him that his life in "my town" is lived at the sufferance of the Anglos and that his success will be measured by the degree to which he has trimmed his own life style to their ways, as his popular brother has already so deftly done. To gain this success Joey must — as he seems already in his heart to have done — deny the roots of his own culture, represented by the Chicano cotton picker, who has already rejected him. Furthermore, the sufferance of the Anglo community might again be suddenly pulled away from him, as it was when Brewer evicted him from the barbershop, should he ever because of his actions, or maybe even his mere appearance, be again confused with those others.

The position of the Mexican-American who is a sell-out, "vendido," to the Anglo community has been treated often, and sometimes quite stridently in Chicano literature. But the treatment which Garza gives the theme in "Everybody Knows Tobie" is the more effective because the story is genuinely a work of literary art in which Joey is not just a person with a label but a boy who has suffered and will probably suffer again.

The genre in which Chicano literature has had its most pronounced development is that of the novel. Though Chicano novelists have dealt strongly, in some of their works, with social issues and have felt personally allied to the Chicano movement, they have allowed themselves a good measure of freedom in choice of theme and have been definitely concerned with the novel as an art form. The Texan writer, Tomás Rivera, has put it this way: "I believe that the most important thing for art and literature is to liberate itself from dogmas and to express freely not only the suffering, the injustice, but rather the totality of the Chicano."[10] In seeking to express this totality, the Chicano novel has ranged not only thematically but geographically. The reader of the Chicano novels comes to understand that the Mexican-American is not a single entity but rather his numbers are deployed over a vast region and he varies culturally from California through Arizona to Texas, and markedly so in New Mexico and southern Colorado.

The earliest novel that is generally listed with Chicano fiction is actually a transitional work. *Pocho* by José Antonio Villareal was published in 1959, before the launching of the Chicano movement. Furthermore, its action dates even farther back, to the period before and during World War II. For these reasons the book provides interesting points of comparison between earlier and later Mexican-American attitudes. We are given a view of the Pachucos of World-War-II fame, and it becomes clear that those exotically assertive types were the forerunners of certain kinds of Chicanos, particularly the *bato loco,* crazy guy, of contemporary Los Angeles.

The word *Pocho* is the generally derisive term used by Mexicans to refer to Mexican-Americans, their culture, or their language. The novel is a sensitively inward book rather than a socially panoramic one in its principal concerns, and yet we are introduced to a considerable variety of people. Richard Rubio, the central figure of the novel, is the son of Juan Rubio, an ex-colonel in Pancho Villa's army. Juan has to flee to El Paso because of a shoot-out in Ciudad Juarez. He eventually settles with his family in Santa Clara, California, and works in the fruit harvests. Unlike later fruit pickers in Chicano fiction, Juan is not desperately poor, so the son, Richard, grows up in at least minimally comfortable circumstances. He is the only boy in a family of five girls. Progressively he grows to be introspective and becomes a great reader as he moves into adolescence. Despite a considerable detachment of nature, he is intensely interested in experience and seeks it out. Unlike the Chicanos who tend to look to each other for companionship, Richard cultivates a wide range of friendships among Anglos, Mexican-Americans, Spanish, Portuguese, Italian, and Japanese. It is from a Portuguese immigrant of an aristocratic background that he is introduced to formal philosophical thought. Just before World War II, now grown into manhood, he enters a group of Pachucos and comes to understand and respect them, recognizing that their bravado is the result of being between two worlds and belonging to neither.

Richard Rubio witnesses the deterioration of his family and ponders it. When his mother begins to assert a sense of emancipation from the traditional Mexican conception of the woman's position, his father deserts her and marries a pretty young girl just up from Mexico, who is very traditional. The girls of the family are thoroughly Americanized and are beginning to marry and move out. Since he plans to enter the navy, Richard knows that his mother will soon be all alone. Surveying the situation, Richard becomes rebellious against the impositions of any culture, being totally unwilling to submit to either traditional Mexican culture or American, chamber-of-commerce, business culture. Instead, he resolves to discover an intensely personal identity.

It is interesting to speculate as to how Richard Rubio would have reacted to the current Chicano scene. Quite possibly the Chicano movement, having rejected both traditional Mexican culture and Anglo culture to form its own culture synthesis, might have provided a solution for him. The Pachucos, though he sympathized with them, did not satisfy him for long. In their showy exhibitionism, they had not developed a truly political, social, and cultural side to their movement as did the Chicanos later. The Chicanos might have rescued Richard Rubio from the isolation of withdrawal into himself.

With the publication of *The Plum Plum Pickers* in 1969, the Chicano novel proper comes into being, although one might quibble that the author, Raymond Barrio, a Spanish-American from New Jersey, is not truly a Chicano. However, he is married to a Mexican wife, calls his children Chicanos, and runs a bilingual household in California. More importantly, the plum pickers in the fields of Santa Clara are beginning to hear, in the novel, about the strike at Delano, directed by Cesar Chávez. The novel presents the beginnings of what later is to be called Chicano consciousness. A final reason for accepting *The Plum Plum Pickers* as a Chicano novel is that the Chicanos themselves consider it to be one.

Laid in the period before unionization on the land, the novel is a chronicle of the abuses suffered by Chicano fruit and cotton pickers in California. Many of the scenes take place in a dusty compound in Santa Clara where the dilapidated shanties of the workers stand in rows. The compound is presided over by the frumpy, seedy, flabby, and basically cowardly Mr. Quill. Though a weakling himself, he is the medium through which the power of Mr. Turner, the boss grower, flows. Therefore, with impunity, he can lay it on the Chicano workers and their families brutally and derive from his cruelty a vicarious sense of power. At the end of the novel, Quill is found in the early morning, hanging from the gallows tree. He has taken the place of the dummy that has hung there for years as an expression of Mr. Turner's Western buff whimsy.

Though the *Plum Plum Pickers* is basically a proletarian novel, Barrio is also interested in aspects of the Chicanos other than their oppressed economic and social condition. In various ways he examines the cultural relations between the Chicanos and the people about them. For example, Lupe Gutiérrez, hard working wife of a much exploited fruit picker and devoted mother, finds out something, shocking to her, about her neighbors the Jonsons. Jonson is a hulking, alcoholic Swede who has been reduced to the level of fruit picker. Some years ago, Lupe is told, Mrs. Jonson gave birth by herself to a baby whose father was not Jonson. The couple agreed to throw the baby out into the garbage to die. This tale gives a wrench to her basic maternal instinct:

> Lupe was horrified.
> She'd never heard of such a terrible thing before. She couldn't imagine its being true. It was an unimaginable, unforgivable act, entirely beyond her mental capacity to understand. How could a woman give up her natural baby? Whatever the provocation? Even dumb beasts fight to the death to protect their young. What kind of unspeakable beings were these people? I'd die first, she whispered, crossing herself...... Where was the love? Was there no horror, no sin these gueros would not commit? No crime?[11]

In another passage, a young Chicana, Margarita Delgado, is pondering a situation which constantly appears as a dilemma in Chicano life and literature:

> Still, there were times she couldn't help feeling she didn't belong, even though she had been born right here in Santa Clara, an American born, a citizen by birth. What good was it? What was

the good of being born a perfectly good, honest, private, legal citizen of the United States of America if everyone was going to snarl Mexican to your face like it was some hateful word? Where did she belong then? Back in her mother's home town? In her father's? In Salpinango? In Guadalajara? Would they send her back there? But what if she wasn't from there, from any of those places either? What then? She didn't belong there, in old Mexico, either.[12]

The fruit pickers of the novel, whose heroism consists in their capacity to endure and even wrench moments of wild enjoyment out of a grinding lot, never succeed in materially improving their situation. But one of the toughest of them, Manuel Gutiérrez, experiences a significant moral triumph, which is an augury of things to come. Gutiérrez has been recruited by the *contradista,* contractor, Roberto Morales, a prosperous, rotund, and cunning agent of the growers. Gutiérrez and his co-workers spend an exhausting day picking buckets of apricots. At the end of the day they are lined up with their buckets to receive their pay. Morales at this point almost deprecatingly tells them that he is going to have to take his cut from each man's pay, a known practice but an illegal procedure. Manuel rebels and kicks over the last bucket he had picked. While Morales rages, he kicks over another. The other workers, to the astonishment of Morales, stand behind their buckets, threatening to kick them over also. Morales backs down, saying "I shall take nothing this time." Manuel Gutiérrez has made a powerful discovery, which gives him something in common with don Gaspar, the first Spaniard to explore and lay claim to that area of California. Barrio recounts Manuel's reaction to his own triumph and proclaims its significance:

> Manuel felt a thrill of power course through his nerves.
> He had never won anything before. He would have to pay for this, for his defiance, somehow, again, later. But he had shown defiance. He had salvaged his money savagely and he had earned respect from his fellow slaves. The gringo hijos de la chingada would never know of this little incident, and would probably be surprised, and perhaps even a little mortified, for a few minutes. But they wouldn't give a damn. It was bread, pan y tortillas out of his children's mouths. But they still wouldn't give a single damn. Manuel had wrenched Morales' greedy fingers away and removed a fat slug of a purse from his sticky grasp. And in his slow way, in his stupid, accidental, dangerous way, Manuel had made an extravagant discovery, as don Gaspar had also made two centuries before, in almost exactly the same spot. And that was — that a man counted for something. For men, Manuel dimly suspected, are built for something more important and less trifling than the mere gathering of prunes and apricots, hour upon hour, decade upon decade, insensibly, mechanically, antlike. Men are built to experience a certain sense of honor and pride.
> Or else they are dead before they die.[13]

Following closely upon *The Plum Plum Pickers* came the novel *Chicano* by Richard Vásquez, 1970. The scene has changed from rural California to metropolitan Los Angeles. *Chicano* has been criticized for cluttering up its pages with a swarm of characters while not achieving individual characterization in depth. The novel is indeed ambitious in its scope, beginning in Sonora at the time of the Mexican Revolution and proceeding through several generations of Mexican-American families to the Los Angeles of our day. It is apparent that the author's interest is not in the close and detailed portrayal of individual characters but rather in social documentation, and this latter is richly achieved. A reader with little prior knowledge of the Chicanos of Los Angeles will come away from the novel greatly informed. Furthermore, Vásquez has that first requisite gift of the novelist, the power of invention. He handles complex plotting with considerable skill. Though the theme of the exploitation of the Chicano is there, the Mexican-American characters in the novel are not idealized but very realistically portrayed.

One of the valuable aspects of the book is that the reader is able to learn how the Chicano feels about traits of his character that have been criticized by outsiders. For example, an Anglo character in the novel is horrified to discover that Chicanos nickname friends and associates according to their physical deformities. Thus there are people who are called to their faces *Cojo* (cripple), *Jorobado* (hunchback), *Cacarizo* (scarface), and *Poca Luz* (little light — thus, mentally retarded). On this subject, the young Chicana, Mariana Sandoval, says to her Anglo boyfriend: " 'Why not? They're very aware of it. Much more so than anybody else, in fact. I think if you call them that, then pretty soon it really doesn't matter any more. It's much less cruel than pretending somebody who's different is really the same. Like you people do.' "[14]

There is one important aspect of the plot where, perhaps, the author's desire to emphasize the theme of exploitation has resulted in rather arbitrary characterization. David Stiger, a university student and sociology major, is portrayed as being deeply in love with the beautiful Mariana Sandoval. Though attending a university in Los Angeles, he is from a wealthy and socially prominent family in the Middle West. Stiger gets Mariana pregnant. When he learns of her condition, he panics and decides that she will be socially unacceptable back home. Though he has withdrawn his love, he pressures her into an illegal abortion, promising marriage. The operation results in a serious infection, and Mariana dies, abandoned by her lover, in a county hospital. In view of the kind of young men found on campuses these days, especially majors in the social sciences, David Stiger comes through as something of a stereotype from the past.

With the work of Tomás Rivera of Texas, the Chicano novel moves in the direction of technical experimentation. "... *and the earth did not part* is a loosely knit and highly subjective novel. As in Sherwood Anderson's *Winesburg, Ohio,* a single consciousness is used to bind together disparate narrative matter. And yet, despite this emphasis upon personal reactions, the reader is always aware of the cultural framework in which events transpire. To secure this context, the author makes an ingenious use of epigraphs. Before a chapter which is going to deal with a primarily inward happening in terms of the narrator's experience, an epigraph will be placed which recounts an external event in the narrator's life. The two will have no episodic relationship with each other. However, in a manner which displays considerable literary and intellectual finesse, the one will complement the other to produce a larger framework of related associations. Thus, by means of this objective-subjective treatment, the sense of a life experience within a given culture is enlarged.

However, the world of the novel is not enclosed within Chicano culture. The series of dramatic commentaries, which the chapters in fact consist of, are divided between confrontations within Chicano culture and confrontations between the Chicano narrator and an Anglo world perceived as alien and hostile. The element of violence in Mexican life, commented on so frequently by Anglo-American writers, is here recounted as seen from within the culture. In a chapter called "His Hand in His Pocket," the narrator is a school boy. So that he can be nearer to his school, he is sent by his father to board in a house owned by a niggardly couple, Don Laito and Doña Boni. Though his father is paying for his board, the narrator is kept underfed and is made to do yard work. Once, with no explanation, he is made to dig a square hole. A "wetback," smelling of cheap perfume, has been coming with some regularity to the house. The narrator learns that he has been using Doña Boni as a whore, with her husband's consent. This man is later murdered and robbed by Don Laito. The narrator is made to drag the body into the square hole and refill it. He is told by the couple that if he doesn't keep quiet, they will call the police and accuse him of the crime. Later, when the narrator is back home, Don Laito comes to visit his father. He gives the narrator a ring which the narrator remembers had belonged to the wetback. He does not dare to not wear the ring, but from then on, when he sees anyone approaching, he puts his hand in his pocket. This grisly tale serves to exemplify the type of assault upon the psyche that a young boy might have to endure growing up in the barrio.

A theme which appears in the work of several of the Chicano writers is that of self-liberation from the authority and dogma of the Catholic Church. Perhaps this is a reflection, on an individual basis, of the historical struggle between church and state in Mexico. The theme is treated in several ways by Rivera in his novel and in fact accounts for the title of the book. In the chapter "It Was a Silvery Night," the young narrator creeps out to the woods at midnight to summon the Devil. When the Devil does not answer the summons, the narrator feels a great sense of liberation. He reasons that if there is no Devil, then. . . . In the chapter that bears the same title as the book, the narrator has been told by his mother, while he was questioning the desperate lot of the Chicano field workers, that if he cursed God, the earth would part and he would be swallowed. After both his father and his nine-year-old brother suffered sunstroke while working in the fields, the narrator cursed God. ". . . and the earth had not parted . . . and for the first time he felt himself capable of doing and undoing whatever he chose."[15]

Rivera uses several episodes that exemplify conflicts between the Chicanos and the Anglo society that surrounds them. In a chapter reminiscent of Garza's story about haircuts, the narrator goes into a barbershop to have a haircut before the movie show started. He thinks at first that his having to wait is due to the fact that the barbers are busy. However, a little later he is abruptly told to get out. He leaves the shop but stays by the theater waiting for the show to start. The barber steps out of his shop and tells him to get out of the neighborhood. The narrator leaves to get his father.

The chapter "It is Painful" is essentially an interior monologue. The young boy, son of fruit pickers, is in Utah for the first time. He reflects upon the embarrassment it has caused him when he had to strip for the school nurse and have his hair searched for lice. Later he is expelled from school because of a fight with Anglo students which was forced upon him. He cannot face his parents and his godfather, who are so proud of him and support his ambitions to become a telephone operator. Throughout the story occurs the painful refrain, as the young boy tries to both deceive and undeceive himself: "But maybe they didn't expel me, *sure they did,* maybe not, *of course they did.*"[16]

The bilingual and bicultural nature of Rivera's novel is emphasized by the fact that it appears in two language versions within the same volume. It was written first in Spanish with the title . . . *y no se lo tragó la tierra.* As the author explains in the preface, Spanish is his first language, and his creative energies discharge themselves much more readily when he is thinking and writing in his native tongue.

New Mexico is the locale of one of the most impressive of the Chicano novels, *Bless Me, Ultima* by Rudolfo Anaya, and it seems not only right but almost inevitable that a literary work of beauty, subtlety, and profundity, written by a native son, should arise from that area. It is almost as though the region had been storing up its ancient treasures all those years waiting for the right hand to touch it so as to yield them up. In New Mexico, not only has there been an established Hispanic settlement for four centuries, long enough to develop a deeply rooted folk culture, but, for ages preceding this settlement, there have been stabilized Indian communities which have been attending to the steady growth of complex forms of religion and art. Anaya was the man with the literary craft and cunning as well as the depth of spirit to tap those resources and remold them according to the designs of his own creation.

In *Bless Me, Ultima,* a basic plot serves to set in motion powerful forces whose meanings are expressed through the symbolism of folk practices and beliefs. The point of view of the novel is expressed through a first person narrator. Antonio Márez, the "I" of the book, is, by the end of the novel, ten years old. Since the novel concerns Tony's discoveries and growth, it contributes to that vigorous tradition in American literature, the initiation novel. Tony's parents come from two different but strong strains out of New Mexico's social history. The Márez are from the *llanos* (plains) and are *vaqueros* (cowboys) dating back to the unfenced era when the cattle were driven over huge distances. The name, with the word *mar* in it, dates back even further to the restless conquistadores. These *vaqueros,* a disappearing breed at the time of the book, represent freedom and mobility. Tony's father, Gabriel, is a frustrated man. Persuaded by his wife, he has moved to the small town of Guadalupe, New Mexico, for the children's sake and has taken a job on a highway gang. He has been bodily hemmed in, but his spirit rebels. Tony's mother is from the stable, agricultural Lunas, loving workers of the soil. But the first of the Lunas of the area was none other than the priest of the region, who fathered forth the clan, a situation which is both a source of pride and embarrassment to the Lunas. Tony's mother thinks that the Márez are shiftless vagrants and wants him to be a Luna and a priest, thus bringing back the tradition of learning to the Lunas. Tony is torn between his father's ideal of freedom and his mother's of stability and piety. Early in the book, Tony's mother, as an act of charity, invites Ultima, an old and homeless curandera, to live with the family. Ultima's presence in the house is to have immense consequences, and she is to be an important mentor to Tony.

There are four places in Guadalupe and in the nearby town of El Puerto which serve as constant points of reference: the church, the school, and Rosie's whorehouse in Guadalupe and Tenorio's saloon in El Puerto. These places, each with its cluster of significances, are played off against each other.

Like Hawthorne and Faulkner, Anaya draws upon folkloric elements to develop universal themes. As in Hawthorne's world, Anaya's is one of good and evil, with those forces being dressed out in deeply traditional forms. Also like Hawthorne, Anaya seems to be giving us a choice as to how literally to take accounts of witchcraft and magic. For example, Tony's father, talking about the curandera, says to Tony:

> "Ultima has sympathy for people, and it is so complete that with it she can touch their souls and cure them —"
> "That is her magic —"
> "Ay, and no greater magic can exist," my father nodded. "But in the end, magic is magic, and one does not explain it so easily."[17]

And surely there are elements in the book drawing upon practices of witchcraft and magic that are not easily explained. The three daughters of Tenorio Trementina, the saloon keeper, who are said to be witches, put a curse on Tony's uncle Lucas. He is brought back from the edge of death by Ultima's cures. Ultima counterattacks by using effigies against the three sisters. When they sicken and die, their father comes after Ultima with a gun. He does not succeed in shooting her, but he does shoot her guardian owl, which turns out to be, in effect, her soul. However one is to take Ultima's owl, aesthetically Anaya uses it to beautiful effect.

Aside from the skillful use of folkloric motifs, Anaya makes use of technical devices which the modern novel has been exploring. For example, he has managed dream sequences to telling effect. In one instance, Tony in his dream saw three of his friends who had died. He questioned them about God, heaven, and hell and got shattering replies. The dream ended in this fashion: "And as the three figures departed my pesadilla [nightmare] they cried out longingly. We live when you dream, Tony, we live only in your dreams —"[18]

Just as in Hawthorne's country village of Salem, Anaya's Guadalupe is a little town in which, beneath the daily happenings among ordinary folk, awesome moral and spiritual forces are grappling for ultimate power. The sense of this combat is sharpened by the deft use of contrast. Places with their differing connotations, as mentioned above, have been used to almost allegorical effect: the school, the church, the brothel, the saloon. As the action of the novel moves toward its climax, hilarity and terror are counterpoised in swift succession. Because of an unusually heavy snowstorm near Christmas time, the girls stay home from school, and only the boys, in their "macho" pride, show up. A nativity play has been scheduled for that day, and the school teacher, Miss Violet, decides that the boys must take the girls' parts. The boys are horrified and attempt to resist, but Miss Violet is insistent. "Bones" perches on a beam over the stage and refuses to come down. Abel says he has to "pee." Miss

Violet, suspecting subterfuge, will not let him leave. He quietly lets go on the stage. "Horse" is made to be the Virgin, much to the taunting of his friends. Tony, not resisting, takes the role of Joseph. One of the kings slips on Abel's "pee." "Bones," distracted, comes hurtling down from the beam. "Horse" slugs Florence (a boy — Florencio in Spanish) when Florence in a loud voice says to him, while handing a gift, "For the Virgin." The play ends in pandemonium. However, as Tony starts to make his way home, things take a sinister turn. The snow, which has been falling steadily, has created such drifts that Tony feels the beginning of fear as he thinks of the long way home. Meanwhile other things have been happening. Tenorio, the saloon keeper, who has been drinking throughout the day to build up his courage, takes his gun and heads for the Márez house, determined to kill Ultima for the bewitchment of his daughters. The lumbering and taciturn Narciso, loyal friend of the Márez family, who has been hearing Tenorio's threats all day, decides to warn Ultima. He first goes to Rosie's whorehouse to get the assistance of Tony's older brother, who, not wanting to be deflected from his pleasures, will not take Narciso seriously. Narciso plunges alone through the snowstorm. When he approaches the Márez home, Tenorio is already there and shoots him to death from ambush. Tony, exhausted, arrives home to witness his father, in turn, shoot Tenorio. Ultima, her guardian owl having been shot by Tenorio, has not long to live.

Though elements in the realm of spirit abound in the novel, they do not, on the whole, take an orthodox form. Tony's mother, to be sure, is very pious. His father is much less so, and the Márez men are rumored to be "free thinkers." This difference in attitudes toward religion between men and women is typical of Latinity. In fact Tony, as with the narrator in ". . . and the earth did not part," undergoes a process of liberating himself from the authority of the church. Father Byrnes, the priest in Gaudalupe, is seen by Tony as a threatening figure. His hell-fire sermon to the children studying for First Communion resembles that in Joyce's *Portrait of the Artist as a Young Man* and has a similar function. As in much literature about Mexican culture, folk religion, in this novel, is pitted against formal religion. When Ultima is called in at the last minute to cure Tony's Uncle Lucas, Tony asks her:

> "But why didn't they call you sooner?" . . .
> "The church would not allow your grandfather to let me use my powers. The church was afraid that —" She did not finish, but I knew what she would have said. The priest at El Puerto did not want the people to place much faith in the powers of la curandera. He wanted the mercy and faith of the church to be the villagers' only guiding light.[19]

In fact, Ultima, in her deep knowledge and love of plants and in her skillful use of herbal medicine, is something of an earth goddess and represents to Tony a liberating alternative to the "jealous God" of the Catholic church. Ultima's sense of nature, perhaps drawn from the Indian heritage, resembles that of the American transcendentalists, particularly Thoreau. Tony says of Ultima: "She taught me to listen to the mystery of the groaning earth and to feel complete in the fulfillment of its time. My soul grew under her careful guidance. I had been afraid of the awful *presence* of the river, but through her I learned that my spirit shared in the spirit of all things."[20]

There is another mysterious force that Tony has sought out, and this influence comes explicitly from the Indian heritage. Tony's hermitic friend Cico, after much inducement, takes him to the secret pool which is the haunt of the giant Golden Carp whose legend goes back to the Indians. The sacred fish acts as another pagan reenforcement to Tony's revolt against orthodoxy. If the young Tony of *Bless Me, Ultima* is in some respects the author himself preparing to be a writer, one might say that by the end of the book Tony is on the way to resolving the problem of his heritage by gaining the freedom of the Márez and the intellectualism of the Lunas.

Another Chicano novel which equally employs experimental methods has the distinction of existing only in a Spanish-language edition. *Peregrinos de Aztlán* (Pilgrims of Aztlán) by Miguel Méndez presents the reader with a great sweep of the border country on both sides of the line and introduces him to a wide variety of characters: general Americans, Chicanos, Mexicans, and the Yaqui Indians, representing various levels of society. The Spanish used also varies as we are given different levels of expression. There is the clear, "standard" Spanish of the passages of narration. There is the powerful poetic voice, Méndez's own, which resounds through memorable inscape passages, and there is, finally, the voice of the Chicanos themselves, faithfully recorded, with its sly inventiveness, its wryly humorous turn of phrase, its free-flowing use of obscenities, and its in-group coinage of a special vocabulary.

Although authorial commentary is given throughout the book, there is another center of consciousness used at critical points. This is the mind of the old Yaqui Indian, Loreto Maldonado, once formidable fighter for his "nation," now reduced to competing with children in a Mexican border town as a car washer, catering to American tourists. Loreto summons up the epical Yaqui past while the reader is being alternatingly introduced to corrupt, haughty, middle-class Mexicans who indulge themselves in the vices made available by a border town which resembles Tijuana, maintaining at the same time a disdainful aloofness from the masses of the wretchedly poor who surround them.

This Mexican middle class milieu is not only contrasted to Loreto's memories of the heroic Yaqui past but also to the Sonora desert itself, Loreto's former domain, which becomes a personage in its own right. In a memorable passage full of skeletal imagery, the reader is reminded that the desert was once covered by ocean but that the present Sonora desert has "robbed the sea of its once commanding presence while feigning the very majesty of its motions."[21]

The desert, of course, is no respecter of international boundaries and extends well into the American Southwest. As such it becomes the scene of a migration which is central to the themes of the novel. If the image of past heroism is that of the Yaquis, that of present heroism is the ordinary "wetback" headed, through the infernal desert, for the cotton and fruit fields of California and Arizona. Of the wetback and his kind, descended largely from Indian stock, Méndez writes: "From the south they came, reversing the route of their ancestors, in a pilgrimage without priests, without prophets, dragging along a history no longer even worth recounting, its tragedy now reduced to the repetitious, the commonplace."[22] There are passages in which the poor migrants mingle their voices, decrying their lot with rage, despair, or sometimes a humorous stoicism.

As the author takes us across the border into the American Southwest, he sets up another series of contrasts. Wetbacks and Chicano workers are compared to their American employers and exploiters. The successful Mexican-American entrepreneur who exploits Mexican migrants is personified in La Vieja, the Old One. She runs a chile-dog business, hires a number of wetbacks, pays them miserably, and lectures them sanctimoniously on how fortunate they are that she has rescued them from starvation. The Anglo-American bosses and authorities tend to run to a type: red faced, aseptic puritans who, on the one hand, are churchgoers and constant Bible readers and, on the other, are ruthless exploiters of their Mexican and Chicano workers.

As the author recounts the hardships of the migrants or takes us to Vietnam where a disillusioned Chicano, Frankie Pérez, dies a lonely death, he carries on his contrapuntal theme of the Yaqui past. For example the Vietnam War is compared to the historical struggle of the Yaquis to preserve their independence against the encroachments of the Spanish and Mexican governments, culminating in the great battles against the forces of the Mexican dictator Porfirio Díaz. During the great revolution that began in 1910, the Yaquis are cajoled by the revolutionaries into joining them in the battle for justice and freedom. The Yaquis fought with ferocious effectiveness only to find that, when the fighting was over, the revolution was betrayed from within.

Aside from Loreto Maldonado, there are other memorable Yaqui figures in the novel. There is Jesús de Belem, the Yaqui curandero, who performs miraculous cures without taking pay. His influence among the Yaquis becomes so strong that Mexican officials consider him dangerous and reenact another brutal version of the Christ story. They execute him by lashing him to a very spiny sahuaro cactus. Jesús de Belem forgives his executioners. Memorable too is the Yaqui soldier Rosario (Chayo) Cuamea who, by his ferocity, rose to be a colonel in the revolutionary armies. It is his fantasy that death is La Flaca — the Thin One — and that he is the impassioned pursuing lover. Colonel Cuamea, after the revolution, is spurned by his old comrades-in-arms, now grown rich, when he tries to reactivate them in the cause of a betrayed revolution. He has the final indignity of growing old and senile in furious frustration and poverty. His death is graphically described in terms of a passionate sexual union with the long sought for "la Flaca." Loreto Maldonado himself finally dies of hunger in the great squalor of a putrefying slum, in his box-like house made of corrugated metal sheets and old food cans whose labels display pictures of steaks and beans and other foods.

There is a scene toward the end of the novel in which Frankie Pérez's father, Pánfilo, is shown as grief-stricken over Frankie's death in the Vietnam War. A friend offers Pánfilo a drink from a bottle of tequila. Pánfilo grabs the bottle and gulps it compulsively. The result is that he experiences a sort of "trip" in which he feels himself as transformed into a great, black bird, flying over the deserts of the Southwest, peering down at the Chicanos as they experience various forms of injustice. Pánfilo is finally driven mad and is taken away in a straitjacket.

The novel ends in a mixture of voices, those of Mexicans who have immigrated to the United States and now cannot understand their Chicano children. An underlying voice supercedes these, declaring that the Chicanos will become a river of resistance. *Peregrinòs de Aztlán* is an unusual mixture of compelling, inward, poetic writing and broad satire tending toward caricature. At its best, particularly in those passages of poetic force which deal with the desert and with the Yaquis, passages which seem most congenial to the art of Miguel Méndez, *Peregrinos de Aztlán* is a deeply moving book.

With the publication of *The Road to Tamazunchale* by Ron Arias, the Chicano novel takes another step in the direction of literary experimentation. This is a non-political novel except, perhaps, by implication. As Tomás Rivera puts it in the Foreword to the novel, *The Road To Tamazunchale* deals with creative dying. Much of the "action" of the novel consists of the dream/vision interior life of the dying old man Fausto Tejada, a one-time bookseller from Los Angeles. The reader is shocked to suddenly find himself switched from modern Los Angeles to colonial Peru, but he soon realizes that he is entering Fausto's dream/

vision world and is sharing in the process of creative dying. Fausto's "travels" reflect the reading he has done when, because of his profession, he had access to many books. Obviously he has been a man of lively interests. He has had, evidently, a good deal of contact with wetbacks, mojados, in his life, and an index to his character is how he "treats" them in this last demi-world of his. He "opens" a deserted theater and puts on a show for them by which they witness — and also take part in — a bus trip that goes through Mexican towns, a show which demonstrates important aspects of their lives to them. Fausto has obviously been a man of compassion. He tells them that he wants to take them on the road to Tamazunchale — actually a town in the Sierras on the road to Mexico City — but we come to understand that the road to Tamazunchale is every man's road of life.

Sometimes aspects of Fausto's "travels" remain with him even when he knows that he is back in Los Angeles. For example, Marcellino, whom he "met" in vice-regal Peru insists on coming back to Los Angeles with Fausto. Marcellino's herd of alpacas are a nuisance on the Los Angeles freeways. We get to know Fausto's family and friends both within and without his fantasy world. There is Carmela, his niece, who takes good care of him with practical, undemonstrative devotion. Her "agringado" boyfriend insists upon being called Jesse, although his name is Jesús. He is something of a "square" but is treated with good-natured tolerance by the author. Then there is Fausto's young Chicano friend Mario, who has much of the *bato loco* in him. Flashily dressed and swaggering, he is full of Los Angeles Chicano "lingo." Though he is a "rip-off" artist, deft and brazen in his stealing, he is basically a loyal and helpful friend to Fausto. Cuca, the earthy midwife and curandera from Chihuahua, is a great raconteur whose stories would undoubtedly have been much appreciated by the Wife of Bath.

Fausto's "experiences" vary greatly in quality. They are sometimes exotic, as in his trip to Peru. Sometimes they are replays of episodes in his life, such as his trip to Mexico with his wife, Evangelina. She hated the dirty toilets. At the very end of his life, these fantasies have gotten so realistic that the reader must be alert to make distinctions. There is a scene in a book store — in fact a vision scene — in which Fausto and a number of his friends are picking up huge numbers of books for him. Two of his friends, Tiburcio and Smaldino, begin looking through an "illustrated sex manual." Tiburcio's wife tells him to come away because "it's pictures like that that give me babies."[23] Fausto's creative dying is the act of his final discharging of a rich nature. Surely Tomás Rivera is correct when he writes that "in this novel, Chicano Literature gains a most creative dimension."[24] This literature, from its crude beginnings, has come of age and is now revitalizing the literary scene in the Southwest.

CHAPTER ELEVEN

## The Southwest as a Literary Region: Local Color or Belles Lettres?

The American writers whose works have been examined in this book have not all, by any means, been regional writers. In fact a significant number of them are writers whose primary concerns have not been regional. Nevertheless, it is to be expected that the Southwestern area of the United States, which daily experiences the presence of Mexico would reflect most persistently the influence of Mexican culture in its literature. It is the purpose of this chapter to appraise the degree of significance of the regional literature of the Southwest and of the role that Mexican culture has played and might, in the future, be expected to play in this literature. Do the regional writers whose works have been considered singly in this book, in reference to images of Mexico, add up to a constellation of artists who have produced a literary expression commensurate to the possibilities of the region?

There is, in fact, a tantalizing quality about the Southwest considered as a literary region. With its varicolored fabric of story and lore, rich in so many ways that can stimulate the literary imagination, it seems, nevertheless, to promise more than it has yet been able to fulfill. "Our Weimar is ready, perhaps," wrote John Chapman referring to the University of Texas in its cultivation of regional material, "but Goethe is lagging."[1] This would seem to be true, at least in terms of the work of Anglo-American writers in the region. Certainly the area cannot be accused of failing to husband its resources. Publications such as *The New Mexico Quarterly, The Texas Quarterly, The Arizona Quarterly, Arizona and the West,* the *Southwest Review,* the *Publications of the Texas Folklore Society* have done an excellent job of garnering and presenting the folkloric material of the Southwest. More recently, *El Grito,* Quinto Sol Publications and others have been furnishing us with the latest examples or critiques of Chicano literature. And yet it seems that the breath of fire which converts tradition and lore into literary art has not touched this region as often or as strongly as might have been expected, although it might well be that Chicano and Amerind literature are ushering in a new era. Though there is disagreement on the literary accomplishments of the region, the discourse on the cultural expectations of

# The Southwest: Local Color or Belles Lettres 333

the Southwest is in itself interesting, and perhaps some readers might agree, now that the argumentation has subsided, that literary works have appeared which in some measure justify earlier hopes. Lawrence Clark Powell in the excellent introduction to his anthology *Southwest Classics* argues persuasively that important work has been done, and his selections would seem to support his argument. To Powell, one of the most important influences upon the literature of the region has been "the Southwest itself, the land and its climate and configurations of desert, mountains, rivers and skies. . . . If land has determined books, then have books also exalted land. Unions forceful and tender have been consummated between writers and a region as magnificent as any on earth."[2] Despite inroads of "progress," much of the geographical magnificence of the Southwest remains and can be expected to continue to exert an influence on literature. Another influence that remains is that of Mexico and its cultural extensions into the Southwest. As to this influence, one of the most prophetic voices that American literature has ever had has again proven to ring true.

In preparation for the celebration of the three hundred and thirty-third anniversary of the settlement of Santa Fé by the Spanish, officials of the city wrote to Walt Whitman asking him to send a poem in commemoration. Instead of sending a poem, Whitman wrote a letter, part of which is reproduced below, to "Messrs. Griffin, Martínez, Prince, and other Gentlemen at Santa Fé," dated Camden, July 20, 1883:

> We Americans have yet to really learn our own antecedents, and sort them, to unify them. They will be found ampler than has been supposed, and in widely different sources. Thus far, impress'd by New England writers and schoolmasters, we tacitly abandon ourselves to the notion that our United States have been fashion'd from the British Islands only, and essentially from a second England only – which is a very great mistake. Many leading traits for our future national personality, and some of the best ones, will certainly prove to have originated from other than British stock. As it is, the British and German, valuable as they are in the concrete, already threaten excess. Today, something outside of them, and to counterbalance them, is seriously needed. . . .
> 
> To that composite American identity of the future, Spanish character will supply some of the most needed parts. No stock shows a grander historic retrospect – grander in religiousness and loyalty, or for patriotism, courage, decorum, gravity and honor. (It is time to dismiss utterly the illusion-compound, half raw-head-and-bloody-bones and half Mysteries-of-Udolpho, inherited from the English writers of the past 200 years. It is time to realize – for it is certainly true – that there will not be found any more cruelty, tyranny, superstition, etc, in the *resume* of past Spanish history than in the corresponding resume of Anglo-Norman history. Nay, I think there will not be found so much.) . . .

> ... As to the Spanish stock of our Southwest, it is certain to me that we do not begin to appreciate the splendor and sterling value of its race element. Who knows but that element, like the course of some subterranean river, dipping invisibly for a hundred or two years, is now to emerge in broadest flow and permanent action?[3]

In 1887, the *New Orleans Picayune* wrote to Whitman asking him to send remembrances of his famed trip to New Orleans in 1848. In the course of his letter of reply, Whitman wrote: "I have an idea that there is much and of importance about the Latin race contributions to American nationality in the South and Southwest that will never be put with sympathetic understanding and tact on record."[4] Thus early in the discourse and from a distinguished quarter the claim was made that the Hispanic Southwest has not been given its due importance in the over-all scheme of American culture. The note has been sounded regularly ever since. Southwest regionalists have deplored the notion of American culture as having had its genesis solely in the Anglo-Saxon cultures of New England and Virginia, and of having unilaterally filled in the vacuum of the West. These regional claimants would substitute a pincer view of our culture with the Anglo-Saxon arm moving westward from the east coast and the Indo-Hispanic arm coming up from the south and west, the arms of the pincer joining with fruitful cultural effects in the American Southwest. That Connecticut Yankee turned passionate Hispanophile, Charles F. Lummis, wrote in 1891:

> I hope some day to see a real history of the United States; a history not written in a closet, from other one-sided affairs, but based on a knowledge of the breadth of our history, and a disposition to do it justice; a book which will realize that the early history of this wonderful country is not limited to a narrow strip on the Atlantic seaboard, but that it began in the great Southwest; and that before the oldest of the Pilgrim Fathers had been born swarthy Spanish heroes were colonizing what is now the United States; in their little corner of which they suffered for three hundred and fifty years such awful dangers and hardships as our Saxon forefathers did not dream of. I hope to see such a history, which will do justice to perhaps the most wonderful pioneers the world has ever produced; but it has not come yet. Why, there is not even one history which gives the correct date of the founding of Santa Fe, which was a Spanish city more than a decade before the landing at Plymouth Rock![5]

The authors of a book on the literary resources of the Southwest published in 1938 express themselves in a similar vein: "It is annoying to find American history and letters continually described as a single tradition with its genesis in the Mayflower compact and the Massachusetts Bay Psalm Book." They go on to mention the parallel development of exploration and settlement by the Spaniards in the Southwest ending the statement with the assertion that "Villagra's account of the heroic capture of Ácoma by Zaldivar and seventy men bears comparison with the scaling of the heights outside Quebec by Wolfe if one keeps all the circumstances in mind."[6]

This excoriating of New England and the East generally for having blinded the country to the wealth of the Hispanic tradition can be viewed somewhat ironically when it is remembered how saturated in Hispanic culture were many of the major literary figures of early New England and New York. Stanley T. Williams in his two-volume work *The Spanish Background of American Literature*[7] ably demonstrates that such august literary personages as Longfellow, Lowell, and Bryant were steeped in Spanish history and literature. When these names are added to those of such well-known Hispanophiles as Prescott, Ticknor, and Irving the total involvement adds up to almost an obsession and suggests that the Puritan soul craved something of Spain's pageantry and passion. To be sure, most of these writers were more interested in the Spanish peninsula itself than in Spain's extensions in the New World, but it is interesting to discover that Washington Irving had planned to write a major epic on the theme of the Conquest but graciously gave up the idea when he found out that Prescott had similar plans. In this affair the American reading public owes a debt to the generous spirit of Washington Irving. Bryant's Hispanic interests extended beyond the Peninsula to include Latin America, and his journals contain interesting commentaries on Cuba and Mexico. And yet in the main, educators and commentators ignored this aspect of the early American writers and emphasized their English ancestry and orientation; so there is some justice to the charge that America's cultural debt to Spain has been generally overlooked.

The first American writers who began to work the vein of Hispanic lore in the Southwest were outlanders. They far from satisfied Allen Tate's requirement for the regional writer that he must have absorbed the culture of the region along with his mother's milk. Yet one of the outlanders, Willa Cather, produced a finished work of literary art in *Death Comes for the Archbishop* from the raw materials of history, tradition and lore in the Southwest, an accomplishment which suggests that one need not have been nurtured on tortillas and beans to respond aesthetically and with comprehension to the indigenous culture of the region. But it must be admitted that most of the early discoverers of the Southwest for literature never lost the air of the perennial amateur, the enthusiast. Charles F. Lummis, the newspaperman, who came to the Southwest in the 1880's by way of Connecticut and the Middlewest, was a progenitor of the type of folk arts and crafts lover which was later to become so familiar in the neighborhood of Santa Fe and Taos We have accounts of him entertaining guests, mostly enthusiasts of Southwestern lore like himself, in his home in Los Angeles, surrounded by artifacts of Indian and Mexican design, dispensing liquor freely and regaling the company with versions of old Mexican folk songs which he had just discovered, accompanying himself on guitar, and singing Spanish lyrics in accents which remained obdurately Yankee. Yet despite the comic air of the wide-eyed collector, his work is not to be totally dismissed. Though much of his literary effort could be described as booster pieces, he produced some writing of merit. Some of the stories in *A New Mexico David* are written in clean, hard prose and show skill in descriptive narrative, and much of *The Land of Poco Tiempo* describing folkways in New Mexico is good reporting. Furthermore, the Southwest Museum in Los Angeles with its important storehouse of early Spanish and Mexican manuscripts of historical and folkloric interest and its examples of early Indian and Mexican crafts owes a great deal to his zeal as a collector.

Another outlander and early comer to the Southwest was Mary Austin. Her experiences growing up in a small town in Michigan are recorded in an autobiography, *Earth Horizon*,[8] which should be required reading for students of the psychology of the revolt from the village in American literature. Her revolt led her as a young woman to an early and unspoiled California. When she arrived in the Southwest, she knew that she had found the land of the heart's desire. After a few years in California, she settled in Santa Fe, which became her permanent home. She shared some of the traits of Charles F. Lummis and in fact was directly influenced by him, having been one of the "ardents" who frequented Lummis's soirées in Los Angeles. She outgrew Lummis, but she never quite outgrew the tendency to rhapsodize. Yet her sensibility was real, and at least two of her works dealing with Southwestern material, *One Smoke Stories*[9] and *The Land of Journey's Ending*,[10] are of permanent value. In *One Smoke Stories* she imposed a form upon herself which curbed the worst tendencies in her writing. When the Navajos told each other stories around the evening fire, they traditionally confined each story to the duration of one pipe smoke. As the bowls of Indian pipes are very small, the narrator had to come to the point of his tale quickly. Having adopted this Navajo convention of brevity in *One Smoke Stories,* Mary Austin produced a series of pithy and delightful tales about Indian and Mexican life in New Mexico.

However, Mary Austin's work is relevant to the present discussion principally because she as well as Lummis was a theorizer about the cultural potential of the Southwest. She was as much a champion of the pincer theory of American culture as was Lummis, and she looked forward to the rise of a new and fruitful culture in the Southwest as the result of cross-fertilization of the three main strains, Indian, Spanish and Anglo:

> Here in the Southwest, and up along the Western coast, where our blood-stream reaches its New-World journey's ending, it finds itself possessed with no effort, along with beauty and food — and power-producing natural resources, of a competent alphabet of cultural expression. Thus it gains so enormously over all other sections, where such notation is still to be produced, that one confidently predicts the rise there, within appreciable time, of the *next* great and fructifying world culture.
>
> It draws, this land of prophecy, from more than the region herein described, from all up the California coast to San Francisco, between the sea and the Sierras, from districts east of the Rio Grande toward Texas, from Chihuahua and Sonora of the South. But by virtue of its acceptance and use of aboriginal material as a medium of spiritual expression, it takes its dominant note from the place of the Sacred Mountains, from the place of our Ancients, the home of the Guardian of the Water Sources. Takes it, in point of time just so much in advance of other American provinces as goes to the development in them, of similar indigenous mediums of cultural expression.
>
> Three strains of comparative purity lie here in absorbing contact, the Indian, the Spanish, and the so-called Nordic-American, for by distance, by terror of vastness and raw surfaces, the more timorous, least adaptive elements of our population are strained out. Of these three the Spanish serves chiefly to molify temperamentally the aboriginal strain, so that in New Mexico and Arizona we approach nearest, in the New World, to the cultural beginnings which produced the glory that was Greece, the energetic blond engrafture on a dark, earth-nurtured race, in a land whose beauty takes the breath like pain.[11]

This kind of writing reminds one of the literary revival in Ireland in the days of its early inspiration, when the young Yeats would talk of the sparks that resulted from the mixing of the golden-haired Milesians with the dark and primitive Firbolg to create a new race and a new culture. It was in this indigenous Irish culture that he sought the basis of a great new art, utilizing to the full the folk memory of the people.

These high hopes existed before the *Playboy of the Western World* was stoned at the Abbey Theater and Sean O'Casey finally retired to England grumbling that his country had been taken over by the "broadcloth Irish," i.e. the bourgeois. The enthusiasts of the Southwest in a similar manner dreamed of a new culture and a new art, reared upon the ancient traditions and the aesthetic sensibility of the Indians and Mexicans as well as upon the folk culture of the unspoiled "Anglo" cattlemen. Mary Austin, when she wrote *The Land of Journeys' Ending* in 1924, had not reckoned on the stream, which was to become a deluge, of standardized American types from the East and especially the Middlewest which was pouring into California, Arizona, and New Mexico. The Chicago businessman or professional man who moved to Arizona to escape the winter winds blowing from Lake Michigan could hardly be classified as a pioneer facing up to the "terror of vastness and raw surfaces." But if Yeats, Synge, and Lady Gregory did not succeed in creating a literature which could be embraced and recognized by the people as their own, they continued their work, once disabused of naïve expectations, and produced literary art of worth and permanence, based on traditional material. The American South, which faces a situation of growing standardization similar to that of the Southwest, still has effective writers who can draw tellingly upon folklore and tradition. What is called for, evidently, is a conscious art that is unconcerned to discover, upon looking behind, that no one is following.

In certain respects, the development of literature in the Southwest has not followed Mary Austin's predictions. Perhaps she had not reckoned upon the emergence of important indigenous writers, the Chicanos and the Amerinds, who were, in significant ways, to mark the course of future writing in the Southwest. These writers, rather than seeking a cultural merging have insisted upon the preservation of a multi-cultural society in which Indian and Chicano cultures remain intact.

Mary Austin herself had, by 1929, second thoughts on the subject of the great "fructifying" culture which was to come into being of itself. In a symposium conducted by the *Southwest Review* in that year on the question of whether there really was a regional culture in the Southwest, she wrote: ". . . the country itself has everything to offer out of which competent regional cultures are built. The landscape is magnificent, the traditions rich and appealing. But I see everywhere too much disposition to overlay the tradition with complacencies of the present hour. . . ."[12] Yet these traditions, however overlaid by complacencies, could, in the right hands, provide material for literary art. Franklin Walker, in assessing the literary resources of California in mid-nineteenth century, wrote: "True belles lettres might still be wanting, but there were other media of expression — the emigrant's diary, the soldier's record, the journalist's chronicle, the traveler's account, and the evanescent and varied forms of folklore. These were both important and interesting; later they were to be used as bases for literary expression in its more conventional forms."[13] This source material still has much to yield to a literary talent capable of exploiting it to the limit of its possibilities. J. Frank Dobie has been sufficiently recognized for his tireless work in the field of Southwestern folklore but not to the extent deserved for the keenness of his literary sense. In his best work he has converted lore into art, while modestly disclaiming that he has had much of a hand in the final outcome. "These tales are not creations of mine," he wrote in the introduction to *Coronado's Children*. "They belong to the soil and to the people of the soil. Like all things that *belong*, they have their roots deep in the place of their being, deep too in the past. They are an outgrowth; they embody the geniuses of divergent races and peoples who even while fiercely opposing each other blended their traditions."[14] But the articulation in literary form of that which is deeply rooted in the spirit of a people, as Faulkner has demonstrated, can be the highest literary art. J. Frank Dobie is not Faulkner, but there is a great deal of literary cunning employed in the seemingly casual manner in which he weaves his folkloric strands into books which are organically whole. It would not be too difficult to defend the claim that Dobie's *Tongues of the Monte* is close to being the best book on Mexico ever produced by an Anglo-American writer.[15]

In a Texas which has been declared totally ruined by oil money and Cadillac culture, younger men, influenced by Dobie, have been continuing his work and are widely read, a situation which can only be understood in the light of one of the interesting phenomena of the modern Southwest. Despite the rapid transformation of its cities, this region, excluding California which has been radically altered by the influx from the East, maintains vast stretches of rural area which remain relatively unchanged. Easterners and Middlewesterners have poured into Houston, Dallas, Fort Worth, Albuquerque, Phoenix and Tucson, where most of them have set up a suburban way of life duplicating what they left behind. But these newcomers do not often venture beyond the periphery of the cities except to go to other cities by plane or highway route or to visit commercialized sites of scenic interest. In the spaces between, regional manners and attitudes survive. Furthermore, among culturally aware people of the cities there is concern about preserving something of the regional traditions of the area. But the problem of standardization remains. Even the most isolated communities have access to the mass media of radio, television, and motion pictures, which are probably the most effective means of standardization in our society, and there is a steady seepage of influence into the rural areas from the big cities. Nor should these changes brought about by industrialization be completely deplored. Nothing is more futile than trying to preserve old things because they are quaint. It is in literature that ways of human life soon to pass are preserved. In the vigor of his imagination the literary artist can confer an immortality beyond the power of the historian, and in illuminating that which is inward in human conditions he registers the effect upon the individual of conflicts between the traditional and the emergent in human society. Furthermore, such writers as Carlos Castañeda and Neil Claremon, in directing our attention to Indian practices and beliefs in the borderlands, have demonstrated that there are in fact some ancient traditions in the area which seem to have effectively resisted the encroachments of modern, standardized, popular culture. In addition, the literary output of the region, which had seemed to be flagging — perhaps due to the effects of standardization — is being recharged through the vigor of the Chicano and Amerind writers. B. A. Botkin, contributing to the symposium conducted by *Southwest Review* mentioned above, may well have exaggerated the role of the folk and underestimated the manipulative function of the conscious artist.

> Side by side with the ancient cultural tradition of the Southwest is a tradition of action unsurpassed in history and equalled only by the Homeric and Elizabethan ages — the epic of romance and path-finding, transportation, Indian-fighting, treasure-hunting, trail driving, and land-booming that have marked the successive stages of pioneering. Heroic, nomadic, pastoral, agrarian, the Southwest has contributed to the saga of the West the vigor and variety of its conquerors and footloose wanderers, lawless adventurers and dauntless builders.... But for the genuine creative flowering of the spirit, without which there can be no true culture, the Southwestern tradition must grow from below rather than be imposed from above and can best be disseminated by an art and literature deriving their materials, methods, motifs, and symbols from communal, popular, and traditional sources and in turn supplying these to American art and literature at large.[16]

Another contributor to the symposium, Howard Mumford Jones, while admitting the advance of "Middle-Western culture of conformity to business standards," holds out the hope that this "avalanche" can be turned aside from "certain favored regions" if artists do their part.

> ... it is not too late, it seems to me, for the artists to bring to this region a sense of the deep spiritual values of that which is too rapidly disappearing.
> 
> The natural landscapes of the Southwest are of a brilliance and color which echo the brilliance and color of the Pueblo and Spanish-Mexican arts. The slow rhythm of cowboy speech corresponds to the slow rhythm of life among the Mexicans and Indians. The dominant qualities of a possible Southwestern culture, so far as the arts are concerned, would seem to me to be therefore brilliance of color and a characteristic rhythm. This color is not alone the literal color of gaudy blankets and pottery: it echoes in the literature or romantic and melodramatic tendency which might, and should, grow out of the traditions of past life in the Southwest.[17]

This concept is vivified in a passage in *Death Comes for the Archbishop* describing Bishop Latour entering Taos:

> When the Bishop dismounted to enter the church, the women threw their shawls on the dusty pathway for him to walk upon, and as he passed through the kneeling congregation, men and women snatched for his hand to kiss the Episcopal ring. In his own country all this would have been highly distasteful to Jean Marie Latour. Here, these demonstrations seemed a part of the high colour that was in landscape and gardens, in the flaming cactus and the gaudily decorated altars, in the agonized Christs and dolorous Virgins and the very human figures of the saints. He had already learned that with this people religion was necessarily theatrical.[18]

This element of vividness and high coloration is, in fact, being reintroduced into the literature of the region by the Chicano and Amerind writers of the region.

Willa Cather's bishop was making a conscious adaptation to the tone of a region, an adaptation which was essentially a practical one, a matter of policy. Some of the critics who have entered the discourse on the cultural potential of the Southwest have denied that this adaptation can be made culturally. In his contribution to the book *Regionalism in America*, Benjamin T. Spenser, discussing Mary Austin's prophesy of cultural fusion, wrote: "Yet, as many Southwestern regionalists admit, the dichotomy of cultures has scarcely been resolved; vigorous twentieth-century conquistadors continue to impose 'derived notions of the good life upon the land.' The Anglo-Spanish-Indian elements have not been culturally fused even to the degree that the Anglo-Negro elements have been synthesized in the Southeast."[19] Yet it will be remembered that the Chicano and Amerind writers actively resist absorption by "twentieth-century conquistadors," thus reversing the trend toward cultural oblivion.

Another demurrer comes from Albert Guérard, making his statement for *Southwest Review's* symposium: "The one bond of unity of the Southwest' is its Mexican tradition — Indian and Spanish. Two civilizations which you cannot adopt as your own; they will have to remain subordinate. . . . Apart from the historical factor, there is no such thing as the Southwest. It is a mosaic, not a synthesis, of many elements."[20] Yet the rise of Chicano and Amerind literatures and the movements behind them have proven that these two civilizations have refused to "remain subordinate," thus giving something of a patronizing air to Guérard's remarks. These literatures make no apologies for not being a "synthesis" and in fact maintain that the element of "mosaic," the multicultural aspect of the region is its very glory.

And yet a degree of synthesis is ascertainable in the evidence of linguistic borrowings and also in the techniques, traditions, and lore passed from Mexican to "Anglo" in the basic Southwestern industry of cattle ranching. There have also been social adaptations both ways, with each stock being somewhat modified by the other in manners and outlook. In his linguistic and, by extension, sociological study, *A Dictionary of Spanish Terms in English With Special Reference to The American Southwest,* Harold W. Bentley records the impressive amount of language borrowing that has occurred in the Southwest. This borrowing has been a two-way affair with many Spanish words having been absorbed into English and a considerable number of English words taken into Mexican Spanish. In this connection, Bentley makes an interesting observation. "The motives prompting English borrowings from Spanish are varied. Absolute necessity is not always the explanation. Picturesqueness and connotations as well as local color are sought after in a great many instances. Spanish borrowings from English, on the other hand, have seldom been made from any other motive than that of necessity."[21] Recoiling defensively from the massive weight of American influence from the north and insisting to themselves that only in technical matters does the United States have anything to offer, Mexican intellectuals, proud and protective of a vital cultural heritage, have been considerably less receptive to American cultural influences than is true of the reverse. On the popular level, however, American influences are pervasive in Mexico even to the extent of having brought in many more English words than were current when Bentley published his book in 1932. In the American Southwest, the situation is reversed. The average Anglo-American, at least in the cities, is relatively unaffected by and often contemptuous of things Mexican, whereas the culture-conscious American of this area is frequently enamoured of Mexicana to the point of fatuity. "In the over-weening zest to be regional," writes T. M. Pearce in *The New Mexico Quarterly,* "it is difficult to see how Americans here differ from Americans becoming regional in Paris or Athens or anywhere else where one people assumes the outer trappings of another people — borrowing its architecture, wearing its ornaments, buying the products of its looms and of its artisans."[22] Yet he sees the shaping of an authentic Southwestern culture but finds "the pattern not yet distinct" and rests his case mainly on the evidence of linguistic borrowings.

In the rural areas of the Southwest, especially near the border, Mexican influence is strong even though often unacknowledged. It is visible in many facets of daily life, in the mud adobe bricks used for building, in fences made of mesquite branches, in food, in place names, and in the words used for common articles of daily usage. What Charles M. Flandrau said about American attitudes toward Mexico might well apply to Anglo attitudes toward Mexican influences in the Southwest. All too often, wrote Flandrau, Americans will "accept the best of everything in Mexico" and yet "stupidly deny its attraction for them, repudiate their sympathy with it."[23] Flandrau's paean to the Mexican plaza might apply as well to many a Southwestern community:

> The plaza is in constant use from morning until late at night. . . . By eleven o'clock at night the whole town will, at various hours, have passed through it, strolled in it, played, sat, rested, talked, or thought in it. . . . The plaza is a kind of social clearinghouse — a resource — a solution. I know of nothing quite like it, and nothing as fertile in the possibilities of innocent diversion.[24]

Mexican influence in the American Southwest is especially strong in anything to do with the raising and marketing of cattle, that basic and traditional industry of the Southwest. The Mexican *vaquero* or cowboy was a type developed in over three hundred years of conditioning in a highly specialized environment. He passed on his techniques, vocabulary and lore to the Anglo-American cattlemen of the Southwest. Tom Lea in *The King Ranch* writes:

> The hacienda's work developed a picturesque and unprecedented type of New World herdsman: the vaquero. It was this vaquero of Mexico who invented a technique for the horsebackhandling of half-wild cattle on an open range. He became adept at tossing a coiled rawhide rope he made with a sliding noose. He sat a saddle with a pommel he designed and built as a sturdy snubbing post for

his rope, to hold what he caught. He rode a strong-legged and tender-mouthed pony he trained for the work of herding and roping. He used the branding iron derived from Spain to burn the mark of ownership into an animal's living hide . . . . The Mexican vaqueros became the prototypes who furnished the ready-made tools, the range techniques, even the lingo, from which sprang the cowboy of song and story. The Mexican haciendas provided the primal outlines for the pattern which produced the later Cattle Kingdom of the American West.[25]

Edward Laroque Tinker describes in detail the apprenticeship that the American cowboy underwent at the hands of the Mexican vaquero:

The North Americans established ranches of their own and stocked them from the great unbranded herds. They needed cowboys to take care of them, but the young men from the Atlantic coast knew nothing of how to manage huge numbers of wild, fierce longhorns roaming an unfenced continent. They had to learn how to ride herd from the Mexican vaquero, how to break a bronco, and to use riatas and branding-irons. They adopted his entire equipment — the ring-bit, that was copied by the Spaniards from the Moors and is still in use in parts of the Southwest, and the stock saddle which is merely a slightly modified form of the Conquistadores', with a horn added for roping. Even the cowboys' work-a-day vocabulary is still generously peppered, in the Southwest, with Spanish words. He wears a *sombrero* and *chaps* (chaparreros), his stirrups are protected by *tapacieros,* and his lariat (from la riata) has a *hondo* on the end, he rides a bronco when he works a rodeo, and disciplines it with a quirt. His saddle has *cinchas, latigos,* and *alforjas;* he calls his string of ponies a *remuda* and the equine stock of a ranch a *caballada,* which he often shortens to cavvy. He has twisted the word *mesteno* into mustang, the generic terms for the descendants of Spanish horses, and savvy, a corruption of *sabe,* is understood by everyone, and has received canonization in Webster's dictionary. I checked a collection of over 3000 cowboy terms and found that approximately one out of every fifteen was of Spanish origin.[26]

Yet the pupils were not inclined to any gracious acknowledgement of the debt they owed their teachers. "They learned the arts of the vaquero," writes Harvey Fergusson, "and they stole his stock. For generations a bitter guerrilla warfare, mostly unrecorded and forgotten, was waged all up and down the lower Rio Grande."[27] That the Mexican tradition in the American cattle industry is far from dead is demonstrated by a recent novel of ranch life in southern Texas as it is lived today, *The Black Bull,* by Frank Goodwyn.[28] This work of fiction is based on the author's own experience growing up on the King Ranch, that vast holding whose history has been so thoroughly documented by Tom Lea. The principal characters are Mexican ranch hands and *caporales,* sub-bosses. The book is interlarded with the sayings, attitudes, and lore of these people, and the author makes it quite evident that the Anglo-Texans and the Mexicans on such a ranch not only work together but intimately share a common culture.

Of less lasting influence but a definite fact of cultural borrowing in the Southwest is the Mexican influence on the development and vocabulary of that other basic industry of the area, mining. In *North From Mexico,* Carey McWilliams reports on this exchange:

> Quite apart from many technical mining expressions in Spanish which passed into American mining law and the vocabulary of American miners, dozens of Spanish-Mexican mining terms found wide popular acceptance in the West. *Bonanza* or rich ore is one such expression; *borrasco* or barren rock is another. Such terms as *placer, xacal* (slack), and *escoria* (slag) are merely a few of many terms that might be cited. In The Big *Bonanza,* Dan De Quille devoted three pages to a glossary of Mexican mining terms in general use in the Washoe territory. Appropriation of these terms was a necessity since there were, of course, no equivalent expressions in Anglo-American speech. Dan De Quille, one of the most accurate of observers, reported that "the business of working silver-mines was then new to our people, and at first they depended much on what was told them by the Mexican silver-miners who flocked to the country." These miners, he wrote, "were in great demand" and much of what was subsequently learned about quartz mining was based on their experience and knowledge.[29]

Modern techniques in mining owe little to early Spanish and Mexican methods, but in such mines as the large open copper pits at Ajo and Morenci in Arizona, the two peoples, Anglo and Mexican, work in close contact with each other, and much of the early vocabulary remains.

However, close contact was not always the case. Just as Anglos borrowed ranching techniques without bestowing respect upon the creators of these techniques, so did they, in the nineteenth century, borrow mining vocabulary and techniques while excluding Mexicans from everything but the periphery of the mining industry. This aspect of the mining scene in northern Arizona has been explored in an excellent novel, *The Blue Chip* by Ysabel Rennie. In the town of Jericho, devoted to copper mining, the Mexican *barrio* is an isolated section of town. Mexicans are not allowed to go into the pits as miners but simply provide services of various kinds. However, the book does give a glimpse of the life inside the *barrio.* One of the partners in the mining company, Jake Feely, a feckless Irishman, has disappeared. Finally his friends do the unthinkable. They look for him in the Mexican quarter. González, the owner of the cantina, is reluctant to say anything more than that Jake has been there recently. Jake is finally found nearby, dying, in the house of a young Mexican girl, María. It develops that Jake, an aging and essentially lonely widower, has been seeing María for a long time. She has been tender to him and given him the affection that he needed. To Jake's partner, Jim Packer, this association immediately lowers Jake in his eyes. The other partner, Bow Miller, more coolly opportunistic, takes in the fact that María, though Mexican, is beautiful. Secretively, he sets her up as his mistress. The general impression given is that to Anglo men in Jericho Mexican women are useful primarily as sexually exploitable commodities. However, there is another view given of the possibilities for a Mexican in Jericho. Toby Heers is a genial and lazy Anglo. He lives in relative comfort, however, because his Mexican wife, Eugenia, is a very shrewd businesswoman. The distinction is made here between the Mexican of the *barrio* and the middle class Mexican.

In discussing the degree of cultural synthesis in the Southwest, one feels on safe ground in citing linguistic borrowings. The evidence is irrefutable. But when the argument is shifted to sociological findings, there can be no such certainty; nor is it within the scope of this work to make detailed examinations of the results of sociological surveys. However, the reactions of literary men to the social scene in the Southwest are within the purview of this book, as are the author's personal observations in this area. John Houghton Allen, in his novel *Southwest*, sees the Texas border area as a land where the "white man" goes to seed and the natives are spoiled. "You are in a country that doesn't belong to the gringo, and that the Mexicans don't seem to want after the gringo is through with it. And better men than you have felt this deadlock, the disintegration, and like going to pieces in this hollow dismal land — in fact, the better they are the faster they go to seed. The only ones who aren't haywire are the morons, they just get louder."[30] Continuing, in this breezy fashion, on the plight of the gringos, he says: "It is too bad they didn't absorb some of the natural graces of the Mexicans in this bitter land, but to mention such a thing is enough to bring out the vigilantes. Not that the Mexicans today are any better than the gringos — both races make you want to go out and eat grass."[31] The flip gesture in Allen's writing, one feels, serves as a check upon the too open exposure of his great nostalgia for old traditions in the American South and in Mexico. A considerably more bitter view of the relationship of the two peoples is expressed by Waldo Frank. In the section of *Our America* called "The Land of Buried Cultures," he mourns the destruction of Mexican culture in the Southwest at the hands of American arrogance and commercialism and declares the Mexicans in that area to be in a state of total moral defeat.

> For the Mexican is cowed, and is beaten. He moves about like one who feels himself a dog among men. He bends the neck to the steel-mill and to the hard, keen masters who are the makers of steel. The Americans live in ugly houses, so he comes to despise the intimate temper that made him beautify his own. The Americans go to the Machine for their pleasure as well as for their food. So he comes to despise the labor of his hand. Nothing that is his meets the approval of the "gringos." He is a "greaser," a half-breed, a "nigger." The Americans are stronger and the Americans do not respect him. What then will it gain him to respect himself? The Mexican, in the United States, sinks thus into the certain ways of one who has lost his faith and given up his pride. He becomes dissolute, shiftless, insolent and cringing....
> The American did not absorb or learn. In his hands, the integral expressions of Mexican life — their remarkable harmony with the native American world — become toys of the picturesque, motives for cheap commercial imitation. And conversely, the growing dominion of the 'gringo' is stamping out the impulse from which this native culture sprang. There are plenty of collectors to rage like locusts through the New Mexican and South-Californian hills, and make their blight of *Santos* and pottery and blankets.
> But America was too long insulated from this spiritual wealth that flowered along the edges of the Great Desert. It has no eyes for the loveliness of 'dobe towns, nor for the fire of this people that still burns under the ban of the Industrial world like jewels in the dark. And now that America is readier to see and learn, the Mexican is already lost in the spell of the tin-can and the lithograph. For what has been buried must die surely.[32]

Fortunately, thanks to the Chicano movement, Mexican-American culture has been rescued at the eleventh hour, but Frank's observations make clear the need for the movement and the reasons for its insistence upon cultural pride.

Native to the Southwest and, as has been seen, one of its prolific writers, Harvey Fergusson, considers aspects of the same situation in *Rio Grande,* a non-fictional analysis in terms of the history and culture of the region surrounding the Rio Grande. He concedes adaptation but not defeat to the Mexican-American of the Southwest and feels that the resiliency of his stock will make him a figure to reckon with in time.

> As you near one of the larger towns, such as Albuquerque, the proportion of Mexicans who own and cultivate land steadily decreases and those you see are obviously products of adaptation. They ride in Fords and if you speak to them in Spanish they reply in excellent idiomatic English, including the latest slang. When

> he comes in contact with the Americans the native of the younger generation shows an adaptability in manner and language as surprising as the earth-rooted resistant conservatism of his fellows back in the hills. When it comes to learning the current values of time and money he is not so quick. He has a tendency to buy whatever takes his eye, on the installment plan, and keep it until they take it away from his again. He seldom becomes a rich man or a thorough-going puritan. The virtues of thrift and repression elude him. He remains always a man of pleasure and leisure. Doubtless he is in process of being absorbed but he seems likely to leave his mark upon the society that absorbs him.

This somewhat stereotyped view of the Mexican-American is gainsaid by the number of serious professional men and women of Mexican origin that the Southwest is producing. In Frank Waters' novel, *The People of the Valley,* one of the characters is Don Eliseo, a Mexican-American judge. Standing astride two traditions, the Mexican-American and the Anglo-American, he is a successful mediator between two cultures because he has formed within himself a working synthesis. Old María del Valle refers to him while rebuking a granddaughter for having mocked the "gringos." She says: "Yes, they are ignorant of some things as we Spanish-Americans are ignorant of others. So do not condemn them unjustly. When we both see all, then will there be no difference between us. . . . The good judge; was he not a ragged little chamaco? Is he not respected now by the Anglos perhaps more than by us? Simply because his eyes, through learning, have seen both ways."[33]

Harvey Fergusson in *Rio Grande* takes up the subject of the Southwest as the cultural front which is increasingly feeling the pressure of an upward surging Hispanic America.

> From the Rio Grande south, clear to the frozen lands of the Argentine, this same man of mixed blood, more Indian than Spanish, is the prevalent, the surviving type. He varies widely in build and complexion according to the aboriginal stocks that went into his making but later immigration has changed him little and everywhere that I have seen him — in Mexico, in Central America and in the islands — he is much the same man. Unmistakably he is an emergent type — a man half-primitive just beginning to grasp the tools of industrial civilization and the mysteries of democratic government. His period of incessant revolution is drawing toward an end. He is just beginning to find himself in the arts. His fertility both spiritual and physical, seems to be unimpaired.
>
> For a hundred years all immigration across the border was southward. Men from the old Southwest, of the Bowie and Crockett type, had pre-empted a large part of Texas before the guns of the Alamo began a revolution. The wagon merchants from

Missouri had taken New Mexico away from the ricos and were supporting the government ten years before Kearny hoisted a new flag at Santa Fe. Lately the spontaneous movement of population has in a measure reversed itself and the fact seems to me not without significance. The Americans who go south now are salesmen rather than settlers while thousands of Mexicans have been crossing the border every year, looking for easy American dollars, alarming Nordic congressmen. These humble track-workers and fruit-pickers are pioneers just as much as the early Texans were and so are the Mexican painters and cartoonists who invade the literary teas in Manhattan. Indo-Spanish America is coming toward us, bringing both its gifts and its needs. The Rio Grande is now, as it has been for a hundred years, the frontier between two races and two cultures and the outcome of that contact is a thing that remains to be seen.[34]

Since *Rio Grande* was written in 1933, the trend of population movement took yet another turn with the great influx of Americans from the East and Middlewest to the Southwest. This movement for a while obscured but did not reduce to insignificance the steady movement of Mexicans across the Rio Grande into the United States. Beginning in the nineteen sixties, this movement picked up tempo again. By the nineteen seventies, immigration, much of it illegal, had reached tremendous proportions. This constant feeding from the motherland has had the effect of strengthening Mexican cultural influence in the American Southwest.

To the long record of the Mexican or the Chicano as figures in American literature has been added the increasingly impressive work of the Chicanos themselves. Some Chicano writers have felt that they alone have the prerogative of setting, for the future, the image of the Chicano in American literature. In view of the many literary distortions that have occurred in the past, which this book has been parading before the reader, one can hardly blame them. But what is overlooked in this view is that all societies need the corrective vision that the outsider, with his greater detachment, can sometimes supply. On the other hand, it is no doubt true that there are certain things about the "feel" of a culture that only a member of it can really know. In any event, American literature dealing with Mexican or Chicano culture now has the advantage of a double vision, the view from within and the view from without.

# EPILOGUE

# Epilogue

In surveying the long literary record in which American writers have registered response to the neighboring and contrasting culture of Mexico, one characteristic is evident. American appreciation of Mexican culture, at least at the level of thought of people who write books, has grown proportionately to America's abandonment of much of its early provincial cockiness. The literary mind, often sensing important new areas to explore before the more literal formulators of ideas have become aware of them, has been among the first in the United States to recognize that Mexican culture is remarkably complementary to that of the United States and has much to teach North Americans in vital areas of human experience. New recognition has also been given to the interlocking situation of the cultures of English-speaking America and those of Latinity to the south, a situation which is being given a rich articulation by the Chicano writers.

In some measure this recognition has been, in fact, implicit in the varying ways in which North American writers, from early times to the present, have treated the epic of the Conquest. Whatever their attitudes or styles, these authors have sensed in the Conquest a prototype of a larger drama staged throughout the Americas. Bird, Maturin, and Ingraham emphasized the ferocity of the Spanish assault against an idealized Tenochtitlan. Here the Conquistador stands as the figure of European man, despoiler of the New World. Despite the fact that bales of American prose, over the decades, have been devoted to American construction, development and progress — all of this expressing an undoubted reality — creative writers have persistently sounded a countertheme: that of the destruction of the ancient ways of indigenous peoples, the raping of the wilderness, the crushing, in more recent times, of long-established rural patterns of life, and of dignified and aesthetically effective folkways before the glacialization of the industrial age, the "cultural rape" — to use an emphatic Chicano phrase — of Mexican-American culture by the pervasive Anglo-American culture. It was to epitomize and in a sense immortalize these losses that Archibald MacLeish and

William Carlos Williams sounded again the death cries of the curiously brilliant capital of the Aztecs. To these poets, the death in humiliating captivity of Moctezuma and the hanging of Cuauhtemoc by Cortez were not merely episodes in history, but parts of an archetypal legend for the Americas, a legend revivified by the Chicano writers in their commitment to the Indian side of their heritage.

Or again, when early North American writers dealing with the Conquest rang out the old battle cry of the Spanish conquistadores, "God and Santiago!" they were inaugurating a theme whose implications were to be explored at length by writers of the New World, that of the perversion of religion to the uses of various forms of conquest. What could be more direct in line of descent from Edward Maturin's wry reference to this Spanish battle cry than Herman Melville's comment on the presence of a naval chaplain upon a man o' war? "Bluntly put, a chaplain is the minister of the Prince of Peace serving in the host of the God of War — Mars. . . . Why then is he there? Because he indirectly subserves the purpose attested by the cannon; because too he lends the sanction of the religion of the meek to that which practically is the abrogation of everything but brute force."[1]

Reading the accounts of the Conquest, whether in the chronicles of Bernal Diaz del Castillo, or in the adaptations of the chronicle by Prescott or MacLeish, one is impressed by descriptions of Aztec Mexico which hold true of Mexico today. Unforgettable are such small touches, in the account of the first entry of the Spaniards into Tenochtitlan, as the report of the muffled but rapid pit-a-pat sound, unfamiliar to the ears of the Conquistadores, of Aztec women in their homes making tortillas, deftly and in rapid-fire manner passing the *masa*, dough, from one palm of the hand to the other with a staccato sound until the lump of dough has become flattened and rounded into a large, thin pancake. In just this manner the tortillas are made today in millions of Mexican homes. One is reminded that those elements of food and drink which are thought of as quintessentially Mexican — tortillas, tacos, enchiladas, tamales, and the alcoholic drinks made from the juices of the maguey plant, such as pulque, tequila, mezcal — all these were being relished in Mexico long before the arrival of the first Europeans. The New World is new only to its conquerors and their descendants. To others, and especially to important sections of the population of the Americas, it is an ancient world.

What more freighted symbol could be found for the confrontation of the old and the new peoples of the Americas than the portentous meeting of Moctezuma and Cortez? It has been skillfully used by writers north and south and is still effective as the symbol of an unresolved social, political, and purely human problem in the Western Hemisphere. The problem itself is many-faceted. To the two principal races of Americas, a third has been added — the Negro. He is one of the most important, and least acknowledged, bonds between the continents of the New World. In slavery, and in varying degrees of emancipation, he has contributed richly to the cultural experience of North and Hispanic America. Henry David Thoreau, and in quite a different mood, the Texas romancers of the mid-nineteenth century, described typical citizens of the United States as reacting similarly to Negroes and to members of the fused Spanish-Indian race of Mexico, with a tendency to render both racial groups alien in their place of dwelling, the place in which the Negro incidentally had been forced to dwell.

Conversely, the first white men in Mexico, the Spaniards, were portrayed by MacLeish in *Conquistador* as being incurably alien to the native people and to the Mexican landscape. These invaders heard everything "with the ears of strangers." Centuries later, in the borderlands, the North Americans were to intrude upon the civilization of Mexico and to react with a similar sense of alien hostility. Though the literary record has revealed recent radical changes in North American attitudes toward Mexico, North American writers on Mexican subjects, despite the decline in hostility, remain, as we are being told by the Chicano writers, to a considerable extent alien. The time is ripe for an extended cultural discourse between North America, the Aztlán of the Chicanos, and the Latin American regions to the south, a discourse which, as it intensifies itself in range and depth, should be received no longer, on any side, "with the ears of strangers."

Standing upon the border between the United States and Mexico and looking south, an imaginative North American can hardly avoid a feeling of awe at the thought that he is facing a vast extension of territory, embracing all types of climate and terrain and stretching the full distance southward to Cape Horn, in which Indio-Latin America is working out its destiny and pressing upward toward him, indeed, in the Southwest, surrounding him. If he is a man of perception, he will recognize that here is an involvement that the United States cannot abrogate at will. If he is a literary man, he will know in his brain and in his viscera that a paramount task of literature in North and in Latin America is to articulate this involvement.

# Notes, Bibliography, and Index

# NOTES

Notes giving publication data follow the first mention in the text of a title and author; all subsequent notes referring to the same work will give page numbers only.

## PROLOGUE

[1] Albuquerque: University of New Mexico Press, 1949.
[2] Tucson: University of Arizona Press, 1963.
[3] Garden City, New York: 1941.
[4] Note: The name of the Aztec emperor who met Cortez is spelled in various ways in English. Any variation is at best a rough phonetic transcription of the Nahuatl word.
[5] *Calavar*, Philadelphia: Lea and Blanchard, 1847 (1st ed. 1834), Introduction, p. iv.
[6] New York: Bantam Books, 1953, p. 96.
[7] *Ibid.*, pp. 97–98.
[8] *The Infidel; or the Fall of Mexico*, Philadelphia: Carey, Lea and Blanchard, 1835, Vol. II, p. 228.
[9] *Montezuma, the Serf*, Boston: H. L. Williams, 1845, Vol. I, p. 116.
[10] New York: Paine and Burgess, 1845, Vol. I, pp. 8–9.
[11] New York: Rinehart, 1947, p. 238.
[12] *The Collected Poems of Hart Crane*, New York: Liveright Publishing Corp., 1933, pp. 146–147.
[13] *Selected Essays of William Carlos Williams*, New York: Random House, 1954, p. 22.
[14] *Ibid.*, p. 143.

## PART I

### CHAPTER 1

[1] Fayette Copeland, *Kendall of the Picayune*, Norman: University of Oklahoma Press, Preface, 1943.
[2] New York: E. P. Dutton & Co., 1956.
[3] Berkeley: University of California Press, 1950, pp. 12–13.
[4] *History of the Conquest of Mexico and History of the Conquest of Peru*, New York: Random House, Modern Library ed., p. 33.
[5] *The Life of Washington Irving*, London: Oxford University Press, 1935, p. 77.
[6] *The Gathering of the Forces*, editorials, essays, literary and dramatic reviews and other material written by Walt Whitman as editor of the *Brooklyn Daily Eagle* in 1846 and 1847, edited by Cleveland Rodgers and John Black in two volumes. New York: G. P. Putnam's Sons, the Knickerbocker Press, 1920, p. 247.
[7] Albert Weinberg, *Manifest Destiny*, Baltimore: Johns Hopkins Press, 1935, p. 55.
[8] *Anti-Slavery and Reform Papers*, ed. H. S. Salt, London: S. Sonnenschein & Co., 1890, p. 27.
[9] *Bulletin of the New York Public Library*, July 1922, p. 555.

## Notes

[10] "The Austin Papers," edited by Eugene C. Barker, *Annual Report for the American Historical Association for the Year 1922*, Washington: United States Government Printing Office, 1928.
[11] *The Life of Stephen F. Austin*, Nashville: Cokesbury Press, 1925, p. 47.
[12] Mattie Austin Hatcher, *Letters of an Early American Traveler—Mary Austin Holley Her Life and Her Works*, Dallas: Southwest Press, 1933.
[13] Postscript, p. 302.
[14] Alleine Howren, "Causes and Origin of the Decree of April 6, 1830," *The Southwestern Historical Quarterly*, Vol. XVI, p. 395.

### CHAPTER 2

[1] Chicago: Lakeside Press, 1929, p. 369. Note: This edition stops at the point that the members of the Expedition, as prisoners of war, arrive at El Paso.
[2] *Narrative of the Texan Santa Fe Expedition*, London: Henry Washbourne, 1847, p. 474. Note: This old edition contains the entire narrative.
[3] New York: E. P. Dutton & Co., 1956, p. 162.
[4] George W. B. Evans, *Mexican Gold Trail, the Journal of a 49er*, San Marino, Calif.: Huntington Library Publication, 1945, pp. 110–111.
[5] *Personal Narrative of Explorations and Incidents in Texas, New Mexico, California, Sonora, and Chihuahua*, New York: Appleton & Co., 1854, Vol. II, pp. 348–349.
[6] *Ibid.*, Vol. I, p. 40.
[7] *Ibid.*, Vol. II, pp. 299–300.
[8] A. J. A. Duganne, "The Peon Prince or the Yankee Knight Errant," *Beadle's Dime Novels*, New York: Beadle & Co., 1861, p. 20.
[9] *Journal of a Voyage Between China and the Northwestern Coast of America, Made in 1804*, Claremont, California: Saunders Studio Press, 1935, p. 59.
[10] New York: MacMillan, 1915, p. 84.
[11] *Ibid.*, p. 91.
[12] *Los Gringos*, London: Richard Bentley, 1849, p. 148.
[13] *The Personal Narrative of James O. Pattie of Kentucky*, ed. Timothy Flint, Chicago: the Lakeside Press, R. R. Donnelley & Sons, 1930, p. 168. Note: First published in 1831 in Cincinnati.
[14] *Narrative of the Texan Santa Fe Expedition*, London: Henry Washbourne, 1847, p. 326.
[15] *A Tour Through Arizona, 1864 or Adventures in the Apache Country*, Tucson: Arizona Silhouettes, 1950, p. 168.
[16] *Op. Cit.*, Vol. I, pp. 39–40.
[17] *Op. Cit.*, p. 142.
[18] Glendale, Calif.: Arthur H. Clark Co., 1931, pp. 87–88.
[19] Boston: Cummings, Hilliard & Co., 1826, Vol. I, p. 12.
[20] *American Local-Color Stories*, ed. Harry H. Warfel and G. Harrison Orians, New York: American Book Co., 1941, pp. 17–18.
[21] *Op. Cit.*, p. 47.
[22] *Piney Woods Tavern; or Sam Slick in Texas*, Philadelphia: T. B. Peterson & Bros., 1858, p. 69.
[23] *Bernard Lile*, Philadelphia: J. B. Lippincott, 1856, p. 214.
[24] *Ibid.*, p. 246.
[25] Vol. I, p. 273.
[26] London edition, p. 477.
[27] *Op. Cit.*, p. 159.
[28] "The French in Mexico," *Overland Monthly*, Vol. I, no. 3, September 1868, p. 233.
[29] *Jack Tier, The Works of James Fenimore Cooper*, Mohawk Ed., New York: G. P. Putnam's Sons, 1896, p. 143.
[30] *Ibid.*, pp. 304–305.
[31] *Op. Cit.*, p. 82.
[32] *Ibid.*, p. 88.

## Notes 361

[33] *Down the Santa Fe Trail and Into Mexico, the Diary of Susan Shelby Magoffin in 1846–1847*, ed. Stella M. Drumm, New Haven: Yale University Press, 1926, pp. 130–132.
[34] *Op. Cit.*, p. 190.
[35] P. 208.
[36] *Wah-To-Yah and the Taos Trail*, Southwest Historical Series, Vol. VI, ed. Ralph P. Beiber, Glendale, California: Arthur H. Clark Co., 1938, p. 238. Note: In 1846 young Garrard traveled from St. Louis to Bent's Fort (now Pueblo, Colorado), Taos, and Santa Fe as part of the annual caravan of Bent, St. Vrain & Co. His book was first published in 1850 by H. W. Derry & Co., Cincinnati, but, until it was reprinted in 1938, it had long been unavailable. High-spirited and informative, it is one of the best and least known of the accounts of life on the Santa Fe Trail.
[37] *Crusoe's Island . . . with Sketches of Adventures in California and Washoe*, New York: Harper & Bros., 1864, p. 238.
[38] *Op. Cit.*, Vol. II, p. 428.
[39] *The Shirley Letters from the California Mines, 1851–1852*, New York: Alfred A. Knopf, 1949, p. 121.
[40] H. H. Bancroft, *History of the North Mexican States and Texas*, San Francisco: 1889, Vol. II, p. 115, ft. note 31.
[41] José María Sanchez, *Viaje a Texas – en 1828–1829, Diario del Teniente D. José María Sanchez, Miembro de la Comisión de Limites*, Mexico: Papeles Historicos, 1939, p. 29. Note: translation mine.
[42] Pattie, *Op. Cit.*, p. 395.
[43] *Ibid.*, p. 327.
[44] London: R. Kennett, 1837, p. 115. Note: This edition is a combination of the *Autobiography* of Crockett, 1834, which was probably dictated or at least authorized by himself, and the undoubtedly spurious *Colonel Crockett's Exploits and Adventures in Texas*, 1836.
[45] *Op. Cit.*, p. 47.
[46] P. 272.
[47] *American Local Color Stories*, pp. 18–19.
[48] Pp. 107–108.
[49] Pp. 113–114.
[50] P. 56.
[51] *Op. Cit.*, Vol. I, p. 449.
[52] New York: Dewitt and Davenport, 1852, p. 70.
[53] P. 266.
[54] P. 196.
[55] New York: Beadle and Adams, 1882.
[56] *Ibid.*, p. 4.
[57] Joseph E. Badger, "Jack Rabbit, the Prairie Sport," *Beadle's Dime Novel Library*, New York: Beadle and Adams, 1878, p. 11.
[58] New York: Alfred A. Knopf, 1953, p. 554.
[59] *Op. Cit.*, p. 240.
[60] *Op. Cit.*, p. 266.
[61] *Op. Cit.*, Vol. II, p. 413.
[62] *The Adventures of Captain Bonneville, U.S.A., in the Rocky Mountains of the Far West*, Works of Washington Irving, Vol. VI, Kinderhook Edition, New York: G. P. Putnam's Sons, 1868, pp. 144–147.
[63] *Op. Cit.*, London ed., p. 418.
[64] *Commerce of the Prairies or the Journal of a Santa Fe Trader, During Eight Expeditions Across the Great Western Prairies and a Residence of Nearly Nine Years in Northern Mexico*, Philadelphia: J. W. Moore, 1851, Vol. II, p. 142.
[65] *Ibid.*, Vol. I, p. 220.
[66] *Texan Santa Fe Expedition*, Lakeside Ed., pp. 168–169.
[67] *Ibid.*, p. 363.
[68] *Op. Cit.*, p. 179.
[69] *Audubon's Western Journals, 1849–1850, Being the MS Record of a Trip from New York to Texas and an Overland Journey Through Mexico and Arizona to the Gold-Fields of California*, Cleveland: Arthur H. Clark Co., 1906, p. 88.

[70] *Ibid.*, p. 93.
[71] *Ibid.*, p. 103.
[72] *Op. Cit.*, Vol. I, pp. 488–489.
[73] *Op. Cit.*, pp. 168–169.
[74] Pp. 102–104.
[75] *Prose Poems and Sketches,* Boston: Light and Horton, 1834, p. 107.
[76] *Op. Cit.*, p. 81.
[77] *Op. Cit.*, p. 81.
[78] Philadelphia: Lea and Blanchard, 1847, Introduction, p. xix.
[79] *Op. Cit.*, pp. 172–173.
[80] Philadelphia: M. Siegfried, p. 66.
[81] P. 215.
[82] Samuel E. Chamberlain, *My Confession,* New York: Harper & Brothers, 1956, pp. 188–191.
[83] *Ibid.*, p. 217.
[84] Pp. 421–422.
[85] Walt Whitman, *Complete Poetry and Prose* (as prepared by him for deathbed edition), New York: Pelligrini and Cudahy, 1948, Vol. I, pp. 95–96.
[86] *Spanish Character and Other Essays,* Boston: Houghton Mifflin Co., 1940, p. 8.
[87] *Op. Cit.*, p. 385.
[88] Vol. II, p. 435.
[89] *The Life and Works of William Cullen Bryant,* New York: D. Appleton & Co., 1884, Vol. II, p. 173.
[90] *An Account of Expeditions to the Sources of the Mississippi and Through the Western Parts of Louisiana to the Sources of the Arkansas, Kans, La Platte, and Pierre Juan Rivers; Performed by order of the Government of the United States During the Years 1805, 1806, 1807 and a Tour through the Interior Parts of New Spain when conducted through these Provinces by order of the Captain General in the Year 1807,* Philadelphia, 1810, p. 208.
[91] "A Mexican Tale," *Prose Sketches and Poems,* p. 101.
[92] *Memoirs of My Life, Including in the Narrative Five Journeys of Western Exploration during the Years 1842, 1843–44, 1845–6–7, 1848–9, 1853–4,* Chicago: Delford, Clarke, & Co., Vol. I (no more Vols. published), 1887, pp. 573–4.
[93] *Memoir of Colonel Ellis P. Bean, Written Himself about the Year 1816,* Ed. W. P. Yoakum, Houston, Texas: 1930, p. 13.
[94] *Texan-Santa Fe Expedition,* London Ed., pp. 389–390.
[95] *Ibid.*, p. 548.
[96] *Ibid.*, p. 549.
[97] *Op. Cit.*, p. 122.
[98] *Op. Cit.*, Vol. I, p. 219.
[99] P. 418.
[100] P. 444.
[101] *Op. Cit.*, pp. 118–119.
[102] *Op. Cit.*, London Ed., p. 475.

CHAPTER 3

[1] Samuel Harmon Lowerie, *Culture Conflict in Texas,* New York: doctoral dissertation for Columbia University, 1932, p. 32.
[2] *Mexico and Texas,* Austin: University of Texas Press, 1934, p. 149.
[3] New York: J. B. Lippincott, 1949.
[4] New York: Harcourt, Brace, 1946.
[5] New York: G. P. Putnam's Sons, 1941.
[6] *The Letters of Hart Crane 1916–1932,* ed. Brown Weber, New York: Hermitage House, 1952, p. 387.
[7] Philadelphia: John C. Winston Co., 1931, p. 3.
[8] *Ibid.*, p. 71.
[9] *Ibid.*, p. 307.
[10] *A Tour Through Arizona, 1864, or Adventures in the Apache Country,* Tucson: Arizona Silhouettes, 1950, p. 22.

[11] *Ibid.*, pp. 171–172.
[12] *Ibid.*, p. 180.
[13] George F. Emery, "The Water Witch," *The Overland Monthly*, San Francisco: A. Roman & Co., 1869, Vol. III, pp. 95–96.
[14] *Personal Narrative of Explorations and Incidents in Texas, New Mexico, California, Sonora, and Chihuahua*, 2 Vols., New York: Appleton & Co., 1854, Vol. I, p. 484.
[15] Philadelphia: T. B. Peterson & Brothers, 1858, p. 280.
[16] Boston: Cummings, Hilliard and Co., 1826, Vol. II, p. 193.
[17] *Prose Poems and Sketches*, Boston: Light and Horton, 1834, p. 102.
[18] P. 310.
[19] Ed. Glenn S. Dumke, San Marino: The Huntington Library, 1945, p. 44.
[20] New York: MacMillan, 1915, p. 85.
[21] *The Works of James Fenimore Cooper*, Mohawk Edition, New York: G. P. Putnam's Sons, p. 25.
[22] *Op. Cit.*, Vol. I, p. 191.
[23] Vol. II, June 1869, p. 567.
[24] Vol. I, p. 232.
[25] Jno. R. Thompson, p. 29.
[26] *Prose Writing of William Cullen Bryant*, ed. Parke Godwin, New York: D. Appleton & Co., 1884, Vol. II, p. 180.
[27] *Commerce of the Prairies*, Philadelphia: J. W. Moore, 1851, Vol. II, pp. 89–90.
[28] Philadelphia: M. Siegfried, pp. 206–207.
[29] New York: Alfred A. Knopf, 1936.
[30] *Followers of the Sun, Wolf Song*, p. 14.
[31] *Ibid.*, pp. 86–87.
[32] *Ibid.*, p. 102.
[33] *Followers of the Sun, In Those Days*, p. 44.
[34] *The Story of Roy Bean: Law West of the Pecos*. Greenwich, Conn.: Fawcett Publications, 1972, p. 46.
[35] *Down the Santa Fe Trail and Into Mexico, The Diary of Susan Shelby Magoffin 1846–1847*, ed. Stella M. Drumm, New Haven: Yale University Press, 1926, p. 95.
[36] Boston: Little, Brown & Co., 1943, p. 321.
[37] New York: E. P. Dutton & Co., 1956, p. 175.
[38] *American Local-Color Stories*, ed. Harry R. Warfel and G. Harrison Orians, New York: American Book Co., 1941, pp. 16–17.
[39] *Op. Cit.*, p. 79.
[40] *Rio Grande*, New York: Alfred A. Knopf, 1933, p. 91.
[41] *The Centuries of Santa Fe*, p. 184.
[42] New York: William Morrow & Co., 1954, pp. 105–106.
[43] Pp. 205–206.
[44] *Bernard Lile, an Historical Romance*, Philadelphia: J. B. Lippincott, 1856, pp. 270–271.
[45] London: Richard Bentley, 1849, p. 147.
[46] *An Account of Expeditions to the Sources of the Mississippi and Through the Western Parts of Louisiana to the Sources of the Arkansas, Kans, La Platte, and Pierre Juan Rivers; Performed by order of the Government of the United States During the Years 1805, 1806, 1807 and a Tour through the Interior Parts of New Spain when conducted through these Provinces by order of the Captain General in the Year 1807*, Philadelphia, 1810, Appendix to Part III, p. 37.
[47] *Followers of the Sun, Wolf Song*, pp. 49–50.
[48] *Ibid.*, p. 60.
[49] *Ibid.*, p. 53.
[50] *Ibid.*, pp. 60–62.
[51] *The Southwest Historical Series*, Vol. VI, ed. Ralph P. Bieber, Glendale, California: Arthur H. Clark Co., 1938, p. 238. Note: originally published 1850.
[52] *Narratives of the Texan Santa Fe Expedition*, Chicago: Lakeside Press, 1929, pp. 428–429.
[53] *Op. Cit.*, p. 86.
[54] *Crusoe's Island . . . with Sketches of Adventure in California and Washoe*, New York: Harper, 1864, p. 240.

## Notes

[55] *Op. Cit.*, p. 324.
[56] *The Conquest of Don Pedro*, p. 4.
[57] *Ibid.*, pp. 66–67.
[58] *Ibid.*, pp. 56–57.
[59] *Ibid.*, pp. 115–116.
[60] *Ibid.*, pp. 144–145.
[61] *Ibid.*, p. 146.
[62] *History of the Conquest of Mexico and History of the Conquest of Peru*, New York: The Modern Library, Random House, p. 50.
[63] P. 118.
[64] *Great River, the Rio Grande in North American History*, New York: Rinehart, 1954, Vol. II, p. 567.
[65] New York: Alfred A. Knopf, 1953, p. 71.
[66] *Ibid.*, p. 315.

## CHAPTER 4

[1] *Rio Grande*, New York: Alfred A. Knopf, 1933, p. 99.
[2] Tucson, 1962, p. 284.
[3] *Ibid.*
[4] *Op. Cit.*, pp. 99–100.
[5] *Ibid.*, p. 78.
[6] *Ibid.*, p. 83.
[7] *Ibid.*, pp. 83–84.
[8] *Ibid.*, p. 114.
[9] *Ibid.*, p. 90.
[10] *Ibid.*
[11] New York: William Morrow & Co., 1950, pp. 32–33.
[12] New York: William Morrow & Co., 1954, p. 191.
[13] New York: Samuel French, 1935, pp. 193–194.
[14] *Ibid.*, pp. 173–174.
[15] *Rio Grande*, p. 99.
[16] *The Liberal Imagination*, New York: The Viking Press, 1948.
[17] *Rio Grande*, p. 81.
[18] *The Great River*, New York: Rinehart & Co., Vol. II, p. 690.
[19] *1846 The Year of Decision*, Boston: Little, Brown & Co., 1943, p. 190.
[20] *Juarez and His Mexico*, New York: The Viking Press, 1947, Vol. I, p. 74.
[21] *Rio Grande*, pp. 76–77.
[22] *Ibid.*, pp. 77–78.
[23] Fergusson, *The Conquest of Don Pedro*, p. 42.
[24] P. 285.
[25] P. 185.
[26] Pp. 116–119.
[27] "Texas and the United States of America in their Relations with the Mexican Republic," *The Mexican Side of the Texan Revolution*, compiled and translated by Castañeda, Dallas: P. L. Turner Co., 1928, p. 288.
[28] Joseph E. Badger, "Jack Rabbit, the Prairie Sport," *Beadle's Dime Library*, New York 1876, p. 125.
[29] Joseph E. Badger, "Joachim, the Saddle King," *Beadle's Dime Library*, New York, 1881, p. 2.
[30] A. J. A. Duganne, "The Peon Prince," *Beadle's Dime Novels*, New York, 1861, p. 15.
[31] Major Sam Hall, "The Serpent of El Paso, *"Beadle's Dime Library*, New York, 1882.
[32] *Rio Grande*, p. 116.
[33] *Memoir of Colonel Ellis P. Bean, Written by Himself about the Year 1816*, ed. W. P. Yoakum, Houston, 1930, p. 42.
[34] *Mexican Gold Trail, The Journal of a '49er*, San Marino, California: Huntington Library Publication, 1945, pp. 83–84.

Notes    365

[35] *Jack Tier*, The Works of James Fenimore Cooper, Mohawk ed., New York: G. P. Putnam's Sons, 1896, preface, pp. iii–iv.
[36] New York: J. B. Lippincott, 1949, p. 75.
[37] *Narrative of the Texan Santa Fe Expedition*, London: Washbourne, 1847, p. 388.
[38] *Los Gringos*, London: Richard Bentley, 1849, p. 170.
[39] Philadelphia: J. B. Lippincott, 1856, p. 216.
[40] New York: Alfred A. Knopf, 1953, p. 11.
[41] P. 47.
[42] *Narrative of the Texan Santa Fe Expedition*, Chicago: Lakeside Press, 1929, p. 478.
[43] *Commerce of the Prairies*, Philadelphia: J. W. Moore, 1851, Vol. II, p. 132.
[44] *Ibid.*, Vol. I, p. 226.
[45] *Ibid.*, p. 235.
[46] New York: MacMillan Co., 1915, p. 185.
[47] *An Account of Expeditions to the Sources of the Mississippi* etc., Philadelphia, 1810, p. 229.
[48] *Texan Santa Fe Expedition*, London ed., p. 383.
[49] *Ibid.*, p. 427.
[50] Mattie Austin Hatcher, *Letters of an Early American Traveller–Mary Austin Holley, Her Life and Her Works*, Dallas: Southwest Press, 1933, p. 56.
[51] "The Austin Papers," ed. Eugene C. Barker, *Annual Report for the American Historical Association for the Year 1922*, Washington, 1928, Vol. II, p. 788.
[52] *Ibid.*, pp. 654–656.
[53] Eugene C. Barker, *The Life of Stephen F. Austin*, Nashville: Cokesbury Press, 1925, p. 47.
[54] *Op. Cit.*, Appendix to Part III, p. 35.
[55] *Op. Cit.*, pp. 100–101.
[56] *Ibid.*, p. 125.
[57] *The Personal Narrative of James O. Pattie of Kentucky*, ed. Timothy Flint, Chicago: The Lakeside Press, 1930, p. 388.
[58] *Ibid.*, p. 361.
[59] *Ibid.*, p. 161.
[60] John Russell Bartlett, *Personal Narrative of Explorations and Incidents in Texas, New Mexico, California, Sonora, and Chihuahua*, New York: Appleton & Co., 1854, Vol. I, p. 43.
[61] Boston: Cummings, Hilliard & Co., 1826, Vol. II, p. 23.
[62] *Ibid.*, Vol. I, p. 111.
[63] Philadelphia: J. B. Lippincott, 1858, pp. 84–85.
[64] "A Visit to Mexico," *The Life and Works of William Cullen Bryant*, New York: D. Appleton & Co., 1884, Vol. II, pp. 156–159.
[65] *Op. Cit.*, pp. 111–112.
[66] *Op. Cit.*, Vol. I, p. 262.
[67] *Ibid.*, p. 264.
[68] *Ibid.*
[69] *Op. Cit.*, p. 173.
[70] Glendale, California: Arthur H. Clark, 1931, p. 102.
[71] *Op. Cit.*, p. 211.
[72] Philadelphia: John C. Winston, 1931, p. 209.
[73] *Op. Cit.*, Vol. I, p. 263.
[74] *American Local-Color Stories*, ed. H. R. Warfel and G. H. Orians, New York: American Book Co., 1941, p. 23.
[75] Philadelphia: J. B. Lippincott, 1858, pp. 215–216.
[76] New York: Leavitt and Allen, 1855, p. 203.
[77] *Texan Santa Fe Expedition*, London ed., p. 550–551.
[78] *Op. Cit.*, p. 76.
[79] *Prose, Poems and Sketches*, Boston: Light and Horton, 1834, p. 109.
[80] New York: Harpers Bros., 1956, pp. 187–188.
[81] *Op. Cit.*, Lakeside Press ed., p. 460.
[82] *Ibid.*, London ed., p. 452.
[83] *Ibid.*, p. 428.

84 *Op. Cit.*, Vol. I, p. 246.
85 *Ibid.*, p. 256.
86 *Ibid.*, p. 257.
87 *Op. Cit.*, Vol. I, p. 427.
88 Philadelphia: M. Siegfried, 1838, p. 54.
89 *Op. Cit.*, London ed., p. 479.
90 *History of the Conquest of Mexico and History of the Conquest of Peru*, Modern Library, New York: Random House, p. 195.
91 *Ibid.*, pp. 685–686.
92 *Ibid.*, p. 79.
93 *Op. Cit.*, Vol. I, p. 260.
94 *Op. Cit.*, Vol. I, p. 243.
95 *Down the Santa Fe Trail and Into Mexico, the Diary of S. S. Magoffin 1846–1847*, New Haven: Yale University Press, 1926, pp. 137–138.
96 *Op. Cit.*, London ed., p. 433.
97 *Op. Cit.*, Vol. I, p. 262.

## PART II

### CHAPTER 5

1 Boston: Little, Brown & Co., 1935, p. 14.
2 New York: MacMillan Co.
3 *Under the Redwoods*, Collected Works, Vol. X, Argonaut edition, New York: P. F. Collier & Son, n. d., pp. 305–306.
4 *The Land of Poco Tiempo*, New York: Charles Scribner's Sons, 1928, pp. 4–5.
5 Boston: Houghton Mifflin Co., 1929, Introduction, p. xiv.
6 *Works of Stephen Crane*, ed. Wilson Follett, New York: Alfred A. Knopf, 1926, Vol. XII, p. 150.
7 *Songs of the Sierra*, Boston: Robert Brothers, 1873, p. 197.
8 Dallas: Southwest Press, 1935, introductory page.
9 New York: Harper & Bros., 1899, Vol. I, p. 193.
10 *The Overland Monthly*, San Francisco: A. Roman & Co., 1873, Vol. X, p. 279.
11 *In the Footprints of the Padres*, San Francisco: A. M. Robertson, 1902, pp. 59–60.
12 "San Antonio de Bexar," *Retrospects and Prospects*, New York: Charles Scribner's Sons, 1899, p. 91.
13 New York: Harper & Bros., 1895, p. 78 & p. 80.
14 "Delmar of Pima," *McClure's Magazine* (February, 1902), Vol. XVIII, No. 4, p. 345.
15 Argonaut Edition of Works, Vol. VI, pp. 218–223.
16 *Collected Poems*, New York: Alfred A. Knopf, 1955, pp. 379–380.
17 *Ibid.*, pp. 102–103.
18 *Figures in a Landscape*, New York: Harper & Bros., 1931, pp. 259–260.
19 *Smoke and Steel, Slabs of the Sunburnt West, Good Morning, America*, New York: Harcourt Brace & Co., n. d., p. 78.
20 "A Beautiful Mexican," New York: Alfred A. Knopf, 1930, p. 12.
21 "In the Sacred Park," *Partisan Review* (Winter, 1958), Vol. XXV, No. 1, pp. 91–98.
22 *Collected Poems*, p. 30.
23 *Ibid.*, p. 101.
24 *Selected Poems*, New York: Farrar & Rinehart, 1938, pp. 91–93.
25 New York: Doubleday, Page & Co., 1904.
26 *Ibid.*, pp. 47–50.
27 *Roan Stallion, Tamar and Other Poems*, New York: The Modern Library, 1935, pp. 192–194.
28 New York: Bantam Books, 1953, p. 52.
29 *Flowering Judas*, New York: The Modern Library, n. d.
30 *I Wonder as I Wander: An Autobiographical Journey*. New York: Hill and Wang, 1956, p. 291.

[31] *Ibid.*, p. 292.
[32] *Followers of the Sun,* New York: Alfred A. Knopf, 1936, pp. ix-x.
[33] New York: Houghton Mifflin Co., 1932, p. 186.
[34] New York: Harcourt, Brace & Co., 1946, pp. 16-17.
[35] *Ibid.*, p. 18.
[36] *Ibid.*, pp. 18–19.
[37] Philadelphia: J. B. Lippincott Co., 1949, p. 36.
[38] P. 21 & p. 23.
[39] P. 26.
[40] *Ibid.*, pp. 420–421.
[41] Argonaut Edition of Works, Vol. XIII, pp. 292–293.
[42] New York: Harper & Bros., 1936, p. 78.
[43] Pp. 45–46.
[44] *Ibid.*, p. 237.
[45] *Ibid.*, p. 239.
[46] *Ibid.*, p. 240.
[47] Pp. 31–32.
[48] *Ibid.*, pp. 81–82.
[49] New York: Alfred A. Knopf, 1957.
[50] Boston: Houghton Mifflin Co., 1956.

## CHAPTER 6

[1] *The New York Times Book Review,* August 27, 1961, p. 1.
[2] *Ibid.*, p. 24.
[3] *The King Ranch,* Boston: Little, Brown & Co., 1957, Vol. I, p. 157.
[4] "The Wolfville Coyote," *Wolfville Days,* New York: Frederick A. Stokes Co., 1902, pp. 66–67.
[5] New York: Frederick A. Stokes Co., 1897, p. 138.
[6] Argonaut Edition of Works, New York: P. F. Collier & Son, Vol. XVIII, p. 285.
[7] New York: G. P. Putnam's Sons, pp. 102–103.
[8] *McClure's Magazine* (February, 1902), Vol. XVIII, No. 4, p. 341.
[9] *The Works of Stephen Crane,* ed. Wilson Follett, New York: Alfred A. Knopf, 1926, Vol. XII, pp. 93–94.
[10] *Ibid.*, p. 120.
[11] *Vaquero of the Brush Country,* Boston: Little, Brown & Co., 1952, p. 43.
[12] *U.S.A.*, New York: The Modern Library, Random House Inc., 1937, p. 306.
[13] Boston: Little, Brown & Co., 1935.
[14] New York: Sheldon & Co., 1871, p. 146.
[15] *Ibid.*, p. 44.
[16] Riverside Edition of Works, Boston: Houghton, Mifflin & Co., 1896, Vol. XIV, p. 324.
[17] Argonaut Edition of Works, Vol. IV, pp. 215–216.
[18] "The Caballero's Way," *Heart of the West,* New York: Doubleday, Page & Co., 1927, pp. 187–188.
[19] *Ibid.*, pp. 126–129.
[20] *Rolling Stones,* New York: P. F. Collier & Son, n. d., pp. 257–258.
[21] Boston: Houghton Mifflin Co., 1943, p. 61.
[22] *With Eyes at the Back of Our Heads,* New York: New Directions, p. 66.
[23] *Op. Cit.,* pp. 296–299.
[24] *Followers of the Sun,* New York: Alfred A. Knopf, 1936, pp. 7–8.
[25] New York: Harcourt, Brace & Co., 1946, pp. 49–50.
[26] *Op. Cit.,* p. 345.
[27] "Antepenultimata," *The Collected Works of Ambrose Bierce,* New York: The Neale Publishing Co., 1912, Vol. XI, p. 95.
[28] P. 142.
[29] New York: Bantam Books, 1953, p. 35.
[30] *Partisan Review* (Summer, 1955), Vol. XXII, No. 3, pp. 320–321.
[31] New York: Harper & Bros., 1931, p. 98.
[32] Pp. 29–33.

[33] London: Martin Secker, 1939, p. 110.
[34] New York: Harcourt Brace & Co., 1947, pp. 80–81 & p. 84.
[35] *The Night-Born,* New York: Grossett & Dunlap, 1913, pp. 261–262.
[36] Philadelphia: J. B. Lippincott Co., 1949, p. 71.
[37] New York: Rinehart & Co., 1947, pp. 304–305.
[38] *Indian Earth,* New York: Alfred A. Knopf, 1930, p. 21.
[39] Philadelphia: J. B. Lippincott, 1966, p. 207.
[40] New York: The Devin-Adair Co., 1958, p. 238.
[41] P. 294.
[42] New York, 1959, p. 236.
[43] New York, 1961, p. 68.
[44] *In All Countries,* New York: Harcourt, Brace & Co., 1934, p. 76.
[45] Boston: Little, Brown & Co., 1949, p. 178.
[46] P. 123.
[47] New York: The John Day Co., 1955, p. 111.
[48] *Retrospects and Prospects,* New York: Charles Scribner's Sons, 1899, p. 47.
[49] New York: Harcourt, Brace & Co., 1924, p. 430.
[50] *The Desert Music and Other Poems,* New York: Random House, 1954, pp. 79–80.
[51] Pp. 219–224.
[52] P. 351.
[53] New York: Readers Club, 1942, p. 44.
[54] "The Summit Redwood," *Cawdor and Other Poems,* New York: Random House, 1934, pp. 139–140.
[55] New York: Harper & Bros., 1945, p. 124.
[56] New York: Harcourt, Brace & Co., 1957.
[57] P. 120.
[58] *Op. Cit.,* p. 404.
[59] *Pony Tracks,* New York: Harper & Bros., 1895, p. 73.
[60] Pp. 141–142.
[61] New York: Signet, 1964, p. 115.
[62] New York: Capricorn Books, 1964, pp. 108–109.
[63] *Sherwood Anderson's Memoirs, A Critical Edition,* ed. Ray Lewis White, Chapel Hill: University of North Carolina Press, 1942, pp. 538–539.
[64] *Op. Cit.,* Vol. XII, p. 128.
[65] *Ibid.,* pp. 206–207.
[66] *Selected Poetry of Robinson Jeffers,* New York: Random House, 1937, pp. 55–56.
[67] Pp. 87–93.
[68] P. 251.
[69] *Five Families,* p. 112.
[70] *Op. Cit.,* p. 19.
[71] New York: Doubleday, Page & Co., 1904, p. 502.
[72] P. 205.
[73] New York: Payson & Clarke Ltd., 1929, p. 209.
[74] London: Martin Secker, 1939, p. 137.
[75] *The Sorrow Dance,* New York: New Directions, 1963, p. 51.
[76] New York: New Directions, 1962, p. 120.
[77] *Gasoline,* San Francisco: City Lights Books, 1958, p. 24.
[78] Chapel Hill: North Carolina University Press, 1945, p. 247.
[79] Boston: Houghton Mifflin Co., 1956, pp. 40–41.
[80] *Op. Cit.,* p. 326.
[81] Pp. 141–142.
[82] *Winner Take Nothing,* New York: Charles Scribner's Sons, 1933, p. 91.
[83] Pp. 21–22.
[84] Boston: Little, Brown & Co., 1952, p. 165.
[85] P. 75.
[86] *The Mexico I Like,* University Press in Dallas, 1942, pp. 63–69.
[87] Pp. 234–235.
[88] *American Local Color Stories,* ed. H. R. Warfel and G. H. Orians, New York: American Book Co., 1941, pp. 753–766.
[89] Follett Edition of Works, Vol. XII, pp. 215–216.
[90] *Ibid.,* p. 169.

[91] *The Land of Poco Tiempo,* New York: Charles Scribner's Sons, 1928, p. 18.
[92] *A New Mexico David,* Charles Scribner's Sons, 1902, pp. 195-196.
[93] *Op. Cit., pp.* 289-290.
[94] Oscar Lewis, p. 38.
[95] Dallas: South-West Press, 1935, p. 118.
[96] *Ibid.,* p. 142.
[97] *Owen Wister Out West, His Journals and Letters,* ed. Fanny Kemble Wister, University of Chicago Press, 1958, pp. 236-237.
[98] *Op. Cit.,* p. 141.
[99] *One Smoke Stories,* Boston: Houghton Mifflin, 1934, pp. 160–169.
[100] *The Best Novels and Stories of Eugene Manlove Rhodes,* ed. J. Frank Dobie. Boston: Houghton Mifflin, 1949.
[101] Boston: Houghton Mifflin, 1922.
[102] New York: Alfred A. Knopf, 1951, pp. 258–259.
[103] New York: Harper & Bros., 1936.
[104] *Selected Poetry,* p. 206.
[105] *Southwest,* p. 43.
[106] *Op. Cit.,* pp. 11–12.

## CHAPTER 7

[1] *Reality Sandwiches,* San Francisco: City Lights Books, 1963, p. 38.
[2] "The Land of Buried Cultures," *Our America,* New York: Boni and Liveright Publications, 1919, p. 94.
[3] *Rio Grande,* New York: Alfred A. Knopf, 1933, pp. 107–108.
[4] New York: Farrar and Rinehart, 1941, p. 254.
[5] New York: Harcourt, Brace & Co., 1924, pp. 405–406.
[6] New York: William Sloane Associates, 1961, p. 13.
[7] *Ibid.,* p. 195.
[8] *Ibid.,* pp. 259–260.
[9] Boston: Little, Brown & Co., 1952, p. 353.
[10] New York: The Viking Press, 1938, pp. 243–256.
[11] London: Martin Secker, 1939, pp. 91–92.
[12] New York: The Viking Press, 1973, p. 129.
[13] *Sketches New and Old,* New York: Harper & Bros., 1905, pp. 149–151.
[14] New York: The Modern Library, n. d., 32–35.
[15] "Purgatorio," *The Collected Poems of Hart Crane,* New York: Liveright Publishing Corp., 1933, p. 151.
[16] *The Letters of Hart Crane, 1916–1932,* ed. Brom Weber, New York: Hermitage House, 1952, p. 368.
[17] *Ibid.,* p. 405.
[18] *Ibid.,* p. 372.
[19] "Reflections on Wallace Stevens," New York: Vintage Books, 1955, pp. 125–126.
[20] *The Collected Poems of Wallace Stevens,* New York: Alfred A. Knopf, 1955, p. 337.
[21] *Flagons and Apples,* Los Angeles: Grafton Publishing Co., 1912, p. 11.
[22] New York: Harper & Bros., 1935, p. 70 & 72.
[23] New York: Harcourt Brace & Co., 1947, p. 116.
[24] *Op. Cit.,* p. 1.
[25] New York: Signet Books, 1958, pp. 229–230.
[26] "An Impression of Mexico – Its People," *Southern Literary Messenger* I (April, 1939), pp. 241–242.
[27] *Pony Tracks,* New York: Harper & Bros., 1895, p. 114 & p. 153.
[28] New York: Charles Scribner's Sons, 1928, p. 3.
[29] *Good Morning, America,* New York: Harcourt Brace & Co., 1928, p. 112 & p. 4.
[30] *The Forgotten Peninsula,* p. 177.
[31] *Op. Cit.,* pp. 9–10 & 13–15.
[32] *The Land of Little Rain,* Boston: Houghton Mifflin & Co., 1903, p. 281.
[33] P. 406.
[34] *Ibid.,* p. 423.
[35] *Ibid.,* pp. 418–420.

[36] University Press in Dallas, 1942, p. 62.
[37] P. 215.
[38] Dallas: The Southwest Press, 1930, p. 156.
[39] New York: Harper & Bros., 1936, p. 71.
[40] New York: Pocket Books Inc., 1951, p. 88.
[41] *Indian Earth,* New York: Alfred A. Knopf, 1930, p. 16.
[42] *Letters,* p. 371.
[43] *The Jacob's Ladder,* New York: New Directions, 1958, p. 26.
[44] New York: Alfred A. Knopf, 1951, p. 206.
[45] *Big Sur and the Oranges of Hieronymus Bosch,* New Directions, 1957, p. 118.
[46] New York: Covici Friede Publishers, 1935, p. 11.
[47] New York: Harcourt, Brace & Co., 1956, p. 27.
[48] *Cawdor and Other Poems,* pp. 128–129.
[49] New York: Harcourt, Brace & Co., 1951, p. 275.
[50] *Man Takes Control* (Minneapolis, 1961), p. 316.
[51] "Land of Great Volcanoes," *In All Countries,* New York: Harcourt, Brace & Co., 1934, pp. 78–79.
[52] *Not With the Fist,* New York: Harcourt, Brace & Co., 1946, p. 106.
[53] *Op. Cit.,* pp. 118–119.
[54] *Southwest,* New York: Bantam Books, 1953, pp. 145–146.
[55] Boston: Little, Brown & Co., 1935, p. 27.
[56] New York: Farrar & Rinehart & Co., 1944.
[57] *Crazy February,* p. 38.
[58] *Flowering Judas,* pp. 103–105.
[59] *Ibid.,* p. 11.
[60] New York: Popular Library, 1955, p. 412 & p. 414.
[61] New York: The Devin-Adair Co., 1958, p. 133.
[62] *The Mexican Night, A Travel Journal,* New York: New Directions, 1962, pp. 18–19.
[63] Pp. 50–51.
[64] *The Jacob's Ladder,* p. 27.
[65] *Great River,* New York: Rinehart & Co., 1954, Vol. II, p. 835.
[66] *The Mexico I Like,* pp. 62–63.
[67] *One-Smoke Stories,* Boston: Houghton, Mifflin Co., 1934, pp. 145–147.
[68] Pp. 75–76.
[69] *The Mexico I Like,* p. 261.
[70] Albuquerque: University of New Mexico Press, 1955.
[71] Pp. 35–36.
[72] *Ibid.,* p. 43.
[73] *Idols Behind Altars,* New York: Payson & Clarke Ltd., 1929, p. 213.
[74] P. xxii.
[75] *Ibid.,* p. 370.
[76] New York: Hastings House Publishers, 1953, p. 79.
[77] Dallas: South-West Press, 1935, p. 20.
[78] *The Land of Journeys' Ending,* New York: The Century Co., 1924, pp. 345–346.
[79] Letter to Solomon Grunberg, April 12, 1932, *Letters,* p. 408.
[80] *Indian Earth,* p. 8.
[81] Pp. 34–35.
[82] *North From Mexico,* Philadelphia: J. B. Lippincott Co., 1949, p. 72.
[83] New York: The John Day Co., 1955, p. 9.
[84] *The Meetings of East and West,* New York: The MacMillan Co., 1946, p. 7.
[85] *Gasoline,* p. 23.
[86] P. ix.

## CHAPTER 8

[1] "Grandeur and Misery of the Count of Villamediana," trans. from the Spanish by F. L. Ganivet, *Partisan Review,* (Summer, 1957), Vol. XXIV, No. 3, p. 383 & p. 386.
[2] *Ibid.,* p. 385.
[3] *The Works of Bret Harte,* Argonaut Ed., New York: P. F. Collier & Son, n. d., Vol. IV, pp. 229–230.

[4] *Roan Stallion, Tamar, and Other Poems,* New York: The Modern Library, 1935, p. 3.
[5] New York: Random House, 1935, p. 45.
[6] New York: Covici Friede Publishers, 1935, p. 233 and p. 236.
[7] New York: Brewer, Warren, & Putnam, 1932.
[8] New York: Bantam Books, 1952.
[9] Pp. 175–190.
[10] University Press in Dallas, 1942, pp. 158–159.
[11] Garden City, New York: Doubleday & Co., 1958, pp. 141–142.
[12] *Ibid.,* p. 107 and p. 109.
[13] New York: Signet Books, 1958, pp. 69–85.
[14] *Hard Candy,* New York: New Directions, 1954, p. 131.
[15] *Ibid.,* p. 132.
[16] *Ibid.,* p. 142.
[17] *Flowering Judas,* New York: The Modern Library, n. d.
[18] New York: New Directions, 1962, p. 121.
[19] *Here and Now,* San Francisco: City Lights Books, 1957, p. 30.
[20] *The Speed of Darkness,* New York: Vintage, 1971, pp. 26-27.
[21] New York: Harper & Bros., 1935, p. 82.
[22] P. 189.
[23] New York: Bantam Books, 1953, pp. 42-43.
[24] P. 134.
[25] Pp. 81-85.
[26] University of North Carolina Press, 1945, p. 320.
[27] New York: Rinehart & Co., 1947, p. 301.
[28] New York: Harcourt Brace & Co., 1947, p. 287.
[29] Boston: Little, Brown & Co., 1939, pp. 329-340.
[30] P. 82.
[31] New York: Harcourt, Brace & Co., 1951, p. 276.
[32] P. 171.
[33] *A Separate Reality,* New York: Simon and Schuster, 1971, p. 220.
[34] *Journey To Ixtlan,* New York: Simon and Schuster, 1972, p. 115.
[35] *Op. Cit.,* pp. 113-114.
[36] Boston: Little, Brown & Co., 1949, pp. 199-200.
[37] *Ibid.,* p. 87.
[38] New York: The John Day Co., 1955, p. 24.
[39] New York: Harcourt, Brace & Co., 1956, pp. 192-193.
[40] P. 197.
[41] *The Meeting of East and West,* New York: The MacMillan Co., 1946, p. 55.
[42] *Serenade,* New York: Alfred A. Knopf, 1937, p. 11.
[43] P. 291.
[44] New York: Vintage Books, 1955, p. 3.
[45] P. 17.
[46] New York: The John Day Co., 1951, p. 51.
[47] New York: The Devin-Adair Co., 1958.
[48] *Discovery No. 4,* July, 1954, pp. 46-56.
[49] Archibald MacLeish, *Conquistador,* Boston: Houghton Mifflin Co., 1932, p. 105.
[50] "The Destruction of Tenochtitlan," *In the American Grain,* Norfolk, Connecticut: New Directions, 1925, p. 33.
[51] *Reality Sandwiches,* pp. 26-27.
[52] *Idols Behind Altars,* New York: Payson & Clarke Ltd., 1929, p. 21.
[53] New York: Popular Library, 1955, p. 344.
[54] *Op. Cit.,* p. 35.
[55] P. 38.
[56] *The Mexico I Like,* p. 170.
[57] *The Letters of Hart Crane,* ed. Brom Weber, New York: Hermitage House, 1952, p. 385.
[58] P. 15.
[59] *The Mexico I Like,* pp. 172-173.
[60] *Journey To Ixtlan,* p. 55.
[61] *A Separate Reality,* pp. 182-183.

[62] *Indian Earth,* New York: Alfred A. Knopf, 1930, p. 17.
[63] *The Desert Music and Other Poems,* New York: Random House, 1954, pp. 89-90.
[64] London: Martin Secker, 1939, pp. 107-108.
[65] Pp. 57-58.
[66] New York: Liveright Publishing Corp., 1946, pp xx-xxi.
[67] *Ibid.,* p. xxi.
[68] P. 15.
[69] P. 19.
[70] Pp. 25-26.
[71] *The Meeting of East and West,* New York: The Macmillan Co., 1946, p. 54.

## CHAPTER 9

[1] San Francisco: A. M. Robertson, 1902, pp. vi–vii.
[2] Pp. 155–156.
[3] New York: Alfred A. Knopf, 1951, pp. 25–26.
[4] New York: Harper & Bros., 1942, p. 284.
[5] New York: Harper & Bros., 1935, p. 77.
[6] P. 156.
[7] New York: Basic Books, 1959, p. 68.
[8] New York: Harper & Bros., 1945, pp. 197–198.
[9] *The Overland Monthly,* Vol. II, April No. 4, 1869, pp. 375–376.
[10] *The Works of Bret Harte,* Argonaut Edition, New York: P. F. Collier & Son, Vol. XVII, p. 299.
[11] *Ibid.,* pp. 287–288.
[12] P. 293.
[13] *Rio Grande,* New York: Alfred A. Knopf, 1933, p. 239.
[14] *Followers of the Sun,* New York: Alfred A. Knopf, 1936, pp. 100–101.
[15] New York: Viking Press, 1947.
[16] Dallas: The Southwest Press, 1930.
[17] University Press in Dallas, 1942, pp. 46–53.
[18] pp. 94-95.
[19] New York: Ballantine Books, 1968, p. 5.
[20] *Journey To Ixtlan,* p. 151.
[21] New York: Bantam Books, 1953, p. 54.
[22] New York: Bantam Books, 1952.
[23] Pp. 138-140.
[24] P. 136.
[25] Carter Wilson, p. 37.
[26] New York: The Viking Press, 1941.
[27] *Indian Earth,* New York: Alfred A. Knopf, 1930, pp. 44-45.
[28] March 5, 1973.
[29] *The Teachings of Don Juan,* p. 255.
[30] *A Separate Reality,* p. 19.
[31] *Psychology Today,* December 1972, Vol. 6, No. 7, p. 102.
[32] *The Teachings of Don Juan,* p. 195.
[33] *Ibid.,* p. 151.
[34] *Ibid.,* p. 250.
[35] *Ibid.,* p. 143.
[36] *Op. Cit.,* p. 100.
[37] *Journey To Ixtlan,* p. 184.
[38] *A Separate Reality,* p. 51.
[39] *Journey To Ixtlan,* p. 302.
[40] *A Separate Reality,* p. 50.
[41] *Journey To Ixtlan,* p. 75.
[42] *Ibid.,* p. 229.
[43] *Ibid.,* p. 232.
[44] *A Separate Reality,* p. 302.
[45] *Ibid.,* p. 160.
[46] *Journey To Ixtlan,* p. 104.
[47] New York: Payson & Clarke Ltd., 1929, p. 37.

[48] *Mexican Journal,* New York: The Devin-Adair Co., 1958, p. 40.
[49] *The Land of Poco Tiempo,* New York: Charles Scribner's Sons, 1928, p. 118.
[50] P. 148.
[51] *The Letters of Hart Crane,* ed. Brom Weber, New York: Hermitage House, 1952, p. 381.
[52] *The Mexican Night,* p. 45.
[53] *Reality Sandwiches,* p. 30.
[54] New York: New Directions, p. 154.
[55] Pp. 83-84.
[56] Pp. 85-86.
[57] New York: Farrar and Rinehart, 1944, p. 19.
[58] *Letters,* pp. 391-392.
[59] Pp. 65-66.
[60] *The Meeting of East and West,* New York: MacMillan Co., 1946, pp. 27-28.
[61] *The Land of Journeys' Ending,* New York: The Century Co., 1924, p. 355.
[62] Austin: University of Texas Press, 1955, pp. 20-22.
[63] Argonaut ed. of *Works,* Vol. IV, pp. 216-217.
[64] *Ibid.,* Vol. VI, pp. 171-172.
[65] Pp. 178-181.
[66] *Land of Journeys' Ending,* p. 197.
[67] P. 316.
[68] P. 37.

## CHAPTER 10

[1] "Mis Ojos Hinchados," *El Espejo: Selected Mexican-American Literature,* Berkeley: Quinto Sol Publications, 1969, p. 172.
[2] "Out The Alley Our Soul Awaits Us," *Nationchild Plumaroja,* San Diego: Toltecas en Aztlan, Inc., 1972, n.p.
[3] "The Girl I Never Knew," *Chicano Poet,* Lubbock, Texas: Trucha Publications, Inc., 1973, pp. 78-79.
[4] *We Are Chicanos,* Philip D. Ortego, ed., New York: Washington Square Press, 1973, p. 178.
[5] New York: Ballantine Books, 1972, pp. 9-10.
[6] *Ibid.,* pp. 58-59.
[7] Jorge A. Huerta, ed., *El Teatro de la Esperanza, An Anthology of Chicano Drama,* Goleta, California: El Teatro de la Esperanza Inc., 1973, p. 44.
[8] *We Are Chicanos,* p. 305.
[9] *Ibid.,* pp. 309-10.
[10] Foreword to *The Road To Tamazunchale* by Ron Arias, Reno, Nevada: West Coast Poetry Review, 1975, p. 9.
[11] Sunnyvale, California: Ventura Press, 1969, p. 36.
[12] *Ibid.,* p. 70.
[13] *Ibid.,* p. 62.
[14] Garden City, New York: Doubleday, p. 275.
[15] Berkeley, California: Quinto Sol Publications, 1971, p. 79.
[16] *Ibid.,* p. 34.
[17] Berkeley, California: Quinto Sol Publications, 1971, p. 237.
[18] *Ibid.,* p. 233.
[19] *Ibid.,* p. 90.
[20] *Ibid.,* p. 14.
[21] Tucson, Arizona: Editorial Peregrinos, 1974, p. 91.
Note: Translations from *Los Peregrinos de Aztlán* are mine.
[22] *Ibid.,* p. 64.
[23] Reno, Nevada: West Coast Poetry Review, 1975, p. 102.
[24] *Ibid.,* p. 9.

## CHAPTER 11

[1] *Southwest Review,* Vol. XIV, No. 4, 1929, p. 488.
[2] Pasadena, California: Ward Ritchie Press, 1974, p. 3.

[3] *The Complete Poetry and Prose of Walt Whitman as prepared by Him for the Deathbed Edition.* Pellegrini and Cudahy, 1948, Vol. II, *November Boughs,* pp. 402-403.
[4] *Ibid.,* pp. 452-453.
[5] Charles L. Lummis, *A New Mexico David,* New York: Charles Scribner's Sons, 1902 (copyright 1891), p. 174.
[6] Mabel Major, Rebecca W. Smith, T. M. Pearce, *Southwest Heritage,* University of New Mexico Press, 1938, p. 33.
[7] New Haven: Yale University Press, 1955.
[8] Boston: Houghton Mifflin, 1932.
[9] Houghton Mifflin, 1934.
[10] New York: The Century Co., 1924.
[11] *The Land of Journeys' Ending,* pp. 441-443.
[12] Vol. XIV, No. 4, p. 477.
[13] *Literary History of Southern California,* Berkeley: University of California Press, 1950, pp. 41-42.
[14] Dallas: The Southwest Press, 1930, p. v.
[15] Note: The title of this book, originally published in 1935, was changed to the less felicitous title, due to publisher's insistence, of *The Mexico I Like,* in 1942. The latest edition has reverted to the original title.
[16] Vol. XIV, No. 4, 1929, pp. 492-493.
[17] *Ibid.,* p. 484.
[18] P. 142.
[19] Ed. Merrill Jensen, Madison: University of Wisconsin Press, 1951, p. 254.
[20] Vol. XIV, No. 4, 1929, p. 486.
[21] New York: Columbia University Press, 1932, p. 5.
[22] Vol. I, No. 3, August, 1931, p. 197.
[23] *Viva Mexico!,* New York and London: D. Appleton and Co., 1926, pp. 259-60.
[24] *Ibid.,* pp. 279-80.
[25] Vol. I, pp. 113-114.
[26] *The Horsemen of the Americas and the Literature They Inspired,* New York: Hastings House, 1953, p. 96.
[27] *Rio Grande,* New York: Alfred A. Knopf, 1933, p. 245.
[28] New York: Doubleday, 1958.
[29] New York: J. B. Lippincott, 1949, p. 138.
[30] P. 2.
[31] P. 6.
[32] Pp. 95-97.
[33] P. 249.
[34] Pp. 125-126.

## EPILOGUE

[1] *Billy Budd, Foretopman,* ed. Frederick Barron Freeman, New York: The Popular Living Classics Library, 1962, p. 81.

# BIBLIOGRAPHY

Abel, Lionel. "In the Sacred Park." *Partisan Review*, XXV (Winter, 1958).
Aiken, Conrad. *A Heart for the Gods of Mexico*. London: Martin Secker, 1939.
Allen, John Houghton, *Southwest*. New York: Bantam Books, 1953.
Alurista (Alfredo Baltazar Urista Heredia). "Mis Ojos Hinchados," *El Espejo: Selected Mexican-American Literature*. Berkeley, California: Quinto Sol Publications, 1969, p. 172.
Alurista. "Out The Alley Our Soul Awaits Us," *Nationchild Plumaroja*. San Diego: Toltecas en Aztlan, Inc., 1972, n. p.
Anaya, Rudolfo A. *Bless Me, Ultima*. Berkeley, California: Quinto Sol Publications, 1971.
Anderson, Maxwell. *Night Over Taos*. New York: Samuel French, 1935.
Anderson, Sherwood. "An Impression of Mexico — Its People," *Southern Literary Messenger I* (April, 1939), pp. 241-242.
Anderson, Sherwood. *Sherwood Anderson's Memoirs, A Critical Edition*. Ray Lewis White, ed. Chapel Hill: University of North Carolina Press, 1942.
Arias, Ron. *The Road to Tamazunchale*. Reno, Nevada: West Coast Poetry Review, 1975.
Arnold, Elliott. *The Time of the Gringo*. New York: Alfred A. Knopf, 1953.
Atherton, Gertrude. *The Splendid Idle Forties*. New York: MacMillan Company, 1902.
Audubon, John W. *Audubon's Western Journals, 1849-1850, Being the MS Record of a Trip from New York to Texas and an Overland Journey Through Mexico and Arizona to the Gold-Fields of California*. Cleveland: Arthur H. Clark Company, 1906.
Austin, Mary. *Earth Horizon*. Boston: Houghton Mifflin and Company, 1932.
———. *One Smoke Stories*. Boston: Houghton Mifflin and Company, 1934.
———. *The Land of Journeys' Ending*. New York: The Century Company, 1924.
———. *The Land of Little Rain*. Boston: Houghton, Mifflin and Company, 1903.
Austin, Stephen F. "The Austin Papers." Edited by Eugene C. Barker, *Annual Report for the American Historical Association for the Year 1922*. Washington: United States Government Printing Office, 1928.
Babbitt, Irving. *Spanish Character and Other Essays*. Houghton Mifflin and Company, 1940.
Badger, Joseph E. "Jack Rabbit, the Prairie Sport." *Beadle's Dime Novel Library*. New York: Beadle and Adams, 1878.
———. "Joachim, the Saddle King." *Beadle's Dime Novel Library*. New York: Beadle and Adams, 1881.
Bancroft, H. H. *History of the North Mexican States and Texas*. 2 volumes. San Francisco, 1889.
Barker, Eugene C. *Mexico and Texas*. Austin: University of Texas Press, 1934.
———. *The Life of Stephen F. Austin*. Nashville: Cokesbury Press, 1925.
Barrio, Raymond. *The Plum Plum Pickers*. Sunnyvale, California: Ventura Press, 1969.
Bartlett, John Russell. *Personal Narrative of Explorations and Incidents in Texas, New Mexico, California, Sonora, and Chihuahua*. 2 volumes. New York: Appleton and Company, 1854.

Bean, Ellis P. *Memoir of Colonel Ellis P. Bean, Written by Himself about the Year 1816.* Edited by W. P. Yoakum. Houston, Texas, 1930.
Bellow, Saul. *The Adventures of Augie March.* New York: Popular Library, 1955.
Bentley, Harold W. *A Dictionary of Spanish Terms in English with Special Reference to the American Southwest.* New York: Columbia University Press, 1932.
Bierce, Ambrose. "Antepenultimata." *The Collected Works of Ambrose Bierce.* 12 volumes. New York: The Neale Publishing Company, 1912.
Bird, Robert Montgomery. *Calavar; or the Knight of the Conquest: a Romance of Mexico.* Philadelphia: Lea and Blanchard, 1847.
──── . *The Infidel; or the Fall of Mexico.* 2 volumes. Philadelphia: Carey, Lea and Blanchard, 1835.
Braddy, Haldeen. *Cock of the Walk.* Albuquerque: University of New Mexico Press, 1955.
Brenner, Anita. *Idols Behind Altars.* New York: Payson and Clarke Limited, 1929.
Browne, J. Ross. *A Tour Through Arizona, 1864 or Adventures in the Apache Country.* Tucson: Arizona Silhouettes, 1950.
Browne, J. Ross. *Crusoe's Island ... with Sketches of Adventure in California and Washoe.* New York: Harper and Brothers, 1864.
Bryant, William Cullen. *The Life and Works of William Cullen Bryant.* Edited by Parke Godwin. 6 volumes. New York: D. Appleton and Company, 1883-89.
*Bulletin of the New York Public Library,* (July, 1922).
Bynner, Witter. *Indian Earth.* New York: Alfred A. Knopf, 1930.
──── . *Journey with Genius: Recollections and Reflections Concerning the D. H. Lawrences.* New York: The John Day Company, 1951.
Cain, James M. *Serenade.* New York: Alfred A. Knopf, 1937.
Castañeda, Carlos. *A Separate Reality: Further Conversations with Don Juan.* New York: Simon & Schuster, 1971.
──── ."An Interview With Carlos Castañeda," *Psychology Today,* December, 1972, vol. 6, no. 7, pp. 101-102.
──── . *Journey to Ixtlan.* New York: Simon & Schuster, 1972.
──── . *The Teachings of Don Juan: A Yaqui Way of Knowledge.* New York: Ballantine Books, 1969.
Cather, Willa Sibert. *Death Comes for the Archbishop.* New York: Alfred A. Knopf, 1951.
──── .*The Professor's House.* New York: Alfred A. Knopf, 1925.
──── . *The Song of the Lark.* Boston: Houghton Mifflin Company, 1943.
Chamberlain, Samuel E. *My Confession.* New York: Harper Brothers, 1956.
Chopin, Kate. *The Awakening.* New York: Capricorn Books, 1964.
Clappe, Louise Amelia Knapp (Smith). *The Shirley Letters From the California Mines 1851-1852.* Introduction and notes by Carl I. Wheat. New York: Alfred A. Knopf, 1949.
Claremon, Neil. *Borderland.* New York: Alfred A. Knopf, 1975.
Clark, Walter van Tilburg. *The Ox-Bow Incident.* New York: Readers Club, 1942.
Clemens, Jeremiah. *Bernard Lile, an Historical Romance.* Philadelphia: J. B. Lippincott and Company, 1856.
──── . *Mustang Grey, a Romance.* Philadelphia: J. B. Lippincott, 1858.
Clemens, Samuel Langhorne (Mark Twain). *Roughing It.* 2 volumes. New York: Harper and Brothers, 1899.
──── . *Sketches New and Old.* New York: Harper and Brothers, 1905.
Cleveland, Richard. *Voyages and Commercial Enterprises, of the Sons of New England.* New York: Leavitt and Allen, 1855.
Cooper, James Fenimore. *Jack Tier, The Works of James Fenimore Cooper.* Mohawk Edition. 32 volumes. New York: G. F. Putnam's Sons, 1896.
──── . *The Prairie, The Works of James Fenimore Cooper.* Mohawk Edition. 32 volumes. New York: G. P. Putnam's Sons.
Copeland, Fayette. *Kendall of the Picayune.* Norman: University of Oklahoma Press, 1943.
Corso, Gregory. *Gasoline.* San Francisco: City Lights Books, 1958.

Crane, Hart. *The Collected Poems of Hart Crane.* Edited with introduction by Waldo Frank. New York: Liveright Publishing Corporation, 1933 (Black and Gold Edition, July, 1946).
———. *The Letters of Hart Crane, 1916-1932.* Edited by Brown Weber, New York: Hermitage House, 1952.
Crane, Stephen. "Mexican Sights and Street Scenes." *Philadelphia Press,* May 19, 1895.
———. *The Works of Stephen Crane.* Edited by Wilson Follett. 12 volumes. New York: Alfred A. Knopf, 1926.
Crockett, David. *Colonel Crockett's Exploits and Adventures in Texas.* London: R. Kennett, 1837.
Dana, Richard Henry. *Two Years Before the Mast.* New York: MacMillan Company, 1915.
DeForest, John William. *Overland.* New York: Sheldon and Company, 1871.
de Leon, Nephtali. *Chicano Poet.* Lubbock, Texas: Trucha Publications, Inc., 1973.
DeVoto, Bernard. *1846 The Year of Decision.* Boston: Little, Brown and Company, 1943.
Dobie, J. Frank. *Apache Gold and Yaqui Silver.* Boston: Little, Brown and Company, 1939.
———. *A Vaquero of the Brush Country.* Boston: Little, Brown and Company, 1952.
———. *Coronado's Children.* Dallas: The Southwest Press, 1930.
———. *The Mexico I Like.* Dallas: University Press, 1942.
Dos Passos, John. *In All Countries.* New York: Harcourt, Brace and Company, 1934.
———. *U.S.A.* New York: Random House, The Modern Library.
Duarte-Clark, Roderigo. "Brujerías," *El Teatro de la Esperanza, An Anthology of Chicano Drama.* Jorge A. Huerta, ed., Goleta, California: El Teatro de la Esperanza, Inc., 1973.
Duganne, A. J. A. "The Peon Prince or the Yankee Knight Errant." *Beadle's Dime Novels.* New York: Beadle and Company, 1861.
Emery, George F. "The Water Witch." *The Overland Monthly,* III, 1969.
Erasmus, Charles J. *Man Takes Control.* University of Minnesota Press, Minneapolis, 1961.
Evans, George W. B. *Mexican Gold Trail, the Journal of a 49er.* Edited by Glenn S. Dumke. San Marino, California: Huntington Library Publication, 1945.
Fergusson, Harvey. *Followers of the Sun, a Trilogy of the San Fe Trail* (includes *Wolf Song,* 1927; *In Those Days,* 1929; *Blood of the Conquerors,* 1921). New York: Alfred A. Knopf, 1936.
———. *Grant of Kingdom.* New York: William Morrow and Company, 1950.
———. *Rio Grande.* New York: Alfred A. Knopf, 1933.
———. *The Conquest of Don Pedro.* New York: William Morrow and Company, 1954.
Ferlinghetti, Lawrence. *The Mexican Night — A Travel Journal.* New York: New Directions, 1962.
Flandrau, Charles M. *Viva Mexico!* New York and London: D. Appleton and Co., 1926.
Fletcher, John Gould. *Selected Poems.* New York: Farrar and Rinehart, 1938.
Flint, Timothy. *Francis Berrian, or The Mexican Patriot.* 2 volumes. Boston: Cummings, Hilliard and Company, 1826.
Frank, Waldo. *Our America.* New York: Boni and Liveright Publishers, 1919.
Frémont, John Charles. *Memoirs of My Life, Including in the Narrative Five Journeys of Western Exploration during the Years 1842, 1843-44, 1845-6-7, 1848-49, 1853-4.* 1 volume (no more volumes published), Chicago: Belford, Clarke, and Company, 1887.
Galarza, Ernesto. *Barrio Boy.* New York: Ballantine Books, 1972.
Ganilh, Anthony. *Mexico Versus Texas.* Philadelphia: M. Siegfried, 1838.

Garland, Hamlin. "Delmar of Pima." *McClure's Magazine*, XVIII, no. 4 (February, 1902).
Garrard, Lewis H. *Wah-To-Yah and the Taos Trail*. Edited by Ralph P. Bieber. Glendale, California: Arthur H. Clark Company, 1938. (Southwest Historical Series, Vol. VI.
Garza, Daniel. "Everybody Knows Tobie." *We Are Chicanos*. Philip D. Ortego, ed. New York: Washington Square Press, 1973, pp. 301-310.
Gillmor, Frances. *Flute of the Smoking Mirror*. University of Arizona Press, 1949.
——. *The King Danced in the Market Place*. University of Arizona Press, 1963.
Ginsberg, Allen. *Reality Sandwiches* (1953-1960). San Francisco: City Lights Books, 1963.
Goodwyn, Frank. *The Black Bull*. Garden City, New York: Doubleday and Company, 1958.
——. *The Magic of Limping John*. New York: Farrar and Rinehart, 1944.
Gregg, Josiah. *Commerce of the Prairies or the Journal of a Santa Fe Trader, During Eight Expeditions across the Great Western Prairies and a Residence of Nearly Nine Years in Northern Mexico*. 2 volumes. Philadelphia: J. W. Moore, 1851.
Hall, Major Sam. "The Serpent of El Paso." *Beadle's Dime Library*. New York: Beadle and Adams, 1882.
Hammett, Samuel A. *Piney Woods Tavern; or Sam Slick in Texas*. Philadelphia: T. B. Peterson and Brothers, 1858.
Hardwick, Elizabeth. Review of *The Children of Sanchez* by Oscar Lewis. *The New York Times Book Review*. August 27, 1961.
Harte, Bret. "Friar Pedro's Ride." *The Overland Monthly*, II (April, 1869).
Harte, Bret. *Works*, Argonaut Edition. 20 volumes. New York: P. F. Collier and Son, 1896-1914.
——. *Gabriel Conroy*. Riverside Edition of Works, XIII and XIV. Boston: Houghton, Mifflin and Company, 1896.
Hatcher, Mattie Austin. *Letters of an Early American Traveler — Mary Austin Holley Her Life and Her Works*. Dallas: Southwest Press, 1933.
Helm, MacKinley. *A Matter of Love*. New York: Harper and Brothers, 1945.
Hemingway, Ernest. *Winner Takes Nothing*. New York: Charles Scribner's Sons, 1933.
Herrick, Robert. *Waste*. New York: Harcourt, Brace and Company, 1924.
Horgan, Paul. *Figures in a Landscape*. New York: Harper and Brothers, 1931.
——. *Great River, the Rio Grande in North American History*. 2 volumes. New York: Rinehart and Company, 1954.
——. *Main Line West*. New York: Harper and Brothers, 1936.
——. *No Quarter Given*. New York: Harper and Brothers, 1935.
——. *The Centuries of Santa Fe*. New York: E. P. Dutton and Company, 1956.
——. *The Common Heart*. New York: Harper and Brothers, 1942.
Horgan, Paul. *The Return of the Weed*. New York: Harper and Brothers, 1936.
Howren, Alleine. "Causes and Origin of the Decree of April 6, 1830." *The Southwestern Historical Quarterly*, XVI, 1913.
Hughes, Langston. *I Wonder As I Wander: An Autobiographical Journey*. New York: Hill and Wang, 1956.
Ingraham, Joseph Holt. *Montezuma, the Serf*. 2 volumes. Boston: H. L. Williams, 1845.
Irving, Washington. *The Works of Washington Irving*. The Kinderhook Edition. 10 volumes. New York: G. P. Putnam's Sons.
Jackson, Helen Hunt. *Ramona*. Boston: Little, Brown and Company, 1935.
Jarrell, Randall. *Poetry and the Age*. New York: Vintage Books, 1955.
Jeffers, Robinson. *Cawdor and Other Poems*. New York: Random House, 1934.
——. *Flagons and Apples*. Los Angeles: Grafton Publishing Company, 1912.
——. *Roan Stallion, Tamar and Other Poems*. New York: The Modern Library, 1935.
——. *The Selected Poetry of Robinson Jeffers*. New York: Random House, 1937.
——. *Women at Point Sur*. New York: Random House, 1935.

Jensen, Merrill, editor. *Regionalism in America.* Madison: University of Wisconsin Press, 1951.
Kemp, Lysander. "The Only Beast." *Discovery No. 4.* New York: Pocket Books, 1954.
Kendall, George Wilkins. *Narrative of the Texan Santa Fe Expedition.* London: Henry Washbourne, 1847.
———. *Narrative of the Texan Santa Fe Expedition.* Chicago: Lakeside Press, 1929.
Kerouac, Jack. *On The Road.* New York: Signet Books, 1958.
Kesey, Ken. *One Flew Over The Cuckoo's Nest.* New York: The Viking Press, 1973.
Krutch, Joseph Wood. *The Forgotten Peninsula.* New York: William Sloane Associates, 1961.
LaFarge, Oliver. *Behind the Mountains.* Boston: Houghton, Mifflin and Company, 1956.
———. Introduction to *Five Families* by Oscar Lewis. New York: Basic Books Inc., 1959.
Lanier, Sidney. "San Antonio de Bexar." *Retrospects and Prospects.* New York: Charles Scribner's Sons, 1899.
Lawrence, D. H. *The Plumed Serpent.* New York: Vintage Books, 1955.
Lea, Tom. *The Brave Bulls.* New York: Pocket Books, 1951.
———. *The King Ranch.* 2 volumes. Boston: Little, Brown and Company, 1957.
———. *The Wonderful Country.* Boston: Little, Brown and Company, 1952.
Lee, Alwyn. "Something for Bradshaw's Tombstone." *Partisan Review,* XXII (Summer, 1955).
Lewis, Alfred Henry. *Wolfville.* New York: Frederick A. Stokes Company, 1897.
———. *Wolfville Days.* New York: Frederick A. Stokes Company, 1902.
Lewis, Oscar. *Five Families.* New York: Basic Books Inc., 1959.
———. *The Children of Sánchez.* New York: Random House, 1961.
Levertov, Denise. *Here and Now.* San Francisco: City Lights Books, 1957.
———. *The Jacob's Ladder.* New York: New Directions, 1958.
———. *The Sorrow Dance.* New York: New Directions, 1963.
———. *With Eyes At The Back of Our Heads.* New York: New Directions, 1958.
Lippard, George. *Legends of Mexico.* Philadelphia: T. B. Peterson, 1847.
London, Jack. *The Night-Born.* New York: Grosset and Dunlap, 1913.
López, Antonio. "Pánfila La Curandera," *El Teatro de la Esperanza, An Anthology of Chicano Drama.* Jorge A. Huerta, ed. Goleta, California: El Teatro de la Esperanza, Inc., 1973.
Lowerie, Samuel Harmon. "Culture Conflict in Texas." Doctoral dissertation, Columbia University, 1932.
Lummis, Charles F. *A New Mexico David.* New York: Charles Scribner's Sons, 1902.
———. *Flowers of Our Lost Romance.* Boston: Houghton Mifflin Company, 1929.
———. *The Land of Poco Tiempo.* New York: Charles Scribner's Sons, 1928.
MacLeish, Archibald. *Conquistador.* Boston: Houghton Mifflin Company, 1932.
Magoffin, Susan Shelby. *Down the Santa Fe Trail and Into Mexico, The Diary of Susan Shelby Magoffin in 1846-1847.* Edited by Stella M. Drumm. New Haven: Yale University Press, 1926.
Major, Mabel, Rebecca W. Smith, and T. M. Pearce. *Southwest Heritage.* Albuquerque: University of New Mexico Press, 1938.
Marañon, Gregorio. "Grandeur and Misery of the Count of Villamediana." Translated from the Spanish by F. L. Ganivet, *Partisan Review,* XXIV (Summer, 1957).
Maturin, Edward, *Montezuma, the Last of the Aztecs.* 2 volumes. New York: Paine and Burgess, 1845.
McWilliams, Carey. *North from Mexico.* Philadelphia: J. B. Lippincott Company, 1949.
Melville, Herman. *Billy Budd, Foretopman.* Edited by Frederick Barron Freeman. New York: The Popular Living Classics Library, 1962.
Méndez M., Miguel. *Peregrinos de Aztlán.* Tucson: Editorial Peregrinos, 1974.
———. "Tata Casehua," *El Espejo: Selected Mexican-American Literature.* Tucson: Editorial Peregrinos, 1974.

Miller, Henry. *Big Sur and the Oranges of Hieronymus Bosch.* New Directions, 1957.
Miller, Henry. *The Colossus of Maroussi.* New York: New Directions, 1941.
Miller, Joaquín. "El Vaquero." *The Overland Monthly,* X, 1873.
———. *Songs of the Sierra.* Boston: Robert Brothers, 1873.
Morris, Wright. *Love Among the Cannibals.* New York: Harcourt, Brace and Company, 1957.
———. *The Field of Vision.* New York: Harcourt, Brace and Company, 1956.
Neiman, Gilbert. *There Is a Tyrant in Every Country.* New York: Harcourt, Brace and Company, 1947.
Niggli, Josephina. *Mexican Village.* Chapel Hill: North Carolina University Press, 1945.
———. *Step Down Elder Brother.* New York: Rinehart and Company, 1947.
Norris, Frank. *McTeague.* New York: Signet, 1964.
———. *The Octopus.* New York: Doubleday, Page and Company, 1904.
Northrop, F. S. C. *The Meeting of East and West.* New York: The MacMillan Company, 1946.
Parkman, Francis. *The Oregon Trail.* Philadelphia: John C. Winston Company, 1931.
Pattie, James O. *The Personal Narrative of James O. Pattie of Kentucky.* Edited by Timothy Flint. Chicago: The Lakeside Press, 1930.
Pearce, T. M. On regionalism in the Southwest. *The New Mexico Quarterly,* I, no. 3 (August, 1931), p. 197.
Pike, Albert. *Prose Poems and Sketches.* Boston: Light and Horton, 1834.
Pike, Zebulon. *An Account of Expeditions to the Sources of the Mississippi and Through the Eastern Parts of Louisiana to the Sources of the Arkansas, Kans, La Platte, and Pierre Juan Rivers; Performed by order of the Government of the United States During the Years 1805, 1806, 1807 and a Tour through the Interior Parts of New Spain when conducted through these Provinces by order of the Captain General in the Year 1807.* Philadelphia, 1810.
Porter, William Sidney (O. Henry). *Heart of the West.* New York: Doubleday, Page and Company, 1927.
———. *Rolling Stones.* New York: P. F. Collier and Son, n. d.
Porter, Katherine Anne. *Flowering Judas and Other Stories.* New York: The Modern Library.
Powell, Lawrence Clark. *Southwest Classics.* Pasadena, California: Ward Ritchie Press, 1974.
Prescott, William H. *History of the Conquest of Mexico and History of the Conquest of Peru.* New York: The Modern Library.
Pritchard, W. T. "In the Backwoods of Mexico." *The Overland Monthly,* II (June, 1869).
Ramirez, Frank. "La Bolsa Negra," *El Teatro de la Esperanza, An Anthology of Chicano Drama.* Jorge A. Huerta, ed. Goleta, California: El Teatro de la Esperanza, Inc. 1973.
Ramsey, Robert. *Fiesta.* New York: The John Day Company, 1955.
Remington, Frederick. *Pony Tracks, Sketches of Pioneer Life.* New York: Harper and Brothers, 1895.
Rennie, Ysabel. *The Blue Chip.* New York: Harper & Bros., 1954.
Rhodes, Eugene Manlove. *Copper Streak Trail.* Boston: Houghton Mifflin Company, 1922.
———. *The Best Novels and Stories of Eugene Manlove Rhodes.* Edited by J. Frank Dobie. Boston: Houghton Mifflin Company, 1949.
Richter, Conrad. *The Lady.* New York: Alfred A. Knopf, 1957.
Rivera, Tomas. ". . . *and the earth did not part.*" Berkeley, California: Quinto Sol Publications, 1971.
Rodman, Selden. *Mexican Journal.* New York: The Devin-Adair Company, 1958.
Roeder, Ralph. *Juárez and His Mexico.* 2 volumes. New York: The Viking Press, 1947.
Romero, Leo. "I Too, America," *We Are Chicanos.* Philip D. Ortego, ed. New York: Washington Square Press, 1973, p. 178.

Rukeyser, Muriel. *The Speed of Darkness.* New York: Vintage, 1971.
Sanchez, José María. *Viaje a Texas — en 1828–1829, Diario del Teniente D. José Maria Sanchez, Miembro de la Comision de Limites.* Mexico: Papeles Historicos, 1939.
Sandburg, Carl. *Smoke and Steel, Slabs of the Sunburnt West, Good Morning, America.* New York: Harcourt, Brace and Company. n. d.
Shaler, William. *Journal of a Voyage Between China and the Northwestern Coast of America, Made in 1804.* Claremont, California: Saunders Studio Press, 1935.
Shulman, Irving. *The Square Trap.* Boston: Little, Brown, and Company. 1935.
Simms, William Gilmore. *Michael Bonham or the Fall of Bexar.* Jno. R. Thompson, 1852.
Simpson, Lesley Byrd. *Many Mexicos.* New York: G. P. Putnam's Sons, 1941.
Sonnichsen, C. L. *The Story of Roy Bean: Law West of the Pecos.* Greenwich, Connecticut: Fawcett Publications, 1972.
Sorensen, Virginia. *The Proper Gods.* New York: Harcourt, Brace and Company, 1951.
*Southwest Review,* XIV, no. 4, 1929.
Spicer, Edward H. *Cycles of Conquest.* University of Arizona Press. Tucson: 1962.
Steinbeck, John. *The Forgotten Village.* New York: The Viking Press, 1941.
———. *The Long Valley.* New York: The Viking Press, 1938.
———. *The Pastures of Heaven.* New York: Brewer, Warren, and Putnam, 1932.
———. *The Pearl.* New York: The Viking Press, 1947.
———. *Tortilla Flat.* New York: Covici Friede Publishers, 1935.
Stevens, Wallace. *The Collected Poems of Wallace Stevens.* New York: Alfred A. Knopf, 1955.
Stoddard, Charles Warren. *In the Footprints of the Padres.* San Francisco: A. M. Robertson, 1902.
Summers, Richard. *Dark Madonna.* New York: Bantam Books, 1952.
Taylor, Bayard. *Eldorado or Adventures in the Path of Empire.* New York: G. P. Putnam's Sons, 1894.
Thoreau, Henry David. *Anti-Slavery and Reform Papers.* Edited by H. S. Salt. London: Swan Sonnenschein and Company, 1890.
*Time,* March 5, 1973, pp. 36-38, 43-45.
Tinker, Edward Larocque. *The Horsemen of the Americas and the Literature They Inspired.* New York: Hastings House, 1953.
Tornel, José María. "Texas and the United States of America in their Relations with the Mexican Republic." *The Mexican Side of the Texas Revolution.* Compiled and translated by Carlos E. Castaneda. Dallas: P. L. Turner Company, 1928.
Trilling, Lionel. *The Liberal Imagination.* New York: The Viking Press, 1948.
Tuck, Ruth D. *Not With the Fist.* New York: Harcourt, Brace and Company, 1946.
Turnbull, W. R. "A Pronunciamiento." *The Overland Monthly* (October, 1870).
Turner, Timothy G. *Bullets, Bottles, and Gardenias.* Dallas: Southwest Press, 1935.
Vaca, Nick. "The Visit," *El Espejo: Selected Mexican-American Literature.* Octavio I. Romano-V., ed. Berkeley, California: Quinto Sol Publications, 1969.
Vaillant, George. *The Aztecs of Mexico.* Garden City, New York: Doubleday Doran and Company, 1941.
Vasquez, Richard. *Chicano.* Garden City, New York: Doubleday, 1970.
Villareal, José Antonio. *Pocho.* Garden City, New York: Doubleday, 1959.
Walker, Franklin. *A Literary History of Southern California.* Berkeley: University of California Press, 1950.
———. *San Francisco's Literary Frontier.* New York: Alfred A. Knopf, 1939.
Warfel, Harry R., and G. Harrison Orians. *American Local-Color Stories.* New York: American Book Company, 1941.
Waters, Frank. *People of the Valley.* New York: Farrar and Rinehart, 1941.
Waugh, Julia Nott, *The Silver Cradle.* Austin: University of Texas Press, 1955.

Webb, James Josiah. *Adventures in the Santa Fe Trade 1844-1847*. Glendale, California: The Arthur H. Clark Company, 1931.

Webber, Charles W. *The Prairie Scout: A Romance of Border Life*. New York: Dewitt and Davenport, 1852.

Weinberg, Albert. *Manifest Destiny*. Baltimore: Johns Hopkins Press, 1935.

Wells, William V. "The French in Mexico." *The Overland Monthly*, I, no. 3 (September, 1868).

Whitman, Walt. *The Complete Poetry and Prose of Walt Whitman as prepared by Him for the Deathbed Edition*. 2 volumes. New York: Pellegrini and Cudahy, 1948.

―――. *The Gathering of the Forces*. Edited by Cleveland Rodgers and John Black. 2 volumes. New York: G. P. Putnam's Sons, 1920.

Williams, Stanley T. *The Life of Washington Irving*. 2 volumes. London: Oxford University Press, 1935.

―――. *The Spanish Background of American Literature*. 2 volumes. New Haven: Yale University Press, 1955.

Williams, Tennessee. "Rubio y Morena," *Hard Candy*. New York: New Directions, 1954.

―――. *The Night of the Iguana*. New York: New Directions, 1962.

Williams, William Carlos. *In the American Grain*. Norfolk, Connecticut: New Directions, 1925.

―――. *Selected Essays of William Carlos Williams*. New York: Random House, 1954.

―――. *The Desert Music and Other Poems*. New York: Random House, 1954.

Wilson, Carter. *Crazy February*. Philadelphia: J. B. Lippincott, 1966.

Wise, Lieutenant H. A. USN. *Los Gringos or An Inside View of Mexico and California With Wanderings in Peru, Chili, and Polynesia*. London: Richard Bentley, 1849.

Wister, Owen. *Owen Wister Out West, His Journals and Letters*. Editors by Fanny Kemble Wister. University of Chicago Press, 1958.

# INDEX

## A

"The Adventure of Padre Vicentio," 285
*Adventures in the Santa Fe Trade:* 21, 37, 57, 126
*The Adventures of Augie March:* 241, 273–74
*The Adventures of Captain Bonneville:* 25, 54, 62, 66
"An Afternoon Miracle," 172
Anaya, Rudolfo: 324–28
*. . . and the earth did not part:* 323–24
Aiken, Conrad: 181, 197–98, 216–17, 277
All Soul's Day: 274–75
Allen, Hervey: 20
Allen, John Houghton: 288–89; on the conquest, 7–9; satire on "romantic" Mexico, 152–53; on the California myth, 156; on Mexican attitudes toward Americans, 180–81; on cruelty, 200; on Americanized Mexicans, 238; on banditry, 243–47; on sex, 247; on bullfights, 265; on result of culture synthesis, 347–49
Alurista: 309, 310
American ethnocentricity: 120–21
Anderson, Maxwell: 106–108, 111–114
Anderson, Sherwood: on Anglo fear of Mexicans, 191; on Mexican endurance, 224–25
*Anthony Adverse:* 20
*Apache Gold and Yaqui Silver:* 263–64
Apaches and Mexicans: 47–48
Arias, Ron: 330–31
Aristocrats *see* ricos
Armijo, Manuel: 19, 37, 38, 111–12
Army *see* military power
Arnold, Elliott: 20, 52; on Mexican psychology, 52; on death, 101; on Armijo, 111; on corruption, 118
Arrieros: 55
Atherton, Gertrude: 139

Audubon, John Wodehouse: 24, 56
Austin, Mary: 249; on the California myth, 154; on courtesy, 207–08; on primitive virtues, 227; on bandits, 244–45; on Catholicism, 306; as a regional writer, 337, 338
Austin, Stephen F.: 28–29, 120–21
*The Awakening:* 191
Aztecs *see* Conquest of Mexico
*The Aztecs of Mexico:* 4
Aztlan: 308

## B

Backnell, William: 21
Ballads: 248
Banditry: 243; Austin on, 244; Allen on, 245; Dobie, 246; Braddy, 246–47, *see also* thievery
"The Bandit's Prayer," 244
Barker, Eugene C.: 69
*Barrio Boy:* 311–13
Barrio, Raymond: 319–21
Bartlett, John Russell: 24, 54; on mechanical ineptness, 34; on laziness, 36–37; on women, 43; on cowardice, 49; on courage, 54; on thievery, 56; on cruelty, 63; racial intolerance, 73; on Catholicism, 123, 130, 133
Beadle and Adams: 27
Bean, Ellis: 18, 64, 115
*Behind the Mountains:* 162, 199
Bellow, Saul: 241, 273–74
Bentley, Harold W.: 342
*Bernard Lile:* 50, 60, 117–18
Bierce, Ambrose: 178
Bird, Robert Montgomery: 4–5; on the Conquest, 10; on violence, 59
*The Blood of the Conquerers:* 77, 160–61, 176–77
*The Black Bull:* 256–57, 344–45
*Bless Me, Ultima:* 324–28
*The Blue Chip:* 345–46

"A Boatman," 276
Borderland: 212, 298, 340
Botkin, B. A.: 340
Braddy, Haldeen: 246–47
*The Brave Bulls:* 186–87, 230–31
Bravery *see* courage
Bravery, cult of: 253
Brenner, Anita: on cruelty, 197; on death 273, 278; on religious fusion, 298
"The Bride Comes to Yellow Sky," 168
*The Bridge:* 13
Browne, J. Ross: 24; on laziness, 36; on women, 43, 88–89; racial intolerance, 71–2
*Brujerias:* 314
Bryant, William Cullen: 63, 76; on clergy, 124–25
Bullfights: 63, 265 ff.; Allen on, 265; Lea on, 265–66; Ramsey, 267–68; Morris, 268; Lawrence, 269–70; Northrop, 268–69; Kemp, 270–72
*Bullets, Bottles and Gardenias:* 141, 206
Bynner, Witter: 147, 291–92; on race, 184; on violence, 195; on simple virtues, 231; on folk music, 249; on bullfights, 269–70; on death, 276

## C

Caballeros: 143 ff.
Cain, James N.: 269
California: 22, 23; attitudes toward Mexicans, 69–70; Helen Hunt Jackson on, 137–39; Harte, 139; Atherton, 139
California myth: 137–39 ff., 154 ff.
*Californians:* 214
Castañeda, Carlos: on destiny, 264–65; on death, 276; on a *diablera*, 288; on sorcery, 294; on being a warrior, 294; on hallucinogenic drugs, 294–95; on the power of place, 296; on Castañeda's relationship to American writers, 296; on looking and seeing, 296; on doing and not doing, 297; earthy humor, 297–98; on Indian resistance to change, 340
Cather, Willa: 249; sympathetic view of Mexicans, 174–76; on charity, 208; on primitive virtues, 213; on Catholicism, 281–83; as a regional writer, 335
Catholicism and the clergy: 120 ff., 284 ff.; Zebulon Pike on, 121; Evans, 112, 125; Pattie, 122–23; Bartlett, 123, 130, 132; Parkman, 126; Webb, 128; Albert Pike, 126, 128–29; Kendall, 127–28, 129–31; Chamberlain, 129; Ganilh, 130–31; Prescott, 131–32; Susan Magoffin, 133; Cather, 281–83; Horgan, 283–84; Harte, 285–86; Fergusson, 286; Steinbeck, 286–87; Austin, 306; *see also* Penitentes
*The Centuries of Santa Fe,* 21, 37, 81
Chamberlain, Samuel E.; 30–31; on horsemanship, 67; on violence, 60–62; on clergy, 124
Charity *see* kindness
Chavez, Cesar: 309, 319–20
Chicano: origin of word, 308
Chicano literature: 309–32
Chicano movement: 308–09
Chicano theater: 313–15
*The Children of Sanchez:* 164–65, 186, 188–89, 206, 223, 247, 255–56, 263
Chopin, Kate: on Mexican treachery, 191
Chroniclers, early: 17
Claremon, Neil: on love for land, 212; on Indianized White man, 298; on Indians' resistance to change, 340
Clark, Walter van Tilburg: 189
Classes and society: 73–74 ff.
Cleanliness: 38–39
Clemens, Jeremiah: on origin of "greaser," 38–39; on cowardice, 50; on violence, 60; on corruption, 117–18; on Jesuits and Catholicism, 124, 126–27
Clemens, Samuel L.: 141
Clergy *see* Catholicism and clergy
Cleveland, Richard, 22, 127
"The Coast-Range Christ," 151–52
*Cock of the Walk,* 246–47
*Colonel Crockett's Exploits,* 46–47
*The Colossus of Maroussi:* 300–01
Comanches and Mexicans: 49
"The Comedian as the Letter C," 148
*Commerce of the Prairies:* 21, 33, 55
*The Common Heart:* 283
*The Conquest of Don Pedro:* 82–83, 89–97, 106
Conquest of Mexico: 3 ff.; Prescott, 3–4; Vaillant, 4; W. C. Williams, 5–6, 7, 13–14; Bird, 4, 18; Jiménez Moreno, 9–10; MacLeish, 11
The Conquest as innocence betrayed: 4, 9
*The Conquest of Mexico:* 3–4, 131–32
*Conquistador:* 6–7, 11, 12
Contacts, early, by land: 18–21
Contacts, early, by sea: 22
Contempt for men contrasted with attitude toward women: 42–43
Contempt for Mexicans: 26, 31, 33, *see*

*also* cowardice, thievery, and similar headings
Contempt for Mexicans, reaction against: 166 ff.; survivals of, 166–67 ff.
"Convert of the Mission," 305–06
Cooper, James Fenimore: 25, 41; on courtesy, 41; on sex, 75; on feudal society, 116
*Copper Streak Trail:* 208
*Coronado's Children:* 230, 287, 339
Corruption: 117 ff.; Herrick on, 188; Lanier on, 188; Lewis, 188–89
Corso, Gregory: cruelty to horses, 198–99; Mexican cultural loss, 250
Cortez: 3, 10, 11
"Countryman," 231
Courage, 30, 53–54, 205 ff.; Bartlett on, 54; Irving on, 54–55; of muleteers, 55; Magoffin on, 52; Garrard, 51, 53–54; Lummis, 205; Turner on, 206, *see also* cowardice
Courtesy: 40–42, 207–09
Cowardice: 44–47, 202–04; Pattie on, 46–48; Garrard on, 47; Albert Pike on, 43; Evans on, 48–49; Bartlett on, 49; Harte on, 202; Stephen Crane on, 202–04
Crane, Hart: on racial fusion, 13; on cultural complexity, 70–71; on the Day of the Dead, 275; on death, 278; on popular religion, 299–300; on the Virgin, 303
Crane, Stephen: admiration for Mexico, 140; on Mexicans in borderlands, 168; on violence, 191–92; on cruelty, 195–96
*Crazy February:* 184, 190, 240, 288, 290
Criollos, 12, 32, 44–45, *see also* feudalist society
Cruelty: 62-3, 195–201; Stephen Crane on, 195–196; Brenner on, 197; Aiken on, 196–197; Niggli on, 199; La Farge on, 199; Lee on, 199; Neiman on, 200–01; Lea on, 201; Allen and Dobie on, 201; Levertov, 198; Gregory Corso: on cruelty to horses, 198–99; on Mexican cultural loss, 250; Tennessee Williams, 198
*Crusoe's Island,* 24
Cultural complexity: 70–71
Culture conflict in Southwest: 104 ff.
Culture fusion: 12–13, 250, 348
Culture synthesis in Southwest: 347 ff.; Allen on results, 346; Frank on results of, 347; Fergusson, 347–48; *see also* linguistic borrowing

Curanderas: 289–91
*Cycles of Conquest:* 103

## D

Dana, Richard Henry: 22; on laziness, 35–36; on courtesy, 41; on classes in California, 74; on women, 88; on funerals, 98–99; on judicial procedure, 119
Dancing: 80–81
*Dark Madonna:* 255, 289
Day of the Dead: 274–75
"The Dead Men's Child," 233–34
Death: 99 ff., 272 ff.; Prescott on, 98; Dana on, 98–99; Kendall, 99; Horgan, 100–01; Magoffin, 101; W. C. Williams on, 272–73; Brenner, 273, 278; Lewis 274; Bellow on, 273–74; Ginsberg on, 272–73, 274; Castañeda, 264–65, 276
Death as a festivity: 275
*Death Comes for the Archbishop:* 53, 208, 232, 249, 282–83, 299, 335–36, 341
DeForest, John W.: 170–71
"Delmar of Pima," 143, 167–68
de Leon, Nephtalí: 310
"The Desert Music," 188, 276–77
*The Desire of the Moth:* 208
"The Destruction of Tenochtitlan," 13
"The Devotion of Enríquez," 143–44
DeVoto, Bernard: 80–81, 109
*A Dictionary of Spanish Terms in English:* 242
Dime novels: 27–28
Dobie, Frank: 168, 201, 229–30, 256; banditry, 246; on fatalism, 263–64; on Day of the Dead, 274–75; on popular religion, 284; as a regional writer, 339
*El Dorado:* 169
Dos Passos, John: 168–69
Duarte-Clark, Roderigo: 314

## E

*Earth Horizon:* 154, 336
Earthiness *see* primitive virtues
Emerson, Ralph Waldo: 26
Erasmus, Charles J.: 237
Ethnocentricity of Americans: 120–21
Etiquette *see* courtesy
Evans, George W. B.: 22–23, 48–49; on mechanical ineptness, 34; on cowardice, 46–47, 48–49; on charity, 65–66; on classes, 74; on dancing, 82; on feudal society, 116; on Catholicism and clergy, 122, 125
"Everybody Knows Tobie," 316–18
Explorers: 23–24

## F

Family: 103–04
Fatalism: 262–63, 264–65
Fergusson, Harvey: 74, 105, 115, 154; on racial conflicts, 77, 78–79; on dancing, 82–83; on sex conventions, 85–87; on Penitentes, 100; on father-children conflict, 104–05; on family, 105–06; on great houses, 110; on Armijo, 112; on corruption, 115; on the passing of feudal society, 158–61; on ambiguous position of Mexicans in the Southwest, 176–77; on primitive virtues, 211–12; on Catholicism, 286; on result of cultural synthesis, 347–48; as agent of culture synthesis, 348–49
Ferlinghetti, Lawrence: on Mexican innocence, 241–42; on primitivism, 242; on Indian religion, 300
Feudal society: 103–04 ff., 115
Feudal society, decline of: 107 ff., 158–63
Feudal society, late survival: 162–63
*The Field of Vision:* 233, 268
*Fiesta:* 187, 250, 267–68
*Figures in a Landscape:* 179–80
*Five Families:* 164, 186, 250, 284
"The Five White Mice," 204
Flandrau, Charles M.: the role of the Mexican plaza, 343
Fletcher, John Gould: 148–49
Flint, Timothy: 23, 38; on courtesy, 39–40; racial intolerance, 73; on Catholicism, 123–24
*Flowering Judas:* 218, 258–59
*Flowers of Our Lost Romance:* 139–40
*Flute of the Smoking Mirror:* 4
Folk arts: 247–50
*Followers of the Sun:* 77
*The Forgotten Peninsula:* 214, 226, 261
*The Forgotten Village:* 290–91
*42nd Parallel:* 168–69
*Francis Berrian:* 25, 38, 39, 40, 73, 123–24
Frank, Waldo: 67, 211, 221, 278, 346–47
Frémont, John Charles: 24; sympathy for Californians, 64; on horsemanship, 66–67
"Friar Pedro's Ride," 284–85
Funerals *see* death
Fusion of races: 12–13

## G

*Gabriel Conroy:* 171, 178, 202
Galarza, Ernesto: 311–13
Gambling: 81
Ganilh, Anthony: on violence, 59–60; racial intolerance, 76–77; sex attitudes, 83–84; on Catholicism, 130–31
Garland, Hamlin: 142–43, 167–68
Garrard, Lewis H.: 21, 51, 53–54; on women, 43, 87–88; on cowardice, 48; on courage, 51, 53–54
Garza, Daniel: 316–18
*Gasoline:* 198–99, 250
Gillmore, Frances: 4
Ginsberg, Allen: on traditions, 211; on death art of Aztecs and Mayas, 272–73; on the mummies of Guanajuato, 274; on Indians and classical world, 300
"The Girl I Never Knew," 310
Gold rush: 22–23
Goodwyn, Frank: 239, 256–57, 302, 344–45
*Grant of Kingdom:* 105–06, 111, 118
Greaser (term): 38–39
*Great River:* 100, 109
Gregg, Josiah: 21; on courage of arrieros, 55; on charity, 66; racial intolerance, 76; on judicial procedures, 118–19; on Catholicism and clergy, 125, 130, 132
*Los Gringos:* 22, 42, 84
Gringos, hatred of: 180 ff.
Guérard, Albert: 342

## H

Hacienda owners *see* ricos
Hall, Sam: 50–51; on cowardice, 51; on violence, 60
Hammett, Samuel A.: on cleanliness, 38; on cowardice, 50; on racial intolerance, 73
*Harmonium:* 221
Harte, Bret: 139, 143–44; as a pivotal writer, 157–58, 171; on sex attitudes, 253–54; on Catholicism, 284–86, 304–06
*A Heart for the Gods of Mexico:* 181, 197–198, 200
Helm, MacKinley: 189, 193, 284, 289–90
Hemingway, Ernest: 200, 265
*Here and Now:* 259–60
Herrick, Robert: on official corruption, 188; on primitive virtues, 213–14, 228–29
Holley, Mary A.: 29, 120

## Index 387

Horgan, Paul: 21, 33; on laziness, 33; on sex attitudes, 81–82; on death, 100–01; on military leaders, 109; on Mexican as picturesque figure, 146–47; on the passing of feudal society, 158; on Mexican feelings for Americans, 179–80; on kindness, 208; on simplicity, 222–23; on primitive virtues, 230; on sex, 260; on Catholicism, 283–84
*The Horseman of the Americas:* 248
Horsemanship: 66–67, 141–42 ff.
"Horses — One Dash," 192, 204
Hospitality: 63–64
Hostility toward Mexicans: 28, 31, 32, *see also* such headings as corruption, Catholicism, laziness, racial intolerance
Hostility toward Mexicans, reaction against: 166 ff.
Hostility toward Mexicans, survivals of: 166–67 ff.
Hughes, Langston: on bohemian life in Mexico City, 153

### I

"I Too, America," 311
*I Wonder As I Wander:* 153
Idolatry *see* Catholicism and clergy
*Idols Behind Altars:* 197, 278, 298
"In Mescala," 184
"An Impression of Mexico — Its People," 224–25
*In the American Grain:* 5–6
*In the Footprints of the Padres:* 280–81
*In Those Days:* 77, 79, 158–60
*Indian Earth:* 292
Indolence *see* laziness
Ingraham, Joseph H.: 10
Innocence: 231–33, 241–42, *see also* primitive virtues
"The Inroad of the Navajo," 38, 48, 82, 126
Irving, Washington: 25, 62, 66

### J

*Jack Tier:* 25–26, 41
Jackson, Helen Hunt: 137–39
*The Jacob's Ladder:* 242
Jeffers, Robinson: on the California myth, 151–52; on thievery, 189; on violence, 192–93; on kindness, 208; on primitive virtues, 216, 233–234; on sex, 254
Jiménez Moreno, Wigberto: 9–10
Jones, Howard Mumford: 340–41

*Journal of a Voyage Between China and the Northwestern Coast:* 22
*Journey To Ixtlan:* 264–65, 276, 296, 297, 297–98
*Journey with Genius:* 269–70
Juárez, Benito: 109–10
Judicial procedures: 118–19

### K

Kemp, Lysander: 270–72
Kendall, George Wilkins: 20, 55; on mechanical ineptness, 33; on laziness, 36; on courtesy, 40; on courage of arrieros, 55; on untruthfulness, 56; on hospitality, 65; on kindness, 65; on charity, 67–68; on opinions of women, 88; on corruption, 117; on judicial procedures, 18; on military power, 119; on clergy, 127–28, 129–30
Kerouac, Jack: 223–24, 257
Kesey, Ken: on Mexican earthiness, 217
Kindness, 64–66, 208–09, *see also* courtesy
*The King Danced in the Market Place:* 4
*The King Ranch:* 343–44
Krutch, Joseph Wood: on unspoiled Baja California, 214, 226; on possessiveness re women, 261

### L

*The Lady:* 161–62
*La Bolsa Negra:* 314
La Farge, Oliver: 250; on feudal survival, 162–63; on cruelty, 199
"Land of Great Volcanos," 186
*The Land of Journey's Ending:* 336, 337
*The Land of Poco Tiempo:* 139, 225–26, 336
Lanier, Sidney: 188
*The Last of the Mohicans:* 75
Law *see* judicial procedures
Lawrence, D. H.: 210, 269–70
Laziness: 22; Shaler on, 35; Dana on, 35–36; Browne, 36; Wise, 36; Kendall, 36; Pattie, 36; Bartlett, 36–37
Lea, Tom: 166, 201; on primitive virtues, 214, 231; on bullfights, 265–66; on linguistic borrowing, 343–44
Lee, Alwyn: 178–79, 199–200, 208–09
"The Legend of Monte del Diablo," 285–86
Levertov, Denise: on the Mexican house snake, 175; on cruelty to animals, 198; on the sordid and the religious, 242; on tropics and sexual passion, 259–60

Lewis, Alfred Henry: 167
Lewis, Oscar: 164–65; on corruption, 188–89; sex attitudes, 255–56, 263
Linguistic borrowings: 342–45
*Literary History of Southern California:* 23
"The Living Shepherdess," 208
London, Jack: 182–83, 205
*The Long Valley:* 215–16
López, Antonio: 315
Love *see* sex attitudes
*Love Among the Cannibals:* 189–90
Lowell, James Russell: 26
Lummis, Charles Fletcher: 138–40; on cowardice, 205; on simple virtues, 225–27; on Penitentes, 299; on Spanish heritage, 334; as regional writer, 336

## M

MacLeish, Archibald: 6–7, 11
McWilliams, Carey: 74; on racial intolerance, 70; on the California myth, 155; on folk art, 249; on linguistic borrowing, 345
Machismo: 84, 205–06
*The Magic of Limping John:* 239, 302
Magoffin, James: 51–52, 101
Magoffin, Susan: on courtesy, 41–42; on sex attitudes, 80; on Catholicism, 133
*Main Line West:* 208
Malinche: 11–12
"A Man and — Some Others," 202–03
Manifest Destiny: 26
Manners, Mexican *see* courtesy
*Many Mexicos:* 70
Marañon, Gregorio: 252
"Maria Concepcion," 219–20, 240–41
Marriage *see* sex attitudes, women
Martínez, Father Antonio: 53, 112–14
*A Matter of Love:* 193–94, 284, 289–90
Maturin, Edward: 10–11
*McTeague:* 191
Mechanical ineptness: 33–34
*The Meeting of East and West:* 306–07
Méndez, Miguel: 316, 328–30
Mestizos: 12–13, 111–12, 182 ff.
"The Mexican," 182–83, 205
Mexican attitudes toward Americans: 179 ff.
*Mexican Gold Trail:* 22–23, 48–49
*Mexican Journal:* 185, 187, 270, 275, 303
*The Mexican Night:* 241–42, 300
"Mexican Quarter," 148–49
"Mexican Sights and Street Scenes," 195–96

"A Mexican Tale," 58, 73, 128–29
*Mexican Village:* 199, 262
Mexicans as children of the earth, *see* primitive virtues
*The Mexico I Like:* 229–30, 256, 263, 287, 301–02
*Mexico Versus Texas:* 59–60, 76–77, 83–84, 130–31, 132
*Michael Bonham:* 76
Mier y Teran, Manuel: 31
Military officers, power of: 183, 119–20, 186–87
Miller, Henry: 232, 237–38, 300–01
Miller, Joaquin: 140, 141
"Mis Ojos Hinchados," 309
Missions: 280–81
Moctezuma, 14 ff.
Montezuma, *see* Moctezuma
*Montezuma, the Last of the Aztecs:* 10–11
"Moonlight on the Snow," 168, 191–96
Moral righteousness of Americans: 177–78
Morris, Wright: 189–90, 233, 268
"The Mother of a Queen," 200
Muleteers: 55
Murder: 59–60
*Mustang Grey:* 124
*My Confession:* 29–31, 129

## N

Nagual: 287–88
*Narrative of the Texas Santa Fe Expedition:* 20, 33, 99
Nationalism, American: 26–28
Negroes: 76
Nieman, Gilbert: 181–82; on thievery, 190; on cruelty, 200–01; on primitive virtues, 223; on sex, 263
"A New Mexico David," 205
Niggli, Josephina: on racial fusion 12–13; on class conflicts, 183–84; on cruelty, 199; on fatalism, 262–63
*The Night of the Iguana:* 198, 259
*Night over Taos:* 107–08, 112–14
*No Quarter Given:* 222–23, 260
Noble savage: 70, 225
Nolan, Philip: 18
Norris, Frank: 141, 149–51, 196–97
*North from Mexico:* 70, 117, 155, 345
Northrup, F. S. C.: 268–69, 279, 303–04, 307
*Not With the Fist:* 70, 154–55, 177

## O

O. Henry: 172–74
*The Octopus:* 196–97
Officials, power of: 186–89
*On the Road:* 223–24, 257
*One Flew Over the Cuckoo's Nest:* 217
*One Smoke Stories:* 336–37
"The Only Beast," 269, 270–72
*The Oregon Trail:* 71, 74, 126
*Our America:* 346–47
"Out the Alley Our Soul Awaits Us," 310
*Overland:* 170–71
*Overland Monthly:* 72–73, 75, 119–20
*The Ox Bow Incident:* 189

## P

Pachuco: 169–70, 238–39
*Pānfila la Curandera:* 315
Parkman, Francis: 71, 74, 126
"The Passing of Enríquez," 157–58
"The Pastor Caballero," 144–45
*The Pastures of Heaven:* 215, 255
Pattie, James Ohio: 23, 46, 48; on laziness, 36; on courtesy, 42; on courage, 46; on cowardice, 48; on violence, 59; on cruelty, 62–63; on Catholicism, 122–23
Pearce, T. M.: 343
*The Pearl:* 286–87
Penitentes: 99–100, 110–11, 132, 299
*People of the Valley:* 212, 348
*Peregrinos de Aztlan:* 328–30
*The Personal Narrative of James O. Pattie:* 23
Pike, Albert: 21, 48; on filthiness, 38; on hospitality, 63; on racial tolerance, 73; sex attitudes, 82; on clergy, 126, 128–29
Pike, Zebulon: 21, 23–24, 104, 119; on hospitality, 63; on treatment of women, 84–85; on Catholicism, 121–22; on clergy, 126
*Piney Woods Tavern:* 73
*The Plum Plum Pickers:* 319–21
*The Plumed Serpent:* 269
*Pocho:* 318–19
Politeness *see* courtesy
"The Politeness of Cuesta La Plata," 207–08
Pony Tracks: 142
Porter, Katherine Anne: 153, 218; on primitive virtues, 218–20; satire on primitivism, 240–41; on sex, 258–59
Porter, William S. *see* O. Henry
Powell, Lawrence Clark: influence of the land upon Southwestern literature, 333
*The Prairie:* 75
*The Prairie Scout:* 50
Prescott, William H.: 3, 4; on death, 98; on Catholicism, 131–32
Priests *see* Catholicism and clergy
Primitive virtues: Frank, 211; Herrick, 213–14; Cather, 213; Steinbeck, 215–16; Aiken, 216–17; Porter, 210–20; Harte Crane, 220–21; Neiman, 223; Kerouac, 223–24; Dobie, 229; Horgan, 230; Sorensen, 234–36; Claremon, 212; Kesey, 217; Waters, 212
Primitivism, reaction against: Porter, 240–41; Bellow, 241; Rodman, 241; Ferlinghetti, 242
Pritchard, W. T.: 75
*The Professor's House:* 213
*The Proper Gods:* 234–36
*Prose Poems and Sketches:* 21
Prospectors: 22–23
"A Pupil of Chestnut Ridge," 171–72, 253–54, 304–05
*Psychology Today:* 295–96

## Q

"The Quarrel," 222

## R

Racial conflict: 77–78
Racial fusion: 12–13, 292 ff.
Racial intolerance: 67, 69 ff., 71 ff.
Racial situation, Mexican, American interest in: 182 ff.
Racial situation: Niggli on, 183–84; Dos Passos on, 186; Lewis on, 186; Rodman on, 184, 187, 240
Ramirez, Frank: 314
*Ramona:* 137–39, 156–57
Ramsey, Robert: 187, 250, 267–68
Rancheros: 55–56
*Reality Sandwiches:* 211, 272–73, 274, 300
*Regionalism in America:* 341
Regionalism in literature: 335 ff.
Religion *see* Catholicism and clergy
Religion, popular: 287 ff.; Dobie, 287, 301–02; Summers, 289; Bynner, 291–92; Brenner, 298; Goodwyn, 302; role of the Virgin, 302 ff.; Austin, 304 *see also* curanderas, Penitentes
Remington, Frederick: 142, 190, 225
Rennie, Ysabel: exclusion of Mexicans from mining industry, 345–46; greater

opportunity for Mexican middle class, 346
*The Return of the Weed:* 158, 230
"The Revolutionists Stop for Orangeade," 145–46
Rhodes, Eugene Manlove: 208
Richter, Conrad: 161–62
Ricos: 105 ff.
*Rio Grande:* 85, 100, 111, 347–49
*The Road to Tamazunchale:* 330–31
"Roan Stallion," 254
Rivera, Tomás: 323–24
Robbery, *see* thievery
Rodman, Selden: on classes, 185; on military power, 187; on primitivism, 241; on bullfights, 270; on Day of the Dead, 275; on popular religion, 303
Roeder, Ralph: 109–10
Romantic Mexico, satire on: 153
Romero, Leo: 311
*Roughing It:* 141
"Rubio y Morena," 257–58
Rukeyser, Muriel: on the passionate women of Chiapas, 260

## S

Salazar, 19–20
"San Antonio de Bexar," 188
Sanchez, José M.: 47–48
Sandburg, Carl: 147, 226
Santa Fe Trail: 20–21
Savagery *see* violence
"Sea Surface Full of Clouds," 148
*A Separate Reality:* 264–65, 276, 296, 297–98
*The Serpent of El Paso:* 50–51, 58, 60
Sex attitudes: 80 ff., 252 ff.; Susan Magoffin, 80; Gregg, 81; Wise, 84; Fergusson, 85–87; Bret Harte, 253–54; Jeffers, 254; Summers, 255; Lewis, 255; Dobie, 256; Goodwyn, 256–57; Kerouac, 257; Porter, 258–59; Levertov, 259–60; Tennessee Williams, 259; Rukeyser, 260
Sex codes: 261–62
Shaler, William: 22, 35
*Sherwood Anderson's Memoirs:* 191
*The Shirley Letters:* 23, 43–44
Shulman, Irving: 169–70, 238–39
*The Silver Cradle:* 304
Simplicity, *see* primitive virtues
Simms, William Gilmore: 76
Simpson, Lesley Bird: 70
Smith, Louise A.: 23, 43–44
*Smoke and Steel:* 147

Soldiers, Mexican: 43–44, 45–46
"Something for Bradshaw's Tombstone," 178–79
*The Song of the Lark:* 174–76
Sonnichsen, C. L.: on the attractions of Mexican life for Roy Bean, 79–80
Sorensen, Virginia: 234–46, 264
*The Sorrow Dance:* 198
Southwest: Lummis on, 334; Whitman on, 333
Southwest, 78, 152–53, 180–81, 201, 245, 261–62
Southwest as a literary region: 332 ff.
*Southwest Classics:* 333
Southwest, rediscovery of: 137 ff.
Spain as the despoiler: 9–10
Spanish as spoken by Americans: 43–44
*The Spanish Background of American Literature:* 335
Spanish terms in English: 342–45
*The Speed of Darkness:* 260
Spenser, Benjamin T.: 341
Spicer, Edward H.: 103, 236–37
*The Splendid Idle Forties:* 139
The Square Trap: 169–70, 238–39
Steinbeck, John: 215–16, 232–33; sex attitudes, 255; on Catholicism, 286–87; on curanderas, 290–91
*Step Down Elder Brother:* 12–13; 183–84, 262–63
Stereotype Mexican: 170–74
Stevens, Wallace: 144–46, 147–48
Stoddard, Charles Warren: 141–42, 280–81
"The Story of a Mine," 167
*The Story of Roy Bean:* 79–80
"Street Musicians," 249
Style of Living: 66–68
Summers, Richard: 255, 289
Sympathy for Mexicans: 165–66, 167 ff.

## T

"The Tale of the Tall Alcalde," 140
"Tamales," 173–74
*Tamar:* 192–93
"Tata Casehua," 319–20
Taylor, Bayard: 167, 177–78, 190, 207
*The Teachings of Don Juan:* 288, 294, 295
Teatro Campesino: 313–14
Teatro de la Esperanza: 314
Texas Santa Fe Expedition: 18–20, 65
Texas romances: 28
"That Tree," 151, 230
*There Is a Tyrant in Every Country:*

181–82, 190, 200–01, 223, 263
Thievery: 56–58, 189–90, 243–45; Audubon, 56; Bartlett, 56; Wise, 56–57; Webb, 57–58; Albert Pike, 58; Evans, 59; Jeffers, 189; Helm, 189; Neiman, 190; Horgan, 243; Dobie, 243–44; *see also* banditry
Thoreau, Henry David: 26
Tijerina, Reis: 309
*The Time of the Gringo:* 20, 52, 101, 111, 118
Tinker, Edward Larocque: 248, 349
*Tongues of the Monte:* 339
*Tortilla Flat:* 232–33, 254
*A Tour Through Arizona:* 24
*Transport to Summer:* 221–22
Tuck, Ruth: 74, 237; on racial intolerance, 70; on the California myth, 154–55; on persistence of stereotype Mexican, 177; on Mexican workers in the U.S., 237
La Tules: 80–81
Turner, Timothy G.: 141, 206, 248
Twain, Mark: 141
*Two Years Before the Mast:* 22, 35–36, 98–99, 119

## U
Untruthfulness: 56

## V
Vaca, Nick: 315–16
Vaillant, George: 4
Valdez, Luis Miguel: 313–14
*El Vaquero:* 141
Vasquez, Richard: 322
*Viaje a Texas:* 47–48
Victor, Orville J.: 27
Villa, Pancho: 245–47
Villainy, Mexican: 18
Villareal, Jose Antonio: 318–19
Violence: 58 ff., 190 ff.; Bird, 59; Pattie, 59; Clemens, 60; Ganilh, 59; Hall, 60; Taylor, 190; Remington, 190; Stephen Crane, 191–92; Jeffers, 192–93; Helm, 193–94; Lewis, 194–95
"The Visit," 315–16
*Viva Mexico:* 343
"Volcano," 195
*Voyages and Commercial Enterprises of the Sons of New England:* 22, 127

## W
*Wah-To-Yah and the Taos Trail:* 21, 47, 51, 53–54, 87–88

Walker, Franklin: 23
*Waste:* 188, 213–14, 218–20, 228–29
Waters, Frank: on love for the land, 212; on cultural fusion, 348
Waugh, Julia Nott: 304
Webb, James J.: 21; on Armijo, 37; on clergy, 126, 128
Webber, Charles W.: 50
Wells, William V.: 40–41, 75
Whitman, Walt: 26, 62, 272, 333–34
Williams, Stanley T.: 335
Williams, Tennessee: on cruelty to animals, 198; on a passionate Mexican woman, 257–58; on the tropics and sexual passion, 259
Williams, William Carlos: on the Conquest, 5–6, 7, 11, 13–15; on death, 260, 272–73, 276–77
Wilson, Carter: on racial tensions, 184; on killing witches, 190; on Mexican Indianists, 240; on Indian with soul of a tiger, 88; on cuaranderos, 290
Wise, H. A.: 22; on laziness, 36; on filthiness, 38; on allure of Mexican women, 42; on untruthfulness, 56; sex attitudes, 84
*With Eyes at the Back of Our Heads:* 175
*Wolf Song:* 77, 85–87
*Wolfville:* 167
Women: 28, 42–43, 87 ff., 260–62; Fergusson, 85–87; Garrard, 87; Kendall, 88; Browne, 88–89; *see also* sex
*Women at Point Sur:* 254
*The Wonderful Country:* 201, 214–15

## Y
Yaquis: 234–47
*The Year of Decision:* 80–81, 109